CW01262901

Investing in Distressed Debt in Europe

The TMA Handbook for Practitioners
Consulting Editor **Ignacio Buil Aldana**

Consulting editor
Ignacio Buil Aldana
Published in association with TMA Europe

Managing director
Sian O'Neill

Investing in Distressed Debt in Europe: The TMA Handbook for Practitioners
is published by
Globe Law and Business Limited
3 Mylor Close
Horsell
Woking
Surrey GU21 4DD
Tel: +44 20 3745 4770
www.globelawandbusiness.com

Printed and bound by Gomer Press

Investing in Distressed Debt in Europe: The TMA Handbook for Practitioners
ISBN 9781911078104

© 2016 Globe Law and Business Ltd

All rights reserved. No part of this publication may be reproduced in any material form (including photocopying, storing in any medium by electronic means or transmitting) without the written permission of the copyright owner, except in accordance with the provisions of the Copyright, Designs and Patents Act 1988 or under terms of a licence issued by the Copyright Licensing Agency Ltd, 6-10 Kirby Street, London EC1N 8TS, United Kingdom (www.cla.co.uk, email: licence@cla.co.uk). Applications for the copyright owner's written permission to reproduce any part of this publication should be addressed to the publisher.

DISCLAIMER
This publication is intended as a general guide only. The information and opinions which it contains are not intended to be a comprehensive study, nor to provide legal advice, and should not be treated as a substitute for legal advice concerning particular situations. Legal advice should always be sought before taking any action based on the information provided. The publishers bear no responsibility for any errors or omissions contained herein.

Table of contents

Foreword _____ 7
    Lukas Fecker
    TMA Europe President

Preface _____ 9
    Ignacio Buil Aldana
    Cuatrecasas, Gonçalves Pereira

Part I: Introduction

Investing in distressed debt _____ 13
in Europe: an overview
    Tom Cox
    Damian Malone
    Mark Sinjakli
    AlixPartners

Part II: Acquisition of distressed debt

Credit agreement and _____ 33
indenture analysis from
a European perspective
    Jacqueline Ingram
    Cadwalader, Wickersham & Taft LLP

Anatomy of an LMA distressed _____ 43
trade transaction and transfer
mechanisms under English law
    Elizabeth Bilbao
    Mandel, Katz & Brosnan LLP

Overview of distressed _____ 59
trading in selected jurisdictions
    France
    Jérémie Bismuth
    Olivia Locatelli
    Dimitrios Logizidis
    Gide Loyrette Nouel

    Germany
    Sacha Lürken
    Wolfgang Nardi
    Oded Schein
    Kirkland & Ellis International LLP

    Italy
    Gregorio Consoli
    Federica Scialpi
    Chiomenti Studio Legale

    Spain
    Beatriz Causapé
    Cuatrecasas, Gonçalves Pereira

Part III: The European non-performing loans (NLP) market

'Bad banks' and their _____ 81
role in the financial sector
deleveraging process in Europe
    Fernando Mínguez
    Cuatrecasas, Gonçalves Pereira

Anatomy of a non- _____ 93
performing loan portfolio sale
    Paul Dunbar
    Vinson & Elkins LLP

Part IV: Direct lending

The direct lending landscape in Europe — 109
    Nerea Pérez de Guzmán
    FTI Consulting

Trends in direct lending — 119
    Andrew Perkins
    Sarah Ward
    Macfarlanes LLP

Legal structuring of direct lending deals in selected European jurisdictions

France — 133
    Jérémie Bismuth
    Marie Dubarry de Lassalle
    Olivia Locatelli
    Caroline Texier
    Gide Loyrette Nouel

Germany — 141
    Sacha Lürken
    Wolfgang Nardi
    Oded Schein
    Kirkland & Ellis International LLP

Italy — 149
    Giorgio Cappelli
    Andrea Martino
    Giovanna Randazzo
    Chiomenti Studio Legale

Spain — 157
    Íñigo de Luisa
    Íñigo Rubio
    Cuatrecasas, Gonçalves Pereira

Part V: Restructuring and workouts

Recent trends in European cross-border restructurings — 167
    Arturo Gayoso
    Deloitte Financial Advisory

Schemes of arrangements: theory and practice — 175
    Graham Lane
    Iben Madsen
    Willkie Farr & Gallagher LLP

Developments in the European legal framework for restructuring

France — 199
    Jérémie Bismuth
    Marie Dubarry de Lassalle
    Olivia Locatelli
    Caroline Texier
    Gide Loyrette Nouel

Germany — 215
    Sacha Lürken
    Kirkland & Ellis International LLP

Italy — 237
    Giulia Battaglia
    Antonio Tavella
    Chiomenti Studio Legale

Spain — 249
    Cristóbal Cotta
    Andrea Perelló
    Fedra Valencia
    Cuatrecasas, Gonçalves Pereira

Restructuring high-yield ——— 261
bonds in Europe
    Paul Durban
    Grégoire Hansen
    Brown Rudnick LLP

The recast EU Insolvency ——— 279
Regulation and its impact
on distressed investing
    James Bell
    Douglas Hawthorn
    Jeremy Walsh
    Travers Smith LLP

Part VI: Taxation

Structuring the acquisition ——— 295
and disposal of distressed debt
    Rebeca Rodríguez
    Cuatrecasas, Gonçalves Pereira
    Luke Vassay
    Milbank, Tweed, Hadley & McCloy LLP

About the authors ——— 317

Foreword

Lukas Fecker
TMA Europe President

As president of Turnaround Management Association (TMA) Europe, it is a pleasure to introduce *Investing in Distressed Debt in Europe: The TMA Handbook for Practitioners* co-published by TMA Europe.

This book comes at a time where the European distressed debt market has developed exponentially during the last few years and has experienced very significant changes, including very relevant amendments to national insolvency and restructuring laws throughout Europe, with the common goal of introducing restructuring tools to enhance out-of-court and in-court restructurings. Furthermore, attention to the non-performing loans market (which has experienced a dramatic increase from 2010 to 2016) and direct lending is also provided, acknowledging the importance and relevance that these fields of distressed investing have achieved in Europe during recent years.

I am grateful to the consulting editor, Ignacio Buil Aldana, and the team of contributors who have participated in this book and authored the different chapters which capture the complexities and intricacies of the European distressed market. These contributors, who represent some of the key European jurisdictions, are all leaders in their field and have taken the time to share with us both their technical knowledge of the matters discussed and the practical aspects they come across in their day-to-day practice. I am sure that, as a result of this, this book will become a practical reference guide for those seeking a better understanding of the commercial and legal complexities involved in the European distressed market.

I want to finish this preface highlighting that this publication is part of TMA's dedication to corporate renewal and turnaround management, shared with more than 9,000 TMA members who comprise a worldwide professional community of turnaround practitioners. In particular, TMA Europe (which represents 12 European chapters) has become the forum for the interchange of ideas across Europe in connection with turnaround and restructuring matters. This book is yet another example of our organisation's commitment to innovation and progress in the law and practice of restructuring and turnaround in Europe and in the cross-border context.

Dr Lukas Fecker, TMA Europe President, owns a turnaround and distressed investment boutique, he is a frequent speaker at sector conferences in Europe and the United States.

Preface

Ignacio Buil Aldana
Cuatrecasas, Gonçalves Pereira

The European distressed debt market has experienced dramatic developments since the financial crisis that began in 2007/2008. This book is a response to these developments and aims to give an overview of the legal background and the challenges and opportunities of investing in distressed debt in Europe, with specific attention to certain European jurisdictions (France, Germany, Italy, Spain and the United Kingdom). In this regard, our book focuses on what are the four key areas of interest for distressed investors: distressed debt trading, direct lending, the non-performing loan portfolio market in the context of bank deleveraging and the European restructuring and workout framework.

1. Distressed debt trading

The development of the European secondary loan market of par and distressed debt (also known as impaired debt or sub-performing debt) during the last few years is remarkable. 'Distressed debt' refers to those loans or credits with uncertain recovery prospects due to the borrower either being in insolvency or in financial distress; this debt being traded as a result at significant discount to face value. The market where this type of debt is traded, once controlled by a small number of participants, is now used by a diverse array of participants, ranging from investment banks to hedge funds, pension funds or private equity houses.

Despite the uniformity provided by the Loan Market Association (LMA) terms and conditions (which is currently the standard used by the market and is analysed in depth in the "Anatomy of an LMA distressed trade transaction" chapter), the European market is far from being uniform (both from a regulatory and legal point of view) which becomes clear in the chapter "Overview of distressed debt trading in selected jurisdictions".

2. Direct lending

The changes in bank regulation have led to a reduction of bank lending opportunities for corporations and especially for small and medium-sized enterprises (SMEs). This retrenchment of traditional banks in the business of lending has resulted in a lack of sources of financing, providing the backdrop for the development of an alternative lending market which has become a permanent feature of the European market and is rapidly evolving to become an asset class with over 300 direct lending professionals active in the European market.

This alternative lending market, commonly known as direct lending, refers to lending provided by non-traditional sources of financing (ie, credit funds) with different lending strategies, such as mezzanine financing, distressed-debt investment or capital relief to name a few. This book provides an overview of the current state of the direct lending market as well as a chapter undertaking an analysis of the trends in the European market relating, for example, to unitranche financing or 'cov loose'/'cov lite' financings, as well as a review of the regulatory and legal regimes applicable in different European jurisdictions.

3. Non-performing loans market

Reducing non-performing loans in the banks' balance sheet has become a hot topic for a broad range of politicians, policymakers and investors. The regulatory focus on the level of non-performing loans in the European banking system is the result of the concerns that these loans hold down credit growth and reduce economic activity.

These concerns and increased regulation – the European Central Bank driven single supervisory mechanism, capital requirements for banks and insurance companies as a result of Basel III, Solvency II and, in the future, IFR39 – continue to stimulate deleveraging, and a strong European non-performing loans market has developed, with the United Kingdom and Ireland heading the tables of non-performing loan transactions and Spain, Benelux the Nordic countries and central and eastern Europe following their lead. This activity is expected to remain high in the next couple of years, and new countries are expected to open up the non-performing loan market in the coming months with their banks becoming active participants (eg, Italy).

Moreover, some European countries have set up so-called bad banks (such as Nama in Ireland or SAREB in Spain) which, as explained in the chapter "Bad banks and their role in the deleveraging process in Europe", is a well-established banking crisis management tool aimed at facilitating the management of legacy assets and their orderly divestment, turnaround or liquidation. These bad banks also play a key role as active participants in the distressed-debt markets.

4. Restructuring and workouts

The scheme of arrangement has been one of the restructuring tools most favoured by market participants during the last few years. Debtors from continental Europe have used this tool to restructure their debt and implement their restructurings, taking advantage of a flexibility that their national restructuring and insolvency regimes did not provide to them. This book acknowledges this and provides a detailed focus on the scheme of arrangement and its latest developments. We also look into the dynamics of high-yield bond restructuring and the influence that the scheme of arrangement and the US Chapter 11 have in the restructuring process.

In this regard, different European countries have enacted amendments to their legislation, introducing new frameworks to facilitate in-court or out-of-court restructuring, in what can be seen as a race to catch up with the English restructuring framework and prevent the 'escape' to English law of many debtors, creditors and their restructurings.

These amendments, which range from the Spanish *homologación judicial* to the

Italian *concordato preventivo*, have also introduced changes in the new money regime, debt-for-equity swaps and other tools with the purpose of enhancing corporate restructuring and facilitating the viability of distressed debtors. All these developments are addressed in this book, and we provide an overview of the many legal changes introduced in recent years in the European market.

Now we have explained what this book is about, two things need to be raised at this point, without which the preface of this book would not be complete. First, Brexit. Brexit is changing, and is going to change further (once the formal exit process is formally started and eventually concluded), the relationship between the United Kingdom and the rest of Europe, both politically and economically. While we have included references to Brexit throughout this book, it will be only in the medium term when we will be in a position to assess the real impact that Brexit will have in the European distressed investing market. At this point, however, to try and picture the impact of Brexit is highly speculative and while all political signs seem to point to a 'hard' Brexit, it is difficult to have much clarity on what this will really mean if this is finally the case.

Secondly, it has not been possible to cover all the countries that comprise Europe and have a say in its distressed market. We acknowledge that chapters on the Nordic or central and eastern European countries may be missing in this first edition of the book; however, while we anticipate that this book may move into future editions that will allow us to analyse these countries as well, we also hope that as it stands this book serves as a valuable introduction to the European distressed market and its key features.

Finally, I would like to extend my gratitude to all the contributors for their support and cooperation in the preparation of this book, to the Turnaround Management Association Europe for their kind sponsorship, and to our publishers for all their help in the completion of this book. Finally, thanks as ever to my wife.

Ignacio Buil Aldana
Cuatrecasas, Gonçalves Pereira
El Tormillo / London

Investing in distressed debt in Europe: an overview

Tom Cox
Damian Malone
Mark Sinjakli
AlixPartners

1. Introduction

The concept of distressed investing in Europe is not new. We have operated in an environment of extreme financial volatility (both boom and bust) from a debt market perspective since the early 1980s, accelerated by the emergence of the European high yield bond market in 1997[1] which heralded a new wave of value investing in Europe. This volatility is not a surprise, one might argue, given the rapid growth of the leveraged buyout market, the subsequent failure of many companies in the mid-1990s and later the boom-bust cycle in the technology, media and telecommunications market at the turn of the 20th century.

Since the financial crisis in 2008 the European distressed debt market has become more dynamic as European and US banks, many of which made significant profits driving leveraged buyout volumes in the mid-2000s, were forced to unwind balance sheets of long positions in leveraged buyout loans, and some of the most complex structured products including mortgage-backed securities and collateralised debt obligations. Arguably US banks (operating in Europe) suffered more heavily than their European counterparts who held onto assets for longer, rather than completing a mark-to-market of their loan books and suffering catastrophic losses at the height of the crisis.

We have witnessed a substantial increase in non-performing loan portfolio trading since the start of the Eurozone crisis, as investors flocked to Europe seeking yield and targeting banks now subject to increasingly stringent capital adequacy requirements and more onerous regulation. The European Central Bank's asset quality review in 2014 identified €879 billion of troubled loans held by 123 banks in the Eurozone's 18 countries, prompting a raft of loan disposals and a flood of capital into Europe. This is hardly a surprise given the growth of the derivatives and securitisation markets in the mid-2000s, as assets on bank balance sheets grew from €18 trillion in 1999 to €45 trillion in 2008.

What is perhaps more surprising is the fact that the speed of bank deleveraging since 2008 (and therefore the opportunity for distressed returns) has not been as rapid as many commentators originally predicted. There has been a great deal of 'amend and extend', in contrast to previous cyclical downturns. However this is

---

1 Edward Altman, "The Anatomy of the High Yield Bond Market", September 21 1998: pages.stern.nyu.edu/~ealtman/anatomy.pdf.

more likely to have been the result of under-provisioning by banks and an inability to absorb losses on disposal of assets rather than through a lack of appetite itself, particularly since such lending ties up capital and prevents it from being recycled into other opportunities. The year 2015 witnessed a substantial uptick in activity with €140 billion of European loan portfolio transactions recorded, up 50% (in absolute value terms) on 2014, but this was largely driven by non-strategic performing residential mortgage portfolios in the United Kingdom rather than non-performing loans.[2]

On the other hand, deleveraging of Italian bank balance sheets accelerated, with €11 billion of unsecured/non-performing loans trading at large discounts to par.[3] In the context of an estimated €1,180 billion of non-performing loan stock held by European banks, less than 30% had traded by the end of 2015, but the speed of disposal is likely to accelerate in the coming years as lenders have continued to rebuild balance sheets and are now generating earnings capable of absorbing losses on non-core portfolios. In the last quarter of 2016 pressure is increasing on Spain's 'bad bank', SAREB, as well as its commercial banks, to recognise significant impairments in respect of their loan books, which in turn may lead to price alignment between buyer and seller, and allow for an uptick in transactions.[4]

The level of genuine distress experienced since 2013 has been relatively muted, driven by ultra-low interest rates and capital availability across a variety of markets, both debt and equity, which provided solutions (albeit including amend and extend in some cases) for the most stressed borrowers. At the same time, looser credit protection in loan documentation (driven by a shift towards covenant-light bond financings in Europe) suppressed distressed trading volumes as return-hungry investors enabled borrowers to avoid or defer complex workouts.

However, the current European distressed industry is one which still presents a raft of opportunities, given the volatility that threatens the European economic system and a general feeling of anxiety across global markets. The United Kingdom's vote to leave the European Union in the June 2016 referendum has triggered turmoil in the UK, European and global markets. Only time will tell what the medium-term impacts will be, with most market commentators predicting a period of uncertainty and in many cases recession. In the hours after the result was announced, the governor of the Bank of England sought to reassure the UK population, asserting the ability of the UK economy to cope with such shocks and to return to stability, yet before the vote he had predicted that recession was a possible outcome of a Brexit vote.

Indeed, such volatility is playing out during a period in which Europe has also witnessed the most extensive monetary policy stimulus in living history, through quantitative easing, which rather than establishing a robust economic platform has delivered only anaemic growth across the continent. As the Chinese market continues to slow down and restructuring activity picks up in the United States (largely driven by low oil prices) it is likely that the European market will again

---

2 PwC, *Portfolio Advisory Group Market update* – Q4 2015.
3 PwC, *Portfolio Advisory Group Market update* – Q4 2015.
4 www.auraree.com/real-estate-news/bank-of-spain-puts-pressure-on-banks-to-speed-up-property-sales/.

provide significant value opportunities for alternative investors over the next five years, although the horizons on which such returns are achieved may necessarily be longer.

With an increasing absence of covenants in many large primary financings (and refinancings) which have closed in the last three to four years, it may be a liquidity crunch (or interest payment default) which ultimately brings distressed investors into play in the current environment. The steady flow of recent high-yield issuances (which has resulted in average annual issuances of €69 billion between 2013 and 2015, compared to €24 billion across 2006 and 2007) will ultimately increase the probability of future distressed opportunities, despite relatively weak volumes in the recent past.

Today's distressed-debt market participants are notably diverse and varied, ranging from more traditional investment banks and hedge funds to private equity groups who have raised 'special situations' or 'distressed opportunity' funds to drive returns through varied investment strategies from super-senior (debtor-in-possession style financing) through to deeply subordinated, payment-in-kind instruments which provide a route to borrower recovery or lender control. An example of the latter is Kohlberg Kravis Roberts & Co's investment in European vending machine operator Selecta in 2014[5] which, while positioned as a long-term refinancing, ultimately resulted in the fund acquiring a majority equity position from the incumbent private equity owner approximately 18 months later.[6]

2. **Market development**

Distressed-debt investing has been a consistent feature of the mainstream UK investment market since the 1990s and accelerated following the financial crisis in 2008. Following the crisis, US capital flooded into Europe attracted by the prospect of super-normal returns resembling those that were generated following recessions in the early 1990s and early 2000s. This influx of capital was also partially driven by a view that European banks would need to deleverage more aggressively than US counterparts, focusing initially on commercial real estate portfolios and then more traditional leveraged buyout positions. The reality is that the European market proved more complex than this, given the divergence in restructuring and insolvency regimes, the difference in accounting practices between European and US banks, and the relative balance sheet fragility of many participants.

Despite more recent reforms in Spain, France and Italy (the latter's regime was amended as recently as 2015 to focus on rescue rather than liquidation) the European distressed market was not as uniformly lucrative as many investors had hoped. As we have articulated, however, the European market remains a compelling investment opportunity, with over 70% of non-performing loans still notionally held by European banks, albeit this figure may be overstated by the multiple single asset disposals and 'bid wanted in competition' trades that have also filtered into the market since 2008.

---

5   media.kkr.com/media/media_releasedetail.cfm?ReleaseID=855882.
6   www.selecta.ch/krrit/.

The secondary market itself, which allows for the sale and trading of debt after the original loan has been syndicated, has continued to evolve since the 1990s in order to provide market stability and to manage lender risk in a more systematic manner. As a result, single asset or sector concentration can be managed more efficiently by lenders, thereby ensuring frequent loan (or tranche) turnover (among participants). This ultimately acts as a catalyst to free up additional capital, in light of the stringent Basel III and CRD IV requirements,[7] and to maintain system liquidity.

With borrowers (and private equity owners) increasingly concerned by the threat of a potential loan-to-own investor suddenly emerging in a lending syndicate, and lenders themselves keen to retain transfer flexibility, it is now not unusual to see transfer 'white lists'[8] running to several hundred qualifying lenders in loan documentation permitting the sale or transfer of debt without borrower consent. Ultimately, this has not stopped aggressive hedge funds or private equity investors buying into situations where new money is desperately needed and a meaningful return can be achieved, but it has ensured that the secondary market operates in a more fluid manner.

More recently we have seen several private debt funds, having initially underwritten mid-market deals, exploit such flexibility post-financing in order to reduce portfolio concentration and to lay off single asset risk by selling down their exposure. The secondary market ultimately provides the mechanism to facilitate risk management in an environment where private debt funds have achieved market share gains over the last two years, forcing the major European banks to fight back with more competitive terms.[9]

Regardless, the European secondary market has become a relatively robust marketplace despite the absence of an automated system to facilitate trading of positions. This has been supported by the development of standard documentation by the Loan Market Association in the United Kingdom and Loan Syndications and Trading Association in the United States, which have helped standardise trading processes and accelerate the timeframe for execution. This has allowed debt to be traded in a commoditised marketplace, allowing investors to take short-term minority positions, or larger stakes seeking significant influence or even control, according to their mandate.

Funds such as Alcentra, Babson Capital and ICG, among others, have also benefited from the re-emergence of collateralised loan obligation issuance in the last two years, allowing them to deploy institutional capital across the market in a range of situations, supported by increased deal flow in the larger syndicated market. This represented a welcome return of collateralised loan obligation liquidity in Europe since issuance collapsed in 2009,[10] following a peak of €35.5 billion in 2006. While increased regulation has somewhat hindered the structuring of new collateralised

---

7   www.eba.europa.eu/regulation-and-policy/implementing-basel-iii-europe.
8   A white list represents a schedule of defined lenders or institutions which is appended to the borrowers' financing agreement and which allows for subsequent transfer or assignment by the lenders of record at completion of their facilities (in the absence of a default). In the event of a default, the white list concept falls away and lenders are free to sell their debt to any party capable of holding the positon.
9   *AlixPartners Midmarket Debt Survey – 2015 (Europe); AlixPartners Midmarket Debt Survey – H1 2016 (Europe).*
10 Only €0.4 billion of collateralised loan obligations were issued in Europe during 2009.

loan obligations since 2012, and will fully manifest itself at the end of 2016 when new risk retention rules are implemented,[11] the re-emergence of the product in 2014 and 2015 (when €14.5 billion and €13.6 billion respectively of new collateralised loan obligations hit the market) provided ample liquidity across the market. The level of issuance softened somewhat in early 2016, with increased macroeconomic volatility linked to the depressed oil price, but rebounded in March. Year to date issuance for the eight months to August had reached €10.1 million and 2016 remains on track to deliver another strong period for new paper, despite the month of August itself delivering the lowest level of monthly issuance since August 2015.

The incidence of loan-to-own investment strategies, discussed in more detail below, has not been as prevalent as one might have expected since 2011. Instead we have seen more bespoke investment strategies employed by hedge, credit and private debt funds, investing on the basis of borrower and market fundamentals, rather than as a route to take control of the borrower itself. This is perhaps a function of the lack of genuine (dis)stress inherent in the system as funds have, outside relatively short term macroeconomic shocks (such as the Greek sovereign debt crisis), invested on a passive pull-to-par basis, where public market intelligence and sector knowledge have been used more efficiently to drive pricing arbitrage when debt positions are under-valued by the market. It also reflects the difficulties experienced in some jurisdictions of removing the incumbent equity holders, even when it is clear the economic interest does not lie with them (even if European jurisdictions are increasingly including mechanisms to disenfranchise shareholders within their local legislation). This was notable in the case of Codere, a Spanish multinational group operating in the private gaming sector, where the restructuring was frustrated for a long time by the inability to effect a debt for equity swap without shareholder consent.

Standard and Poor's European Leveraged Loan Index (ELLI) which tracks institutional loan defaults and restructurings has shown a progressive decline since 2011, with the ELLI distress ratio[12] declining from a peak of 31.5% in December 2011 to a low of 2.7% in June 2016, suggesting the market has simply not provided the volume of opportunities one might have expected for activist investors.

3. European distressed industry

Given the scale of bank lending through the mid to late 2000s it is unsurprising that the deleveraging of non-core assets by European banks is likely to continue for many years to come. The UK, Irish and Spanish markets proved the most active in the early stages of the European economic recovery, but the Italian, Dutch and central and eastern European markets have seen more transaction activity in 2015 and 2016 as a result of the intense level of competition and number of investors seeking to deploy capital.

High-profile funds, such as Apollo Global Management, Cerberus Capital

---

11   Risk retention regulation will require collateralised loan obligation managers to hold a 5% stake in each vehicle managed.
12   This ratio represents the share of credits in the ELLI by deal count that are marked below 80 cents/€.

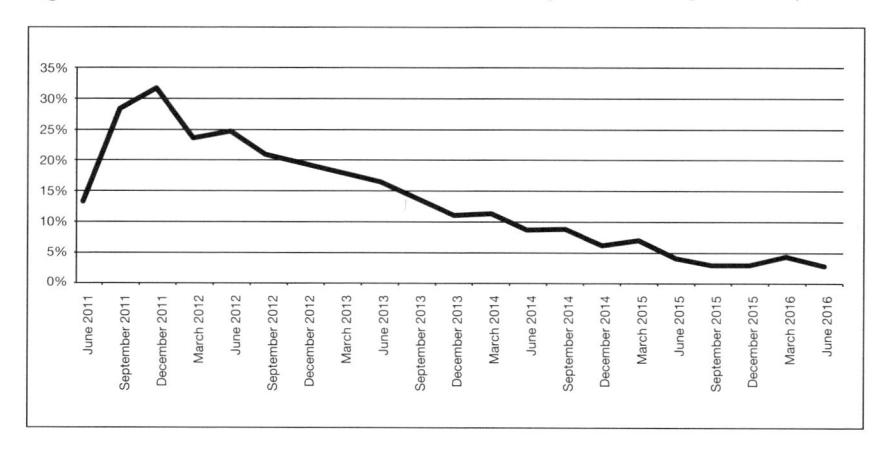

Figure 1: Standard and Poor distress ratio – ELLI (June 2011 to June 2016)

Management, Lone Star and Oaktree Capital, have proved to be active investors in the European distressed market since 2011, largely in commercial real estate. But we have also seen other vehicles emerge, such as Pillarstone, backed by Kohlberg Kravis Roberts & Co, specifically targeting banking assets in more peripheral geographies such as Italy and Greece with genuine operational turnaround potential. Given the level of competition there is a real possibility that investors will continue to look further afield over the next five years as distressed markets continue to mature in central and eastern Europe.

At the same time, given the emergence of private debt in the European mid-market[13] since 2010, and a continuing transition towards a US-style institutional lending market, we may see a new wave of distressed opportunities emerge in the next 10 years if these private funds, currently eager to deploy large pools of capital, end up stretching leverage to unsustainable levels and borrower distress follows. It remains to be seen whether such funds, without the portfolio management and restructuring resources of major European banks, will seek to work out such loans, or simply to take control where equity upside can be generated. It seems that such funds do not currently have the bandwidth to manage multiple restructurings at this stage of the credit cycle, and there will continue to be insufficient liquidity or appetite in the secondary market to provide an efficiently priced exit mechanism for lenders.

What is clear, however, is that companies will continue to find themselves in distress, whether it is driven by an unforeseen closure of capital markets with increased refinancing risk, wider macroeconomic factors, or changes in industry dynamics making the existing proposition incompatible with the market demand. This will present opportunities for distressed investors able to cherry-pick assets to create synergies and optimise value with existing investments, or simply to wind down structured assets and deliver a value recovery relative to the bid price.

---

13   Classified as bilateral financings, club deals or syndications valued below €300 million.

4. Why do companies become distressed?

While the debt markets themselves may often be to blame, in creating unsustainable capital structures that are unable to survive more cyclical economic factors, distress can occur for a variety of reasons, with both internal and external factors playing a part.

4.1 Obsolescence of business model

Societal change and technological obsolescence (which some might argue have accelerated exponentially in the last 20 years) have rendered some business models obsolete in a short space of time, as has been observed for example in the telephone directory 'yellow pages' market. Here, operators such as Hibu have been forced to transition to new business models simply to remain relevant, or at worst just to remain in existence. Such groups' capital structure reflected the expectation of repeat, maintainable cash generation year-on-year. To the extent that old revenue streams were reducing and new ones not sufficiently developed to replace them, debt restructuring became an inevitability.

Parallels of industry-wide change can be seen in the decline of physical digital media (CDs and DVDs), the decline in paper printing and, to a lesser extent, high street retail, with an expanded fixed cost base due to the need to offer a multichannel retailing experience (online, delivery, click and collect, longer opening hours for physical stores etc). It is often the inability of operators to amend such overheads to match industry change which provides the catalyst for distress, including an inability to unwind large leasehold commitments (taken on in boom times to help drive an equity return for investors), which has proven the death knell for many retail chains over the last 10 years.

The pace of technological change is set to increase dramatically, and self-driving cars, predictive coding reviews of legal documents for relevance, rapid, insightful big data analysis and accurate medical diagnosis by robots are no longer part of science fiction. With such change, many once seemingly future-proof companies, if not industries, are likely to become casualties of their unwillingness or inability to move away from what was previously successful and to invest quickly in radical new ways forward.[14]

4.2 Macroeconomic factors

For many businesses, distress follows changes in market fundamentals.

We are all familiar with the macroeconomic trends of the past 50 years, which have had implications for workforces beyond those of providers of capital. Previously profitable manufacturing in western Europe has been significantly supplanted, largely as a result of access to cheap labour in the east. Service jobs have been significantly outsourced to India.

In recent years, we have seen other macroeconomic phenomena: an imbalance

---

14   For a discussion of technological changes and their likely impact on the economy and society see Erik Brynjolfsson and Andrew McAfee, *The Second Machine Age: Work, Progress, and Prosperity in a Time of Brilliant Technologies* (WW Norton & Co, 2014).

between supply and demand in the property market (notably in parts of Spain and China), sustained low oil prices and the market uncertainty which was associated with the build-up to the Brexit referendum, and is now set to be exacerbated by a further period of uncertainty as the United Kingdom renegotiates its place in the world and the European Union seeks to steady the ship and avoid further disintegration.

Such trends tend to result in industry-wide consolidation, with those with the strongest balance sheets able to take the long view, ride out the storm and survive, often acquiring rivals and vertically integrating suppliers in the process.

4.3 Strategic errors

Poor decision-making or omissions in strategy often lead to distress. These include overly-aggressive expansion into new or existing markets, products and geographies (often funded with increased debt), failure to hedge against exchange rate movements or to fix commodity or energy prices in benign times, or poor management of working capital leading to a liquidity crisis.

4.4 Failures in governance (and/or management)

In some cases, distress is the direct result of errors, or occasionally misconduct, in the business. This can occur because of an inadequate governance framework or where decisions are made by a dominant chief executive officer. Such traits are sometimes seen in businesses where the founder has grown the business from a relatively small concern to a size and presence where the market demands a more sophisticated compliance structure.

Depending on the nature of the misconduct, capital structures may have been established on the basis of projections which are, or become, unrealistic. Examples include products with safety issues requiring a recall, or manipulation of data to understate provisions against asset values, for example in respect of the recoverability of a retail loan book, as was seen in the case of non-standard lender Welcome Financial Services.

The misconduct may be limited to one division or department, but prompt action is required to limit the contagion effect which can rapidly damage the whole business. The problem can be exacerbated when so called bear-raiders seek to take advantage of the woes of ailing corporates through short-selling strategies, sparking exaggerated but then self-fulfilling rumours of a corporate's decline.

The directors often need to be replaced and an exercise undertaken to understand the underlying value of the business, before a discussion can be held on the likely returns to creditors and a recovery strategy. This typically involves salvaging those operations that are worthy of continuation and not irretrievably tainted (perhaps by those distressed investors who can still see value in both core and ancillary assets despite all the background noise). In these situations litigation may also represent a further route to recoveries.

Replacing the directors can often be part and parcel of a more widespread review of the senior management of a business, since many individuals simply do not have the skills necessary to deliver a turnaround or manage a company in crisis situations.

While macroeconomic factors often have a major impact on trading performance, it is equally true that poor management is a major contributing factor in the slide into distress.

At times the appointment of a chief restructuring officer (an independent director parachuted in for a short period to support the board in delivering a turnaround) can help navigate this path to recovery, but fundamental questions must still be asked as to whether the incumbent management team are fit to lead a business out of distress. More often than not, replacements will be required, or additional skills will need to be brought into a business to support a recovery.

4.5 Off-balance-sheet liabilities

In response to the collapse of Enron in 2001, accounting and regulatory changes sought to limit (in many cases successfully) the extent to which liabilities could be held off-balance-sheet by corporates.

However, no reporting regime is perfect, and debates around what constitutes an appropriate and transparent reporting structure will always remain. In January 2016 an international financial reporting standard was issued in respect of leases, which when fully implemented will, it is estimated, have the effect of bringing $3 trillion of leasing commitments on to the balance sheets of listed companies.[15]

Clearly transparency in financial reporting can only assist the potential investor community in assessing the opportunities and risks that any opportunity may bring. At the same time, changes to a company's reporting requirements can also cause sudden and significant changes to the reported balance sheet, which in turn can result in companies that were previously fully compliant with their loan covenants (such as asset cover ratios) suddenly being in default. This can, in turn, cause lenders to reappraise the loan and relationship, resulting in a range of consequences from price increases through to asking the corporate to refinance.

4.6 Lack of access to capital markets

Many countries in continental Europe are dominated by family-owned small or medium-sized enterprises (SMEs). In Italy, for example, around 80% of corporates are family-owned, and 63% of gross domestic product is contributed by SMEs (by way of comparison, in Germany it is 31%).

Such entities have of course traditionally relied upon local banking relationships, but when these banks have not been in a position to provide funding (and in many cases are being required to divest themselves of existing loans), SMEs can struggle to attract alternative investors from global capital markets.

Often the scale of these enterprises makes them unattractive to investors, given the time commitment that is required to manage each connection. Historically regulation has not favoured overseas investors, and owner-entrepreneurs may be wary of foreign investment, in environments where a perception of such investors as 'vulture funds' is commonplace.

---

15 www.ifrs.org/alerts/pressrelease/pages/iasb-shines-light-on-leases-by-bringing-them-onto-the-balance-sheet.aspx.

Having said that, the lack of alternatives for local entrepreneurs, the limited number of large-scale opportunities being pursued by a large number of investors, and the impressive level of recent regulatory reforms on continental Europe, has resulted in an increasing number of SMEs seeking and attracting overseas funding.

In 2013, in an interesting variation on the theme, Apollo Global Management LLC acquired Evo Banco, a Spanish bank, providing them with access to an existing book of retail and commercial loans, as well as a local platform from which to make further loans.

4.7 Why do companies become distressed – conclusion

Distress in a large business typically has many contributing factors. The issues may be capable of being addressed within the existing capital structure by strict financial discipline and an operational turnaround plan. Sometimes the shareholders may inject sufficient funds to address the issues.

However, often these issues leave a company with a debt burden which it has no realistic prospect of servicing. In such cases, a financial restructuring is required alongside the appointment of a new management team; and often with a new money need, which is typically provided by the type of distressed investors that can also help implement genuine structural change in a business, rather than simply deferring an otherwise inevitable slide into insolvency.

5. Due diligence for distressed companies

As highlighted below, prospective investors or incumbent lenders may seek to complete an independent business review when a company is faced with financial stress, albeit this may be largely the outcome of a default on existing facilities and the output of the review may come too late to save a company from a slide into insolvency if there is an immediate liquidity issue.

Where action has been taken by a company early in the process an independent business review will often be the only due diligence available to distressed investors examining an investment opportunity, unless the company itself, or its shareholders, have commissioned other third-party due diligence reviews (commercial, operational or strategic) in advance as part of a more coordinated capital-raising process.

In reality the due diligence available to a distressed investor will often be very limited, and many market participants will rely on their own internal sector expertise and analyst resource to provide industry insight and context for the performance or operation of a potential investment target. There is often simply insufficient time to complete more detailed due diligence. As a result, certain investors will also seek to partner up with industry experts (individuals) from within their network (eg, plural non-executives or fund advisers) to provide investment guidance, based on prior knowledge of the asset or experience from having worked with its competitors.

More often than not, the absence of detailed analytics and diligence materials prior to investment will result in investors triangulating their views on the potential turnaround or value-recovery story based on multiple data points which do not emanate from the company itself. In-house sector expertise can therefore make a real difference in making critical investment decisions in short timeframes.

6. Investment strategies

6.1 Introduction

The investment strategy of any capital provider will be driven by a combination of the funds it has available to invest, the ultimate beneficiaries' appetite for risk, the timescales within which a return is required, the fund's investment criteria, and the skill set and resources of the team.

As mentioned earlier, the emergence of onerous capital adequacy requirements following the financial crisis meant those institutions with the largest exposures (clearing banks) had to set aside specific capital provisions to protect against default risk. Where the customer is in distress and there is a high probability of default, the required capital hold is greater – often in excess of 100% of the par value of the loan. Conservative lenders who invested before distress was apparent may therefore find themselves in an unsustainable position, and prefer to exit at a manageable loss rather than take their chances in a protracted restructuring process, which would require them to set aside precious capital throughout the process, with a significant resultant opportunity cost regardless of the final outcome.

As such, there are opportunities for investors who are relatively unconstrained by considerations of capital adequacy, represent investors with a suitable risk appetite, and have a distress-specific skill set.

6.2 The context of a business requiring debt restructuring

In order to explain some of the main strategies available to distressed lenders, it is necessary first to explain at a very high level the dynamics involved when a company recognises it has to restructure its balance sheet.

In many cases the capital structure of a business means that it has no prospect of meeting an imminent interest or capital repayment, or, at worst, its debt facilities are maturing with little hope of refinancing the par value in full. In such cases some level of restructuring of the affected debt, at the very least a deferral of repayments, is required. The alternative may be an unplanned insolvency process, often with catastrophic consequences for a company and its existing investors.

When the debt is in the form of a syndicated, traded debt instrument, it can be complex to achieve the required restructuring. Typically, finance documents are drafted so that any decision to vary the terms of the debt (extending repayment terms, reducing interest rates or accepting a reduction in the value of debt – a 'haircut') requires the unanimous approval of all holders of that debt instrument. As such, holders of relatively small stakes can (tactically or otherwise) prevent a restructuring under the terms of the finance documents.

In these situations, depending on the governing jurisdiction and the applicable law, 'cram-down' mechanisms may be available. These are typically court-governed processes which allow debt to be restructured, notwithstanding the presence of a dissenting minority of debtholders. The exact approval threshold, and which subset of creditors it applies to, varies by jurisdiction.

This is the backdrop against which investments into larger distressed companies are usually made. The strategies outlined below are described in respect of individual groups. Investors may acquire a portfolio of non-performing loans and seek to apply a combination of these strategies as appropriate.

6.3 Some of the more common investment strategies

(a) *Short-term investment in liquid debt instruments*
This is a common strategy of the trading desks of investment banks, as well as fixed-income investors. These investments are made based on publicly available information and typically involve taking minority stakes in liquid, tradable debt instruments. The aspiration here is to spot opportunities where the market may have mispriced the debt. There is no desire to hold a stake for the long term, to have influence or control, or to have input into any longer term financial or operational restructuring.

(b) *Holdout or blocking stake*
In this scenario, an investor or a group of investors acquire traded debt instruments at a discount, and are able to prevent a solvent restructuring on terms put forward by the company, or exert significant influence on the terms offered.

The amount of debt the holdout group needs in order to have a blocking stake depends on the restructuring options available to the company in question. Under perhaps the best known European cram-down mechanism, the UK's scheme of arrangement, up to 25% of creditors by value of those voting within each class[16] of creditor can be forced to compromise their debt, if 75% vote in favour of a proposed restructuring.

The aspirations of the holdout group vary from case to case, but they may include:
- limiting the amount of day one write-down in debt;
- accelerated payments compared to the timescale put forward in the company's proposals;
- being part of any new money solution;
- taking an equity stake;
- having the ability to convert debt to equity;
- tighter covenants in respect of post-restructured debt management;
- the appointment of a chief restructuring officer to manage any proposed restructuring;
- additional security over the company's assets; and
- maintaining control for existing equity.

(c) *Loan-to-own*
In this scenario an investor or group of investors buys a majority stake in a tranche of debt, where the value is believed to break, with the aim of acquiring an equity

---

16　The constitution of classes of creditors under a UK scheme of arrangement is a technical area beyond the scope of this chapter. For a discussion of this topic see Christian Pilkington, *Schemes of Arrangement in Corporate Restructuring* (Sweet & Maxwell, 2013).

stake in the business. The debt seller, aware of the risk of not being fully repaid, often sells their position at a significant discount to par. They may not have the appetite or mandate to take equity stakes themselves. Exactly what rights the investor acquires will depend on the specifics of the debt instrument, including inter-creditor provisions.

The investor, now in the role of lender, will then require a detailed independent review in order to consider where the value of the company lies. That review will usually show that the investor's debt will not be capable of being repaid at par on the timescales set out in the documentation (if at all).

In reaching a restructuring proposal, the company will have to take account of this shortfall to the debtholders, which is typically done by giving the opportunity to exchange some of their debt for an equity stake in the business. Depending on the level of the shortfall, this may need to be a majority equity stake.

Junior debtholders and shareholders have some opportunity to negotiate, but their 'out of the money' status (ie, having no economic interest) often means they do so from a position of relative weakness. Ultimately, depending on the jurisdiction, they may be forced to suffer a dilution of their stake, since the alternative, an insolvency process, would see their returns reduced to nil.[17]

(d) *Strategic use of an insolvency process*[18]

There are circumstances where an investor, having bought into debt, can emerge as the owner of the business through an insolvency process.

Where (in the United Kingdom) an administrator is appointed and puts the business up for sale, the secured lender has the opportunity to 'credit bid' in order to acquire the business. That is, as the beneficiary of any sales proceeds (subject to dilution by certain other preferential creditors which must be paid in cash), the secured lender can bid up to the value of the amount it is owed in order to acquire the business. A competing bidder would have to bid, in cash, above the value of the debt, thus repaying the investor (who has invested at a discount) at the par debt value. If no alternative cash bidder emerges, the secured lender can absorb the business and assets into a newly formed company. Under certain circumstances this might be conducted on an accelerated basis by means of a pre-packaged (prearranged) administration, which is when a marketing process is undertaken and a sale negotiated before the insolvency appointment, allowing the sale to be executed shortly after appointment. A pre-packaged administration can also be used to remove operational subsidiary companies from an over-leveraged structure with group lending into an entity towards the top of the structure. 'Pre-packs' (as they are known) are often an expedient way of moving a business forward with minimum

---

17   This applies to the UK context. In practice the ability of shareholders to frustrate a restructuring process and force a better deal when being out of the money according to the insolvency waterfall analysis varies immensely between jurisdictions. In this regard, in other European jurisdictions the inability to cram-down equity and the lack of alignment between the economic position of shareholders and their rights under a restructuring process provide shareholders very relevant negotiation leverage and impact the restructuring dynamics.
18   This analysis describes the UK context. The legal framework and application varies greatly by jurisdiction.

disruption with a sustainable capital structure, although there have been examples of abuse of process, which led to the Graham review being commissioned by the UK government and additional compliance measures being brought into place.

In other jurisdictions, the mechanisms to allow a similar restructuring do not exist, or the implementation is more difficult. In the past companies have transferred their centre of main interest to the United Kingdom to take advantage of the regulations in place (such as WIND Hellas), although there are strict criteria in place, and the migration of a company solely to take advantage of another country's insolvency laws often attracts controversy.

An insolvency process can also be seen as an opportunity to acquire only those parts of the business which are attractive to an investor. For example, an investor may seek to acquire only those stores in the portfolio of a multi-site retailer that are profitable (or capable of turnaround). Of course, the administrator will consider each bid on its merits, and may favour a bid which takes more or all stores, if one is forthcoming.

The approaches of credit bidding and selective acquisition of part of a store portfolio were seen in the 2012 administration of Clinton's Cards. Another way of exiting certain sites, in the United Kingdom, while renegotiating rents on others is through an alternative insolvency process, a company voluntary arrangement, which is a debtor-in-possession process, albeit typically with an insolvency practitioner acting as supervisor.

(e) *Providing debtor-in-possession financing*
In a US Chapter 11 restructuring, in order to allow a business to address a liquidity crisis and continue trading in the short to medium term, there is a well-established process for the providing of debtor-in-possession financing. This is often (but not exclusively) provided by existing lenders. The debtor-in-possession finance provider will normally seek super-priority and liens on assets which are already pledged to existing lenders, who as such may object. In this case the court will decide whether to allow the funding to be provided on the proposed terms.

Very few European jurisdictions have fully developed debtor-in-possession-style financing mechanisms, and it can be difficult to structure the loan so as to ensure its recovery, limiting the market for debtor-in-possession financing in Europe. Typically, the incumbent lender(s) provide the required funding through any restructuring, often through existing facilities, on the basis that in the long term the funded strategy will lead to a better return than an unfunded liquidation.

(f) *Providing post-restructuring debt*
Some distressed investors make good returns by lending money to businesses who have been through a restructuring process but, as a result, do not have an established credit profile, and as such are avoided by mainstream banks without the mandate to lend in perceived higher risk situations.

Debt is provided at an interest rate above that which the mainstream lending market would provide (at the time of writing say between 10% and 14% as an all-in effective rate). Once the business has established its creditworthiness (after between

12 and 18 months of successful debt service and achieving its business plan), it will be able to refinance to a cheaper, mainstream debt provider (say at between 5% and 8% initially and with scope for further reductions over time).

7. Valuation methodologies of a distressed business

7.1 Introduction

Setting aside the multiple strategies which investors may deploy in acquiring distressed assets, all investments (other than perhaps very short-term opportunistic ones) will be underpinned by potential assessment of value, both today and in the future. The valuation of distressed businesses is a complex, multifaceted, imperfect and contentious process. This is particularly true when we consider that the theory underpinning the majority of conventional valuation methodologies and techniques is predominantly based on an adaptation of a 'going concern' approach.

Regardless, any distressed valuation is fundamentally impacted by situational factors, including:
- valuation timing (ie, pre- or post-investment assessment), which can be significantly impacted by asymmetric information or uncertainty regarding the future business plan;
- the investment parameters (eg, to justify a bid price relative to return requirements); and/or
- the underlying purpose (eg, to drive a short- or long-term investment return, or to help position negotiations as part of a wider restructuring which shifts the balance of power toward certain stakeholders).

Despite all these factors, distressed asset valuations are still likely to be triangulated using some of the more conventional techniques which include the discounted cash-flow, relative valuation and liquidation methods. Other, less common, methods for valuing distressed entities include option pricing and Monte Carlo simulations, both of which are outside the scope of this chapter.

It should be noted however that conventional methods often fail to consider certain traits of distressed businesses, and therefore are not the complete answer to valuation in all distressed scenarios. A skilled valuation will use conventional approaches as a starting point; however, it will also amend certain elements of the process to reflect situational factors and nature of the target business.

Set out below is a high-level review of some of the core valuation techniques which can be employed, and some potential adjustments that can be made in order to consider the impact of distress. We also address some of the issues commonly encountered when undertaking such valuations, from an investors' perspective.

In the end there is no single method to value a business, and due to various weaknesses in each methodology a valuer will often triangulate the outcomes of each approach, evidencing the old cliché that valuation is an art and not a science.

7.2 Key considerations

As highlighted above, the appropriate valuation method will depend crucially on the purpose and intended use of the valuation, the level of access to information and the overall facts and circumstances surrounding the valuation. An initial assessment must also be made of any business to determine whether it is in terminal decline, or whether it remains economically viable and merely requires a balance-sheet restructuring.

7.3 Valuation techniques in distress

The core valuation techniques[19] considered in distress may include the following.

(a) Discounted cash-flow valuation

The discounted cash-flow approach is a fundamental valuation methodology used around the globe to ascertain the intrinsic value of a business, derived from the present value of its projected free cash-flow. There are a number of variations of the discounted cash-flow approach that can be used to calculate the intrinsic value of a business, including the leveraged buyout and adjusted present value methodologies.

The discounted cash-flow approach requires the same fundamental steps to value a business regardless of whether the company is considered healthy or distressed. This includes initial due diligence on the target entity to analyse historical performance and determine key performance drivers relative to its sector, before projecting free cash-flows over a forecast period. Depending on the perspective of the potential investor, this phase of the valuation presents an opportunity to overlay expected operational improvements and the potential effects of a new management team, or alternative strategic positioning, to determine potential upsides should the asset be acquired. This may impact on the amount an investor is willing to pay to acquire a distressed asset.

Ultimately any investor or incumbent stakeholder will seek to consider the return on capital deployed (or retained) to assess the price that they may be willing to offer to acquire a company or the negotiating position they will take in restructuring negotiations, considering their own cost of funding and return requirements. While the discounted cash-flow method is perhaps the purest theoretical tool for assessing value, given the sensitivity to input assumptions involved (eg, the cost of equity/debt, beta factors, target capital structure and terminal value), it must always be considered alongside other valuation methods to conclude on an applicable valuation range.

Indeed, one of the key limitations often cited in utilising the discounted cash-flow approach in a distressed valuation is that forecast cash-flows, which are traditionally forecast to infinity, are at greater risk due to default and therefore might never be realised, thereby potentially skewing any valuation. There is always a risk of failure which must also be factored in, which will normally manifest itself on the discount rate applied in assessing the present value of future cash-flows.

---

19 Aswath Damodaran, *The Dark Side of Valuation: Valuing Young, Distressed and Complex Businesses* (FT Press, 2009) provides a much deeper analysis on the key methodology underlying distressed valuations including the application of probabilities of distress under both the discounted cash-flow and relative valuation approaches.

(b)   *Relative valuation*
Another common approach for valuing companies is relative valuation based on two comparisons:
- the comparable company (valuation multiples for a basket of companies with similar characteristics or profile); and
- the comparable transaction (valuation multiples achieved on similar businesses in the same sector).

Both comparisons invoke the core foundation of finance theory which postulates that in efficient financial markets two assets with identical cash flows must trade at the same price.

The approach is often considered the most straightforward method by which to value both going concerns and distressed businesses. The relative valuation method is widely used and often preferred by practitioners as it requires fewer assets, time and information than the discounted cash-flow approach.

Furthermore, the relative approach is much less subjective than the discounted cash-flow approach, and is considered easier for wider audiences to comprehend, particularly when it utilises well known listed companies or recently completed transactions as a reference point.

Under both comparisons, an estimate of firm value is reached by multiplying a ratio estimated from comparable firms (a valuation multiple) by earnings before interest, taxation, depreciation and amortisation (EBITDA), or another appropriate multiple, to arrive at an enterprise value for the business.

In a distressed situation, directly comparable company data is often unavailable. Therefore it is necessary to make subjective adjustments to incorporate the impact of distress on the market multiples. Making such adjustments can often lead to over- or under-valuation, and enables personal biases to emerge in the analysis. In order to mitigate these risks, it is preferable to have a sector specialist opine on this situation, in addition to analysing historical data on similarly restructured publicly listed entities.

Other adjustments to consider include consideration of net working capital and capital expenditure. Whereas the comparable company approach assumes a normalised working capital position, it is often the case that a distressed business is suffering from both a working capital 'stretch' and capital under-investment, meaning initial investment is required to normalise the position.

More importantly, the relative valuation method requires a detailed assessment of the target's key financials to determine the appropriate EBITDA (or equivalent) on which the valuation will be based. When undertaking a valuation, it is imperative that non-recurring items are excluded in order to determine the normalised EBITDA of the business. Additionally, it is often the case that adjustments are required to the financial statements in order to make them truly comparable with international companies (if applicable) while also ensuring that year-end calendar adjustments are taken into account.

In a distressed context, comparable transactions may provide the most appropriate guide to multiples in a valuation, as there is often data on companies that have previously been acquired in distressed situations, therefore providing a reasonable proxy for the valuation.

(c) **Liquidation valuation**
When a business is in terminal decline, or where a substantial break-up of the business seems inevitable, then using either a discounted cash-flow or a relative valuation approach may be inappropriate. In these circumstances the most applicable method is a liquidation approach, involving a valuation of any profitable and separable business divisions and break-up values of the company's residual assets (a 'sum of all parts' valuation). This may also be completed in conjunction with an estimated outcome analysis utilising insolvency experts to assess potential asset value discounts in liquidation and overlaying potential additional costs to liquidate (including administrator costs and various statutory deductions), all of which can vary by jurisdiction.

The liquidation value may be the worst-case scenario in valuing any business or assets, but will itself be fraught with input assumption complexities. In the end it will often simply be used as another data point to assess asset recovery value and to support investment or restructuring decision-making. However, liquidation valuations (and estimated returns to creditors) also inform the offers made to creditor classes in many company-led restructurings, since there is often a minimum statutory requirement that each class of creditor has an outcome which is better (or at least not worse) than that which they would receive in a liquidation).

8. Impact of valuation on restructuring transactions
The value of a company on a debt-free basis plays a key part in any restructuring, since it is in effect a forecast; it serves as a projection of what is likely to be returned to each stakeholder within the current capital structure. Projections (usually competing ones) are then used to form the basis for negotiations amongst different stakeholders to determine the holdings that each party will have in the newly restructured business. As discussed above, valuation is a very subjective process, and there is scope for a wide range of views which will often be fiercely contested, sensitised and flexed in order best to serve the purpose of each stakeholder, and also to drive negotiations when the perceived value break implies that some stakeholders have no economic interest.

Typically, a senior lender's adviser will be more inclined to take a realistic but conservative view of projected forecast performance in light of historic underperformance. This may result in an implied value break in the senior debt, which would justify a revised capital structure where the future economic interest of the business would lie primarily in the hands of the senior lender. In other words the senior lender would become the sole lender and majority equity holder (or beneficiary of equity value) in the new structure. This is typically achieved through a debt-for-equity swap. Junior lenders and existing equity holders would be offered subordinated debt instruments and/or minority equity holdings in the new structure, often having minimal value unless the company goes on to exceed expectations in performance terms, but preferable to being eliminated from the equation altogether through an insolvency process.

Junior lenders and equity holders will be independently advised, and will typically argue that the senior lender's view is overly pessimistic, that (depending on the situation) it is possible that the senior lender will be repaid in full over a longer period, and therefore that the more junior ranking debt and current equity ought to retain a substantial element (or indeed all) of their existing holdings (albeit potentially subject to revised terms in the case of junior debt holders).

The senior creditor will respond that, if that were truly the case, the company would have been able to refinance the senior portion of its debt with other debt providers. They will invite existing equity holders to inject the funds to reduce the senior lender's exposure to more manageable levels.

The senior lender may insist on a market-testing exercise where a select group of industry and financial players are invited to bid for the business, thus demonstrating the market's view of value. These valuations will be impacted by the perception of distress. Such an exercise can pave the way for senior lender ownership, either by setting the parameters for a solvent restructuring or (in some jurisdictions) providing a benchmark for the consideration in a pre-packaged sale of the business through an insolvency process. The process can also bring the distress of the business into the public eye and increase operational and creditor pressure, exacerbating the situation. As such it will typically be resisted by equity, whose future returns depend on the valuation of the business following a turnaround process rather than a sale in its distressed state (or a restructuring based on the distressed value).

The power dynamic in this negotiation is complex and highly dependent on the jurisdiction, the restructuring tools and insolvency procedures available, and the potential need for new money investment to drive future value out of situation. Typically, after protracted negotiation, to move beyond a deadlock, one party (often the company or the senior creditor) may present other stakeholders with an ultimatum, in the form of a best and final restructuring proposal, offering a much reduced stake in the business. The implied alternative is an insolvency process where returns to equity or junior creditors may be little or nothing, but the senior lender may be substantially repaid and/or able to take ownership of the business. Whether this is capable of being implemented is situation-specific.[20]

Traditional providers of senior debt may be reluctant to take such a stance, or have a policy which prohibits the taking of (majority) equity stakes. In such circumstances an alternative capital provider may take the role by acquiring the senior debt, typically at a sub-par price, with the clearing bank content to remove the risk in its position by recognising a loss that has already been provided for.

The valuation ascribed to a company or asset will significantly influence each stakeholders' decision-making process at the outset, and will potentially dictate their strategy during negotiations. It is not uncommon to see multiple valuations in restructuring situations, which can ultimately be held up in court if a restructuring reaches an impasse or dissenting stakeholders look to block a course of action which is pushed forward by other participants. Valuations are, in the absence of any other

---

20 For a more comprehensive explanation of the practice of restructuring in the UK context, see Chris Howard and Bob Hedger, *Restructuring Law and Practice*, second edition (LexisNexis, 2014).

tool which can influence decision-making, often used to positon the balance of power in negotiations, and will often be driven by the intended strategy of each stakeholder.

Ultimately distressed investors will look to take a view on value to assess the bid-ask spread before they purchase a position in a restructuring situation, but will also then look to develop their valuation thesis once they have a seat at the table. These two views on value might be very different and will be impacted by the information at hand, but they will inform negotiations throughout, and also support the ultimate exit and recovery story for each participant.

9. Overall conclusion

Despite an active distressed market operating in Europe since the late 1990s the last six to eight years have proven more complex for investors given the sheer scale of the economic crisis, unprecedented quantitative easing and a period of interest rate depression that may not be witnessed again for generations.

However, with continuing global economic uncertainty, Eurozone and sovereign debt travails, the likely protracted post-referendum Brexit negotiations, a correction in Chinese demand and a significant volume of non-performing loan assets still absorbing capital on bank balance sheets, there is likely to be a raft of opportunities for distressed investors.

High levels of corporate bond issuances have increased the opportunity to invest in tradable, multi-stakeholder debt, but this does not address a business's issue of over-leverage, it merely postpones the issue until the bond maturity is pending. Short-term and systemic shocks will continue to generate idiosyncratic opportunities for both passive and active investors alike over the next five years.

Attempts to invest in these situations have also laid bare the very different laws and regulations that prevail in Europe on a country-by-country basis, and are often a reflection of deeply held cultural values.

Valuing these opportunities, understanding the potential upsides and pitfalls, and interacting with the various stakeholders to ensure a successful outcome is a complex matter. There is no substitute for situational and jurisdictional expertise. No two situations are alike, and advice from senior professionals is key. There can be no comprehensive guidebook.

Recognising that context, this book represents a highly valuable, suitably focused contribution to those who aspire to have an understanding of the European distressed debt environment.

Credit agreement and indenture analysis from a European perspective

Jacqueline Ingram
Cadwalader, Wickersham & Taft LLP

1. Introduction

When times are good, lenders can be forgiven for thinking that modern credit agreements, so long and so complicated, are just another excuse for lawyers to burn fees by nit-picking every complex detail. When a company is performing well and complying with all its covenants, the focus is on when lenders will get repaid. In the distressed world, however, the range of who gets paid, how much and when can seem alarmingly wide, and the leverage of different stakeholders can sometimes turn on a host of complex details and intricate points of interpretation.

To grasp the details that matter the most, conducting a credit review is essential. A credit review is a process where the terms of the relevant credit documents (loan agreement, indenture, intercreditor agreement) are reviewed and analysed by a legal team, and their analysis fed back to the investment team looking at a particular investment opportunity.

The fundamental purpose of conducting a credit review is to get as full a picture as possible of the credit that you, as a participant in the world of distressed debt, are considering. The legal analysis is separate from business and market diligence, and focuses on the exact bundle of rights that is being acquired. It allows you to think through potential scenarios and use this knowledge, combined with other diligence, to assess the risks and rewards of a potential investment opportunity. Exactly what scenarios are rehearsed, and to what depth they are analysed, will depend on many factors. However, a broad understanding of the way a credit works is important for any investor.

This chapter provides an introduction to some of the key topics that are usually covered in a credit review. By definition, it is not exhaustive, as the overlaying and overlapping factors and issues that build up a credit review depend very much on the particular opportunity being considered. Its primary aim is to explain the hot topics and red-flag issues that are particular to the pan-European debt market (as opposed to single-jurisdiction or American market).

2. Non-documentary factors

Before focus turns to the legal documents, it is worth noting a few of the extraneous factors that create the context in which a credit review should be read: investor strategy, the specific nature of the business, equity control and access to information.

The first factor is the strategy that the investor is pursuing with a particular investment. An investor with a loan-to-own strategy who is considering a significantly distressed business will focus on different areas than a minority investor who is considering a strong business whose distress is temporary and caused by general market conditions.

The second factor is the type of business being considered. The nature of the business and the industry in which it operates influences both the strategy and the nature of the review. Certain market practices, standards and norms have developed in relation to borrowers operating in particular industries or market sectors. For example, real estate finance documents for property development or property-holding companies have a number of features that distinguish them from the standard leveraged buy-out documentation structure. The type of business being financed may also influence how tight or loose covenants may be in the legal documents; for example, a full-scale operating business is likely to need more flexibility in terms of covenants than a real estate special purpose vehicle.

Equity control is a further significant factor, as shareholders and management play a particularly central role in most distressed scenarios. Although the legal documents may not disclose how shareholders view the future of the business, an assessment can be made of how much leverage they may be able to assert in a downside scenario. An investor can then take the raw data of a credit review and analyse how likely or unlikely it may be that a particular shareholder exploits an identified vulnerability, or how reasonable that shareholder may be in a situation of financial distress. There can be a big difference in approach between equity holders who are a disparate group holding publicly-traded shares, a family who built the business from scratch and a private equity sponsor.

The nature of the equity control may also have an impact on the credit documents. For example, sophisticated sponsors often push for 'house' documents that give significant covenant flexibilities and aim to allow shareholders to retain control in a downside scenario. These documents often push the boundaries in terms of the permissions and carve-outs from restrictions, with varying degrees of success according to when in the credit cycle the deal was done. When conducting a review, it is worth bearing in mind the date of the credit documents in terms of how sponsor-friendly the market was at that point.

The last factor may be the most decisive in terms of the ability actually to conduct a detailed review; the extent of access to documentation and the time available. Accessing documents for listed or publicly traded debt instruments is often straightforward. A significant amount of information about public debt may be readily available, including offering memoranda, indentures and periodic reporting published on issuer websites. However, some key finance documents, such as intercreditor agreements and security documents, may not be publicly available, and investors may be concerned about accessing non-public information if this could restrict their ability to trade the debt. In the private debt context, access to information is less clear-cut. Investors often rely on disclosure from selling lenders and brokers that may be patchy or incomplete. In either situation, the ability fully to review and analyse the credit documents may be severely limited by time constraints imposed by sellers, auction processes or the investor's own internal decision-making processes.

3. Overview of capital structure

The starting point for any credit review is gaining an overall picture of the structure of the debtor group. An investor's ability to determine group capital structure depends very much on what information is available to it, whether through the seller or underwriter, company disclosure, accounts or publicly available commercial registries.

Typically, large European deals involve debtor groups with subsidiaries in multiple European and non-European jurisdictions. The extent of publicly available information varies significantly among jurisdictions. However, in many jurisdictions, annual accounts are publicly available and provide a good basis for understanding where the debtor group trades and where significant assets may be located.

It is important to build up an overview of the debt structure within the group. The first stage of this is to identify which group entities are direct borrowers. Creditors with claims against companies higher up in the group structure are structurally subordinated to creditors with claims against operating subsidiaries. This is because the value of the group is usually concentrated in the operating entities. The claims against the operating entities would have to be satisfied first before value can reach those with claims further up the shareholding chain. Structural subordination is the reason that many junior ranking debt tranches are borrowed at holding company level within the debtor group.

Understanding the type of instrument pursuant to which debt is issued is also important because, even if the particular documentation is not publicly available, assumptions and educated guesses can be made about the structure and terms of the debt. For example, bonds are often issued by a special purpose vehicle relatively high up in the group structure. The bond proceeds are then lent in to the main group structure and are channelled down or up in the group through a proceeds loan. In contrast, bank loans tend to be lent within the main shareholding or group structure. Further, certain facilities within bank loans, such as working capital or revolving credit facilities, are likely to be borrowed by operating entities who need those facilities for day-to-day operations.

A key issue to investigate is for what purpose the proceeds of the financing arrangements were used. It can be significant whether the funds were used for working capital or specific capex items, or whether they went to fund an acquisition. This is particularly the case where, for example, local laws restrict the ability of a company to provide financial assistance for the acquisition of its shares. Financial assistance has been broadly construed in a number of jurisdictions and can encompass the giving of guarantees and security. As a result, the number of entities which are available to be included in the security and guarantee net may be significantly reduced, along with the value of claims against such entities.

4. Guarantees and security

Financial assistance and corporate benefit concerns are often addressed by including standard guarantee limitation wording in legal documents. Guarantee limitations contractually limit the value of a guarantee given by a particular entity. They allow a guarantee to be given, but do not resolve the underlying financial assistance or corporate benefit issue. Where such wording has been included, it is important to consider the impact of those limitations on the validity and extent of claims against members of the debtor group. These limitations are relevant to a number of European jurisdictions and can have quite a significant impact on the ability of creditors to claim and recover in a downside scenario.

Many complex financial structures have a pool of shared guarantors, who guarantee a number of different debt instruments that may be subject to different priorities and rankings. Where this is the case, it is important to know whether the guarantor group is homogenous, or whether certain instruments benefit from guarantees from different entities, thereby effectively priming the other debt classes who do not have a competing claim. Even where the guarantors are homogenous, the relative rankings of the guarantees should be appraised to determine, for example whether intercreditor arrangements are in place to subordinate the guarantees of junior creditors and restrict their ability to enforce security. It is also important to know whether there is a guarantor coverage covenant in the credit documents, that requires the debtor group to ensure that the guarantors account for at least a certain percentage of assets, earnings before interest, taxes, depreciation and amortisation (EBITDA), and/or turnover, as this provides some guidance as to the scope of claims into the debtor group.

Depending on the nature of the investment and the business of the underlying debtor group, investors may conduct a full security review. In essence, a security review examines the scope and the effectiveness of a security package and its effectiveness. Such a review generally involves obtaining copies of the relevant security documents, and then conducting a detailed review of those documents and any ancillary steps taken by deal counsel to perfect the security.

A secondary buyer of debt often has limited ability to take steps to remedy any deficiencies in the security package. The security review acts like a due diligence report in highlighting the commercial risks to be borne in mind when considering an investment. It will highlight any risks that security may not be valid, or may be vulnerable to challenge in a downside scenario. It may also identify significant assets within the debtor group that are not validly or effectively secured.

Even where a full-scale security review is not undertaken, a credit review should include a high-level analysis of the scope of the security package in place. Security can be used by lenders in a proactive and a defensive manner. Proactive security is security that the lenders are likely to use in the context of a restructuring; the most typical is a holding-company share pledge. Enforcement of such security would allow the lender group to cut off the existing shareholders and take control of the debtor group by stepping into the shoes of the shareholder. When looking at proactive security enforcement, the key issues are whether it has been granted over all ownership interests, and whether the enforcement process in the relevant jurisdiction allows for a quick, clean enforcement.

Defensive security is relevant for controlling competing claims and protecting the lenders' potential recovery in insolvency. Lenders often take security over significant tangible assets to defend against key assets within the debtor group being secured in favour of other creditors. This is an important way of controlling the competing claims of creditors. In addition, most European jurisdictions allocate some form of preferred or priority position to secured creditors in insolvency processes. In most jurisdictions, creditors with fixed charges over tangible assets have a claim in the insolvency that enables them to get recoveries ahead of general unsecured creditors.

5. **Covenants and carve-outs**

Competing claims against a debtor group can also be controlled by limiting the ability to incur indebtedness through the use of negative covenants in the credit documents.

In loan documents, the indebtedness covenant is usually structured as an outright prohibition on the obligors (the borrower and guarantors) or the debtor group from incurring indebtedness, subject to specific carve-outs. It is worth noting that the prohibition usually relates to financial indebtedness, which is often explicitly defined as narrower than general indebtedness. The carve-outs from the covenant are usually the subject of significant negotiation at the origination of the transaction. The scope of the carve-outs should strike a balance between enabling the debtor and its group to function in the ordinary course of business and assuring the creditors that the debtor group cannot significantly increase leverage of the debtor group by incurring additional debt.

Bond-style covenants are generally considered more permissive than loan covenants. The general principle behind these covenants is the preservation of cash flow for debt service. The debt covenant typically starts with a limitation on indebtedness except where the debtor and members of its group are in compliance with certain financial ratios, which indicate the financial health of the debtor group. The most common formulation is that the debtor and its restricted subsidiaries (broadly, those of its subsidiaries to whom the covenants apply) would be in compliance with a fixed charge cover ratio or leverage ratio if the debt were incurred. The covenant then lists a number of carve-outs that allow debt incurrence even where the ratio cannot be complied with.

In both loan-style and bond-style indebtedness covenants, the carve-outs often take the form of specific 'baskets' that allow incurrence of certain types of indebtedness up to a certain amount. These basket amounts are the subject of significant negotiation at origination, and are often the focus for investors because they are usually the carve-outs that allow for the incurrence of significant amounts of debt. The baskets may be fixed to a finite limit for each year or over the life of the deal. Alternatively, they may be 'grower' baskets where the limit is the greater of a fixed amount and a percentage that allows the limit to grow with the business, for example a certain percentage of total assets. It is important to note that if debt has been incurred under a grower basket in good times, this debt remains permitted even when performance of the debtor group deteriorates.

In addition to the incurrence of indebtedness, investors often focus on the ability of the debtor group to leak value to shareholders. Most credit documents restrict how much value can be extracted by the shareholder from the debtor group while the debt remains outstanding. However, they also contain carve-outs and baskets that allow certain payments to be made.

As with the indebtedness covenant, loan-style restrictions tend to block distributions and payments to shareholders (those companies outside the 'banking group' of borrowers and guarantors), with specific permissions which allow some leakage. These permissions can take the form of fixed baskets (such as an agreed annual management fee). They can also be more flexible and lift restrictions if, for example, the debtor group achieves a certain leverage ratio.

In bond-style covenants, leakage to shareholders is primarily captured by the restricted payments covenant. This covenant identifies what is considered a 'restricted payment' (which includes a restricted investment), which includes payments to creditors junior to the bonds and investments in non-subsidiaries. Secondly, it sets out the conditions that must be satisfied for a restricted payment to be made. These conditions typically include there being no default, room under the fixed charge cover ratio to incur $1 of debt and there being sufficient headroom in the 'restricted payment builder basket'. Finally, the restricted payments covenant then lists payments that are not subject to those limitations. These baskets are always available, whether there is room under the restricted payment builder basket or not. There are therefore a number of possible routes through the covenant: permitted investment baskets, permitted payment baskets and availability under the restricted payment builder basket.

6. Amendments to credit documents

Credit documents almost always allow the covenants and other provisions to be amended, subject to certain creditor consent thresholds being reached. Minority investors should be aware that, no matter what the legal documents say, fundamental terms can often be amended without their specific consent.

The provisions that regulate the amendments process usually distinguish between lower-level consents that require a majority (which can range from 50.1% to $66^2/3\%$) and those requiring higher level of consent. At the top end of the spectrum are amendments to the 'money terms' of the debt, such as a reduction of margin or extension of maturity. Often these money terms cannot be amended or waived without the consent of all creditors, because they are considered fundamental to the rights of the creditors against the debtor group.

Where large lending syndicates are involved, obtaining the consent of all lenders can be impractical or even impossible. The requirement for total consent can give small debtholders the opportunity to extract special treatment or gain leverage. Several mechanisms have been developed to deal with situations like these – primarily 'structural adjustment' or 'facility change' provisions. Clauses such as these allow certain key changes to be made with the consent of all those affected plus, usually, an overall majority of the creditors. This lower consent threshold allows the debtor group flexibility to work with cooperative or proactive creditors to make amendments.

In addition, it is also worth noting two other mechanisms that have become common in the amendments provisions in credit documents. The first is the 'yank-the-bank' clause, whereby a non-consenting creditor can be repaid at par by the debtor. The second is the 'snooze-and-lose' clause, whereby silence, or a failure to respond to a request for consent beyond a certain fixed deadline, results in the creditor's debt holding being disregarded for the purposes of determining whether the appropriate majority (or, in some cases, unanimity) has been reached.

Although credit documents may require the consent of all creditors or a high percentage of them, certain procedures can be used to override these thresholds. For example, the English law scheme of arrangement can be used to bind creditors (including secured creditors) to a compromise or some other arrangement, so long as certain (lower) thresholds of consent are met. Therefore, simply reading the amendments provisions of the credit agreement may not be sufficient to understand all of the potential ways changes can be effected without the consent of all creditors.

7. **Security enforcement and control of creditors**
One of the defining characteristics of the European distressed debt arena is the absence of a unified restructuring or insolvency process that allows for the compromise of creditor claims in a cohesive process. The EC regulation on insolvency proceedings has made significant progress in bringing some unity to an otherwise diverse and sometimes contradictory set of national insolvency regimes, but it falls short of offering one pan-European debt restructuring process.

This lack of coherent process stands in contrast to the Chapter 11 bankruptcy proceedings in the United States, which provide a tried and tested way to manage different stakeholder groups and to impose a plan for restructuring distressed companies. A central feature of this process is the bankruptcy court's authority to cram down 'out-of-the-money' creditors – that is to impose a compromise on certain creditor classes without requiring the consent of that class. Simply put, such a cram-down can allow 'in-the-money' creditors to impose a restructuring on out-of-the-money creditors, thereby diminishing hold-out value for these out-of-the-money creditors. In contrast to some European jurisdictions, Chapter 11 proceedings also reflect an absolute priority principle, which means that junior creditors and, importantly, equity should not benefit ahead of senior creditors.

In the European context, other than in purely domestic transactions, it is less common that one process can deliver the same certainty of result. Accordingly, the European market has developed contractual frameworks that bind creditors to pre-agreed outcomes and has relied on having security arrangements, such as structural share pledges, to disenfranchise equity. The contractual frameworks are set out in intercreditor agreements, which have become increasingly complex and developed since the financial crisis.

Each intercreditor agreement calls for analysis alert to the agreement's unique capital structure and the investment opportunity being considered. However, as explained in the sub-sections that follow, three key provisions are common to most of these arrangements: control of security enforcement, standstills and releases.

The general principle within intercreditor arrangements is that the most senior class of creditors controls the enforcement of security. The scope of the senior creditors' ability to take action and lead an enforcement of security is usually very wide. They dictate what is enforced, the timing and the manner of enforcement.

The structure described above may differ, depending on the nature of the specific transaction being considered. For example, in transactions involving super-senior revolving credit facilities and senior secured high-yield bonds, it is more likely that holders of the senior secured bonds have the ability to control enforcement despite being junior in ranking to the revolving credit facility. In such scenarios, the intercreditor arrangements can become quite complex, since consultation between creditor classes may be required, or other creditor classes may be able to step in and lead security enforcement if the lead constituency is not acting expeditiously.

Standstills are a contractual agreement that stays the ability of junior creditor classes to accelerate and take enforcement action following the occurrence of defaults. The duration of the standstill and extent of action that is restricted during the standstill period is the subject of commercial negotiation at the time of documenting the deal. However, it is not uncommon for junior creditor classes to be restricted from taking any meaningful action for quite significant periods.

Release provisions are contractual agreements that allow the security agent to release security and, in certain circumstances, to release borrowing and guarantee claims of creditors against the debtor group. The main purpose of these provisions is to ensure that senior creditors can enforce security and sell the debtor group unencumbered by the claims of junior creditors. Release rights are triggered by the enforcement of a share pledge, or by the disposal of shares of an obligor or member of the group. It is important to note the precise drafting of the clause, as the trigger event for the release right can be quite narrowly prescribed. It is also important to consider the extent to which the release covers all liabilities that encumber the value of the entities subject to the proposed disposal. These liabilities may include junior creditor claims and also liabilities under shareholder loans or intra-group liabilities.

In certain deals, release provisions are triggered only under certain conditions. These conditions often seek to ensure that a more senior creditor class cannot release junior claims without some evidence that the value for which the assets are being disposed of is fair. Although such conditions vary, they often require a release of all claims (meaning the assets are being sold on a debt-free basis) and some form of fair value opinion provided by an appropriate expert.

8. Transfers

Credit agreements contain provisions that regulate how creditors can transfer their debt holdings to other creditors. The key considerations in transfer provisions, as set out below, are the method of transfer, documentary restrictions and local law requirements.

English law-governed loan documents usually allow for transfers by assignment or novation. Both methods achieve a similar result, but there is a legal difference between the two that can be quite significant. An assignment does not give rise to a new contract, whereas a novation extinguishes the old contract and replaces it with a new contract on the same terms. The creation of a new contract can have significant implications in certain jurisdictions, raising questions as to whether ancillary rights, such as guarantees and security, are transferred along with the main rights.

Restrictions on transfers can take many forms. A typical formulation may require the consent of a debtor company, or consultation prior to transfer, often for a specified period. Certain debtor groups or their sponsor may be concerned about who is part of their lender group due to the degree of information shared under the loan agreement. Restrictions on competitors becoming lenders are often included in the credit agreement to address such concerns. Alternatively, transfer restrictions may take the form of 'white lists' of pre-approved investors and 'black lists' of investors who are not allowed to become lenders.

Transfer provisions may contain technicalities in relation to the transfers, such as minimum transfer amounts or minimum hold amounts. Close attention should be paid to the drafting of these provisions, as drafting errors can have a significant impact on a creditor's future ability to trade.

The ability to become a lender under a credit agreement can also be affected by local regulatory regimes in the jurisdictions in which the debtors are located. A number of European jurisdictions impose limits on what sort of entity can lend money to borrowers in its jurisdiction, and the permitted lending structure. Local regulatory issues are outside the scope of the current chapter, but are a very relevant part of the credit review analysis.

9. Conclusion

A credit review should be more than just a verbatim recitation of certain clauses in the credit documents. It should allow you to understand how the credit documents deal with the issues important to you and the strategy you are pursuing. The credit review should consider the micro level by analysing the wording of the clauses, and the macro level by highlighting broader legal issues of relevance. It should analyse the different leverage positions of key stakeholders, potential scenarios that might play out if the debtor group becomes distressed and what position you may find yourself in should the debtor group fail. By doing so, you should be in a better position fully to understand the credit you are considering, and the nature of the investment opportunity with which you are presented.

Anatomy of an LMA distressed trade transaction and transfer mechanisms under English law

Elizabeth Bilbao
Mandel, Katz & Brosnan LLP

1. Introduction

The loan trading market has been in existence for over two decades. Developed in the United Kingdom in the early 1990s it has grown significantly since the financial meltdown of 2007/2008 as a result of regulatory changes and the need for lenders (especially regulated financial institutions) to reduce their exposure and free up capital to diversify investments.

Together with the Loan Syndications and Trading Association Inc (LSTA), the Loan Market Association (LMA) is responsible for producing and maintaining standard documentation used for loan trading.

The LMA was established in 1996 to improve efficiency of the primary and secondary syndicated loan markets in Europe, the Middle East and Africa. The LMA's mission is to promote the syndicated loan as a key debt product available to borrowers across Europe, the Middle East and Africa and develop market norms and standardised documentation in this regard.

The LMA first developed a set of secondary loan trade documentation in the early 2000s. Keeping its documentation under continuous review, it updates its forms regularly through a committee of lawyers and market practitioners. The majority of the European loan trading is carried out based on the LMA conventions and settles using the LMA standard forms of documentation.

The LMA documentation was developed to work as a comprehensive suite of documents. The LMA secondary loan trading documents include six templates for confidentiality agreements, three options for trade confirmations, seven different types of participation agreements with related templates for different types of termination agreements (bilateral and multilateral), bilateral and multilateral netting agreements and two forms of assignment agreements (bank debt/claims).

The central document for an LMA transaction is the trade confirmation, which will govern the transaction and which incorporates the LMA standard terms and conditions. It is governed by English law and parties submit to the jurisdiction of the English courts.

This article will explore the anatomy of an LMA distressed trade transaction and explain the different stages of the distressed trade lifecycle, from pre-trade due diligence to settlement of the transaction.

The first part will outline the due diligence process and confidentiality issues that arise before a trade is agreed, focusing on the most relevant confidentiality issues, and identify critical provisions in a confidentiality agreement.

The second part looks at the oral agreement between the seller and the buyer, its meaning and the enforceability of the oral agreement between the parties.

This second part will also describe the elements of an LMA trade confirmation as well as the different transfer mechanisms available under English law. Reference will be made to the LMA standard terms and conditions and the most relevant representations and warranties applicable to a distressed trade transaction.

The third part will explore the different transfer mechanisms for settling an LMA transaction.

Finally, this article will touch on any post-settlement issues that may be required to complete the trade lifecycle and perfect the transfer of the loan and any security attached to it.

2. Phase I: pre-trade

2.1 Preparation for the transaction

(a) *Perform due diligence in relation to the counterparty (whether buyer or seller)*
Prior to trading, the buyer and the seller should have identified which entities will engage in the transaction and their respective jurisdictions of incorporation/formation. They should have also completed know-your-customer and anti-money-laundering checks.

(b) *What is the buyer purchasing?*
In a typical distressed situation the borrower will already have defaulted on its obligations under the credit documentation, and in some circumstances will be close to an insolvency scenario. In this context, it is especially important that a buyer carries out an extensive due diligence on the asset and understands the nature of the asset being acquired.

Due diligence on the asset should be concluded prior to trading. Standard LMA trading conventions assume that review of credit documentation is not a condition to a trade, and instead assume that both parties are sophisticated investors, have all the relevant information to enter into the transaction and have made an informed decision to trade with each other.

The starting point for any due diligence review is to understand the business of the borrower, its capital structure and the position of the asset to be purchased in such structure. Some of the customary due diligence questions to be answered during the review include the following: What is the status of its financial obligations? Has any event of default occurred and is it continuing? Is the obligation that is to be purchased a loan or bond, or is it a derivative? What kind of instrument is available to buy?

(c) *Status of the borrower*
Another series of due diligence queries relate to the status of the borrower: Is the

borrower in default? Is such default remediable? Are there any insolvency proceedings, or is there any restructuring process in place? Are there related obligors in similar proceedings in other jurisdictions?

At this point it is important that a prospective buyer analyses the credit documentation and concludes whether the trade will be compliant with any contractual or regulatory restrictions in the relevant jurisdiction of the borrower.

(d) *Is the loan secured?*

If the loan is secured, the security package should be analysed to confirm that any security or guarantees are assignable.

Knowledge of the structure of the security package is important to determine what a buyer's position in a potential enforcement scenario will be. A review of the security package will also allow a buyer to determine the costs of the transaction, including security registration and assignment costs.

The majority of the loans traded in the UK secondary market include a security trust structure whereby the security is taken in the name of a security agent which holds the security on trust for the benefit of the lenders from time to time. Upon transfer of a loan from one lender to a new lender, the security agent will update its records reflecting the new lender as a beneficiary of the security under such agency structure. This arrangement guarantees that any new lender that buys in the secondary market will have the benefit of the same security as the original lenders. It also avoids re-registration of the security each time a lender assigns its rights to a new lender because the security remains registered in the name of the security agent.

A security trust structure may not work in all jurisdictions. Certain civil law jurisdictions do not recognise the concept of a trust, which in practical terms means that in the absence of a security agent holding the security on behalf of the lenders, the security is created in the name of each individual lender. Upon transfer of a loan or a position in a loan, the security package will also need to be transferred. In the case of a security subject to registration, any new lender wishing to benefit from such security will have to re-register the security in its own name upon settlement of the loan assignment.

Transferring the security attracts additional costs and formalities that will have to be priced and taken into consideration for settlement. These costs can be substantial and can impact the projected economics of the trade depending on the size of the security package and the jurisdiction where re-registration needs to take place.

2.2 Confidentiality

Any due diligence will require access to the relevant documentation. The nature of the loans traded in the secondary market will most likely require access to non-public confidential information, which is invariably available only under a confidentiality agreement.

(a) *Does a prospective buyer need to sign a confidentiality agreement?*

The majority of LMA-based credit documentation contains provisions that allow the disclosure of information in certain circumstances, including in relation to a potential sale of a loan. In the absence of such provisions, the rule under English law is that the borrower's consent must be obtained before a seller/lender can disclose any information relating to the borrower or its group, including copies of the relevant credit documentation. LMA-based credit agreements usually require that an LMA form of confidentiality agreement be used by a seller/lender in delivering credit documentation to a prospective buyer.

(b)   What is the definition and scope of confidential information?
In some cases the definition of confidential information is so broad that it can practically prevent a seller/lender from sharing credit documentation to a prospective buyer for its due diligence review.

(c)   How will a buyer use the information?
The LMA confidentiality agreements restrict the use of any information for the sole purpose of considering and evaluating whether to enter into the purchase or sale of the loan.

(d)   With whom can a buyer share the information?
LMA-based credit documentation allows for the information to be shared with the prospective buyer's professional advisers as well as with any potential further assignees, transferees or sub-participants, or those with whom the prospective buyer enters into any other transaction under which payments are or may be made by reference to the credit agreement or the obligor, provided that any such third party enters into a confidentiality agreement.

(e)   How will confidentiality be maintained?
When reviewing a confidentiality agreement the prospective buyer needs to pay particular attention to whether it includes any releases or waivers that will prejudice them in the future. Can the confidential information be disclosed to any potential buyer? What are the obligations to return the information if the buyer decides not to enter into the transaction with the prospective seller? A buyer needs to be sure that it can comply with the confidentiality agreement restrictions from its internal operation requirements.

The LMA forms of confidentiality agreements provide that sellers may further disclose the terms of the transaction with its prospective buyers if they comply with confidentiality restrictions in the relevant confidentiality agreement the seller signed in order to receive the confidential information.

(f)   For how long will the confidentiality agreement last?
The obligations under the confidentiality agreements will cease upon the buyer becoming a lender of record or, in the event of a participation agreement, 12 months after the termination of that participation. In any other case, the confidentiality agreement will generally terminate on the date falling 12 months after the date of final receipt of any confidential information.

If the prospective buyer does not complete the transaction, the seller can request that the confidential information be returned or destroyed. A prospective buyer needs to determine if its internal or external compliance requirements will require retention of any needed confidential information.

2.3 Private information

Loans are private obligations that give access to confidential information relating to a borrower. To comply with insider trading and market abuse laws, market participants need to have measures in place with respect to trading in publicly listed securities issued by a loan borrower. Measures typically entail raising Chinese walls between trading desks to restrict free flow of information.

2.4 LMA transparency guidelines

The LMA has issued Guidelines on Transparency and the Use of Information. These transparency guidelines (which are voluntary and not regulatory) identify three levels of recipients of information in the loan market:

- market participants who receive information that is available to all lenders under a credit agreement;
- lenders who choose to remain public and not receive information available under the credit documentation (perhaps because they own publicly-listed securities); and
- lenders or market participants who have material information that it is not available to the whole syndicate – information, which is referred to as 'borrower confidential information' (information above and beyond that which is circulated to lenders generally, such as information provided to a steering committee, board members, shareholders, etc).

The transparency guidelines provide that any market participant in possession of borrower confidential information may trade its loans with other market participants regardless of whether these counterparties are in possession of borrower confidential information provided that:

- the relevant lender discloses to the counterparty that it is in possession of borrower confidential information (though the borrower confidential information itself need not be disclosed);
- if the counterparty enters into any related upstream or downstream trade, it will disclose to its further counterparty that some or all of the relevant loans are being either sourced from or sold to a lender holding borrower confidential information; and
- the relevant lender has reasonably made a judgment (consistent with appropriate standards of professional integrity and fair dealings) that the transaction will not adversely affect other members of the syndicate/market.

The guidelines seek to identify areas of best practice but are not intended to be prescriptive as to how such best practice is achieved.

2.5 Know-your-customer and anti-money-laundering checks

Any internal know-your-customer and anti-money-laundering checks on the borrower (if required) and the counterparty should be commenced as soon as is possible in the trade cycle.

2.6 The asset

(a) Review of the transfer restrictions

Regulatory restrictions: Although not the case in England, there are certain jurisdictions where lending activities are reserved for licensed local banks. Banking monopoly rules can effectively prohibit certain entities from becoming direct lenders of record in jurisdictions where these rules apply.

Contractual restrictions: The underlying credit agreement will provide the terms and conditions applicable for any transfer among lenders or to third parties. Common transfer restrictions include the following:

- Borrower's consent – In some instances the borrower will reserve its right to consent to any new lender joining the syndicate. The majority of loan agreements where this provision is incorporated will include a provision that consent to a new lender must not be unreasonably withheld or denied, forcing the borrower to give its reasons for not consenting. In practice, however, this test is easily met by the borrower simply considering the request on its merits in the context of the borrower's own concerns; not those of the seller or buyer.
- Buyer must be a bank or financial institution – Certain credit agreements restrict the ability to become a lender to certain categories of potential transferees, in some cases limiting transferee lenders to banks or financial institutions.

    In *Argo Fund Ltd v Essar Steel Ltd* [2006] EWCA CIV 241, the Court of Appeal held that a Cayman investment fund was a financial institution under a loan agreement that limited any transfer from the syndicate of banks to another "bank or other financial institution". The court gave the term "financial institution" a broad definition.

    Through applicable case law, English law allows for a financial institution that is not a bank (in the strict conventional sense of lending money or accepting deposits for investment) to be considered a financial institution and will allow a hedge fund that invests in loan transactions to be considered a financial institution.
- Minimum transfer amounts and minimum holds – These types of limitations require that transfers cannot be made unless: either the loan amount transferred is over a specified minimum amount, or a lender has a specified minimum holding amount after the proposed transfer takes place.

    Minimum transfer amounts can cause issues for buyers who buy at the minimum threshold when there is a subsequent permanent commitment reduction which reduces their purchase amount prior to formalisation of the transfer.

The aim of a minimum transfer and minimum holding amounts from the borrower's point of view is to prevent a large number of small trades, which in turn could result in a potentially large number of investors as part of the syndicate.

- Know your customer – In many instances, an agent is not required to sign or deliver a transfer document until it is satisfied with all necessary know-your-customer or similar checks in relation to a new lender. It is advisable to ask an agent to start its know-your-customer checks as early as possible once the trade has been agreed.
- Withholding tax effectively prohibiting transfers – Although this circumstance is rare these days, a credit agreement can require that transfers be made only to entities that can be paid gross of withholding tax.
- Lock-up/standstill – The buyer should also take into consideration any standstill or lock-up in place as these will effectively prevent settlement until they have been lifted.

3. Phase II: the trade

3.1 Oral agreement

Condition 2 of the LMA standard terms and conditions provides that:

A binding contract for the sale or participation by the Seller to the Buyer of the Purchased Assets and the Purchased Obligations shall come into effect between the Seller and the Buyer upon oral or, in the absence of such oral agreement, written agreement of the terms on the Trade Date and shall be documented and completed in accordance with these Conditions.

There is supporting case law pursuant to *Bear Stearns Bank plc v Forum Global Equity Ltd* 2007 EWCH 1576, where the English High Court ruled that the parties intended to be contractually committed and that a contract existed even though not all aspects of the transaction had been agreed.

The date of the oral agreement is the trade date, and is the moment from which the buyer is 'on risk'. No credit event between trade date and the future settlement date will relieve a party of its respective obligations.

3.2 Status of confirmation

The LMA trade confirmation is the document that memorialises the terms of the oral agreement between the parties. It is not subject to negotiation of further terms. It remains the central document for an LMA trade and incorporates by reference the LMA standard terms and conditions in force at the trade date. Its terms, conditions, representations, warranties, covenants and indemnities will remain standing even after settlement of the transaction, and its terms prevail over any other settlement document.

The LMA standard terms and conditions are based on the principle that a trade is a trade, so if any third-party consent or condition is not satisfied, the parties must find a way to settle the trade by:

- LMA funded participation; or
- if legal transfer only is specified, or if a form of participation cannot be agreed, a mutually acceptable alternative arrangement having the economic equivalent of the agreed trade. Examples of alternative settlement structures include among others, cash settlement, synthetic structures (ie, total return swaps), and multilateral netting agreements.

3.3 Terms of the trade confirmation

(a) Core information
The trade confirmation identifies:
- the type of transaction (par/distressed);
- a description of the asset – sufficient description and information should be included adequately to identify the asset subject to the trade; this is especially important in the event the borrower in question has entered into multiple credit agreements;
- the trade date – as outlined above, this is the date on which the oral agreement takes place, and is the date from which the buyer is on risk;
- the settlement date – the LMA standard provides for transactions to be closed "as soon as reasonably practicable". If a transaction has not closed 20 business days after the trade date (T+20) (for distressed transactions), delayed settlement compensation will start accruing from this date onwards, so the seller pays any accruing interest from T+20 to the buyer and (unless funding benchmarks are negative) the buyer pays average daily funding costs (such as the euro interbank offered rate – EURIBOR) on the purchase price to the seller;
- the parties, details of the traded portion, the price agreed for the acquisition and interest treatment, which may be:
  - 'settled without accrued interests', which provides for the seller to keep any accrued interest up to the settlement date (as adjusted by delayed settlement compensation);
  - 'trades flat', which provides for the buyer to own any interest paid on or after the trade date (irrespective of when it accrued); or
  - 'paid on settlement', which provides for the buyer to pay to the seller its interest entitlement for its period of ownership of the then current interest period at settlement.

(b) Form of purchase
The form of purchase and ways to acquire the debt are:
- Legal transfer – This means that the seller acquires title to the asset and becomes a party to the finance documentation as a lender of record having a direct relationship with the borrower and agent and voting rights under those documents.
- Participation – Under English law, a participation is a private contractual relationship in which an entity has a bilateral contract with a lender of record

to share in the risk and rewards of an underlying loan. The disadvantage for a participant is that it has no direct nexus with the borrower (which may delay receipt of information), takes the credit risk of the lender of record and the borrower, and may find that the lender of record's other holdings dilute its voting power or control. The LMA funded participation may limit the participant's ability to call the underlying loan, and may contain unfavourable termination rights.
- Fall-back to alternative means of settlement – If settlement of the transaction is not possible by a legal transfer or participation of the loan, Condition 6 of the LMA standard terms and conditions requires the parties to enter into an alternative economic arrangement that will provide both parties with the same economic equivalent of the agreed-upon trade (an alternative settlement).
- Legal transfer only – This option may be elected in addition to legal transfer if the parties do not wish to close by participation. Legal transfer only does not negate the obligation under Condition 6 for the parties to enter into an alternative settlement if a legal transfer is not possible.

(c) *Elections*

Process agents: If the parties are located outside England, they may elect to appoint a process agent in England to take any service of proceedings if there is a dispute before the English courts.

Insolvency election: The parties can elect whether the transaction will terminate upon insolvency of the other party either automatically or by notice.

The LMA determines that an insolvency event has occurred in relation to a party when that party is, among other things, dissolved, or becomes insolvent or is unable to pay its debts, or enters into a composition with its creditors, or, either voluntarily or by the force of law, institutes or has instituted against it insolvency or bankruptcy proceedings.

Transfer fees: The default position is that both parties will share any transfer and registration fees in equal parts, provided that a party making multiple allocations bears the additional transfer fees. Any arrangement other than the default position should be reflected in this section.

(d) *Other terms of trade*

This section will contain any additional representations, conditions, covenants or agreements that the parties may have agreed to include in the transaction. This section enables the seller and the buyer to address credit-specific scenarios.

(e) *Representations and warranties*

A robust set of representations and warranties are an essential element of any secondary debt transaction, particularly for distressed debt trades. The LMA standard terms and conditions contain a strong set of representations and warranties that complements the buyer's due diligence review. The LMA representations and warranties provide contractual comfort and protection and become the basis of the buyer's contractual remedies and indemnities if there is a breach.

The seller is required to make representations as to itself and any previous owner of the debt, (referred to as a 'predecessor in title'). A chain of contingent claims is created whereby each successive buyer will have recourse against its immediate predecessor in title, leading ultimately to the original holder of the loans. The identity of the predecessor in title is never revealed and recovery is against the immediate predecessor in title, so there is no visibility along the chain of title.[1]

The LMA representations and warranties cover the following areas.

The parties:
- Mutual representations for all trades:
    - due incorporation;
    - power to enter into the transaction;
    - legal, valid, binding and enforceable obligations;
    - no broker, finder or other third-party fees or commission payable for the transaction; and
    - no approval of any governmental authority needed to enter into the transaction.
- Buyer's representations for all trades:
    - no use of any information for any unlawful purpose or in breach of any confidentiality agreement; and
    - status under the US Employee Retirement Income Security Act (ERISA).

The asset:
- Seller's representations for all trades:
    - Unencumbered title – The seller represents that it has good title to the loan and other ancillary rights (in this section referred to as the 'asset') and that it transfers the asset to the buyer with full title guarantee and has not made any prior sale, transfer or sub-participation of the asset which is subsisting;
    - No other documents – The seller represents that there are no other documents executed by it or any predecessor in title which would materially and adversely affect the asset. The seller also represents that neither it or any predecessor in title has executed any documentation relating to the credit agreement which has also not been executed by lenders generally;
    - No default – The seller represents that neither it nor any predecessor in title is in default of its obligations in relation to the asset;
    - Alienability – The seller represents that the asset is capable of being transferred;

---

[1] Under the LSTA documentation, the structure is different and the seller discloses/assigns the chain of title of upstream predecessor documents back to the time at which the asset became distressed (known as the 'shift date'), and enters into a purchase and sale agreement. This purchase and sale agreement is successively assigned in the secondary market to the next buyer.

- Pricing letter and payment-in-kind (PIK) interest – The seller represents that the amounts utilised in the pricing calculations are true and correct as of the date of the pricing letter and that such amounts take into consideration any payment in kind that has capitalised on or after the trade date but on or prior to the settlement date.
- ERISA – The seller represents that it is compliant with ERISA to the extent such legislation is relevant.

• Additional representations for distressed transactions:
- Provision of credit agreement – The seller represents that it has provided to the buyer the credit agreement, all inter-creditor and subordination agreements and material waivers and amendment documentation that are in force and any other documents reasonably requested by the buyer;
- No connected parties – The seller represents that neither it nor any predecessor in title is or has been at any time 'connected' with any obligor, as the term 'connected' is used in the Insolvency Act 1986 as amended (or similar provision in any relevant jurisdiction).[2]

  This representation protects the buyer from unfavourable treatment due to the seller's status as an insider of any obligor in any subsequent insolvency proceedings;
- No bad acts – The seller represents that neither it nor its predecessor in title has engaged in any acts or conduct or made any omission independently of other lenders (or similar creditors, in the case of a claims trade) that would result in the buyer receiving proportionately less in payments or distributions, or less favourable treatment, in respect of the asset than any other lender holding advances or a participation of a similar nature to the loan being traded, or similar claims under the credit agreement (or than any other similar creditor, in the case of a claims trade). The seller also represents that such act, conduct or omission would not result in the asset being sold or any part thereof being subject to a material impairment, and that neither the seller nor any predecessor in title has set-off any amount against the asset.

  Taken together with the title representation, this representation is seen as the most important since it addresses the risk of a buyer being precluded from recovering on the same terms as other lenders holding loans of the same nature or in the case of claims creditors holding similar claims;
- No rights of set-off – The seller represents that no rights of set-off exist (including, to the best of its knowledge, in relation to its predecessors in title) in relation to the asset;
- No impairment – The seller represents that neither it nor any predecessor in title has received any notice and is not otherwise, to the best of its

---

2 Under Section 249 of the Insolvency Act 1986, a person is 'connected' with a company if:
   "(a) he is a director or shadow director of the company, or an associate of such a director or shadow director, or (b) he is an associate of the company."

knowledge, aware that the asset is subject to any material impairment or is invalid or void.

An impairment, in the context of this section, is any right or any claim or any action of any person or authority the effect of which, if determined adversely, is or would be to reduce, impair or otherwise materially and prejudicially affect the asset or any part thereof or any related security, and includes rights of set-off.

- No funding obligations – The seller represents that, other than those obligations assumed by the buyer, no further funding obligations exist under the credit agreement for which the buyer will be responsible;
- No litigation – The seller represents that no proceedings of or before any governmental authority have been commenced or, to the best of the seller's knowledge, are threatened against the seller or any predecessor in title which would adversely affect the asset or any rights of the buyer under any of the transaction documentation for the loan sale.

The LMA representations and warranties survive the completion of the transaction.

3.4 Article 55 of the EU Bank Recovery and Resolution Directive (BRRD)

From January 1 2016, European member states are required to implement Article 55 of the BRRD. In the United Kingdom the BRRD was implemented through amendments to the Banking Act 2009, among other legislation.

The directive provides for financial institutions to include language in their non-EU-law-governed contracts, acknowledging that the institution's liabilities may be subject to 'bail in' whereby claims of a banks' shareholders and unsecured creditors may be cancelled, reduced, and/or converted into other types of securities to protect the solvency of the financial institution and avoid a bail-out by the taxpayer.

The LMA and the LSTA have produced a model clause for inclusion in their non-EU-law-governed documentation to assist members with compliance of Article 55 of the BRRD.

4. Phase 3: settling a transaction

4.1 Methods for buying and selling

The main methods for buying and selling distressed assets are as detailed below.

(a) Legal transfer

Assignment: In an assignment the seller assigns to the buyer all or part of its rights to the loans that are the subject of the trade, and the buyer assumes the related obligations under the credit agreement. Some credit agreements provide prescribed forms of assignment documents, which are usually found in an annex to the credit agreement.

In certain jurisdictions, the assignment needs to be notified to the borrower in order to perfect the assignment.

Party A assigns the loans subject of the trade to Party B – assignment of rights (the right of repayment) and assumption of obligations.

Assignment of rights and assumption of obligations

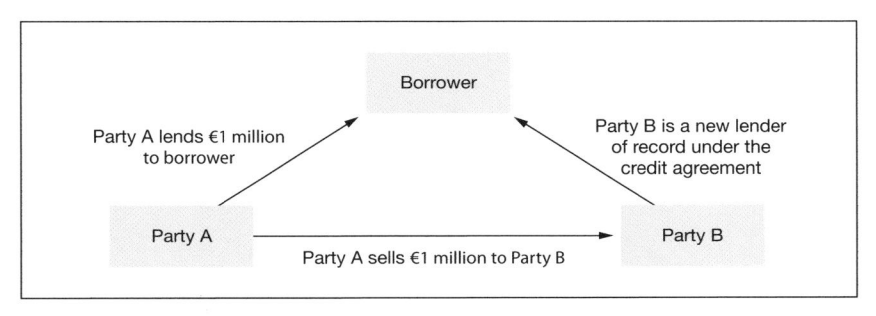

```
                          Borrower
                         ↗        ↖
  Party A lends €1 million        Party B is a new lender
       to borrower                of record under the
                                   credit agreement

     Party A  ─────────────────────▶  Party B
              Party A sells €1 million to Party B
```

Novation (English law concept): In a novation, the seller, the buyer and the borrower agree to novate the loans that are the subject of the trade to the buyer. By means of the novation, the original loans between Party A and the borrower are extinguished and a new relationship is created between Party B and the borrower (which will replace the original obligation between Party A and the borrower). A novation is usually effected pursuant to a transfer certificate. As is the case with an assignment, some credit agreements provide prescribed forms of transfer certificates.

Transfer of rights and obligations

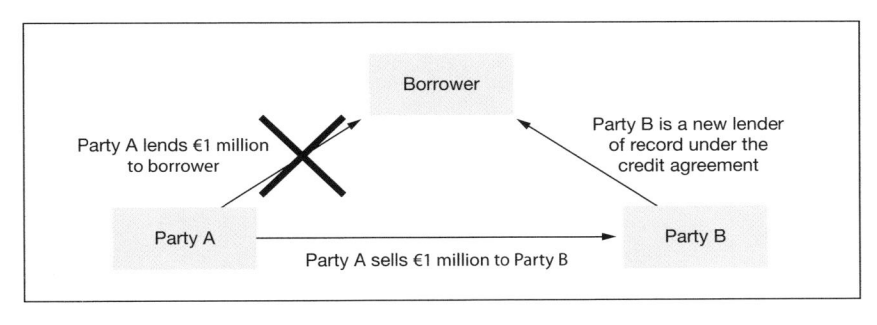

```
                          Borrower
                         ↗  ✕     ↖
  Party A lends €1 million        Party B is a new lender
       to borrower                of record under the
                                   credit agreement

     Party A  ─────────────────────▶  Party B
              Party A sells €1 million to Party B
```

NB: If the security package has not been created under a trust in the name of the security agent, there is a risk that the security package is also discharged and needs to be renewed.

(b)   ***Participation***

As outlined under heading 3.3(b) (form of purchase) above, a participation under English law is a bilateral agreement whereby the buyer as 'participant' funds the seller/lender of record as 'grantor' so that the grantor can fund all or part of a loan made to a borrower. In exchange, the grantor agrees to pay to the participant amounts equal to the participant's portion of any loan repayments or related interest received by the grantor from the borrower.

Debtor/creditor: The relationship between the grantor and the participant is that of debtor and creditor. If the grantor becomes insolvent, the participant is an unsecured creditor of the grantor and has no direct claim against the borrower. The participant takes double credit risk as it is exposed to the credit risk of both the borrower and the grantor. In addition, the participant has no recourse to the grantor if the borrower fails to comply with its obligations under the credit agreement.

Beneficial ownership: The grantor does not transfer or assign any rights or obligations under the credit agreement, and the participant will have no proprietary interest in the benefit of the credit agreement or in any monies or distributions, whether cash or non-cash, received by the grantor under or in relation to the credit agreement.[3]

Obligations under the credit agreement: The grantor remains the lender of record under the credit agreement, and it is not released by virtue of the participation agreement from its obligations owed to the borrower under the credit agreement.

Aim of the participation: The aim is to transfer the risk of the loan being traded from the grantor to the participant without transferring the legal title of the loan.

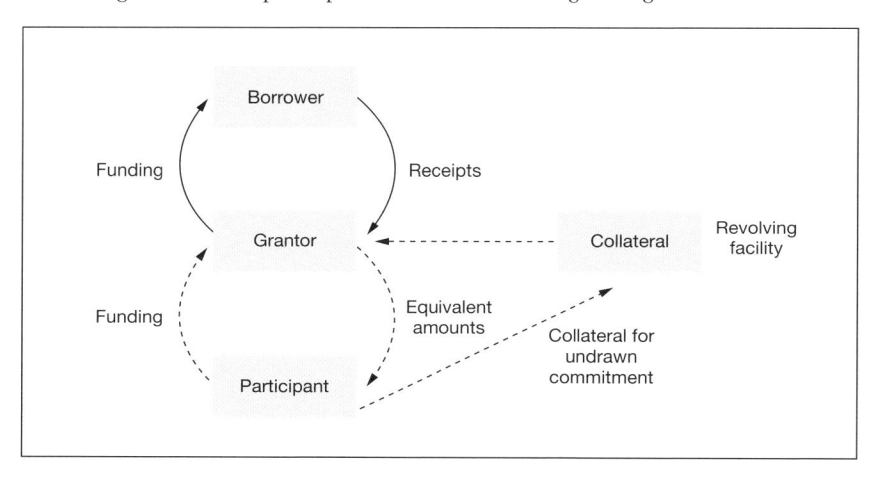

Collateral: When the participation agreement includes a participation in a debt that is partially/fully unfunded, the grantor will usually ask for collateral to secure any commitments and the participant's parallel funding obligations. The grantor will use any such collateral to be certain that it has funds to meet a borrower's demands whether or not the participant is creditworthy. While the LMA does not have a form

---

3   The main difference with the LSTA participation agreement is that a New York law participation agreement assigns beneficial ownership of the loan to the participant and, as such, grants protection against the grantor's insolvency. However, this structure may not work under a non-US credit agreement, as transfer of proprietary interest in the underlying loan is considered an equitable assignment and may be captured under the transfer restrictions provided in the relevant credit agreement.

of documentation with respect to such collateral, some market participants have developed their own forms of collateral agreements, which will be negotiated on a case-by-case basis.

Voting rights and information rights: The participation agreement will provide for any voting rights granted to the participant in connection with the credit agreement. Any voting rights in a participation agreement should be addressed in the LMA trade confirmation. It will also address the information rights that the participant will have and any possible restrictions on the use of such information. Information rights will be subject to the terms of any confidentiality agreement between the seller and the buyer. Voting rights are subject to negotiation, and the usual approach for a distressed trade (although there is no LMA default) is for the LMA-funded participation to grant majority voting rights. Certain grantors will not grant voting rights to their participants, and will retain the right to vote at their discretion or add language to include an overriding right to take or refrain from taking any action that may prejudice the grantor's relationship with any regulatory or governmental authority, or in the grantor's opinion will damage its reputation.

(c) *Alternative settlement*
If settlement of the transaction by participation is not possible because:
- the parties cannot agree the form of LMA-funded participation to be used;
- participations require consent that is not forthcoming;
- the parties have elected for legal transfer only; and/or
- the parties otherwise agree,

the LMA requirement, as set out in the LMA standard terms and conditions, is that the transaction must settle by some mutually acceptable alternative which provides the seller and the buyer with the economic equivalent of the agreed-upon trade.

These alternative settlement modes may include a sale back by the original buyer to the original seller at the latest prevailing price, a synthetic swap transaction or, most commonly, a netting arrangement whereby Party B (which has agreed to buy a loan from Party A) sells the loans subject of the original trade to Party C so that Party A, Party B, and Party C agree to settle the transaction by Party C taking delivery of the loan directly from Party A.

This multilateral arrangement will be set out in a tripartite multilateral netting agreement. The relevant transfer document will be between Party A and Party C, and the payments of the purchase price will continue to flow from Party C to Party B and from Party B to Party A. (Shown overleaf.)

4.2

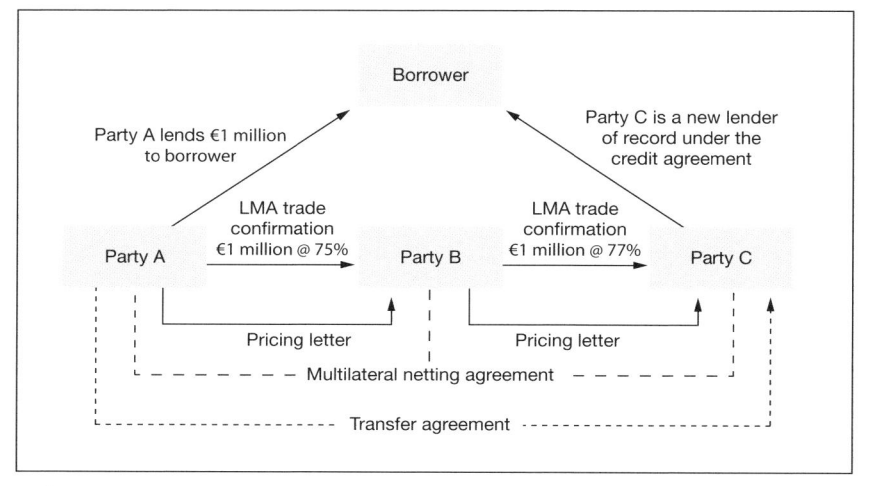

```
                              Borrower
                             ↗        ↖
       Party A lends €1 million      Party C is a new lender
            to borrower              of record under the
                                     credit agreement

                    LMA trade              LMA trade
                   confirmation           confirmation
      Party A    €1 million @ 75%  Party B  €1 million @ 77%   Party C
         │    ─────────────────→      │   ─────────────────→       │
         │                            ↑                            │
         │          Pricing letter    │    Pricing letter          │
         │                            │                            │
         └ ─ ─ ─ ─ ─ ─ Multilateral netting agreement ─ ─ ─ ─ ─ ─ ┘
         └ ─ ─ ─ ─ ─ ─ ─ ─ ─ Transfer agreement ─ ─ ─ ─ ─ ─ ─ ─ ─ ┘
```

Settlement

For a sale and purchase by full transfer, the parties will execute the agreed form of transfer document (a transfer certificate for a novation, or an assignment agreement for an assignment) and submit it to the agent appointed under the credit agreement with a request for a settlement date. Upon review of the transfer documentation and performance of any relevant know-your-client checks on the new lender, the agent will countersign the transfer document and will indicate a settlement date on which it will update its records to show the buyer as the owner of the loans that are the subject of the trade.

For a participation, the parties will execute the agreed form of LMA-funded participation and decide on a mutually acceptable settlement date on which the funded participation comes into force and the buyer pays the seller.

In both transfers and participations, the parties will sign pricing letters, which will contain the calculations of the purchase price including any permanent commitment reductions, contribution to transfer fees, interest and delayed settlement compensation. The parties will arrange funding of the purchase price on the settlement date.

The parties should undertake any post-closing formalities required with respect to any relevant jurisdiction of the borrower/obligor, or under the governing law of the credit agreement, immediately after settlement.

The successful purchase and sale of the loan asset is the conclusion of the trade lifecycle.

Overview of distressed trading in selected jurisdictions: France, Germany, Italy and Spain

France
Jérémie Bismuth
Olivia Locatelli
Dimitrios Logizidis
Gide Loyrette Nouel

Germany
Sacha Lürken
Wolfgang Nardi
Oded Schein
Kirkland & Ellis International LLP

Italy
Gregorio Consoli
Federica Scialpi
Chiomenti Studio Legale

Spain
Beatriz Causapé
Cuatrecasas, Goncalves Pereira

The secondary debt market was traditionally linked to the original syndication of large loans and the transfer by banks of participations in such loans to the secondary market, allowing them to divest some of their exposure. In recent years, however, there have been fewer new primary deals and secondary trading has become more commonly related to loans where syndication has already been completed. Sellers have been motivated by a desire to limit their exposure to bad or doubtful debts and risky assets, and in the last five years Spain, Germany, France and Italy have become the main countries of opportunity and speculation for investors, essentially funds.

The purpose of this chapter is to analyse the restrictions and mechanisms available in the different legal systems for investing in debt in Spain, Germany, France and Italy.

1. Regulatory restrictions on lending activities

Before a non-banking investor such as a hedge fund makes the decision to invest in debt in one of these countries, it should confirm in advance whether or not the purchase of loans activity is reserved to particular entities.

1.1 Spain

Unlike in Germany, Italy and France, in Spain such activity is not subject to any regulatory restrictions irrespective of whether the loan is fully funded or unfunded. Therefore, funds can freely purchase loans in Spain.

1.2 Germany

The applicable regulations under the German Banking Act distinguish between buying fully funded loans and origination of loans and acquiring unfunded commitments.

Buying, holding and collecting fully funded loans is not subject to any regulatory restrictions on the buyer. However, certain decisions with respect to the loan – such as an extension of maturity – may be regarded as a new credit decision and are then subject to the same requirements as the origination of new loans.

Origination of loans or buying of unfunded loan commitments (subject to certain minimum thresholds) is considered a banking activity under German law, and requires the buyer to be licensed as a credit institution in Germany or (if eligible for the passporting regime) the European Economic Area.

Assignments to a non-licensed institution which are made in breach of the banking licence requirements are legally valid, but the regulator can impose fines of up to €500,000 for any wilful breach or up to €250,000 for any negligent breach, and it can issue an order to unwind the assignment or immediately to terminate the underlying lending business. Administrative fines for a breach of such an order may be up to €250,000.

Investors in the German market, however, either use private bond issuances, fronting banks and participation agreements, or rely on the 'reverse solicitation exemption'. While lenders are restricted from making loans to borrowers unless licensed, borrowers are not restricted from soliciting offers from non-licensed lenders. Upon regulatory action, the lender has to demonstrate that it was approached by the borrower and not the other way round. It is therefore market practice to document how a borrower approached an investor, and to obtain from it or its representatives or advisers written confirmation of the underlying facts.

1.3 Italy

The activity of granting loans in whatever form to the public is restricted to banks authorised in Italy, or in other EU countries upon fulfilment of the conditions provided under EU Capital Requirements Directive (2013/36/EU) for the EU passport, and financial intermediaries enrolled in a register held by the Bank of Italy. The establishment in Italy of a branch of a non-EU bank must be authorised by the Bank of Italy.

Any financing activity carried out in breach of the restrictions imposed by Italian law amounts to a criminal offence punishable with imprisonment (of between six months and four years) and fines (of between €2,000 and €10,000) and there are some court precedents in respect of such convictions. Moreover, any contract concluded in breach of the restricted activity regime may be declared null and void.

As to how investors deal with these restrictions, there has been certain progress in Italy. Law Decree 91/2014 has been recently passed with the purpose of allowing several entities, other than banks and financial intermediaries, to grant loans. This new regulation has introduced the following provisions, among others:

- Special purpose vehicles incorporated under Italian securitisation law may advance loans (though not in the form of the issuance of guarantees) in favour of borrowers other than individuals and microenterprises, provided that the borrowers are selected by a bank or financial intermediary, retaining 'a significant economic interest in the transaction' (in accordance with certain further conditions published by the Bank of Italy), and the securities issued to finance the lending are purchased only by qualified investors; and

- As also provided in Law Decree 18/2016, Italian alternative investment funds set up in closed-end form and with a limited recourse to leverage, may invest in loans, including those 'extended out of relevant capital', other than loans to consumers.

1.4 France

The purchase of French law governed outstanding loan receivables in the secondary markets is considered under French law as a regulated activity which can only be performed in France by a licensed credit institution or financing company.[1] This restriction, which applies also to lending activities, is known as the French banking monopoly.

Breach of the provisions regarding the French banking monopoly is a criminal offence punishable by up to three years' imprisonment and a fine of an amount up to €375,000 for an individual, and by a fine of an amount up to €1,875,000 for a company. Additional penalties can be incurred, such as a prohibition on carrying out, directly or indirectly, the activity concerned by the breach of the banking monopoly regulations, either permanently or for a maximum period of five years.

A number of exemptions have however been implemented either by French law or by French courts in order reduce the scope of the French banking monopoly and to authorise entities, other than licensed credit institutions or financing companies, to perform lending activities and to purchase debts in the secondary markets in France.

In respect of the transfer of French law governed outstanding loan receivables, French market practice follows the view that the purchase abroad, in compliance with local regulations, of fully drawn loans – even those granted to French companies – should not fall within the scope of the French regulations on the banking monopoly. For the purpose of this exemption, the following conditions must be met:
- the transferor is located outside France and is duly authorised to provide credit transactions in France under Directive 2013/36/EU;
- the transferee is also located outside France;
- the purchase agreement used for the acquisition of the loan receivables is governed by a non-French law; and
- the purchase price paid by the transferee to the transferor in consideration of the purchase of the loan receivable is not payable in France.

Please note also that the French banking regulator and French case law have ruled that the purchase of fully matured loan receivables does not trigger any banking licensing requirement on the part of the purchaser in France, and such loans can therefore be freely traded.

1.5 Participation agreements

Participation agreements deserve special reference in this chapter as they constitute

---

1   The categories of credit institutions authorised to lend money in France are described in the section on France in the "Legal structuring of direct lending deals in selected European jurisdictions" chapter.

the principal alternative for investing in a particular target by investors that cannot, or do not want, to become a lender of record to the borrower for any reason. Generally, these reasons are either objections from a regulatory or contractual perspective, or the mere desire of the investor not to be visible to the borrower.

The lender is referred to as the 'grantor' and the third-party investor is referred to as the 'participant'. These agreements involve the participant funding the grantor with an amount equal to the amount lent by the grantor to the borrower, or with the amount resulting after deduction of the discount applied where the loan is traded in a distressed state. The grantor's obligation is to repay the participant to the extent that the grantor receives repayment from the borrower. If the borrower does not repay, the grantor has no liability to the participant. Thus, participant takes a double risk, consisting of both the borrower and the participant possibly failing to pay.

Generally, participation agreements do not give the participant any rights in respect of the rights and obligations under the loan agreement. If a participation agreement regarding a local law-governed loan is governed by New York or English law, English or New York law will determine which party can exercise the rights arising from the loan.

In addition, foreign investors will want to know whether or not a participation agreement offends any banking monopoly rules in the jurisdictions of reference.

In Spain, provided that the lending activity is not restricted, non-banking entities may freely enter into participation agreements in respect of those loans. The same applies in Germany where participation agreements are not subject to any regulatory restrictions (though see further below).

(a) *Italy*

As for Italy, as long as the participation agreement does not transfer a beneficial interest, it would not seem to conflict with any Italian monopoly rule. However, in case of participation agreements governed by New York law – where a beneficial interest in the loan is transferred to the participant – a potential violation of the monopoly rules may be envisaged, as direct lending is a reserved activity in Italy.

The possibility of entering into a participation agreement in Italy should be assessed on a case-by-case basis, in light of the restricted lending activity regime, and bearing in mind not only to the structure and provisions of the agreement, but all the actual circumstances surrounding the deal; in this respect, however, the governing law elected by the parties does not represent, as such, a material element.

(b) *France*

The legal classification of participation agreements in French law has been debated in the literature and in the courts. A conservative but safe approach is to take the view that participation agreements qualify as banking transactions and are therefore subject to the banking monopoly rules, and can be performed on a regular basis only by licensed credit institutions.

The submission of a participation agreement to either English law or US law does not impact this analysis: the participation agreement will still fall within the baking monopoly rules.

(c)   Germany

Participation agreements are not subject to any regulatory restrictions in Germany.

A German law governed participation agreement is classified as a civil law partnership between the grantor and the participant. It does not give the participant any rights with respect to the rights and obligations under the loan agreement. In practice, German law governed participation agreements are very rarely used for subparticipations in loans.

If a participation agreement with respect to a German law-governed loan is governed by New York or English law, English or New York law is decisive in determining who can exercise the rights with respect to the loan.

2.   Assignment of credits

2.1   Spain

There are no formalities generally required for perfecting a sale of rights and obligations under a loan in Spain. Notwithstanding the foregoing, recording the transaction in written form and formalising it in a public document before a Spanish public notary is standard.

Under the Spanish Commercial Code and the Civil Code, the seller remains liable to the buyer for the existence of the relevant credits arising from the loan and validity of the seller's legal title. On the other hand, unless it is expressly agreed in the assignment agreement between the parties, the buyer will not have recourse against the seller: the seller will not be liable to the buyer in the event of the insolvency of the borrower.

In addition, under Article 1526 of the Spanish Civil Code, the assignment of a loan will be fully effective as against third parties as from the date on which the transaction deemed certain. In this regard, Articles 1218 and 1227 of the Spanish Civil Code set out that the execution date of a document will be deemed certain where the document is executed before a Spanish public notary.

The requirements for the sale of a mortgage loan include the execution of the transfer in a public document executed before a Spanish public notary and the registration of that transfer with the relevant land registry. If the sale of the mortgage loan does not meet these conditions, the transfer of the loan will not be effective as against third parties, and enforcement of the mortgage may be seriously hindered. If the loan was secured by a mortgage or a non-possessory pledge over movable assets, the same conditions (public document and registration) apply. However, in such a case the registration shall be with the movable assets registry instead of the land registry.

The borrower's consent is not required to execute a valid transfer of a loan, unless it was otherwise agreed by the parties to the original contract. Where consent is required in accordance with the original contract, it is unclear under Spanish law whether a transfer made without that consent remains valid and enforceable against the borrower (who will have a legal action against the original creditor for breaching the contractual provision requiring consent), or whether the lack of consent renders the transfer invalid and, therefore, not enforceable. Case law has not provided a consistent answer to this question.

Giving notice to the borrower is not required for the transfer of a loan to be valid. However, a borrower will be deemed to have validly discharged its obligations under a loan if it has made the payment to the seller before it is notified, or it becomes aware, of the transfer. A borrower may also set off its obligations under a loan against the seller until it is notified of the transfer. In both cases, the buyer will not have any legal action against the borrower to claim the amount paid (or set off), but it would be entitled to claim from the seller the amount received by it from the borrower or (as applicable) the amount set off. Therefore, serving notice of the transfer to the borrower is advisable and enhances the buyer's legal position.

As a matter of practice, it is also advisable to notify the assignment to any guarantors of the mortgage as they signed the relevant mortgage agreement and assumed certain obligations towards the mortgagee such as diligence and care with regard to the real estate asset. Therefore, it is recommended that the assignee and new mortgagee informs the mortgagor's guarantors as to who is the new counterparty under the agreement.

Spanish law does not require any specific formality in connection with service of a notice of transfer. However, as a matter of practice, it is advisable to serve notice in a manner that will provide evidence as to the date of the notice, the date of reception of the notice by the borrower and the latter's consent. Standard procedures for this include requesting a public notary to serve the notice.

2.2 Germany

Typically, when selling a position under a financing agreement, a lender may want to sell and transfer both its rights and obligations (such as the obligation to extend a loan) under the financing agreement. Under German law, the legal technique for such a trade is assumption of contract, which technically is a combination of a transfer of rights and a transfer of obligations.

Subject to more restrictive requirements in the underlying loan documentation, claims can be assigned and transferred by agreement between the seller and the buyer. Notice to the borrower is not a requirement for the validity of the transfer. However, in practice, notice is given to the borrower.

The transfer of a lender's obligations requires the consent of the borrower(s). Syndicated facility agreements usually provide for anticipated consents by the borrower if (possible) additional consent requirements for the transfer of claims are met.

A transfer of a lender's obligations without the borrower's consent is invalid. However, the borrower(s) usually consent to the transfer of obligations if the conditions for a transfer of the debt are met.

A transfer of claims in breach of the transfer restrictions in the financing agreement between a bank and a borrower which is a merchant does not affect the validity of the transfer unless the transfer restriction at issue was agreed after August 19 2008 (Section 354a of the German Commercial Code). In that case, and in any case where the borrower is not a merchant, the assignment of the relevant claims is void, so that the borrower's creditor remains the transferring bank. The borrower in such cases is also able to take legal action against the transferor for breach of contract in terminating the underlying agreement, and/or to claim damages.

2.3 Italy

As a general rule, the borrower's consent is not required for the assignment to be valid. According to Article 1264 of the Italian Civil Code, the consent of, or the notification to, the assigned debtor is required only for the effectiveness and enforceability of the assignment against the debtor and any third party.

Under Article 1265 of the Italian Civil Code, should a loan have been the object of more than one assignment, the first one in respect of which the debtor has been notified, or which the debtor has accepted with an instrument bearing a date that is certain at law, shall prevail. The same provision applies under Spanish law (Article 1473 of the Spanish Civil Code).

However, different rules and formalities apply depending on the nature of the loan that is the object of the assignment, and also depending on the features of the assignment transaction.

If the assignment is carried out according to the special framework set out for the assignment of receivables among banks by Article 58 of Legislative Decree 385/1993, under which the sale of receivables as a pool (ie, their sale *en bloc*) together with the relevant ancillary rights and guarantees is perfected upon registration of the transfer agreement with the competent companies' register and publication of a notice of the assignment in the *Gazzetta Ufficiale della Repubblica Italiana* (the official gazette).

The simplified assignment formalities provided for under Article 58 Legislative Decree 385/1993 are also applicable to assignments perfected in the context of a securitisation transaction, as a consequence of the reference to that provision in the Italian Securitisation Law.

In addition, the Italian Securitisation Law also provides the possibility to formalise assignments of trade receivables (as defined in the Italian Factoring Law) in the context of a securitisation transaction, even if they cannot be identified *en bloc*.

In particular, assignments of trade receivables may be perfected through:

- publication in the official gazette of a simplified notice of assignment containing only an indication of the originator, the buyer and the transfer date; or
- if the parties so elect, payment at a date that is certain at law, in accordance with the Italian Factoring Law (for the purposes of establishing a date that is certain at law, it is sufficient to record the payment in the relevant account of the seller).

In the case of receivables owed by public entities, Royal Decree 2440 of 24 November 1923 provides that an assignment is effective against those public entities if:

- the relevant assignment agreement is entered into by means of a public deed or a notarised private deed;
- all the assigned receivables are owed by a single public debtor; and
- the assignment is accepted by the public debtor on a date that is certain at law, or notice thereof is given to the public entity through notification made by a court bailiff.

By way of exception to these provisions, according to a recent amendment to Law 130/1999 (introduced by Law 9 of February 21 2014), the above formalities do not apply if the assignment of receivables owed by public entities is made in the context of securitisation transactions. In this scenario, it will be sufficient to carry out the transfer formalities provided for under the Italian Securitisation Law; namely, publication of a notice in the Italian official gazette, deposit thereof with the local Companies' Register and notification to the public entity by registered letter, informing it of the appointment or replacement of the servicer in the context of the securitisation transaction. No other provisions requiring formalities different from, or additional to, those provided for under the Securitisation Law shall apply in this case. Considering the notable simplification introduced for a securitisation where the underlying assets are receivables owed by public entities, the new regime is now applied quite often in practice.

Moreover, under Article 117 of Legislative Decree 163/2006, a contractor may assign receivables arising from a public contract to banks or other financial intermediaries only. Such an agreement must be executed by means of a public deed or a notarised private deed, notified to the relevant debtor, which will be deemed to be perfected upon the expiry of a 45-day term starting from the date of notification, during which period the public debtor has the right to challenge the assignment.

2.4 France

Under French law, a transfer of debt can be performed by several legal mechanisms. For the purpose of this section, we will limit our review to the most commonly used transfer methods that allow a valid and enforceable transfer of debts under French law.

(a) Civil law assignment

The assignment of debt in accordance with Articles 1689 and 1690 of the French Civil Code is the most commonly used method to transfer loan receivables under French law, as this procedure does not impose any restriction concerning the purchaser of the loan receivables (the purchaser does not have to be a credit institution) provided that the conditions mentioned above in respect of the French banking monopoly are met.

The assignment of debt under the common civil law regime of Articles 1689 and 1690 of the French Civil Code provides a valid transfer of such receivable between the assignor and the assignee, and is enforceable against the underlying borrower and third parties as from the date on which the assignment is notified to the underlying borrower by a court bailiff, or as from the date of acceptance of the assignment by the underlying borrower.

Civil law assignment has been amended by Ordinance 2016-131 dated February 10 2016 (the Civil Law Reform Ordinance) as follows:
- notification of the assignment by way of a court bailiff is no longer required: the assignment will be enforceable against third parties as from the date of the assignment and against the underlying borrower as from the date of notification (which can be done by registered letter with acknowledgement of receipt); and
- in order to be valid, the assignment needs to be made in writing.

These new rules are applicable to all agreements entered into after October 1 2016. The previous regime will therefore be applicable for all agreements entered into before that date.

(b) **Dailly assignment**

Dailly assignment is a simplified procedure to assign a loan receivable provided that the purchaser is:
- an authorised credit institution licensed in France;
- a financing company; or
- any credit institution licensed in any other member state of the European Union.

The transfer of debt is performed by way of a transfer deed delivered by the seller to the purchaser, identifying the loan receivable to be assigned. The assignment becomes enforceable against third parties without any further formalities as from the date affixed by the purchaser on the transfer deed.

Notification of the transfer to the underlying borrower is not required for the validity or perfection of the assignment, however notification of the underlying borrower (which can be done by registered letter) is often recommended in order to ensure that the latter will pay the purchaser and not the original lender.

(c) **Transfer to a French securitisation vehicle**

It is possible to assign loan receivables by using a French securitisation vehicle. In this scenario, the loan receivables are assigned to the securitisation vehicle, which issues notes or units to be subscribed to by a third party which can be an entity not holding a banking licence in or outside France.

The transfer of receivables is performed by delivery of a transfer deed exchanged between the seller and the purchaser identifying the loan receivables to be assigned. The assignment is enforceable against third parties as from the date affixed on the transfer deed without any further formalities.

(d) **Transfer of loan receivables arising from a mortgaged loan**

Under Law 76-519 dated June 15 1976, loan receivables arising from a mortgaged loan can be transferred through a simplified method of notarial endorsement. Once the mortgaged loan has been fully drawn, it is possible for a bank to assign the loan receivables to a transferee through the endorsement of a certificate evidencing the loan receivables, duly notarised by a French notary.

(e) **Transfer of receivables through novation**

Under the novation mechanism, the parties decide to substitute a new obligation for an existing obligation, which extinguishes the latter. Novation implies the transfer of both rights and obligations.

The consent of the borrower is required for the validity of the transfer of rights and obligations, and the novation must result from an express agreement between the borrower and the lender.

In case of novation, the ancillary rights (such as security interests) granted to the original creditor will not benefit any of the transferees or assignees; therefore any security interests put in place to secure the existing debt will need to be re-executed.

The Civil Law Reform Ordinance provides for additional rules applicable to the novation mechanism as follows:
- the consent of the borrower can be obtained in advance, before the novation;
- the novation is enforceable against third parties as from the date of the novation agreement; and
- the security interests put in place to secure any existing debt can be used for the new debt (transferred by way of novation), provided that the consent of the security providers has been obtained.

These new rules are applicable to all agreements entered into after October 1 2016. The previous regime will therefore continue to be applicable for all agreements entered into before such date.

3. Security issues

3.1 Spain

According to Article 1528 of the Spanish Civil Code, *in rem* security interests are ancillary to the main secured obligation and, hence, the transfer of the main secured obligation automatically entails the transfer of the security interests ancillary to it.

However, it is advisable for enforcement purposes to notarise the assignment so that the assignee has evidence, for enforcement purposes, that it benefits from the security (otherwise, the assignee may not have access to direct enforcement proceedings). If the security is a mortgage, a chattel mortgage or a non-possessory pledge, it is also advisable, for the same enforcement purposes, to register the transfer in the land registry or the movable assets registry (as appropriate). Finally, real estate law provides that (unless otherwise agreed) the transfer of an obligation secured by a real estate mortgage should be notified to the obligor.

Fig.1 Registration process

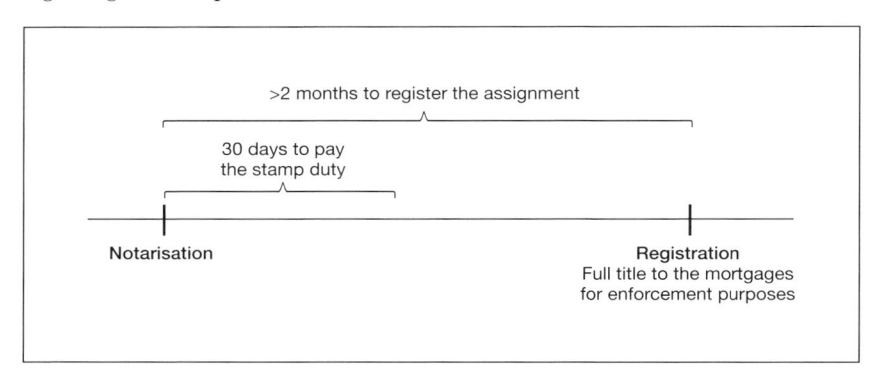

```
                >2 months to register the assignment
        ┌───────────────────────────────────────────────┐
            30 days to pay
            the stamp duty
        ┌─────────────────────┐
  ──────┼─────────────────────┼───────────────────┼──────
        Notarisation                              Registration
                                                  Full title to the mortgages
                                                  for enforcement purposes
```

Spanish law is not familiar with the concept of 'trust', and it does not recognise the creation of a dual ownership (a beneficial owner and a legal owner). Therefore, trusts are not used in Spanish practice, and the security package is usually granted in favour of all lenders according to their participation in the financing (and not in favour of a security agent). This fact has an impact when dealing with English law governed novation agreements and Spanish security, as we will explain later in this section.

Although lenders in Spain tend to appoint a security agent to represent them and to channel communications with the borrower regarding the security package, it is important to bear in mind that this security agent will not be able to represent the lenders in court and enforce their rights on their behalf just because the lenders have appointed it as such in a security agreement. In an enforcement scenario, if the lenders want to have the security agent representing them in court, each lender will have to grant special powers of attorney to the agent for these purposes. In practice this does not happen, as banks do not empower other banks to act on their behalf when it comes to appearing in court and claiming for their respective rights. This is, in essence, the reason why all lenders sign and are a party to the security documents in Spanish law-governed financings.

Generally, all Spanish security can be assigned to any persons or entities, irrespective of their nature.

However, there is a kind of real estate mortgage called a 'floating mortgage' that can only be created in favour of 'credit entities' as they are described in Act 2/1981. These are: banks, official credit entities, savings banks, the *Confederación Española de Cajas de Ahorros* (Spanish confederation of savings banks), credit cooperatives and financial credit establishments.

The main difference between floating mortgages and ordinary mortgages is that while the first ones can secure more than one obligation, ordinary mortgages can only secure one obligation.

When assessing an individual debt it is important to check whether the mortgages attached to it are floating or not, since funds will not be able to become mortgagors and would have to rely on the provisions of an intercreditor agreement, and as a consequence they may face the risk of not being recognised as holders of a privileged credit regarding the floating mortgage.

The scenario becomes even more troublesome if the floating mortgage is a 'floating joint mortgage'. This type of mortgage is incorporated as a 'Germanic community' meaning that all of its mortgagees are joined by a personal relationship such that only collectively are they authorised to exercise the legal faculties attributed to them under the mortgage. This instrument makes sense in scenarios such as refinancing, where lenders want to act together while the borrower is in a delicate financial situation.

If a fund – which would not be eligible to hold a floating mortgage – acquires debt that is secured by a floating joint mortgage, the enforcement of the mortgage may be jeopardised on the grounds that the community is incomplete and lacks of one of its members (ie, the assignor) who must appear in court together with the rest of the mortgagors.

Regarding costs, it is important to bear in mind that only public deeds executed before Spanish public notaries have access to the Spanish public registries.

In particular, public deeds involve notarial fees which amount to approximately 0.03% of the secured liability, although, when that liability is more than €6 million, the fees may be substantially reduced through negotiation with the notary (which always happens in practice).

Additionally, if the relevant assignment is registered with either the land registry or the movable assets registry, registry fees have to be paid to the registrar. These fees very much depend on the volume and complexity of the security package being transferred, and on the number of registries involved in the relevant transaction.

Types of security interests	
Registrable	**Non-registrable**
• real estate mortgages • mortgages over intellectual property rights • chattel mortgages over industrial machinery • non-possessory pledges over inventory • non-possessory pledges over industrial machinery	• personal guarantees • promises to mortgage • pledges over shares, receivables, bank accounts

Assignment costs				
	Notarial fees (negotiable)	Registry fees (variable depending on the land registry)	Clerical services agency fees (minor amount and negotiable)	Stamp duty tax (calculated from the mortgaged liability with reference to the outstanding debt)
Registrable security	√	√	√	√
Non-registrable security	√	n/a	n/a	n/a

3.2 Germany

As for Germany, there are no limitations on any investor holding security interests governed by German law. German law distinguishes between:
- 'accessory security', which transfers by operation of law together with the secured debt, includes pledges, and is typically granted over immaterial assets, such as shares and receivables from bank accounts; and
- non-accessory security, such as assignments or transfers for security, which is typically used for movable assets and trade receivables.

Accessory security is sometimes granted to each lender individually and will transfer upon a transfer of the new debt. These accessory security contracts often contain a 'future pledgee' concept, whereby the security agent accepts the pledges not only on behalf of the lenders existing at the time, but also on behalf of future lenders who becomes lenders by operation of transfers.

When transferring accessory security, the buyer should accede to the security agreement unless the future pledgee concept has been used (though the benefit of the security transfers even without accession). If the security agreement is notarised, accession will trigger notarial fees.

In addition, or *in lieu* thereof, the security agent often receives the benefit of 'parallel debt', whereby the security charger promises to pay to the security agent an amount equal to the secured obligations. Even though it is customary, the parallel debt construct has so far not been tested in court.

Non-accessory security is typically only granted to a security agent. Generally, the trust relationship, whereby a security agent will have the right to claim the full amount of debt owed to all lenders secured by the security, is recognised by German law.

3.3 Italy

In Italy, as a general principle, loans are transferred together with all associated privileges, charges and security interests, unless certain formalities are specifically required for the effectiveness of the relevant transfer.

As a general rule, the security package is transferred together with the relevant loan. Therefore, the same regulatory restrictions for entities which acquire loans referred under heading 1.3 above apply.

In addition to the above, certain additional limitations on the transfer of security may arise both by operation of law (see under heading 2.3 above in respect to the assignments in relation to public entities) or by virtue of contract.

With respect to mortgages, the assignment must be registered in the relevant land registry.

With regard to the transfer of security interests arising from pledges, the formalities will vary depending on the type of assets subject to the security. As a general rule, pledges are assigned by delivering to the pledgee the pledge assets for security purposes.

Under Italian law, each creditor must be the beneficiary of the security and, as such, is entitled to benefit from the rights provided under the security, including the enforcement rights.

However, it is permissible – and it is customary in financing transactions – for the secured creditors to appoint a third-party agent to act in their name and on their behalf in the exercise of the rights provided thereunder and for the enforcement of their security interests.

3.4 France

Under French civil law, the debt is transferred to the assignee with its security documents, which are considered as rights ancillary to the debt.

However, depending on the nature of the transferred security documents, notification may be required to enforce the assignment against third parties and/or the borrower (notably in case of pledges over bank accounts, pledges of financial accounts, or pledges of receivables). Some pledge agreements also require registration of any transfer at the relevant commercial court (such as mortgages, pledges over intellectual property rights, pledges over businesses etc).

Multiple lenders can benefit from security either as parties to the relevant security arrangements or through a security agent appointed in accordance with Article 2328-1 of the French Civil Code. According to this provision, the security agent is entitled to create, register, manage and enforce security *in rem* on behalf of the lenders (and their successors). The appointment of the security agent must be evidenced in the relevant facility agreement concerning the debt secured by the security held in the name of the security agent. The security agent is not however required to meet any specific regulatory requirements.

Please note also that the notion of security agency governed by Article 2328-1 of the French Civil Code does not apply to 'personal security' (such as guarantees).

As to parallel debt mechanisms, the French Supreme Court, in a decision dated September 13 2011 (in the case known as the *Belvédère Case*) has recognised the enforceability, from a French law perspective, of such mechanisms in certain circumstances (such as where parallel debt is valid under the jurisdiction that governs it).[2]

3.5 Multi-jurisdictional considerations regarding transfer of security documents

Having looked at the formalities for assigning a security package governed by the law of the local jurisdictions, a further important question that needs to be resolved arising from the multi-jurisdictional character of the trading market. This is, what happens if the loan assignment is executed by the seller and the buyer entering into an English law novation? Does this have an impact on the local security package?

---

[2] In this case, a company (SA Belvédère) issued New York law notes, and French law security instruments were granted to secure the obligations of the company under the notes. Natixis SA was appointed as French security agent in respect of the security instruments. The contractual documentation included a parallel debt mechanism to the benefit of the French security agent.

Following the opening of a safeguard proceeding against the SA Belvédère and its French affiliate (the centre of main interests of the group being located in France), Natixis, as security agent, submitted its claim before the French court, in its own name and in the name of the noteholders in accordance with the parallel debt clause. The company disputed before the French courts the validity of the parallel debt mechanism.

The French Supreme Court in this decision recognised the enforceability from a French law perspective of the parallel debt mechanism provided that the clause was valid under New York law (the parallel debt clause must be valid under the jurisdiction that governs it).

J Bismuth, O Locatelli, D Logizidis, S Lürken, W Nardi, O Schein, G Consoli, F Scialpi, B Causapé

As described elsewhere in this book, par and distressed debt transactions in the European market are usually completed using the secondary trading documents published by the Loan Market Association, which are governed by English law. However, the underlying credit documents may be subject to different laws. In particular, the security package is always subject to the borrower's local law, on the basis of the principle of the *lex rei sitae* (the law of the place where the property is situated), while English law frequently governs the financing agreement. In these multi-jurisdictional legal structures, buyers should be extremely careful when formalising the transfer of the loan. It is essential to consider the transaction as a whole, to ensure that all formalities required by the relevant law are complied with for the purposes of assigning to the buyer all the seller's rights – not only those under the financing, but also those under the security package granted for the loan.

English law-governed facility agreements usually provide lenders with the ability to transfer a loan either by assignment of rights and benefits or by novation of rights, benefits and obligations. A debt is a chose in action, and an assignment transfers the existing debt and replaces the current lender with a new lender without extinguishing the original contract.

In contrast, a novation essentially creates a new contract between three parties resulting in the existing debt being cancelled and a 'new' debt being created. Under English law, only the benefit of a claim to repayment of a loan is assignable and it is not possible to assign an obligation to lend to a third party. As such, a transfer by way of novation is generally preferred. Under a typical English law syndicated loan structure, the agreements will create the security interest in favour of a security trustee (security agent). As the trustee has title to the security and is the beneficiary of the covenant to pay, transfers by novation or assignment do not impair the security package from an English law perspective, as the trustee holds the security and any payments it receives on trust for the lenders under the facility.

The main disadvantage of the English law financing structure is that from a Spanish law perspective the trust may not be recognised. Accessory security and security registered in the name of the lenders must be held by the creditor directly and not by a trustee. A transfer by novation will release the seller's debt as well as the security and a new unsecured debt will arise in favour of the buyer. In contrast, a transfer by assignment does not extinguish the original debt and the security is preserved.

Therefore, a transfer by novation has potentially serious negative consequences from a Spanish law perspective, as it essentially discharges the original debt and security package and the security would need to be renewed. In practice this would require the borrower and the buyer to re-grant all the security interests before a notary as a new transaction. Formalities for the renewal would need to be complied with, including receiving the borrower's consent and the consent of the other lenders (which may not be forthcoming). Novation also results in the resetting of hardening periods to zero, and notarial fees, registry costs and taxes would be payable.

Under German law, accessory security interests may be also affected if the seller transfers the debt to the buyer through an English law-governed novation agreement. This issue is typically addressed with the future pledgee concept outlined above. In particular in the case of pledge agreements that have to be notarised (such as pledges over private companies with limited liability) some voices in German legal literature have expressed doubt as to the validity of the future pledgee concept. German courts have not decided on this issue yet.

4. Assignment of claims in bankruptcy

No additional assignment formalities are triggered in Spain, Germany, Italy or France by merely filing for insolvency. A creditor of a claim admitted to bankruptcy proceedings is entitled to assign that claim to a third party.

However, for that assignment to be effective in the context of bankruptcy proceedings, notice must be served by the seller and the buyer to the parties involved in those proceedings.

Once the claim that is to be transferred has been registered or admitted in the proceedings, administrators and insolvency courts usually require the documentation attesting the execution of the assignment.

In all jurisdictions (with the exception of France) it is common practice for a public notary to certify the veracity of the signatures on the assignment documentation and, if the notary is not a notary of the place where the insolvency proceedings are taking place, the relevant apostille is usually required. Once the administrator and the insolvency courts are aware of the assignment of the claim, the administrator amends the list of creditors accordingly and pays the claim directly to the buyer in accordance with the provisions of the relevant applicable bankruptcy law.

4.1 Assignment conditions in the context of an Insolvency proceeding

Notwithstanding the above and the lack of specific formalities when trading claims, there is a practical question that players usually face when dealing with claims: what happens with the assignment conditions provided in the financing agreement? Is the financing agreement superseded by the admission of the claim by the insolvency court?

(a) *Spain*

In Spain the answer is not clear and most market players follow a conservative approach in this regard, with the seller trying to comply with all (practicable) assignment conditions provided in the underlying financing agreement from which the claim arises.

(b) *Germany*

In Germany, admission of the claim does not have any effect on the financing agreement, so that any relevant assignment conditions remain in force. If, for instance, the financing agreement requires the borrower's consent for assignment, that consent will have to be obtained, although in this case it would be obtained from the administrator (if one has been appointed) or the borrower (in debtor-in-possession proceedings).

(c) **Italy**

By way of contrast, in Italy, after the declaration of insolvency, on the admission of the claim relating to a financing agreement to the bankruptcy proceedings, the provisions of that financing agreement will be superseded.

(d) **France**

In France, the admission of the claim does not have any effect on the financing agreement, so that any relevant assignment conditions remain in force. If, for instance, the agreement requires the borrower's consent, that consent will have to be obtained although in this case it would be obtained from the administrator (if one has been appointed).

4.2 Voting rights

There is another important question arising from the purchase of a claim that is especially relevant for those investors whose strategy involves having an important role in a composition agreement: voting rights, do they travel with the claim?

(a) **Spain**

Spanish Royal Decree-Law 11/2014 significantly reformed the Spanish Insolvency Law to facilitate the continuity of financially viable companies. The reform in respect of voting rights was significant for players in the distressed debt market. Up to 2014 'entities not subject to financial supervision' could not vote for a composition agreement if they acquired the relevant claim after the declaration of insolvency. Royal Decree-Law 11/2014 changed this by giving those buyers of claims, whether subject to financial supervision or not, the option to vote for a composition agreement even if they acquired the claim after the declaration of insolvency (this without prejudice to the buyer being a related party to the debtor, in which case it would not be able to vote). This reform has certainly made the Spanish claims market more liquid.

(b) **Germany**

In Germany, generally, voting rights travel with the debt. An exception applies for voting rights in a reorganisation plan: if the claim was owed prior to the borrower's insolvency by one creditor and that creditor has assigned it in portions to several buyers, these buyers must vote uniformly (Section 244(2) of the German Insolvency Code).

(c) **Italy**

In general terms and in accordance with the Italian Insolvency Law, creditors are entitled to exercise voting rights following admission to the bankruptcy procedure.

In this regard, given the regulatory differences, it could be useful to make a distinction between composition agreements and pre-insolvency workout agreements with creditors:

- as to composition agreements, under Article 127 of the Italian Bankruptcy Law, debts transferred after the declaration of insolvency do not confer any

voting rights; by way of exception, if the relevant assignment has been made in favour of banks or other financial intermediaries, those entities are entitled to exercise the relevant voting rights;
- as to pre-insolvency workout agreements with creditors, Italian case law and legal scholars do not provide for a unanimous interpretation in relation to an assignee's voting rights, in the event that the transfer of the claim occurs after the filing with the court of the debtor's proposal; notwithstanding the absence of any specific provisions in this respect, the case law and legal scholars (where they take the view that the voting rights are transferred to the assignee) consider it necessary for the assignee to prove the relevant assignment before the date of creditors' hearing in order to exercise its voting right.

(d) *France*

In respect of voting rights in a composition agreement, under French law, the rights and obligations of a creditor are transferred with the claim. The purchaser must therefore notify the insolvency officer of its acquisition of those voting rights if it wishes to be consulted. Creditors which are members of creditors' committees must draw up the list of claims eight days before the date of the vote. The information used to determine this list must be available beforehand.

5. **Tax matters**

The main general tax issues that should be taken into account when trading loans in the different jurisdictions are outlined in the following paragraphs.

5.1 **Withholding taxes**

(a) *Spain*

According to the Spanish Non-Resident Income Tax Act, income obtained by a buyer who is not resident in Spain for tax purposes (either interest income or capital gains) would be exempt from taxation in Spain to the extent that the buyer:
- is resident for tax purposes in an EU member state, other than in a territory classed as a tax haven; and
- does not act, in regards to the purchase of the loan, through a permanent establishment located in Spain or outside the European Union.

Where the buyer is resident for tax purposes in a non-EU member state, it may be subject to withholding tax in Spain in accordance with the provisions set out in the relevant convention for the avoidance of double taxation.

Where the buyer cannot show that it is resident for tax purposes in either an EU member state or in a jurisdiction with which Spain has a convention for the avoidance of double taxation in force, the buyer would be subject to withholding tax on the income derived from the transaction at the general current tax rate of 19%.

(b) *Germany*

Germany does not levy withholding tax on interest payments for loans that are granted to non-bank institutions. German withholding tax may apply if the debt terms embed features of hybrid instruments, such as profit or income participating loans.

If debt is secured with German real estate, with German rights under civil law that are treated like German real estate or with vessels that are registered in the German shipping register, lenders who are resident in foreign jurisdictions are taxed in Germany on any interest income or capital gain/repayment gain that is earned on the (distressed) debt. This applies even if the borrower is resident outside Germany. However, in such cases the lender may benefit from a tax exemption for interest received (or a reduction of the applicable German tax rate) under a double tax treaty between Germany and the country where the lender is resident.

(c) *Italy*

Under the relevant tax law framework, a 26% final withholding tax is ordinarily applicable to interest (and other proceeds) paid by an Italian borrower to foreign lenders. This withholding tax can be reduced in line with any relevant tax treaty entered into between Italy and the state of residence of the lender.

However, the 26% final withholding tax is not applicable to interest (and other proceeds) arising from mid- and long-term facilities (those with a maturity period exceeding 18 months) granted to an Italian enterprise by:
- banks established in a EU member state;
- insurance companies incorporated in a EU member state and authorised under the legislative provisions of a EU member state;
- entities listed under Article 2(5)(4) to (23) of Directive 2013/36/EU; and
- institutional foreign investors (such as investment collective funds) which, irrespective of their taxable status, are established in a country which recognises the Italian tax authorities' right to an adequate exchange of information and are therein subject to regulatory surveillance.

(d) *France*

France does not apply withholding tax to either interest payments or capital gains realised upon the sale of a loan.

By way of exception, a withholding tax is levied at a rate of 75% on interest paid by borrowers established in France if the purchaser is established in a non-cooperative state or territory,[3] unless the borrower can demonstrate that the main purpose and consequences of the transaction is not to transfer and localise the income in that non-cooperative state or territory (Article 125 A, III and III *bis*, 11° of the French Tax Code).

5.2 VAT

(a) *Spain*

Under Spanish legislation on value added tax (VAT), the transfer of the creditor

---

[3] The list of non-cooperative states or territories is amended on an annual basis. At the date of writing, the list is the following: Botswana, Brunei, Guatemala, Marshall Islands, Nauru and Niue.

position would be VAT-exempt to the extent that the seller fully transfers the risks and benefits which would derive from an eventual insolvency of the borrower.

(b) **Germany**

While it is generally possible for a transferor of claims to opt for VAT on such a transfer to another party, it is usual in Germany not to exercise this option. The transfer of claims is therefore effectively free of VAT. However, it is unclear whether the transfer of all rights and obligations under a debt agreement may in fact be subject to VAT based on the judgment of the European Court of Justice (ECJ) of October 22 2009 in case C-242/08 *Swiss Re Germany Holding GmbH v Finanzamt München für Körperschaften*. According to this judgment, the assumption of life reinsurance contracts is generally subject to VAT. While it is the general view of German tax practitioners that the reasoning of this decision should not apply to the transfer of debt agreements, recent transactions involving the transfer of (distressed) claims provide for VAT through language that specifically takes into account the risk of triggering VAT on the transfer of debt agreements (ie, providing for either a grossing-up to account for VAT where it is payable, or no such grossing-up for VAT, depending on the commercial agreement between the transferor of the claim and the transferee). It can be expected that German tax practitioners will continue to use these contractual provisions to deal with the risk of VAT until the German tax authorities (or tax courts) issue a binding statement as to whether the reasoning of the ECJ decision applies to the transfer of debt agreements.

(c) **Italy**

A transfer of claims in the context of a financial transaction, in principle, falls within the scope of VAT under the Italian VAT Decree but qualifies as a VAT-exempt transaction.

This exemption regime applies to the extent that the transfer of claims represents a supply of services for VAT purposes rendered by the buyer in order to provide the seller with the required funds, giving the transaction a clear financial purpose. It must be noted that the qualification of a transfer of claims as a financial transaction for VAT purposes is debated in the jurisprudence and in the official clarifications rendered by the Italian tax authorities, leaving a certain margin of uncertainty.

In addition, the remuneration for the financial transaction comprising the assignment of a claim would be any existing positive difference between the face value of the claim and the purchase price paid by the purchaser for its purchase (ie, the discount) as well as any commission paid by the seller with the purpose of remunerating the buyer for the payment being made in advance, before the expiry of the claim, which in substance constitutes a financing. Circular Letter 32/E of March 11 2011 seems to imply that in the absence of remuneration for the financing granted through the transfer of claims, that transfer cannot result in the supply of a financial transaction for VAT purposes. With particular respect to this point, it must be pointed out that in the decision of October 27 2011, in Case C-93/10 *Finanzamt Essen-NordOst v GFKL Financial Services AG*, the ECJ took an even more restrictive view on this matter, by stating that the assignment of non-performing receivables at a discounted value does not result in the supply of a service for VAT purposes if the price paid represents fair value for those receivables.

The VAT treatment of the assignment of claims is also relevant for registration tax purposes. In a case of a transfer of claims subject to VAT, the registration tax due on the assignment of the claims would be a lump sum of €200.

On the other hand, the assignment, even by way of security, of a claim not subject to VAT is, in general terms, subject to registration tax at a rate of 0.5% on the amount of the receivables assigned, under Presidential Decree 131/1986 and to Part I of the tariff attached to that decree. This tax has to be paid on the execution of the assignment, or potentially later where a number of conditions apply.

Where the assignment is executed outside Italian territory or by way of exchange of correspondence (where the signatures of the parties to any of the documents are each in a separate document), registration tax may become payable if the assignment:

- is filed for voluntary registration;
- is detailed in any other document entered into between the same parties and filed for any reason with the registration tax office or in any proceedings before an Italian court; or
- is filed with an Italian court, when carrying out an administrative activity under Presidential Decree 131/1986, or before an administrative authority, unless the filing is mandatory by law.

Where the agreement is registered, a fixed stamp duty of €16 for every four pages of the assignment will apply.

(d) *France*

The transfer of a loan in France would be exempt from VAT to the extent that the purchase price corresponds to the effective economic value of the loan at the date of the transaction (Article 261 C, 1°, c, of the French Tax Code).

5.3 Stamp duty

(a) *Spain*

According to the provisions of the Spanish Transfer Tax and Stamp Duty Law, a public deed whose main object is a valuable asset or amount and which refers to registrable acts or agreements, is subject to stamp duty.

Therefore, a mortgage credit assignment transaction formalised as a public deed would be subject to stamp duty irrespective of whether it is finally registered within the relevant land registry or not.

Stamp duty ranges between 0.75% and 1.5% of the secured liability (principal, interest and any related costs) depending on the region (autonomous community) where the mortgaged asset is located.

In the case of assignment of mortgage credits, stamp duty due should apparently be calculated on the total assigned secured liability, without taking into account the price paid by the transferee for the relevant mortgaged credit or its outstanding balance. However, in recent binding tax rulings (V0966/2015 and V1263/2015) the Spanish tax authorities have ruled that the taxable base for stamp duty shall be the outstanding balance under the assigned mortgaged credit rather than the total assigned secured liability.

(b) *Germany*
Germany does not levy stamp duty on the transfer of interest or debt.

(c) *France*
Transfers of debt obligations are not subject to stamp duty in France.

However, the parties can voluntarily register the transaction and pay a €125 stamp duty (Article 680 of the French Tax Code).

Furthermore, stamp duty may apply if the transfer of the loan implies a mortgage transfer.

'Bad banks' and their role in the financial sector deleveraging process in Europe

Fernando Mínguez
Cuatrecasas, Gonçalves Pereira, Spain

1. **Introduction**

A good bank/bad bank scheme is a well-established banking crisis management tool, repeatedly used in the past throughout financial systems. Moreover, it has received legal recognition and is expressly contemplated in the 'resolution toolbox' of the EU resolution directive[1] (the 'BRRD'). The spin-off of an ailing institution into two vehicles – whether those vehicles are actual companies or not – may not be, in itself, enough as a resolution tool, but it is a relatively frequent step and resolution strategies often involve its use. The fundamentals of the idea are rather simple: damaged or legacy assets demand effort and management to maximise recovery and, when commingled with the healthy part of a banking business, they are not only unproductive but also drag in financial, technical and managerial resources that would more profitably be devoted to assets that can deliver better returns and, above all, to the origination of new business. Therefore, it is often – though, needless to say, not always – useful to establish a separation between legacy assets and healthy ones, and to put each under the appropriate managerial structure, so that the bad assets may be divested in an orderly fashion, turned around, or liquidated in the least harmful way possible, whereas the good ones, unencumbered, may form a new, viable institution.

While 'good banks' are invariably banks, 'bad banks' often are not. This is because in order to maximise recovery, managers of bad banks need to be freed from the constraints of banking regulation that apply to banks which are a going concern. This is easier, of course, when the bad bank and the good bank operate as separate legal entities, but that need not be the case.

In this article we shall briefly examine the notion and its use in the crisis management of banks, in particular since 2007, and with special focus on the Spanish case which, in addition to being the closest to the author's experience, is, to his knowledge, the most relevant in recent history in terms of the volume of assets involved.

2. **Shaping the notion**[2]

As commented, the essence of the good bank/bad bank technique consists in the

---

[1] Directive 2014/59/EU of the European Parliament and of the Council of 15 May 2014 establishing a framework for the recovery and resolution of credit institutions and investment firms. See, in particular, Article 42 and references to the "asset separation tool" and asset management vehicles.

[2] For an introductory yet systematic approach, see G Brenna, T Poppensieker and S Schneider (McKinsey & Co) (2009): www.mckinsey.com/insights/financial_services/understanding_the_bad_bank.

separation of a bank's troubled assets (the term 'asset' is to be construed here in the widest sense possible, meaning strictly assets, portfolios or entire business lines) from the performing ones. In our opinion, the application of the good bank/bad bank technique does not require the use of separate legal entities, but it does require the setting up of different managerial structures, which is not necessarily the same thing. In other words, whether or not the good and the bad banks are different legal entities, they should operate as entirely separate business units under different rules.

This principle of managerial isolation helps us to differentiate the good bank/bad bank technique from other tools available and used for resolution or restructuring purposes which also involve the identification – but not necessarily the segregation – of a perimeter of troubled assets.

A salient example of the latter are asset protection schemes.[3] An asset protection scheme requires the identification of a set of assets that the scheme will apply to. But those assets are normally not managed separately. Moreover, it may be of the essence in the asset protection scheme rules that assets subject to protection are not managed separately. The beneficiary of an asset protection scheme is generally required not to discriminate protected assets from unprotected ones so as not to alter recovery rates.

Bad banks (or asset management companies) and asset protection schemes or, in other words, separation (or asset removal) and protection are two alternative forms of asset support. In some respects, asset separation can be seen as the more, and an asset protection scheme the less, invasive solutions to the same problem. Market conditions and circumstances should dictate when to use one or the other. According to O'Brien and Wezel,[4] asset separation may become desirable in contexts of depressed marked prices, when there is little market access, when the amount of impaired assets is really too large for the bank's resources and when management may benefit from economies of scale (provided a single or a reduced number of asset repositories are established, as seems invariably to happen).

On the other hand, splitting a bank into two or more units does not necessarily imply that those units are defined on managerial criteria. The units may be homogeneous and established just for the purposes of facilitating a sale (such as in the case of the break-up of a large organisation into smaller, homogeneous units).

Banks may set up, on their sole initiative, legacy units that function as bad banks, either within their own legal structures or as separate legal entities within their consolidated groups. Operationally, these may offer perfect examples of the good bank/bad bank principle and may achieve the same management goals. Nevertheless, in such examples, the concept falls short from delivering its full results,

---

[3] An asset protection scheme is an agreement or a statutory instrument pursuant to which a guarantor (generally, a public institution), guarantees the value of a given set of assets of a bank, be it in the context of the transfer of control to a new investor or in another scenario. We have briefly examined and provided further reference on the nature of asset protection schemes in a previous work (in Spanish), see F Mínguez, "Herramientas Contractuales de Apoyo Financiero a Entidades en Crisis: los Esquemas de Protección de Activos" ("Contractual Tools of Financial Support to Ailing Institutions: Asset Protection Schemes") in A Recalde *et al* (editors), *Crisis y Reforma del Sistema Financiero* ("Crisis and Reform of the Financial System") (Madrid, Thomson Reuters – Universidad Autónoma, 2014).

[4] E O'Brien and T Wezel, "Asset Support Schemes in the Euro Area", *ECB Financial Stability Review*, May 2013.

which may be achieved only when there is some regulatory back-up permitting the exclusion of the legacy assets from the banking regulatory perimeter.

In other words, although the concept may be expanded, the examples that are of primary interest for us for the purposes of this chapter are those experiences backed by some regulatory coverage or directly regulatory-driven.

3. Pre-2007 experiences

According to commentators, the first notable use of the good bank/bad bank technique was that by Mellon Bank (now part of Bank of New York Mellon) as early as 1988. That year Mellon Bank spun off $1.4 billion of bad loans to a newly created institution – chartered as a bank, albeit it did not take deposits – named Grant Street National Bank. Mellon's shareholders received, by way of dividend, a share in Grant Street per share in Mellon.[5] Although the structure did not benefit from any particular regulatory reliefs, it received some endorsement from the Federal Reserve (which accepted that Grant Bank could be chartered). Once isolated, and equipped with most of Mellon's collection teams, Grant Bank could concentrate on recoveries. By 1995, Grant Bank was dissolved.

However, possibly the best known, and – according to the general consensus – most successful to date, application of the notion (in the restricted sense contemplated here) took place in the aftermath of the Swedish banking crisis. The Swedish authorities created two bad banks (actually special purpose vehicles, not banks this time) to receive the non-performing assets from, respectively, Gota Bank and Nordbanken (still in business as Nordea). A similar approach was followed in Finland, also in the early 1990s.

One of the Swedish asset management companies, Securum, became a kind of archetype, although it was based on on earlier precedents. Securum[6] was entrusted with the management of roughly Skr 50 billion in impaired assets[7] – an astonishing amount for 1992 Sweden – and given a 15-year mandate to divest them. Although it was 100% owned by the Swedish state, management was independent and entirely professional, and the company was freed from any banking regulation constraints. Though divesting its assets was its primary purpose, Securum was legally able to manage its legacy in a wider sense and could turn around assets or develop them to maximise return, even if that required additional investments. By 1994, a good part of the task had been successfully accomplished, and in 1997 Securum itself was wound up.

4. Ireland and NAMA

Post-2007, much attention was gathered by the creation of the Irish National Asset Management Agency (NAMA). Pretty much in line with what happened in other countries, and very particularly in Spain, the Irish real estate market collapsed shortly

---

5   Allegedly, the effect on Mellon's share was positive.
6   The Securum case was discussed, among others, by Bergström, Englund and Thorell in a 2003 paper commissioned by the Stockholm-based Centre for Business and Policy Studies, a summary of which is available at: www.sns.se/sites/default/files/securum_eng.pdf.
7   The number of obligors was, however, fairly limited by comparison to what happened later in Spain, for example; less than 1,500.

after the outbreak of the general financial crisis, causing serious trouble to the six Irish banks at the time and, ultimately, to the Irish state itself.

Over a process spanning several years NAMA took care of a face value of €77 billion in loans for a transfer value of €31.8 billion (hence a 57% average discount). Consideration to contributing banks is satisfied in the form of bonds guaranteed by the Irish state. Assets were acquired in the form of loans exclusively. Hence NAMA became the direct owner of properties only after the relevant enforcement and repossession processes.

NAMA was established as a public statutory body by means of an *ad hoc* act (the National Asset Management Agency Act 2009) which also governed the process of separation of assets from the banks subject to the measure. NAMA, as an agency, is under the control of the Irish Treasury. However, the actual structure of the Irish bad bank is rather more complex. NAMA holds 49% of a company named National Asset Management Agency Investment Ltd (NAMAIL), the other 51% of which is held by private investors. Nevertheless, there is a shareholders' agreement between NAMA and the private investors that entrusts NAMA with certain veto rights.[8] The structure under NAMAIL consists in a multiplicity of vehicles with servicing, debt-issuance or asset-holding functions.

The transfer of assets into the NAMA structure was carried out on a case-by-case (bank-by-bank) basis, pursuant to an *ad hoc* due diligence and valuation. This is why, although the primary vehicle was established as early as 2009, it was not until 2011 that NAMA gathered the whole portfolio it currently has under management. This time-span had an impact on asset valuation, so the final discount applied for transfer purposes (an estimate of the assets' long-term value) was larger than expected.

After its long implementation process, NAMA seems to be successfully fulfilling its role, deleveraging at reasonable speed and making consistent profits.

5. The Spanish experience: Sareb

5.1 Background

As early as 2009, the profile of the Spanish banking crisis and where the core of the problem lay were apparent to most well informed observers. As logic dictated, in view of the composition of the balances of the banks, a very significant proportion of real estate or real estate-backed assets turned out to be non-performing. The problem was therefore quite similar to Ireland's but of a different size by several orders of magnitude.

Given that, regardless of size, the problem seemingly stemmed from an identifiable group of assets or asset classes, it was also quite logical that a good bank/bad bank scheme was postulated relatively early in the process as a natural remedy. However, it took some time to put things in operation for reasons related initially to regulatory decisions and later to fiscal issues.

Sparing any political angle to the matter, it seems evident now that Spanish

---

[8] Such veto rights and the general structure were approved by Eurostat for the group headed by NAMA not to be considered a part of the public sector for national accounts purposes. However, for the purposes of corporate accounts, NAMA is deemed to have control over NAMAIL (see NAMA various annual reports at www.nama.ie).

regulatory authorities were, in the early stages of the crisis, either reluctant to disclose the estimated amount of assets affected or misled about what that amount was. Whatever the cause, they thought the creation of a bad bank was not appropriate. If they really thought the dimension of the problem was much lower than it was later considered to be, a bad bank would probably have been unnecessary since there would have been reasons to believe banks could cope with their troubled assets by other means. If they were aware of the magnitude of the matter but, for whatever reason, were not willing to disclose it, a bad bank did not make sense either, simply because a condition for the success of the good bank/bad bank strategy is that it provides a real relief to banks by taking in all, or most, of their impaired assets. If a significant amount of troubled assets is left out, it is hard to see the point of the exercise of separation.

After 2011, the regulatory strategy shifted dramatically: banks were required to clean up their balance-sheets as much as possible and to make substantial provisions for nearly all real estate-related asset categories in a broad sense. Troubled asset classes were clearly labelled as such and the problem was thus disclosed. There was relative consensus, by that time, about the convenience of setting up a bad bank. The problem then turned on its funding or, more precisely, how to make up for the heavy losses banks were to book when writing off, wholly or partially, their assets upon their transfer to the bad bank.[9] Spain was, at the time, under serious budgetary stress and struggling to overcome the fiscal crisis that affected the peripheral euro economies. Ireland, Greece and Portugal had already been forced into wide-ranging EU rescue packages and all the pressure was now on Spain and, next in line, Italy.

By mid-2012, Spain applied for a €100 billion[10] EU credit line for the restructuring of the banking sector. The facility was granted upon Spain's acceptance of certain conditions, as had been the case with the rescue packages for other euro countries, but these were limited to the policy area concerned:[11] banking regulation and banking policy matters. The conditions were set out in a memorandum of understanding entered into between Spain and the European Union. One of the conditions imposed by the memorandum of understanding was that certain impaired assets of banks that were bailed out or had received or were expected to receive public support in the context of the 2012 stress tests[12] had to be transferred to a bad bank (more technically, an 'asset management company').

---

9   In fact, assets could have been transferred at any nominal value but, at some point, the loss implicit in the difference between the book value and the fair value (even after several years of accounting for impairment and making provisions and write-offs, the real estate portfolio of banks was deemed to be overvalued) would have to arise. It was then a matter of choice: banks could be requested to mark-down their assets prior to the transfer and, as a result, become unable to meet regulatory capital standards or plainly insolvent (hence becoming candidates for a bail-out), or losses could crystallise once in the bad bank which, in turn, risked being insufficiently capitalised from the outset.
10 Of which only a part was used.
11 Spain did not apply for a general bail-out programme and hence was not subject to general economic policy conditions as Ireland, Portugal and Greece had been.
12 On the basis of the results of stress tests carried out in 2012, significant Spanish banks were classified into four groups: Group 0 were the healthy banks, ie banks that successfully met the test; Group 1 were the banks that, at the time, were already state-owned due to previous bail-out processes; Group 2 were the banks that failed the test and were deemed to need some form of public support to be kept in business; and, finally, Group 3 were the banks that, while falling short of the test's requirements, were believed to be able to overcome the situation on their own. The banks that had to transfer assets to an asset management company were those in Groups 1 and 2.

The memorandum of understanding was signed in late June 2012 and the legislation implementing it was enacted as early as August 31 of that same year by means of Royal Decree-Law 24/2012 (later re-enacted as a parliamentary act, Act 9/2012).[13] Mere legislative references may fail to convey the magnitude of the accomplishment: Royal Decree-Law 24/2012 was not a typical piece of executive legislation, but a fully-fledged act on bank resolution, incorporating most of what was already in the text of the BRRD, as then available.

As noted above, in the introduction, the BRRD contemplates – and had already contemplated in its earlier drafts – the transfer of assets into an asset management company as part of its resolution toolbox. Royal Decree-Law 24/2014, anticipating that, provided for the regulation of asset management companies as such a resolution tool and, furthermore, mandated that one such company be immediately set up and that certain banks should transfer assets identified as problematic to the new company. The company was effectively incorporated shortly before the end of 2012 as *Sociedad de Gestión de Activos Procedentes de la Reestructuración Bancaria SA* (better known by the acronym 'Sareb').

Time was of the essence in the process and, of course, it proved to be a constraint that influenced the design of Sareb.

5.2 The vehicle

Coming only a short time later, Sareb owes a lot to NAMA's example. The Irish precedent was the primary reference for the Spanish authorities (and their advisers), whether it was to apply the same solutions, or consciously to depart from them.

Unlike NAMA's, Sareb's legal nature and regime were not developed entirely *ad hoc*. There was simply not enough time to cope with the technicalities inherent to the implementation of a newly designed type of institution. Following the path of Securum, Sareb is incorporated as a public limited company (*sociedad anónima*) with very few special provisions. It has a limited life span (15 years from its incorporation) and it has received certain waivers from general company law provisions that are normally only available to listed companies.

The share capital in the company is held by the state (through the *Fondo de reestructuración ordenada bancaria* or 'FROB', meaning the fund for orderly bank restructuring') and private investors on a 45/55 basis. Hence, Sareb is a private company for the purposes of EU national accounts classification. The private investors (holding 55% of the capital and voting rights) mainly come from the healthy part of the financial system.[14]

Sareb is, in addition and at least theoretically, the first of a kind. As noted, neither Act 9/2012 nor Act 11/2015 regulate Sareb as such, but asset management companies in general. However, Royal Decree 1559/2012 of November 15 2012, in addition to developing the legal regime of such companies in general does contain certain provisions applying to Sareb specifically (hence, at least in theory, not necessarily applying to any future asset management company). This special regime does not

---

13 Subsequently repealed upon the enactment of Act 11/2015, implementing the BRRD.
14 Some other institutional investors hold minor stakes.

really create a unique set of rules departing to those applicable to companies in general, but rather consists in an extension to Sareb of certain features that are typical of listed companies (see further below).

In contrast with the complexity of NAMA, the structure of Sareb is rather simple. There are no substructures involved. The Spanish bad bank is single vehicle, encompassing the assets, the liabilities arising from the transfer and the management structure.

5.3 The transfer

The assets transferred to Sareb were real estate or real estate-related, mostly in the form of non-performing loans to developers. The value for transfer purposes was €50.8 billion, of which €11.3 billion corresponded to properties and the remaining €39.4 billion corresponded to loans (assets were valued at discounts ranging from 45% to 80% of their face or original appraisal values). The law foresaw the possible acquisition of shares in real estate companies as well, but this possibility was not used in practice. Assets under a certain threshold (€100,000 for properties and €250,000 for loans) were exempted from transfer, on the assumption that banks were able to divest those themselves quite efficiently.[15] Banks had to mark the assets down to their transfer value, if necessary, in their own books, prior to the transfer – hence losses crystallised at that point.[16]

Unlike in the case of NAMA, and because of the time constraints imposed by the memorandum of understanding, the transfer was a one-off process,[17] virtually simultaneous with the incorporation of the vehicle. No due diligence was carried out beforehand, nor was there an asset by asset appraisal or valuation. Rather, the transfer value was determined in the context of an exercise carried out by Bank of Spain, and Sareb carried out retrospective due diligence, having a 36-month period to put return any assets not meeting the transfer criteria (this put right of return was exercised in practice, leading to adjustments that, while not very significant in the overall context, were not immaterial).

On the basis of the transfer values at its inception, Sareb is larger than NAMA (€50.8 billion in the case of Sareb as opposed to €31.6 billion for the Irish institution) but the difference in size is not commensurate with differences between Spain and Ireland in terms of GDP, population or the size of the banking sector. The differences in structure and complexity of the assets are more relevant. Sareb is not only bigger than NAMA but also more complex. Whereas NAMA received only loans concentrated to a significant degree in relatively few obligors, Sareb had to cope with some 200,000 assets[18] in the form of properties (of various classes) and loans secured

---

15 An assumption likely to hold, since assets under that threshold normally correspond to individual dwellings that banks commercialise through their extensive networks of branches, or to individual mortgages.
16 As a matter of fact, due to the application of extraordinary accounting rules earlier that year, assets had already been marked down, so the transfer to Sareb did not result in significant additional losses.
17 Technically, the transfer of assets took place in two stages. A first stage by the end of 2012, comprising the banks that, at the time, were already majority owned by the FROB (the Group 1 banks) and a second stage in February 2013 with Group 2.
18 Due attention should be paid to the fact that the notion of 'asset' when we come to counting them is not unproblematic, so that figure is always an approximation. By way of example, a loan to a developer (a single asset) may become, after repossession, a much larger number of residential properties (houses) to be sold one by one, so that single asset could be considered, functionally, a multiplicity.

by another 400,000 properties. The Spanish exercise was, therefore, more demanding in terms of analysis and due diligence, due to a much higher degree of granularity.

While, as noted above, there is little originality in the vehicle, legal effort was put into making the transfer secure. Although there is a contract between Sareb and each contributing entity, regulating the particulars, the transfer of assets to Sareb was ultimately made by operation of the law; a statutory transfer subject to certain provisions that represent relevant exemptions to general, common statutory rules applicable to asset transfers. In this respect:

- the transfer was mandatory for the contributing banks and subject to no consent from any third party;
- the transfer was not subject to insolvency claw-back provisions;
- no third-party rights (such as rights of first refusal) could be opposed to the transfer;
- even if some of the assets might be held to constitute a productive unit or a 'business', no labour law, tax or social security liability could be attached and, in particular, no employee could claim a right to be employed by Sareb as a result of the transfer; and
- Sareb is not affected, in the context of insolvency proceedings against its debtors, by the statutory subordination that might otherwise have affected the transferor if the transferor was a party related to the insolvent debtor.

On the other hand, the transfer was a true sale for the banks that ceased to be involved with the assets transferred; Sareb assumed all the risk and rewards, notwithstanding banks' transitional role as servicers.

5.4   Funding

The basic source of funding of Sareb is through bonds issued to the asset transferors as consideration for the assets. The bonds are guaranteed by the Kingdom of Spain and, as such, may be posted as collateral for European Central Bank funding.

As noted above, equity (share capital) is distributed in a 45/55 proportion between the FROB (the Spanish state) and private investors. The capital base was reinforced with convertible financing for an amount of three times the share capital (€3.6 billion for €1.2 billion). Convertible bonds were also issued in a 45/55 basis to the FROB and private investors (although the individual private investors' holdings in convertibles and capital are not exactly the same). Banco Santander is the largest capital and convertibles holder, with 17.3% and 16% of the share capital and the convertibles, respectively, as at Sareb's inception.

5.5   Governance and management structure

As a company, Sareb has the same governance structure as any other Spanish corporation. All shares are equal in rights and every shareholder has the same rights to attend and vote at the general shareholders' meeting, which therefore reflects strictly the 45/55 capital composition.

The company is not listed and may not be in its present configuration, since shares may only circulate among certain categories of institutional investors.

Nevertheless, the law imposes a governance structure that is virtually the same as that applying to listed companies.

The board of directors must have between five and 15 seats, of which a minimum of one third must be assigned to independent directors. Currently, Sareb has 14 directors, five of which are independent. The FROB is a director. Under the board of directors, there is a structure of supporting committees, established by mandate of Section 23 of Royal Decree 1559/2012 (management, risks, investments and assets and liabilities). In addition, like listed companies, the company has an audit and an appointments and compensation committee, consisting of a majority of independent directors and chaired by one of them. Sareb must report to the public at large along the same lines listed companies do.

The Bank of Spain does not have over Sareb the same supervisory powers it has over credit institutions (exercised within the framework of the Single Supervisory Mechanism) or other financial intermediaries. However, it oversees the company's activities, monitored the asset transfer exercise and has authority to dictate Sareb's accounting standards. This last point has led to debate during Sareb's early stages. Not being a listed company and not having consolidated accounts[19] (hence, not falling within the scope of the International Financial Reporting Standards under EU Regulation 1606/2002), the company would have had to abide by the accounting standards set out in the Spanish Code of Commerce and the General Accounting Plan. Being freed from regulatory constraints – in particular, banking provisioning and asset impairment criteria – was viewed as one of the main advantages of a vehicle of this kind. However, Item 10 of the seventh additional provision to Act 9/2012 (introduced by Act 26/2016) foresaw a series of specific rules, to be developed by Bank of Spain. This authority fulfilled that mandate by issuing Circular 5/2015 which sets, among other particulars, provisioning criteria tailored for Sareb which, while being different from banking standards, are more stringent than the general ones.

At its inception, the massive transfer of assets from the contributing banks and time constraints left little choice but to keep the transferors as servicers. Sareb lacked the resources to take over management functions and, moreover, it was never the intention to let the structure grow to the point where it would be able to manage the vehicle's huge portfolio using solely internal means.[20] The first major project undertaken by Sareb – apart from the due diligence – was the re-engineering of it servicing structure. The contributing entities were, in the course of 2014, replaced by four general servicers selected in a competitive process and each awarded a long-term servicing contract.

Being a company, and hence subject to private law, Sareb has ample leeway to manage its assets and divest them as it thinks appropriate. It currently operates both in wholesale and retail property markets, and has become a relevant player in the secondary market for loans and loan portfolios. Though these are more delicate operations from the perspective of a vehicle born to liquidate, Sareb is also able, with no restriction, to transform and turn around assets to make them more fit for the purpose of being divested, even if that requires further investments.

---

19 Sareb has no subsidiaries.
20 That said, Sareb's internal structure grew quickly to some 300 employees.

Although the company has not yet reached breakeven (mostly due to the application of Bank of Spain's 2015 criteria) it has already divested assets by the thousands and has repaid several billions in debt according to the relevant schedules.

6. 'Bad banks' as deleveraging tools: the debate

Asset separation seems to be an advisable technique when banks are faced with a stock of impaired assets that go beyond a certain level, paired with markets that are depressed or otherwise do not offer prospects for quick divesting. These circumstances often amount to a system-wide problem, as was the case in Sweden in 1992 and, more recently, in Ireland or Spain.

Asset reparation provides transferring banks – albeit possibly at the cost of crystallising losses – first with capital requirements relief and a boost in liquidity, to the extent that assets are swapped for cash or low risk-weight bearing securities easily convertible into cash, and, perhaps more importantly, with free management resources which may be re-applied to return-making activities.

If the bad bank is engineered so as to provide a clear break, with no further involvement of the transferring banks with the assets (other than, eventually, as servicers), the deleveraging effect on the banking system is immediate. Needless to say, from a wider perspective, the bad bank is not, by its mere creation, a solution to the problem posed by the assets, merely a change of co-ordinates. The assets leave the banking sector but do not vanish. Someone must bear their risk thereafter and that someone is, very often, the taxpayer. Even though NAMA and Sareb – as the latest and most relevant examples – have been designed to meet Eurostat tests and it must be accepted that they operate under no undue public sector influence, it is no less true that, in both cases, the Irish or Spanish taxpayer owns roughly a half of the vehicle and, which is more relevant, stands behind its balance sheet in the form of public guarantees.

The implementation of bad banks, at least in the versions for which NAMA and Sareb (and Securum before them) provide examples, has led to debate in the respective jurisdictions, and even to bitter argument. In Ireland, the creation of NAMA was the object of open criticism from economists and other commentators. Some objections are, in fact, not addressed at bad banks in particular but to bank bail-outs in general.[21] Others may be better described as technical. For instance, the Bank of Spain, while not expressing any objection in principle against the tool, considered it not appropriate for a long time in the Spanish context. From another angle, some commentators held that Sareb, rather than being half public and half privately owned, should have been made fully public and given a different, more social, mandate. Some academics in Ireland, in a commentary published in *The Irish Times* argued that they would have rather seen banks subject to outright nationalisation, than the limited intervention NAMA represented:

We can summarise our arguments in favour of nationalisation, and against the Government's current approach of limited recapitalisation and the introduction of an

---

21 Eg the position of Joseph Stiglitz about the NAMA bill, expressed publicly at Trinity College on October 7 2009.

asset management agency, under four headings. We consider that nationalisation will better protect taxpayers' interests, produce a more efficient and longer lasting solution to our banking problems, be more transparent in relation to pricing of distressed assets, and be far more likely to produce a banking system free from the toxic reputation that our current financial institutions have deservedly earned.[22]

The public or private nature of the vehicle – or the appropriateness of its mere existence – are not the only matters for debate. When, as was the case in Spain, the vehicle has to coexist with the rest of the system, part of which has not been subject to any form of aid, competition and conflict of interest issues may arise. Unlike in Ireland – where all the banks were given the opportunity to transfer impaired assets into NAMA – in Spain only certain institutions could contribute to Sareb. The healthy part of the system was not only not given the opportunity to transfer assets but, with some salient exceptions, become the private shareholders and subordinated bondholders of the vehicle. And it is worth bearing in mind that, in this context, 'healthy' means unaided rather than untroubled. Spanish banks saw the establishment of a €50 billion competitor in the same market where they were meant to divest their own legacy assets.

On the other hand, it has been said that economies of scale dictate that there is little logic in implementing a large number of asset management companies within a system. A single vehicle appears to be a better option. But, beyond a certain point, the management of that single vehicle may become very complex, as it inherits and concentrates not only troubled assets themselves, but also the problems banks face to make them liquid.

7. Conclusion

The good bank/bad bank arrangement has been repeatedly used in the past to cope with banking failures and crises. And asset separation has proven a good strategy, backed by success in several contexts. The salient examples discussed in this chapter are too recent and have not carried out their mandates for long enough to establish whether they too will be successful. Moreover, it may not be easy to call this experience a success, since there will always be little chance to see the results that alternative strategies might have delivered.

Theory states that when certain circumstances concur, as was the case in Ireland and Spain (a system-wide crisis, accumulation of large stocks of legacy assets and stagnant markets) asset separation is advisable. Some virtuous effects of asset separation are automatic, namely the relief to contributing banks, but their ultimate success (even in merely operational terms) depends on a multiplicity of factors: correct asset valuation at inception, establishment of an efficient management structure and, last but not least, a well-defined management and strategy.

At least when these vehicles attain a certain size, due attention should be paid to potential side-effects in those parts of the financial system that do not benefit directly from the scheme and over the economy at large.

---

22 *The Irish Times*, April 17 2009 (www.irishtimes.com/opinion/nationalising-banks-is-the-best-option-1.747194).

Anatomy of a non-performing loan portfolio sale

Paul Dunbar
Vinson & Elkins LLP

1. Trends in the European non-performing loan market

1.1 Increasing range of active jurisdictions

The European market for loan portfolio transactions continues to be very active, with 2015 seeing over €100 billion in completed loan disposals across Europe. The United Kingdom and Ireland have led the way with the highest value transactions, such as the sale of UK Asset Resolution's £13 billion Project Granite and Lloyds Banking Group's sale of the €4.2 billion Project Poseidon in Ireland.

Other key jurisdictions include Spain, the Netherlands, Germany and Italy, but with highly competitive auction processes in all of these jurisdictions driving up pricing, buyers are looking to an increasing range of opportunities in less familiar jurisdictions, in particular in central and eastern Europe.

1.2 Diverse assets and structures

While loans secured on commercial real estate still form the major part of the European non-performing loan market, portfolio transactions are diverse in range, and can include secured and unsecured consumer or individual borrower loan assets, loans secured on shipping or aviation or other assets, and corporate borrower loans. Portfolios often include far more than just the core loan assets, with transactions that include hedging positions, real estate owned properties, litigation claims, current account overdrafts, agency roles, letters of credit, minority and controlling equity positions, unfunded commitments and employees.

Moving into 2016, a key trend has been the increased number of share transactions where sellers are seeking to sell an entire corporate group structure, containing loan assets and underlying real estate and other assets where security has already been enforced, together with asset management and other employees, an example being the auction of Propertize BV by the government of the Netherlands.

There are also a limited number of secondary portfolio sales in the European market, akin to private equity secondary buyouts, where an investor has acquired portfolios over time and combined loans from different portfolios into a new portfolio, which is then sold in a secondary transaction to a new buyer.

1.3 Continuing buy-side demand and pressure to sell

Buy-side demand and sell-side pressure are expected to lead to a very active loan portfolio market throughout 2016 and beyond. On the sell-side the bad banks and other state-supported entities are planning continued asset sales and wind-down processes. Changing regulatory and economic circumstances, in particular regulatory capital requirements, mean that European banks and other financial institutions will continue to dispose of non-core assets as they focus on new strategies and priorities. On the buy-side, an increased range of investors are competing in the portfolio auction processes, made up of private equity and special situation funds, investment arms of insurance companies, investment banks with special situation groups and smaller local market participants, all of whom have significant amounts of capital to invest.

While non-performing loan portfolio transactions are increasingly varied in structure, jurisdiction and the nature of the portfolios being sold, the market for loan portfolio transactions has evolved since the financial crisis in such a way that there are certain typical transaction processes and key issues that arise on most deals. These key features and issues are assessed below, together with a consideration of the new themes and issues that are arising as the structure of deals, asset classes, financing and jurisdictions involved continue to broaden.

2. Transaction structure

2.1 Bad banks and private sales

State-sponsored bad banks have been set up in several European countries over the past five years as a key strategy in resolving the issue of non-performing loans on European bank balance sheets. The non-performing loans are transferred to the bad banks and are subsequently being disposed of by the bad banks to private buyers in accordance with the wind-down mandate for each bad bank. Particularly active bad banks have included UKAR in the United Kingdom, NAMA in Ireland and SAREB in Spain. Other bad banks have been established more recently, such as HETA in Austria, and are becoming more active, with HETA expected to push on with the disposal of assets in Slovenia, Hungary, Croatia, Bulgaria and other central and eastern European countries.

Where non-performing loans have not first been transferred to a bad bank, they are typically sold by the relevant originating bank directly to private buyers.

2.2 Basic structure

The seller of a non-performing loan portfolio will typically want an outright sale of the loan assets by means of legal assignment and assumption of liabilities. An outright sale is not always possible though, for example due to borrower consent requirements in the underlying loan documentation, or regulatory issues in a particular jurisdiction, and alternative structures are sometimes used. Alternatives include the use of participation agreements that should remove the need to obtain borrower consents, although these are unpopular with buyers if they are required for longer than an interim period before a subsequent elevation, due to the indirect exercise of voting and other rights in a participation structure. A hive-down of the relevant assets to a special purpose vehicle and subsequent share sale may be an option not requiring borrower consent, but change of control issues will still need to be considered. Less frequently, other options are seen, including total return swaps and declarations of trust. With all structures, the tax and regulatory implications will need to be carefully considered by both the seller and buyer.

2.3 Bidco structuring

The bidco entity will usually be a special purpose vehicle, established in a jurisdiction that is tax-efficient for the buyer, taking into account the assets in the portfolio and its upper tier structure, and the necessary governance, financing and regulatory requirements for the transaction. In many cases several special purpose vehicle holding companies will be established, either as part of the buyer's group or as part of an orphan structure. Key tax considerations in the structuring process will include any potential withholding tax on interest payments to the buyer and possible transfer taxes related to the transfer of security or assets.

Another possibility is the use of a securitisation structure to take advantage of particular regulatory requirements or hurdles. In Italy, for example, the government announced a state guarantee in February 2016 in respect of securitised non-performing loans, with the objective being to assist the removal of non-performing loans from the balance sheets of Italian banks. The government guarantee will apply in respect of the senior notes issued by the securitisation special purpose vehicle. Under a securitisation structure, the non-performing loans would be transferred to a securitisation special purpose vehicle in the relevant jurisdiction. The special purpose vehicle would fund the purchase of the portfolio through the issue of different classes of notes with a different seniority ranking to investors in the securitisation. The cash-flow generated by the non-performing loans is collected by a servicer, on behalf of the special purpose vehicle, and applied to the payment of interest and principal on the notes, as well as the running costs of the special purpose vehicle, in accordance with their terms.

In certain jurisdictions, notably Spain, there are a growing number of large portfolios that contain real estate that is already owned by the seller (real estate owned properties), which have been acquired through the enforcement of security. Each real estate owned property is typically held by a special purpose vehicle (REOCo). Portfolios including real estate-owned properties usually transfer them directly as an asset transfer to the buyer, using separate asset transfer agreements, in addition to the main sale and purchase agreement, to effect the transfer of the real estate-owned properties in each applicable jurisdiction. Note that in certain jurisdictions it may be advantageous for transfer tax or other reasons to transfer the shares in the REOCo itself, rather than make an asset transfer of the real estate-owned property.

2.4 Regulatory issues

In structuring a bid for a non-performing loan portfolio, a buyer will need to consider the regulatory regime applicable to the jurisdiction, the nature of the loans and any underlying assets on which the loans are secured. Certain jurisdictions may require the holder of legal title to the loans to have a licence in order to carry out lending activities. What constitutes lending activities may be interpreted broadly in a particular jurisdiction to include not just making an advance under a loan facility, but also the restructuring of a loan or acquisition of a loan.

If the portfolio contains consumer loans or regulated mortgages, additional authorisations will almost certainly be required, and the entity that is to hold legal title to the acquired loans will be required to hold the relevant authorisations. Where the buyer is part of a banking group, the holder of legal title for such loans will often be a regulated banking entity within that group. For a buyer that is not part of a banking group or has not teamed up with a bank as a co-investor, the third-party servicer that will be servicing the portfolio from closing will typically have the necessary authorisations and will be able to hold legal title to the regulated mortgages instead of the buyer. The receivables from the loans will then be transferred to the buyer on a rolling basis to reflect the desired economics of the transaction.

Data protection, bank secrecy and confidentiality rules concerning the disclosure of customer information also need to be considered, as this may prevent the transfer to a purchaser of key information about the loans or underlying borrowers prior to completion, which in turn may cause issues for the buyer's know-your-customer process. However, in many situations there are exemptions to such requirements due to the need to be able to transfer non-performing loan portfolios. In all cases, the scope of the regulatory regime that applies for a particular portfolio transaction should be identified and considered by both the seller and buyer early on in the sale process.

With appropriate structuring, it may be possible for a buyer to team up with a third-party servicer or co-investor in order to meet the relevant regulatory requirements and to ensure it is able to give comfort to the seller on the regulatory compliance matters, which will be one of the priorities for a seller considering opposing bids in an auction process.

3. Due diligence

3.1 Diligence process

In highly competitive non-performing loan auctions, due diligence often remains a buyer's primary source of comfort with respect to the assets that are being acquired, as sellers typically give very limited contractual protections to the buyer in the sale and purchase agreement (see under heading 4 below for a detailed discussion of terms and conditions in the sale and purchase agreement). The results of the due diligence process are crucial in allowing bidders to determine their pricing assumptions, and will also be very important in the buyer's structuring of the transaction.

The seller will customarily provide a data tape setting out key information about the loans in the portfolio at a given date (usually the effective date for the economic transfer of the portfolio to the buyer). Key data points will include the amounts outstanding, interest rates, maturity dates and undrawn commitments. The data tape will be the key piece of information used by bidders in determining its bid purchase price. As a result, contractual protections in the form of robust warranties with respect to the data tape information should be included in the sale and purchase agreement.

Vendor due diligence reports vary in usefulness and scope, and indeed are not even always provided other than in the form of a basic information memorandum. Where full legal vendor due diligence reports are provided, they may be too narrow in scope or subject to low caps on liability to give significant comfort to the buyer. As a result, detailed due diligence by the buyer remains the key due diligence work-stream.

The scope and extent of due diligence carried out by a buyer and its advisers will be driven by:
- the buyer's risk appetite, taking into account the overall level of comfort with the transaction and the seller;
- cost sensitivities;
- attractiveness of the portfolio to a particular buyer and whether they believe they have a good chance of winning the auction;
- the extent and quality of vendor due diligence;
- transaction structure;
- the degree of contractual protections proposed in the seller's draft sale and purchase agreement.

In all cases, the buyer will likely want to ensure it carries out efficient and targeted diligence at an early stage, in order to enable it to determine its appetite with respect to the portfolio and whether its proposed strategies for working out the portfolio post-closing are viable.

Where multiple jurisdictions are involved, it is essential for the buyer's main transaction counsel to take a lead coordinating role, seamlessly integrating advice from leading local counsel in the relevant jurisdictions.

As well as legal due diligence, a buyer will carry out detailed financial and asset-level due diligence, often with external financial advisers and sector specialists, although certain buyers have existing in-house underwriting teams that carry out a large part of this financial and asset diligence work-stream.

3.2 Scope and common red flags to resolve

The scope of due diligence will vary depending on the specific nature of the loans and/or the underlying assets in the portfolio. Set out below are some of the key diligence points and common issues that may arise.

(a) Real estate assets

In respect of real estate assets, due diligence will require:
- a review of title and mortgage status;
- public register searches;
- third-party valuations;
- flagging of cross-collateralisation or cross-guarantees within borrower/obligor groups; and
- a sample review where standard-form documentation is used.

Common issues include:
- security over only a part of a property and/or defects in leasehold title which limit use and therefore value of a property;
- incorrectly executed and/or registered security;
- waiver of some or all enforcement rights;
- inter-creditor arrangements containing gaps so that ranking is not clear or not consistent; and
- missing original documentation.

(b) *Shipping/aviation assets*

With shipping and aviation assets, due diligence will include:
- physical inspection of the vessel/aeroplane;
- third-party valuations;
- an insurance review; and
- an understanding of corporate holding structures and security.

Common issues include:
- the borrower and vessel jurisdictions and the jurisdiction of operations, which may raise particular issues (such as anti-bribery and corruption and/or sanction issues in certain jurisdictions);
- incorrectly executed and/or registered security;
- waiver of some or all enforcement rights;
- inter-creditor arrangements containing gaps so that ranking not clear or not consistent; and
- missing original documentation.

(c) *Consumer/regulated loans*

With consumer and other regulated loans, due diligence should encompass:
- confirming relevant documentation exists;
- reviewing standard forms and samples of loan documentation; and
- reviewing compliance practices.

Common issues include:
- evidence of breach of consumer laws or rules which may make the loan unenforceable;
- origination and/or mis-selling issues; and
- where there are issues, understanding the status of discussions with the regulator and the steps required to remedy the situation.

(d) *Current account overdrafts*

Where borrowers hold current accounts with a selling bank, the outstanding balance will often be turned into a term loan by the seller prior to completion, and the interest in that loan transferred to the buyer. A buyer may want to discuss the impact of the removal of an overdraft facility with the relevant borrower as well as the seller, as it may have a negative impact on the borrower's business that is not helpful for the borrower or buyer.

(e) ***Set-off and cross-collateral***
In a situation where security for a loan is transferred, but other facilities or interests are retained by a seller, this may complicate steps to work out the relevant connection, as there will likely be conflicting interests between the seller and buyer. In addition, where a seller intends to retain certain facilities that are secured by the same assets as the main loan being sold to a buyer, inter-creditor issues will arise that are unlikely to be provided for in existing documentation.

(f) ***Unfunded commitments***
Unfunded commitments raise increased potential problems for the buyer of a non-performing loans portfolio. In particular, it is more likely that the buyer will need a banking licence to hold and fund the commitment.

(g) ***Hedging***
In many non-performing loan portfolios, certain loans may be hedged by an interest rate and/or currency swap. In such cases, the seller will typically want to transfer the swap as part of the overall portfolio. The swap counterparty's consent will usually be necessary in order to enable an outright transfer of the hedging transaction, and so pass-through swap confirmations are usually used to transfer the economic risk and reward of the swap prior to an outright transfer of the hedging transaction.

A buyer will need to consider the regulatory requirements of acquiring and being party to a swap, in particular under the European Market Infrastructure Regulation. This requires swap counterparties periodically to reconcile their positions under the swap documentation, and to set out specified dispute-resolution procedures should any disputes arise from such reconciliation processes. The swap counterparties will also be required to report specified data in respect of the transaction to a trade depositary, either directly or through a delegate.

(h) ***Secured loans***
If any of the loans in a portfolio are secured, key issues to confirm are whether the security has been effectively created over the whole of the relevant asset, whether the security has the correct ranking with relevant inter-creditor provisions, how the security will be transferred to the buyer, and whether and how the security is enforceable. The answer to these questions will be vital in helping the buyer determine whether its investment strategy is viable.

A frequent issue in non-performing loan transactions relating to secured loans is missing original documentation. The consequences of this vary by jurisdiction – in England for example copy documents should be sufficient, but in Germany an absence of original documents may hinder a buyer's ability to enforce certain types of security.

Where security documents have not been registered correctly, it may be void against certain persons. For example in England with respect to a mortgage granted by a corporate borrower, although this may be registered at the Land Registry, if it has not been registered at Companies House within the applicable time period, while the loan remains enforceable against the borrower entity, the security will be void against an administrator, liquidator or other creditor.

The nature of the secured assets and the relevant jurisdiction will determine the technical steps to transfer the security to the buyer. If the security is held by a security agent or trustee, the transfer will need to comply with the express mechanics in the relevant documents for the benefit of the security to transfer to the buyer. If the role of security agent or trustee is held by the seller and will transfer to the buyer, then the direct security rights will need to be transferred to the new buyer and technical steps taken to perfect that transfer. The transfer of direct security rights may be relatively expensive and require new registrations or the taking of new security. The latter may require borrower consent, and may also trigger insolvency hardening periods.

Where a non-performing loan portfolio contains secured loans, a buyer will need to understand the options available to it for enforcement, so that it can determine its optimal strategy with respect to working out the portfolio. Security enforcement ranges from relatively complicated court proceedings or public auctions, through to a private sale or straightforward transfer of the secured asset.

(i) *Active restructurings/insolvency proceedings*

Where a borrower is in an active restructuring or settlement discussions with the seller in the period prior to closing, it is essential for the buyer to understand the status of the negotiations taking place, and any initial agreements reached or term sheets signed in respect of a restructuring. Typically a sale and purchase agreement will include express provisions relating to active negotiations and restructurings that will bind the buyer into a particular course of action with the borrower following closing.

It is also essential to understand whether any borrowers in the portfolio are insolvent and whether any insolvency proceedings have been commenced or threatened in the relevant jurisdiction, as this can directly affect the enforcement rights of the buyer. In Spain, for example, where a borrower becomes insolvent, a court-appointed Receiver is required to obtain a valuation of the underlying real estate held by the borrower, and the outstanding loan is then revised to the applicable fair value based on the new valuation.

4. The auction

The majority of non-performing loan portfolios are sold through a competitive auction process, similar in style to those used in private mergers and acquisitions auction transactions.

The start of the auction will see the seller and/or its financial adviser approaching potential bidders and inviting them to participate in the first phase of the auction on the basis set out in an initial process letter and subject to the potential bidder first entering into a non-disclosure agreement with the seller. Bidders agreeing to take part and who have entered into the required non-disclosure agreement will be provided with basic information on the portfolio, usually in the form of an information memorandum. The bidders are invited to submit non-binding indications of interest based on the information disclosed to them in that first phase.

Several bidders will typically then progress to a second phase, the formalities for

which will be set out in a second phase process letter, and during which they may be provided with a vendor due diligence report, but in any case will be provided with access to a virtual data room in which more detailed information on the portfolio and the underlying assets will be available, typically covering the following areas:
- relevant underlying loan documentation;
- communications with/from borrowers and/or regulators;
- other material information relating to the portfolio;
- a form of sale and purchase agreement for the acquisition of the portfolio;
- a pricing template with certain inbuilt assumptions for use in calculating the second round bid.

The bidders carry out a detailed diligence process during this second phase (see the due diligence section above for more information on the diligence process) and produce a mark-up of the sale and purchase agreement and possibly related transaction agreements to submit with their binding second phase bid (see the section on the acquisition agreements below for an overview of the key terms in these agreements). In certain well run auctions the sellers will seek an interim mark-up of the acquisition agreements from the bidders prior to submission of the binding bids, and will give feedback on these initial mark-ups in advance of the phase two bid date, in order that the mark-ups are as advanced as far as possible at the point the bids are made.

The seller and its financial adviser will take numerous factors into account in assessing the competing bids including:
- compliance with the structure and terms of the proposed transaction set out in the process letters;
- completion certainty;
- the identity of the bidder, their co-investors and third-party servicers (if applicable), and their reputation and experience in acquiring and working out previous portfolios;
- the proposed purchase price and mark-up of the transaction documents;
- the source of financing/commitments in respect of the bid;
- the ability and/or willingness of the bidder to become lenders of record under the terms of the loans included in the portfolio, to take on agency roles related to the loans in the portfolio, and to acquire hedging transactions related to the loans in the portfolio; and
- any other assumptions on which the bid is based.

The third and final phase of the auction sees the seller seeking to negotiate and exchange contracts with a preferred bidder as quickly as possible, while keeping in touch with the other bidders in case a deal with the preferred bidder is not reached. In this phase the sale and purchase agreement, all related transaction agreements and, in certain transactions, detailed transfer procedures in respect of the loans, are all negotiated and agreed. Where there may be a significant time-period prior to signing or conditions to signing, the seller and preferred bidder will often enter into exclusivity arrangements to give themselves time to negotiate and commit resources to the execution of the transaction.

While transactions vary greatly depending on the specifics of the portfolio, transaction and seller, a typical timetable for an auction might be as follows:

Step	Duration
Invitations to potential bidders to participate in first phase, and entering into a non-disclosure agreement	Between one and four weeks
First phase of auction process: initial due diligence and submission of non-binding indications of interest	Between two and six weeks
Second phase of auction process: detailed due diligence, mark-ups of transaction documents, meetings with seller/management teams and submission of binding bid	Between four and 10 weeks
Final phase of auction process: selection of preferred bidder, possible period of exclusivity, negotiation of final form transaction documents and signing of sale and purchase agreement	Between one and four weeks
Completion of transaction following satisfaction of conditions precedent	Between one and 12 weeks
Elevation of assets (if applicable) following satisfaction of transfer requirements	Between two and 12 weeks

5. The sale and purchase agreement

The main agreement setting out the terms and conditions for the acquisition of the portfolio will be a sale and purchase agreement. Some or all of the following ancillary agreements, depending on the nature of the portfolio, the assets contained in it, the time frame and structure for the transaction and the parties involved, may also be used to implement the transaction:

- funded or risk participation agreements;
- pass-through swap confirmations;
- hedging transaction transfer agreements;
- forms of transfer instruments to transfer legal title; and
- transitional services agreements, in particular where the migration of consumer loan portfolios will take place following completion.

The following key provisions will typically be covered in the sale and purchase agreement.

5.1 Effective date for transfer of economic risk/reward
The sale and purchase agreement is typically structured with the economic risk and reward transferring to the buyer on a pricing date in advance of signing, similar to the effective date in a 'locked-box' sale and purchase agreement.

5.2 Conditions
Regulatory conditions, in particular antitrust conditions, may be required, depending on the assets being acquired or where the bidder entity is a formal joint venture between bidders.

5.3 Interim covenants
Interim covenants are particularly important where there are ongoing live restructurings or negotiations with borrowers or where a portfolio is already in an ongoing wind-down plan. The bidder will want as much influence as possible over the operation of the business and in particular live restructurings and negotiations with material borrowers, while the seller will want to maintain limits on the freedom of the bidder in such a scenario, often due to the seller's concerns about its reputation with its customer and in case the transaction fails to complete.

5.4 Transfer procedures and participations
The seller and buyer will need to consider both the specific steps needed to transfer each debt, equity or hedge asset and any relevant security in the portfolio. Such steps and additional instruments are typically set out in a detailed transfer procedures document. Where third-party consents or notifications are required to allow the transfer of full legal title, participations are frequently used so as not to delay completion, with elevation to full legal title at a later date once the relevant consent has been obtained or the notice period has expired.

5.5 Warranties and limitations on liabilities
Auction processes are typically extremely competitive and, due to the distressed nature of the portfolios and/or the status of the seller entity, often being a bad bank, the warranties provided are usually very limited in scope (frequently being pared back from the Loan Market Association distressed trade warranties) and are subject to relatively seller-friendly private mergers and acquisitions style limitations of liability.
Key warranties include:
- clean ownership/title;
- the accuracy of the most important line items in the data tape provided to the buyer, which forms the initial basis for pricing the portfolio;
- the provision and accuracy of information contained in the virtual data room;
- that there are no litigation proceedings ongoing or threatened that might affect the loan assets; and
- that there are no funding obligations, no bad acts, no connected parties, no impairment and no default in each case in respect of the loan assets, other than as disclosed to the buyer.

Key elements of the limitations on seller liability include:
- a relatively short time period in which to bring claims against the seller – typically between 12 and 18 months from signing or closing;
- a customary minimum threshold and aggregate or basket threshold;
- a maximum cap on liability, with a relatively low maximum cap for non-fundamental warranties of between 10% and 30% of the purchase price, and for fundamental warranties (the scope of which will be heavily negotiated but should include ownership/title warranties) a maximum cap of 100% of the purchase price;
- customary limitations relating to a buyer's recovery from insurance, requiring a buyer to mitigate any loss suffered and placing the risk of matters arising after signing on the buyer;
- a take-back right for the seller, whereby the seller has the right to take back an asset from the portfolio and return the purchase price for that asset instead of resisting or paying out under a claim in respect of that asset (if applicable); and
- a relatively broad limitation for buyer knowledge and disclosed information, which the seller will seek, to include the knowledge of the buyer's advisers and also the findings of searches that a prudent buyer should have sought and undertaken (all of which a buyer will strongly resist).

5.6 Indemnities

It is typical for the seller to indemnify the buyer in respect of excluded liabilities – principally covering liabilities of the seller with respect to acts or omissions of the seller before the pricing date – and for the buyer to indemnify the seller in respect of the liabilities relating to the assets that it assumes under the sale and purchase agreement. Additional specific indemnities may be negotiated, such as transfer of undertakings (TUPE) indemnities, environmental indemnities and indemnities relating to specific regulatory investigations or litigation, which will be based on the specific red flags raised through the due diligence of the portfolio.

5.7 Further assurance provisions

A general further assurance clause to give the buyer the benefit of the terms and conditions of the sale and purchase agreement will be included, but this should be supplemented by specific post-completion undertakings where there are practical issues to resolve that have not been dealt with as pre-completion conditions or undertakings. A frequent issue in non-performing loan transactions is that of missing original documents that relate to assets in the portfolio, which could cause issues enforcing security on the asset (see the section above on issues related to security). Where relevant, the bidder should seek undertakings from the seller to search for any such missing original documents and to assist the bidder in obtaining replacement originals and/or taking other steps to rectify any issues resulting from the missing original documents to ensure that the security is fully enforceable.

5.8 Transitional arrangements and notices to borrowers

A particular issue with portfolios in respect of which there are consumer or individual borrowers is the process to migrate the borrowers at or following completion, together with transitional arrangements between the seller and buyer if migration takes place after completion. Customary 'hello and goodbye' letters will be used to inform the borrowers of the transfer that is taking place, together with any formal notices of assignment that are required to perfect the transfer of legal title. Examples of post-completion transitional services that may be required include:

- collection of payments;
- cash management and account maintenance;
- handling and responding to customer queries;
- implementation of instructions from the buyer on an execution-only basis;
- customer payments processing and reconciliations; and
- management of cash sweeps to the buyer.

Terms and conditions will also need to be agreed to deal with data protection prior to migration.

5.9 Succession to litigation proceedings

Where a portfolio includes litigation claims of the seller relating to loan assets that are being transferred in the portfolio, there will typically be a separate agreement dealing with the assignment and procedural substitution or succession to the relevant claim. The specific mechanics for such substitution will be determined by the relevant jurisdiction, but will include interim covenant provisions, information undertakings and the relevant formal mechanics to be substituted as claimant. In addition, provisions will need to be included for the seller to provide and preserve evidence, and to assist with disclosure in connection with any acquired claims following completion. In the event that an assignment of a claim or a related substitution is blocked, it is typical to provide that the relevant claim will be repurchased by the seller and therefore effectively removed from the portfolio sale.

6. Servicing

A bidder has three main options with respect to servicing a portfolio following completion, and the choice will be driven largely by the nature of the assets in the portfolio and the regulatory requirements for servicing such a portfolio.

In many cases a third-party servicer will be retained by a bidder both to help underwrite aspects of the portfolio and to manage the assets from completion. Where a portfolio contains regulated loans or consumers, a servicer holding the necessary regulatory authorisations can also take legal ownership of the loans in the portfolio, with the beneficial interest or receivables being transferred to the bidder's bidco on an ongoing basis.

A second option is to service the portfolio in-house or to set up a new servicing platform, potentially in conjunction with a joint bidder if there is one. This is only likely to be a practical option where the portfolio is very concentrated, such as with corporate portfolios with a limited number of corporate borrowers, unless a bidder has an existing large in-house asset-management team.

A third option is to acquire an existing asset manager in a relevant jurisdiction, often at the same time as an initial large portfolio. In most cases where a portfolio is contained within a corporate group that is being sold in an equity transaction, the assets will inevitably come complete with an existing asset-management team. This may be useful for a bidder without an asset-management team, but it can also raise problems where the existing employees will be surplus to requirements after completion.

7. Equity transactions

While the majority of non-performing loan portfolio transactions are still structured as an asset sale, in certain circumstances sellers are structuring the transactions as a share sale or a transfer of debt instruments at the level of a parent holding company. The reasons for this vary. For example there have been secondary transactions where an existing collection of non-performing loans is held through subsidiaries under a parent holding company structure, where all or part of the existing holding structure is transferred directly to the buyer. This can be achieved through a transfer of shares in the parent company or, where the parent company is an orphan special purpose vehicle, by a transfer of the profit-participating notes or other capital instrument through which the seller holds its economic interest in the orphan special purpose vehicle.

In other situations, a seller may want to transfer existing employees that manage the portfolio and the companies holding the non-performing loans. This has been seen where banks have sold off whole distressed debt divisions, or where governments have nationalised asset management companies or sold bad banks.

Where a portfolio sale is structured through a share sale, the buyer needs to approach the due diligence process aware of the differences between asset and share deals. The key issue being that the historic liabilities of the target group will remain in the target group and are therefore essentially allocated to the buyer, unless contractual provisions are included in the sale and purchase agreement allocating risk to the seller. Note that in share deals it is often the case that indemnities for potential historic liabilities are only rarely given, and usually only in specific areas where there is a known liability that has not or cannot be factored into the purchase price. This contrasts with the market approach to asset transactions, reflected in typical loan sale and purchase agreements, where there will be a broad indemnity given by the seller to the buyer for historic liabilities arising prior to the pricing date.

As a result, the due diligence process for share sales needs to focus far more on possible liabilities within the target group, seeking to understand known liabilities and to identify possible unknown liabilities, as well as examining the assets in the group to verify the value attributed to them. Warranties will be used to flush out information and allocate risk for unknown liabilities.

Where a target group is acquired, a key post-completion step will be an audit of the target group business and activities against the warranties and indemnities received from the seller in the sale and purchase agreement. It is important to carry this out within the applicable time limitation periods in the sale and purchase agreement. In addition, the target group employees will need to be onboarded and internal processes vetted, in particular to align anti-corruption and compliance policies with the buyer's requirements.

8. **Co-investors**

   With respect to larger loan portfolio transactions, it is not unusual to see bidders partnering for a particular bid, often at the start of the second phase of the auction process. This has obvious pricing and risk advantages, but can also be a practical and competitive advantage in a bid, by removing a potential competitor and, where the partner is a bank or holds particular regulatory permissions, can be a useful way to overcome regulatory issues in certain jurisdictions. Such a bidder may also be able to take on agent roles or hedging positions more easily. In addition, co-investors may have different appetites for different parts or assets in a particular portfolio, particularly if part of a portfolio is performing and part non-performing, and, as noted in the financing section below, one bidder may also provide senior debt financing to the other.

   It is relatively rare for co-investors to form a formal joint venture entity for the purposes of a bid, although this does happen in certain situations, especially where the joint bidders are setting up a platform to manage the acquired assets. More frequently, contractual arrangements such as relationship or co-investor agreements will be used to set out the terms between the joint bidders.

   The key terms and conditions to be agreed between the bidders will include:
   - the allocation of the assets in the portfolio;
   - sharing of purchase price and other buyer liabilities under the acquisition agreements; and
   - most importantly, mechanics by which the bidders can bring a claim in respect of an asset against the seller.

   In many cases, however, one joint bidder will not be a counterparty directly with the seller, and instead there will need to be a purely back-to-back structure between the two joint bidders, with only one bidder fronting the transaction. A key issue to resolve with wholly back-to-back structures is how the other bidder has contractual recourse in the event that a claim for breach of warranty, undertaking or indemnity needs to be brought. Consideration will also have to be given as to how any seller liability cap is apportioned between claims by each bidder, and who has control over the conduct of any such claims. The best solution for the non-counterparty bidder is to have direct recourse against the seller through the sale and purchase agreement as a named beneficiary of the seller warranties, indemnities and undertakings in respect of the assets it will acquire. While this may not be possible where the non-counterparty bidder wishes to conceal its identity, it removes issues that can arise with back-to-back warranties or an assignment of rights to bring a claim. Where this is not possible, other options to protect the interests of the non-counterparty bidder are available, and will be influenced by the jurisdiction of the bidders and the governing law of the sale and purchase agreement.

9. Financing

In order to achieve a higher return on the portfolios being acquired, certain buyers are increasingly seeking debt finance and aiming for a higher level of leverage. In certain situations, a co-investor will both provide debt finance and take a share of the equity in the acquisition (see above for further information on co-investment structures).

The nature of any financing used varies widely for each particular transaction, ranging from relatively vanilla senior secured loans where a special purpose vehicle bidco is the borrower and security is provided over the assets, through to bespoke structured securitisations or other bespoke special purpose vehicle structures where total return notes or profit-participating loans are used. Such arrangements, particularly where the finance provider is also an equity co-investor, often reflect the close relationship between the parties, and will be on very different terms to what might be available through typical third-party bank finance.

The direct lending landscape in Europe

Nerea Pérez de Guzmán
FTI Consulting

1. **Introduction**

   Global financial crisis and changes in bank regulation have led to a reduction of bank lending opportunities for corporates and especially for small and medium-sized enterprises (SMEs). During the crisis, big corporates therefore changed from traditional bank lending to using the capital markets (bond issuance, raising new capital). SMEs, however, cannot access that source of financing. This has opened up an opportunity for an alternative lending market: direct lending.

   Direct lending refers to loans given by lenders that are not banks. The direct lending funds that have been raised have different lending strategies: private debt, mezzanine financing, distressed debt investment, or securitisation and capital relief.

2. **Overview of European banks**

   Banking regulation in Europe has tightened since the financial crisis, affecting the capacity of banks to lend. As shown in the graph below, the evolution of debt available to corporates has decreased in the Euro area from €4,900,000 million to €4,300,000 million from January 2009 to January 2016.

   Figure 1: Changes in credit standards applied to the approval of loans or credit lines to corporates (EU)

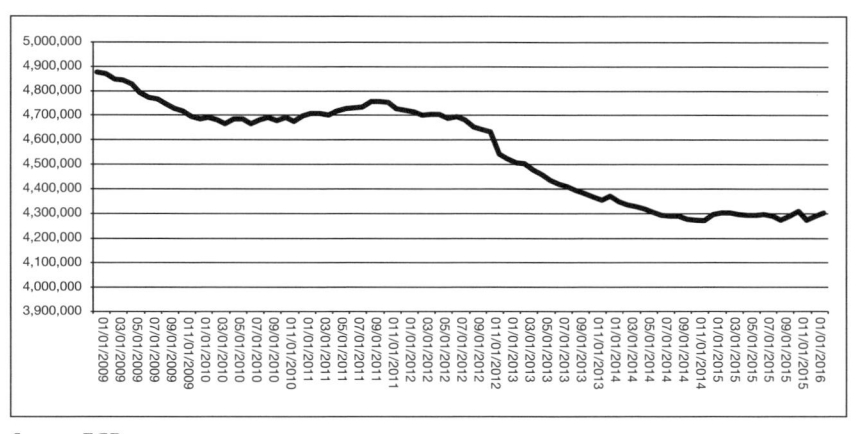

   Source: ECB

Figure 2: Basel III phase-in arrangements

	Phases	2013	2014	2015	2016	2017	2018	2019
Capital	Leverage Ratio	Parallel run Jan 1 2013 – Jan 1 2017 Disclosure starts Jan 1 2015					Migration to Pillar 1	
	Minimum Common Equity Capital Ratio	3.5%	4.0%	4.5%	4.5%	4.5%	4.5%	4.5%
	Capital Conservation Buffer				0.625%	1.25%	1.875%	7.0%
	Minimum common equity plus capital conservation buffer	3.5%	4.0%	4.5%	5.125%	5.75%	6.375%	7.0%
	Phase-in of deductions from CET1*		20%	40%	60%	80%	100%	100%
	Minimum Tier 1 Capital	4.5%	5.5%	6.0%	6.0%	6.0%	6.0%	6.0%
	Minimum Total Capital	8.0%	8.0%	8.0%	8.0%	8.0%	8.0%	8.0%
	Minimum Total Capital plus conservation buffer	8.0%	8.0%	8.0%	8.625%	9.25%	9.875%	10.5%
	Capital instruments that no longer qualify as non-core Tier 1 capital or Tier 2 capital	Phased out over 10 year horizon beginning 2013						
Liquidity	Liquidity coverage ratio – minimum requirement			60%	70%	80%	90%	100%
	Net stable funding ratio						Introduce minimum standard	

* Including amounts exceeding the limit for deferred tax assets (DTAs), mortgage servicing rights (MSRs) and financials
■ ■ transition periods

Source: Basel Committee on Banking Supervision[1]

[1] www.bis.org/bcbs/basel3/basel3_phase_in_arrangements.pdf.

The decrease in lending from banks has come in response to capital constraints and a deterioration of the quality of the banks' assets in their balance sheets.

Basel III has increased capital requirements and liquidity ratios for banks as shown in the graph on the previous page, and these requirements will grow further in future years.

For example, in 2013 the minimum common equity plus capital conservation buffer was 3.5%, a requirement that will have to double by 2019. This new level of capital conservation buffer has a direct impact on dividend distribution and raising new capital, but also has an indirect impact on managing the risk of lending, and has therefore led to tightening of lending conditions.

Basel III has also had an impact in the form of an increase in the supervision of banks, which are now being monitored more than before. Its mandate is to strengthen the regulation, supervision and practices of banks worldwide, with the aim of enhancing financial stability.

In the following chart, we show the changes in credit standards applied to the approval of loans or credit lines to corporates. After 2007, with the financial crisis, the changes in credit standards to approve loans to corporates increased up to the first quarter of 2014. The changes in credit standards have decreased the ability of corporates to get finance, but have made it almost impossible for SMEs to get bank loans.

Figure 3: Changes in credit standards applied to the approval of loans or credit lines to corporates (EU)

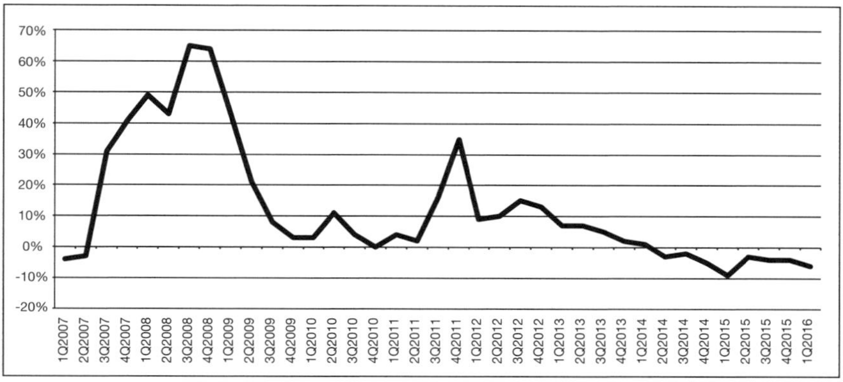

Source: ECB

In addition to regulation, the quality of banks' assets have deteriorated across Europe. The graph below shows non-performing loans as a percentage of total gross loans for each EU country, indicating a negative impact on credit growth.

Countries like Ireland, Greece or Cyprus have significant amounts of non-performing loans as a percentage of total loans. It is mandatory for banks to decrease their stock of non-performing loans, and therefore there has been and it is forecast that there will continue to be sales of non-performing loans. These non-performing loans are normally acquired by funds from banks at a very high discount rate.

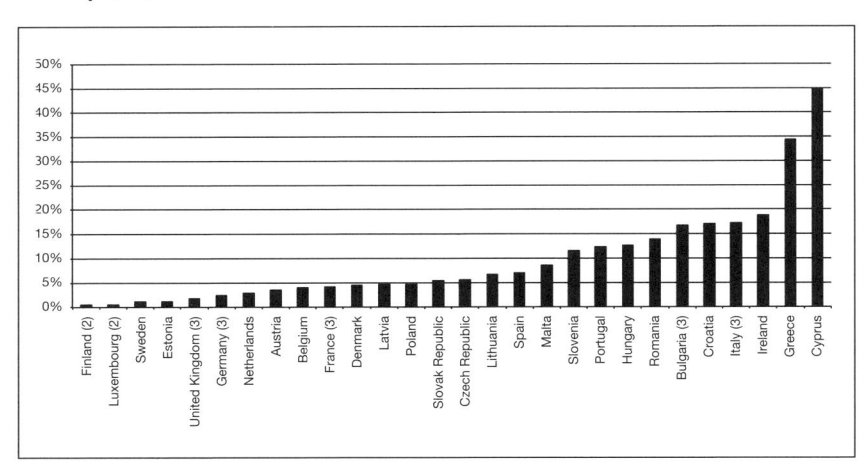

Figure 4: 2015 non-performing loans as percentage of total gross loans by country (EU)

Source: World Bank[2]

In certain countries (Ireland, Spain and Slovenia), an entity has been created for asset disposal and recovery to which non-performing assets from a large number of banks have been transferred.

In Ireland, the Irish National Asset Management Agency, (NAMA), was established in 2009 as one of a number of initiatives taken by the government to address the serious crisis in Irish banking which had become increasingly evident over the course of 2008 and early 2009. The entity is fully government-owned, and participating banks were paid with government-guaranteed securities issued by NAMA.

In Spain, SAREB was founded in November 2012 to help clean up the Spanish banking sector and, more specifically, the banks with problems due to their over-exposure to the real estate sector. Its mission is to divest an asset portfolio with a value of €50.781 billion in 15 years. The creation of the company was brought about through a memorandum of understanding which the Spanish government signed in July 2012 with its European partners, in order to receive financial aid for the banking sector. The memorandum of understanding promised the founding of a management company to which banks that were in financial difficulty could transfer their real estate assets, with the aim of mitigating the risks associated with those assets and carrying out an orderly divestment of them.

In Slovenia, the Bank Assets Management Company (BAMC) was established in March 2013 as a company owned by Republic of Slovenia with the task of facilitating the restructuring of banks with systemic importance that were facing severe solvency and liquidity problems. By the end of 2013, the two largest banks had been recapitalised by the government and a substantial part of their non-performing assets

---

2 Last available data 2013 (Finland and Luxemburg); 2014 (UK, Germany, France, Bulgaria and Italy).

had been transferred to BAMC. They entered 2014 with strengthened balance sheets and with sufficient capital and liquidity to start new lending and thus facilitate renewed economic growth in Slovenia.

Financial instability and poor macroeconomic forecasts in the Euro area have also contributed to a decrease of financing available, especially to small and medium corporates.

This lack of financing from traditional lenders and poor rates for savings have given opportunities to alternative lenders that are looking for higher returns and are willing to take on increased risk.

In the graph below, we show the profitability of 10-year bonds issued by Spain, Germany, France, the United Kingdom, Italy and Portugal. There is a substantial difference between the profitability of 10-year bonds between countries, due to their different financial situations. For example, in 2011 Portugal had to be rescued by the European Union, which led to a risk premium on its 10-year bonds of more than 1,000 basis points. In other words, Portugal had to pay 1,000 basis points more than Germany to get investors to buy its bonds.

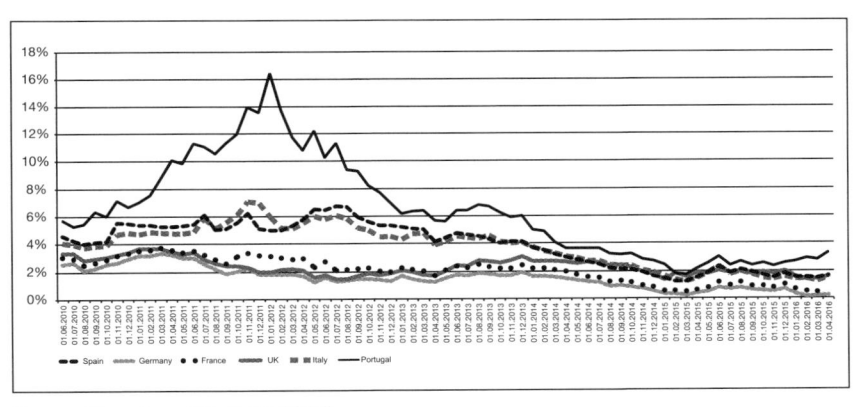

Figure 5: Profitability of 10-year bonds

Source: Bloomberg (April 26 2016)

Traditionally companies in Europe have been very reliant on banks to finance their operations, however with the constraints under which banks are now operating with respect to loans, they have had to find new ways of finance.

3. **Direct lending: borrowers**

Corporates use direct lending funds for a number of purposes, including:
- financing their investments through asset-backed lending structures – The loan or credit line is secured by an asset, through an enforceable security interest. The assets used as collateral would be the investments made by the corporate. Certain funds have specific requirements as to the type of asset that can be collateralised, requiring in certain circumstances that the asset be essential for the activity of the corporate (for example, medical equipment for

a hospital). This type of financing is generally available at single digit interest rates;
- financing of working capital – This is generally structured as a credit line or a revolving line, backed by receivables or inventories. The amount that can be drawn will be determined as a percentage of the value of the collateral that has been pledged (between 70% and 80%). As the assets fluctuate, the lenders periodically review the accounts receivable to update the value of the collateral. The cost of this type of financing would depend of the size of the loan, the credit risk of the drawee and the percentage pledged. The interest rate could go from 7% up to 17%. Alternatively, the corporate could sell their receivables at a discount, depending on the risk of the drawee. This approach is generally used when the working capital financing structure cannot be used, as the cost is greater and only provides cash when the receivable is sold;
- financing of acquisitions through mezzanine, unitranche type loans (normally for deals below €2.5 billion);
- refinancing of their current debt (bridging loans, first or second lien loans).

4. Direct lending: funds

As has already been mentioned, direct lending refers to loans given by lenders that are not banks. These new lenders[3] are financed from institutional investors such as pension funds or insurance companies, private funds or sovereign wealth funds. As seen in Figure 5, the profitability of European 10-year bonds has decreased, with the profitability of a 10-year German bond being close to 0% in April 2016. The low returns on European government bonds has also contributed to institutional investors diversifying their investment criteria, utilising direct lending funds in order to increase their average return.

The lack of finance from traditional lending providers (banks) in Europe, together with the increase in investors looking for higher returns, has resulted in a boom in the creation of funds that have come to Europe to benefit from this opportunity.

Direct lending funds lend at interest rates higher than 8%, which can go up to 20% for distressed situations. The loans can also have fees (arrangement, management or performance), that could increase the cost of the financing.

In the US market, corporates have more options to get finance than in Europe. If we look at the graph below, bank financing was equivalent to only 78% of gross domestic product in the United States in 2014, whereas in Europe, bank financing was equivalent to 138% of gross domestic product in 2014. Historically, as is shown in the graph, bank financing was even greater, having reached a peak of 166% of gross domestic product in 2006.

In Europe, alternative credit providers first appeared in the United Kingdom and Germany, and are still expanding their coverage in continental Europe. As can be seen from Appendix 1, most of the funds have a presence in the United Kingdom and Germany, however they are still looking to grow in other European countries.

---

3   Full list of direct lending funds (European coverage) is provided in Annex 1.

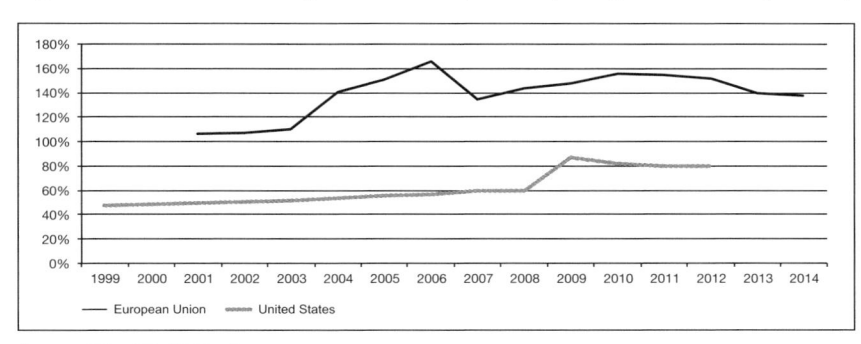

Figure 6: Domestic credit to private sector by banks (% of gross domestic product)

Source: The World Bank

Local presence in the countries concerned is considered to be necessary for funds to offer finance, as the greatest need for alternative finance providers is among SMEs. SMEs have traditionally relied on banks to finance their operations, and have not normally had information on alternative finance providers and could not access the bond or equity markets. Funds have therefore opened offices in various countries to get access to operations there, and to explain and market their financial products. The information shown in Appendix 1 will be soon be outdated, as funds are deploying offices very quickly on the European continent.

5. Direct lending strategies

There are three types of alternative credit providers, which can be summarised as follows:

- mezzanine funds, which provide funding that can be converted into equity;
- distressed or special situation funds, which provide capital focused on a specific market;
- asset-backed lending funds, which provide loans secured by an asset, and which are senior to existing financing.

These funds are more flexible than banks in the way they structure the finance, have higher interest rates, and are often faster than banks in their decision-making.

The most common structure used by direct lending funds, excluding asset-backed lending transactions, is unitranche lending. Unitranche lending is a very flexible product, and often the fastest way to close a deal (usually taking approximatively four weeks), generally has a bullet repayment, with a leverage of around 5 × earnings before interest, taxation, depreciation and amortisation (EBITDA) and high interest. Normally this structure is used for deals of less than €250 million. If the deal is bigger, then the structure that would be used would be a senior loan or mezzanine financing, normally syndicated. These structures are slower to close and have lower leverage than unitranche loans, but have lower interest and generally involve more fees. The debt will typically have an amortisation schedule, cash sweeps and tight covenants in place.

In deals involving distressed debt, special situations or acquisition of non-performing loans, for example in a debt buy-back process, the fund will negotiate with the bank the price to be paid for the nominal value of the debt (generally at a very high discount of between 7% and 10%). The fund would normally hire a legal adviser to prepare the offer and contracts, and a financial adviser to work out the best structure for the deal. In certain deals, the debt is fronted by an investment bank.

6. Pros and cons of direct lending

This new way of sourcing financing has multiple pros and cons.

The advantages are:
- direct lending funds are not subject to banking regulations, which allows them to analyse the operations faster (the average time is two or three weeks);
- the loans have a longer amortisation period and even bullet structures (the loan being paid in its entirety at maturity); and
- there is more flexibility on interest payment ('pay if you can' structures, or a combination of cash interest and bullet interest).

On the other hand, the disadvantages are:
- the cost of direct lending is above the cost of bank financing; and
- sometimes it is necessary to conduct an audit or due diligence before the fund will provide the funding.

Additionally, it is important to highlight the following type of direct lending operations that have been standardised due to market trends:
- long-term financing: operations which involve long-term loans (between three and 10 years), focused on established companies with growth projects or with real, solid collateral;
- short-term financing: operations which involve short-term loans (between three and 36 months), focused on financing orders and contracts from both domestic and international markets;
- commercial discount: factoring, usually without recourse; the fund focuses on a risk analysis not so much of the solvency of the assignor but of the solvency of the debtor of the commercial titles;
- bridge financing: operations backed by some type of solvent and liquid collateral that allow the raising of funding for a specific project, or that anticipate future receipts, and the like.

7. Conclusion

The direct lending landscape in Europe is going through a structural change. Corporates are more open to looking for different lending solutions. However, the evolution of the direct lending market will completely depend on the ability of banks to lend money, to raise their capital requirements and to comply with new regulations. Certain players think that direct lending is not just a temporary trend, and could become a permanent lending alternative, as it has proven to be in the United States.

Appendix 1 – Direct lending funds: breakdown of European coverage

Name	Coverage	Name	Coverage
Alcentra	UK	HIG WhiteHorse	UK, Germany, Spain, Italy, France
Amundi	France	ICG	UK, Germany, Spain, Benelux, France
ARDIAN	UK, Germany, France	Idinvest Partners	UK
ARES	UK, Germany, Nordics, France	Incus Capital	Spain, Portugal
Artemind	France	Indivest Partners	Germany, Spain, France
Avenue Capital	UK, Germany, Spain	KKR	UK, Spain, Ireland, France
Babson Capital Management	UK	M&G Investments	UK
BBP Capital	Ireland	Macquarie	UK
Beechbrook Capital	UK	BlackRock	UK, Germany, France
Muzinich & Co	UK, Spain, Italy, France	BlueBay	UK
MV Credit	UK	Bravo Capital	Spain
Capital Four	Nordics	Njord Partners	UK, Nordics
Cardinal Capital Group	Ireland	Nordic Mezzanine	UK, Nordics
Cerea Partenaire	France	Oquendo Capital	Spain
Cescent Capital Group	UK	Origin Capital	Ireland
Citi	UK	Partners Group	UK, Switzerland, France
Cordet Capital Partners	UK, Benelux	Pemberton	UK, Germany, Spain, Italy, France, Netherlands
CVC Credit Partners	UK	Permira	UK, Germany, France
Delta Lloyd	Benelux	Praesidian Capital	UK
EQT	UK, Germany	Proventus	Nordics
European Capital	UK, France	Renatus Capital Partners	Ireland
Federis Gestion	France	Rothschild	UK, France
Grove Point	UK	Sankaty Advisors	UK
GSO Capital Partners	UK, France	Tikehau Capital Partners	UK, Italy, Benelux, France
Guggenheim	UK	TPG	UK
HAYFIN	UK, Germany, Spain, Benelux, France	Trea Capita	Spain

Source: FTI elaboration

Trends in direct lending

Andrew Perkins
Sarah Ward
Macfarlanes LLP

1. Background

1.1 What is direct lending?

In the aftermath of the credit crunch in 2008 and the ensuing global financial crisis, access to traditional bank funding became markedly more difficult for borrowers. Banks came under greater scrutiny in respect of their lending activities. Increased regulatory and capital controls imposed on banks restricted their ability to meet the demand for debt finance from borrowers. Bank deleveraging was widely seen across the industry and the effect on mid-market loans (which typically range in quantum from €30,000,000 to €200,000,000) was particularly apparent.

In light of the reduced capacity and appetite for the banks to lend in the mid-market, borrowers turned to alternative sources of financing. Asset managers responded to borrower demand by launching direct lending funds to bridge the liquidity gap. Investors, struggling to receive strong returns in a low interest rate environment, were searching for yield, and many investors who may previously have been reticent to invest in illiquid loan assets were attracted by the higher returns which were on offer from the credit funds.

The term 'direct lending' is commonly used to refer to the debt financing provided by a credit fund established to raise funds for this purpose. These funds operate in a range of industry sectors and offer a range of financial products, some of which will be explored further in this chapter.

The impact of these new entrants to the European loan market has been widely seen in the products and the terms now available to borrowers. The largest direct lending funds are now able to compete with the traditional bank lenders in terms of the quantum of debt they are able to provide, and can also offer certain other advantages for mid-market borrowers.

1.2 What are the key advantages of direct lending?

From a borrower's perspective, there are some key advantages of debt financing provided by a direct lender.

(a) Structure

The term loan facilities provided by a direct lender will typically be non-amortising, bullet repayment facilities. Investors in the direct lending fund want to see their capital put to work for the duration of the investment period. Investors do not require that the loan facilities are deleveraged in the same manner as a traditional bank lender may require.

(b) *Tenor*
Typically, direct lending funds are able to provide borrowers with longer tenors for non-amortising debt than can be offered by traditional bank lenders.

(c) *Hold*
Historically, direct lending funds were not able to provide the same hold levels as those which could be offered by the traditional bank lenders. However, as the direct lending funds have matured and have been able to demonstrate consistent track records to potential investors, it has become possible for larger direct lending funds to be raised. Increasingly, the largest direct lending funds are able to offer hold sizes comparable to or greater than those offered by traditional bank lenders. The direct lenders may seek subsequently to sell down part of their hold; however it is no longer the case that direct lending funds are not able to compete with the banks in this area.

(d) *Capital structure*
A traditional bank lender will typically provide senior secured term and revolving credit facilities. The direct lenders take a more flexible approach and often have the capability to lend at different levels in the capital structure. This can take the form of mezzanine financing, unitranche financing (which we will focus on later in this chapter) or holding payment-in-kind (PIK) notes, and can also include investment in the equity in addition to the debt.

(e) *Speed*
The credit processes of a direct lending fund are typically more streamlined than those of the traditional bank lenders, and borrowers often have more direct access to the key credit decision-makers in a fund than they may do with a bank. This leads to direct lending funds being able to transact on shorter timescales. This speed of execution applies at all stages in the cycle, from initial approval at term sheet stage through to credit committee approval, and in responding to consent and amendment requests over the life of the facilities.

(f) *Flexibility*
Often, direct lending funds will be in a position to offer borrowers greater flexibility on key terms in the facility agreement. This can lead to (for example) a less restrictive negative covenant package, with greater flexibility on incurrence of additional indebtedness, making acquisitions and disposals. The financial covenant package offered by a direct lender may also be more attractive to a borrower.

1.3 **What are the key disadvantages of direct lending?**
However, again from a borrower's perspective, there are some disadvantages of debt financing provided by a direct lender.

(a) *Yield*
The investors in a direct lending fund expect a required level of return on their capital. The result of this is that the yield paid on the debt financing provided by a direct lender will typically be higher to that required by a traditional bank lender. London interbank offered rate (LIBOR) and euro interbank offered rate (EURIBOR) floors are also prevalent.

(b) *Non-call protection*
The investors in a direct lending fund expect their capital to be put to work for a period of time. This has advantages for the borrower (as outlined above); however the disadvantage of this feature is that direct lenders will seek protection for early prepayment of the facilities. The call protection features which are required by direct lenders are discussed in more detail below in the context of unitranche financing.

(c) *Facilities and intercreditor issues*
A borrower will generally need to have certain ancillary facilities (letters of credit, bank guarantees and overdraft facilities, for example) to operate its business, which are often provided as a carve-out from a revolving credit facility. Direct lenders are not able to provide these types of ancillary facilities, and so borrowers will typically need to engage with a bank in order to have access to them. Where these ancillary facilities are provided on a secured basis, the ancillary facilities provider will share a first ranking cross-guarantee and security package with the direct lender. This can lead to intercreditor issues between the bank and the direct lender. These issues are explored in more detail later in this chapter in relation to unitranche financing.

(d) *Track record*
The direct lending funds are relatively new participants in the debt finance market, and the performance of many direct lending funds has not been tested at all points in the lending cycle. In particular, experience of how a direct lending fund will operate where the debt becomes distressed or in an enforcement scenario is limited. The intercreditor arrangements which are being entered into in connection with unitranche financing have not been extensively tested in the UK market.

1.4 Response of bank lenders

The emergence of direct lending funds and the advantages offered from a borrower's perspective in transacting with a direct lending fund have led to traditional bank lenders looking to enhance their own debt finance offering to strong credits. In particular, a number of traditional banks have looked at how they can work with the direct lenders to provide the working capital facilities and hedging facilities a borrower may require, alongside the term facilities being made available by the direct lender.

2. Trends in direct lending: covenant-lite loans

Trends in leveraged financing often originate in the US loan market and then appear as features in the European loan market. The current trends in direct lending appear to mirror this migration and, increasingly, there is a convergence in terms between the US and European markets.

In addition, in the last few years, terms in the US and European loan markets are being dictated by a resurgence in the negotiating power of borrowers. There are a number of factors which are driving this.

First, there is an increased level of liquidity in the market. Traditional bank lenders are now coming under increased pressure to resume or increase lending activities after years of consolidation and rebuilding the strength of their balance sheets. However, the direct lending funds which were established to plug the liquidity gap in the wake of the credit crunch are also active, and will be in direct competition with the bank lenders. The increased availability of funding and increased competition between the traditional and direct lenders leaves borrowers in an attractive negotiating position.

With the general move toward more borrower-friendly terms, one of the key trends in direct lending is the return of so-called covenant-lite or covenant-loose loans. In addition, European corporates and sponsors have had access to the US loan market since the effects of the credit crunch eased in the United States. This has caused European leveraged loan products to compete with the US term loan B products. Covenant-lite and incurrence-based ratio tests have been a common feature of US term loan B products for some time.

2.1 What is a covenant-lite loan?

'Covenant-lite' or 'cov-lite' loans developed in the early 2000s in the US loan market; however the growth in cov-lite loans was largely halted by the credit crunch in 2008.

The distinguishing features of a cov-lite loan is that it either has no financial covenants or, alternatively, a springing leverage covenant for the benefit of the revolving credit facility lenders only.

Since 2014, the US market has reported growth in cov-lite loans, but true cov-lite loans are still relatively rare in the European mid-market, where covenant-loose loans are more prevalent.

2.2 What is a covenant-loose loan?

Unlike the US cov-lite loan market which is relatively well established, the covenant-loose or 'cov-loose' loan market in Europe is a lot less uniform. A cov-loose loan will usually have up to three maintenance financial covenants, which will benefit both the term and revolving credit facility lenders. The financial covenant package will usually include a leverage covenant, perhaps also an interest cover test or, alternatively, a cash-flow cover test and a restriction on the amount of capital expenditure a borrower group can incur in any financial year.

2.3 Summary – key provisions in covenant-lite and covenant-loose loans

	Covenant-lite	Covenant loose
Financial covenants	Either no financial covenants or a springing leverage covenant	Typically, a leverage covenant and either an interest cover test or cash-flow covenant
Additional indebtedness	Subject to an incurrence ratio test, usually based on a leverage test	Fixed cap on permitted additional indebtedness
Permitted acquisitions	Generally permitted, subject to incurrence ratio condition and no event of default	Fixed cap on expenditure on acquisitions over the life of the facilities
Equity cure	No requirement to prepay facilities Cure amount deemed to increase earnings before interest, taxes, depreciation and amortisation (EBITDA)	Requirement to prepay facilities Reduction of debt side of leverage test, and not (typically) deemed to increase EBITDA

2.4 Key provisions in covenant-lite and covenant-loose loans

The next section of this chapter takes a more detailed look at some of the key provisions for cov-lite and cov-loose loans and the differences between these.

(a) Incremental debt

The presence of an accordion option or incremental facility is now a key trend in facilities provided by direct lenders, and is an increasingly common feature in mid-market and large cap facility agreements in both the United States and in Europe.

The inclusion of limited conditionality in some accordion options also demonstrates that terms are becoming more borrower-friendly. It has been typical for some time for borrowers to be able to negotiate the ability to look outside the existing syndicate for preferential terms when exercising an accordion option in a facility agreement, provided that the existing syndicate is offered a right to match or right of first refusal in respect of the accordion facility. There may be agreed parameters (such as an overall cap on the yield and fees payable), however, if the borrower negotiates preferential terms with a non-syndicate lender which cannot be matched by an existing syndicate member, the borrower can bring in this new lender on those preferential terms. The acceptance of these features in an accordion facility demonstrates the competitive environment in which lenders now operate.

In the European market, one key consideration for the lenders in exercising an accordion or incremental facility option will be the potential impact on the guarantee and security package. In certain jurisdictions, while the facility agreement may, on its face, appear to extend guarantees and security to the accordion facilities, there may be limits on the amount of accordion facilities which may be provided without the need for guarantees to be re-confirmed and security retaken. Under English law, for example, there is an unfortunate lack of certainty on what these limits are, largely as a result of case law which is often contradictory on this point. Depending on the terms of the accordion facility, it may be necessary for a lender to take legal advice in a number of different jurisdictions as to the legal consequences of the proposed exercise of the accordion facility, which will, inevitably, have time and cost implications for the borrower.

(b) *Additional indebtedness*
Mandatory deleveraging in covenant-lite loans is not often seen. Instead, an incurrence ratio test will apply and the borrower will have the ability to incur additional indebtedness over the life of the facilities subject to *pro forma* compliance with this ratio test at the point of incurrence of the indebtedness. Typically, the test will be a leverage test. The additional indebtedness may be incurred by way of the accordion or incremental facility or other debt, which may be senior secured debt, junior secured debt, or subordinated or junior unsecured debt.

In the European market, adopting the same approach to the incurrence of additional indebtedness may present significant issues for lenders, depending on the composition of the obligor group. If the obligor group comprises entities in a number of different jurisdictions, the insolvency regimes in each of those jurisdictions will need to be accounted for. Out-of-court enforcement processes are more common in European jurisdictions than in the United States. This means that the intercreditor arrangements will be paramount, and the most senior class of creditors will need to be confident that the intercreditor arrangements will protect their position. In particular, in respect of any junior secured (or unsecured) debt in the structure, the senior lenders will want to have the ability to enforce a standstill on the junior lenders in an enforcement scenario, and also to have the ability to release claims of the junior lenders (subject to certain value protection provisions which are examined in greater detail later in this chapter).

In cov-loose loans, it is therefore common to include a hard cap on the amount of additional indebtedness which can be incurred by an obligor group, rather than an incurrence ratio-based test.

(c) *Acquisitions*
In cov-lite facility agreements, it is now common for acquisitions to be generally permitted, subject to no event of default having occurred and compliance with an incurrence-based ratio condition. The ratio is typically a leverage test.

In cov-loose facility agreements, permitted acquisitions will still be subject to compliance with a fixed cap on the expenditure by the group in a financial year and/or over the life of the facilities. Additional conditionality, such as an event of default blocker, requirement to deliver diligence and compliance with a *pro forma* leverage test are also frequently required.

(d) **Equity cures**

As mentioned above, the only financial covenant which may appear in a cov-lite facility agreement will be a springing financial covenant for the benefit of the revolving credit facility lenders. The covenant (typically a leverage test) will apply if the utilisation of the revolving credit facility exceeds a certain threshold amount at the end of the relevant testing period. The financial covenant will be a maintenance test.

Cov-loose loans will be subject to up to three maintenance financial covenants, typically including a leverage and/or an interest cover test.

Because of the different financial covenants, the approaches to the ability to apply an equity cure to a breach of a financial covenant differ between cov-lite and cov-loose facility agreements. In cov-loose facility agreements, there will typically be a requirement to apply a certain proportion of the amount of the equity cure in prepayment of the term facilities. In line with the continued move towards more borrower-friendly terms in facility agreements, borrowers can often negotiate the amount of the prepayment required to 50% or less of the amount of the equity cure proceeds. When the covenant is re-tested, the full amount of the equity cure proceeds are deemed to be applied in prepayment of the term facilities, meaning the borrower obtains the benefit of 100% of the equity cure proceeds through the covenants, notwithstanding only a limited percentage being actually applied in prepayment of the term loan facilities.

In cov-lite facility agreements, where the springing leverage covenant is present solely for the benefit of the revolving credit facility lenders, there will not be a requirement to prepay loans using the proceeds of an equity cure. Instead, the amount of the equity cure is deemed to increase EBITDA, and the leverage covenant is re-tested on that basis. The ability to cure a covenant breach by way of a deemed increase to EBITDA has also started to appear in a number of European loan market transactions in the last few years, however the EBITDA add-back will be limited in its application (for example, a borrower may negotiate the ability to deem an increase to EBITDA once or twice over the term of the facilities).

In the US market, a borrower will not typically be permitted to over-cure a breach of the leverage covenant, and the amount invested in the group by way of an equity cure will be no greater than the amount required to remedy the relevant breach of covenant. In contrast, in the European market, the ability to over-cure is now often accepted by lenders, particularly where the requirement to prepay the term facilities applies to an agreed percentage of the full amount of the equity cure.

(e) **Portability**

In the US loan market, change of control will trigger an event of default that can lead to the majority lenders (a simple majority under US loan agreements, as opposed to the 66^2/3% threshold commonly seen in European transactions) accelerating the facilities and taking enforcement action. In the European market, change of control usually leads to a mandatory prepayment event in respect of all of the facilities. The key benefit of the European approach is that, provided the borrower has funds available to it to prepay the facilities when due, the change of control itself does not lead to a cross-default in other agreements.

Portability has been a feature in the European market since 2010. It is more typically found in bond documentation, but particularly strong borrowers have also been able to negotiate portability features into facility agreements. Portability means that a change of control may, subject to certain conditions, take place without either an event of default or a mandatory prepayment event occurring. These conditions typically include a *pro forma* leverage test and a restriction on use of the portability exception to once over the life of the facilities. Consequently, if the conditions are met, the initial owners of the borrower may exit the transaction and the lenders are obliged to continue to fund the group under the new owner.

3. Trends in direct lending: unitranche financing

3.1 What is a unitranche loan?

Unitranche financing is yet another example of a product which initially originated in the US loan market and has migrated over to the European loan market. Unitranche financing was first seen in the US loan markets in 2003/2004. The initial unitranche financings in the European market were seen approximately five years after this.

Unitranche financing aims to consolidate a traditional senior and mezzanine structure into one single term loan, provided under a single set of finance documents.

The unitranche product is the predominant finance product provided by direct lending funds and, as a consequence, a number of its key features reflect the investment objectives and requirements of the investors in such funds. Some of the typical features of a unitranche loan are set out below.

3.2 Key features of a unitranche financing

(a) Quantum

Unitranche loans are used for mid-market transactions of a quantum of €30 millon to €200 millon.

(b) Tenor

The tenor of a unitranche loan is typically between five and seven years.

(c) Margin

The margin for a unitranche facility will be higher than the margin for senior facilities but lower than the margin for mezzanine facilities, reflecting how the traditional senior/mezzanine structure is consolidated into a unitranche structure. Unitranche facilities are often described as being provided with a 'blended' margin for this reason. In addition, it is a common feature of unitranche financing that the margin is split into a cash payment margin (which is paid by the borrower at the end of each interest period for the duration of the loan) and a capitalised margin (which is capitalised and added to the principal amount of the loan outstanding as at the end of an interest period). A borrower under a unitranche loan may also look to negotiate features which are typically seen in mezzanine facilities, for example a PIK toggle whereby a borrower can elect to convert cash payment interest into capitalised interest on satisfying certain conditions under the facility agreement.

(d) *LIBOR/EURIBOR floor*
A unitranche loan will typically contain LIBOR and/or EURIBOR floor protection for the unitranche lenders of between 0.75% and 1.50%.

(e) *Call protection*
Due to the investment objectives of a direct lending fund, a key feature of a unitranche loan will be the call protection required by the direct lender. The call protection sought by the direct lender is typically a combination of a make-whole provision and a flat prepayment fee. For example, a direct lender may require make-whole yield protection for an initial period of the term of its facilities, usually between 12 and 24 months (the 'non-call period'). This means that, if the borrower makes a prepayment during this period, it will need to pay to the direct lender an amount equal to the interest the lender would have received had the debt been outstanding for the duration of that non-call period. The make whole payment is typically calculated on a net present value basis.

Following the non-call period, the direct lender may also require a prepayment fee, which will be a percentage of the principal amount of the facilities which are being prepaid, in respect of any prepayments made from the end of the non-call period to (for example) between 12 and 24 months thereafter.

The time periods for the non-call period and any subsequent period in which a prepayment fee may be paid, and the amounts of such fees, are negotiated between the borrower and the direct lender. The borrower can also negotiate the circumstances in which the make-whole and/or prepayment fee will be paid. The starting point for a borrower in these negotiations may be that such fees should only apply on a voluntary prepayment of the facilities, but this is often expanded to cover prepayments made as a result of a change of control, flotation or sale of all or substantially all of the assets of a group.

(f) *Purpose*
A unitranche loan may be used for the same purposes as a typical senior term loan facility. For example, unitranche financings have been used recently to finance or re-finance private equity buyouts and bolt-on acquisitions, to provide financing for capital expenditure and for dividend recapitalisations. Because of the flexibility of unitranche financings and the terms that can be offered by the direct lenders, unitranche financing is often provided to smaller businesses to fund the next stage of their growth, perhaps following an initial buyout by a private equity sponsor.

Borrowers may find that a typical senior term loan is the more attractive option if pricing is the main driver, or if they are looking to delever over the life of the facility through amortisation or prepayments out of excess cash.

(g) ***Super senior facilities***

A traditional bank lender will need to provide the borrower with the working capital facilities required by the borrower to operate its business. The borrower may also need to put hedging in place on a secured basis to mitigate either foreign currency or interest rate risks, in connection with both its business requirements and in connection with servicing its debt facilities. In a typical senior/mezzanine structure, the working capital facilities and hedging liabilities would rank equally with the senior term facilities. With a unitranche financing, the working capital facilities (being a revolving credit facility out of which typical ancillary facilities can be carved out) are provided on a super-senior basis. The ranking of hedging liabilities can be more complicated and is discussed in further detail below.

3.3 Intercreditor issues on unitranche financings

Given that a direct lender will be the lender of record in respect of the unitranche loan, a borrower will usually need a traditional bank lender to provide revolving credit and/or ancillary facilities, and such facilities will typically be provided on a super-senior basis.

In summary, in the context of unitranche financing structures, 'super-senior' means that, on an enforcement of the transaction security, the proceeds of the enforcement will be used to repay all liabilities owed to the revolving credit or ancillary facility providers (referred to in this chapter as the 'super-senior lenders') before the repayment of any liabilities owed to the unitranche lenders.

(a) ***Payments***

The super-senior lenders and unitranche lenders will rank equally in terms of payments throughout the life of the facilities. In contrast to senior/mezzanine structures, neither the super-senior nor unitranche lenders will have the right to switch off or block payments to each other on the occurrence of a default, event of default or acceleration of the facilities.

(b) ***Security***

The super-senior lenders and the unitranche lenders will (to the extent possible and subject to any jurisdictional issues) share a first ranking cross-guarantee and security package.

(c) ***Enforcement***

The super-senior lenders will only have the right to enforce the transaction security if one of a limited number of events of default (often referred to as 'material events of default') has occurred and subject to a negotiated standstill period.

The material events of default are subject to negotiation between the super-senior and unitranche lenders, but typically include:

- non-payment of the super-senior liabilities;
- breach of a financial covenant (or delivery of evidence of compliance with this covenant) which is included solely for the benefit of the super-senior lenders, which typically will be either a leverage covenant calculated with additional headroom or a minimum EBITDA covenant;
- insolvency and related events of default;
- breach of the negative pledge;
- breach of the restrictions on disposals in the facilities agreement; although the trigger for the material event of default is often set at a looser level than that set out in the facilities agreement, such that a breach of the disposals covenant will only be a material event of default if it has occurred in relation to the disposal of companies or assets which generate EBITDA in excess of a certain threshold amount; and
- unlawfulness and invalidity of a finance document.

Standstill periods are typically set at between 60 and 90 days for a non-payment default and between 90 and 120 days for other material events of default. At the end of the applicable period, provided that the unitranche lenders have not taken any steps to enforce the transaction security, the super-senior lenders may commence enforcement action. There will also usually be an additional long-stop standstill period whereby, if an enforcement process has been commenced on the instructions of a unitranche lender, a material event of default has occurred and the super-senior lenders have not been repaid by the end of that standstill period, the super-senior lenders can then take over control of the enforcement process.

In circumstances where the super-senior lenders are controlling the enforcement process, the unitranche lenders will receive the benefit of value-protection provisions in the intercreditor agreement to ensure that fair value for the assets is received as a result of the enforcement process. These value-protection provisions are similar to those sought by mezzanine lenders in a senior/mezzanine structure. The provisions typically state that, if the super-senior lenders are enforcing the transaction security, the claims of the unitranche lenders may only be released as part of the enforcement process if:

- the enforcement process is a court-approved process (for example, a scheme of arrangement);
- the enforcement process is a disposal made as a result of a public auction for the group or for the assets of the group; or
- the security agent obtains an opinion from an independent financial adviser that the proceeds received as a result of the enforcement process represent fair market consideration in the prevailing market conditions for the group or for the assets of the group.

(d) *Amendment and waivers*

One of the key features of unitranche financing is that the unitranche and revolving credit facilities are provided in one set of finance documents. As a general rule, amendments to the finance documents will require the consent of the parent company in the obligor group and of the majority of lenders (usually lenders holding 66^2/3% of the total commitments of all of the super-senior and unitranche lenders). Typically the super-senior lenders will not hold enough of the total commitments to give them a blocking vote on any amendment and waiver decisions (because the commitments held by the super-senior lenders will comprise less than the 33^1/3% of the total commitments). This would give the unitranche lenders the right to drag the super-senior lenders on lender voting decisions. From the super-senior lenders' perspective, there are a number of reasons why this would not be attractive. For example, the super-senior lenders have a great deal of protection by virtue of their position at the top of the payment waterfall, which gives them the right to receive any enforcement proceeds on a priority basis, but if the unitranche lenders could amend the payment waterfall without the consent of the super-senior lenders, this protection could be removed. A super-senior lender will therefore negotiate into the finance documents a set of entrenched voting rights so that certain specified amendments and waivers cannot be made without their consent. These will include:

- any amendments to the material events of default which give the super-senior lenders the independent enforcement rights referred to above and any other provisions relating to the enforcement mechanic given to the super-senior lenders (for example, changes to standstill periods);
- the super-senior financial covenant and how this is calculated and reported;
- amendments to the payment waterfall;
- the independent right of the super-senior lenders to accelerate the facilities;
- the group of creditors who can instruct the security agent to enforce the security; and
- changes to the guarantee and security package.

In addition, a super-senior lender will want to ensure that a market-standard set of amendments which require the consent of all of the lenders (for example, extensions to payment dates, reductions in margin, increases in commitments etc) are included in the facility agreement.

(e) **Hedging**
Hedging facilities provided on a secured basis in relation to interest rate and exchange rate risks incurred in connection with the term facilities being provided to the borrower will usually rank equally with the senior term and revolving facilities. All other hedging (for example, any foreign exchange rate hedging entered into the ordinary course of a borrower's trading) is either provided on an unsecured basis or, alternatively, the borrower may negotiate that a certain proportion of its trading hedging liabilities may share in the benefit of the transaction security on an equal footing, with the remainder of the trading hedging liabilities being subordinated to the term and revolving facilities.

In unitranche financings, the unitranche facility provider is typically a direct lender or another entity which does not have the capability to provide hedging facilities to the borrower. It is often the case that the super-senior lender will be able (and will want) to provide the hedging facilities required by the borrower. However, the super-senior lender will usually only be prepared to do so if the liabilities owed to it in respect of the hedging facilities rank equally with the other liabilities owed to it as an institution, meaning that the hedging facilities would also rank on a super-senior basis. Given the nature of foreign exchange hedging in particular, if adverse market movements lead to an unforeseen increase in the amount of liabilities which rank on a super-senior basis, this can present significant additional risks for the unitranche lenders. This issue is often addressed by unitranche lenders by including a monetary cap on hedging liabilities which can rank on a super-senior basis. All hedging liabilities incurred in excess of this cap will typically rank equally with the unitranche liabilities or, occasionally, will be subordinated to the unitranche liabilities.

3.4 Re-tranching and agreements among lenders

As mentioned above, one of the key features of a unitranche financing is that the unitranche loan is a single term loan facility. This is how the facility will be presented to the borrower. However it is common for the single unitranche loan to be re-tranched into so-called 'first out' and 'last out' tranches. This re-tranching will be either in the facility agreement to which the borrower is party, or in a separate agreement known as the agreement among lenders or 'AAL'. The borrower is not party to the AAL and so may not be aware that the unitranche facility has been re-tranched, or know the terms of the re-tranching between the lenders.

The AAL will (among other things) reallocate the margin payments received during the life of the facility to reflect the different risk profiles of the first-out and last-out loans. The borrower will still make a single interest payment, but the AAL will provide that a greater proportion of this is paid over to the last-out lenders, to reflect the higher level of risk being taken on by them. The AAL will also include provisions relating to ranking of payments, enforcement of transaction security and the voting rights of the relevant classes of lenders.

AALs are more typical in US unitranche financings. In the European market, it is more typical for the intercreditor arrangements outlined above to be included in the typical intercreditor agreement to which the borrower will be party.

Legal structuring of direct lending deals: France

Jérémie Bismuth
Marie Dubarry de Lassalle
Olivia Locatelli
Caroline Texier
Gide Loyrette Nouel

1.   Lending activity in France: regulatory regime

The lending of money on French territory is a regulated activity under French law, falling within the scope of regulations on the banking monopoly and can therefore only be performed in France by a licensed credit institution or financing companies.

As mentioned in the "Overview of distressed trading: France" chapter, breach of the provisions relating to the banking monopoly rules can result in criminal sanctions of up to three years' imprisonment and a fine of up to €375,000 for an individual, or a fine of up to €1,875,000 for a company. Additional penalties can be incurred such as a prohibition on carrying out, directly or indirectly, the activity concerned by the breach of banking monopoly regulations, either permanently or for a maximum period of five years.

1.1   Categories of credit institutions authorised to lend money in France

(a)   French lenders

Under Article L.511-5 of the Monetary and Financial Code, only credit institutions or financing companies licensed by the French banking regulator (the ACPR), and/or the European Central Bank (ECB), under Regulation 468/2014 of the European Central Bank of April 16 2014, are authorised to lend money on French territory.

(b)   Foreign EU lenders

Credit institutions licensed in a member state of the European Union or the European Economic Area are duly authorised in France to perform credit operations, provided that they have given the notification required by European rules for being authorised in France.

(c)   Non-EU foreign lenders

Credit institutions licensed in a country which is not a member state of the European Union or the European Economic Area need to obtain a banking licence from the ACPR in order to grant loans on a regular basis on French territory. The ACPR lists each year on its website[1] the non-EU foreign credit institutions which have obtained a banking licence in France.

---

1   acpr.banque-france.fr/agrements-et-autorisations/registres-et-listes/regafi-et-liste-des-agents-financiers.html.

1.2 Legal exceptions relating to lending activities

French law provides for a lot of exemptions to the French banking monopoly, allowing certain companies to perform lending activities on French territory, either due to their nature (such as insurance companies) or due to the context of specific transactions (such as intra-group cash pooling or supplier credits).

More recently, Law 2015-990 dated August 6 2015 introduced an additional exemption under which joint-stock companies or limited liability companies may grant loans to small and medium-sized enterprises subject to certain conditions (such as sufficient economic links between both companies and the tenor of the loans being less than two years).

We note also that following EU Regulation 2015/760 dated April 29 2015 introducing the European long-term investment fund ('the ELTIF Regulation') and the Amending Finance Law for 2015 (Law 2015-1786) dated December 29 2015, a European long-term investment fund (ELTIF) can lend money in France provided that it has been approved as an ELTIF by the French financial markets authority (the AMF).

To qualify as an ELTIF, a fund must (among other things set out in the ELTIF Regulation), invest at least 70% of its capital in eligible investment assets, defined in Article 10 of the ELTIF Regulation as:
- eligible equity or quasi-equity debt instruments;
- loans granted by the ELTIF;
- units of shares of certain European funds; and
- assets of a value of at least €10 million.

Additionally, the fund may not engage in short selling, and must observe strict limitations on its use of leverage and derivatives. The ELTIF Regulation is directly applicable in France without having to be transposed into French domestic law. Consequently, as from January 1 2016, French professional specialised funds, professional private equity funds and securitisation vehicles have been entitled to grant loans under the conditions set out in the ELTIF Regulation, when they have received authorisation from the AMF to use the ELTIF label.

The ELTIF Regulation has also resulted in amendments to the Monetary and Financial Code for the same categories of French investment funds when they are not authorised to use the ELTIF label, in order to allow these funds to be entitled to grant loans under conditions to be set out in a decree which has not yet been issued by French authorities.

Non-French investment funds, even those which would be authorised to use the ELTIF label by their home state regulator, are currently outside the scope of these proposals. However, on March 30 2016, the French government published a bill promoting transparency, anti-corruption and economic modernisation known as the 'Sapin II bill'. This bill is currently being discussed before the French Parliament, and the situation of non-French investment funds willing to grant loans in France could become much clearer as a result. The Sapin II bill, once passed, will enable the government to specify the conditions under which such an investment fund can grant loans in France.

1.3 Market practice exceptions relating to lending activities

Foreign funds that want to lend money to a French company usually structure their transactions with the help of a fronting bank.

Concomitantly to the granting of the loan by the fronting bank to the French company, the loan (once it has been fully drawn down by the borrower) can be transferred to the foreign fund provided certain conditions are met, namely:

- the fronting bank is located outside France and is duly authorised to provide credit transactions in France under Directive 2013/36/EU;
- the purchaser is located outside of France;
- the purchase agreement used for the acquisition of the loan receivables is governed by a non-French law; and
- the purchase price paid by the transferee to the transferor in consideration of the purchase of the loan receivables is not payable in France.

This exception is frequently used in syndicated loans governed by French law and granted to a French borrower in which a foreign fund (not licensed in France) wishes to participate.

In that situation, the foreign fund appoints a foreign credit institution (licensed in France but located outside France) as the fronting bank. This foreign credit institution participates in the syndication, and, as soon as its commitment in the loan has been fully drawn down by the borrower, transfers its rights in the loan to the foreign fund. In order to be outside the scope of the French banking monopoly, the parties must be careful that they do not link this transfer to French territory (ie, payment must be made outside France and the purchase agreement covering the loan must not be governed by French law).

1.4 Relevant limitations that should be considered by an investor

In general, payments made by borrowers to lenders are not subject to withholding tax. As an exception, payments (excluding payments of principal) made to lenders established in a 'non-cooperative state or territory' are subject to a 75% withholding tax.[2]

2. Lending activity in France: French market practice

For a French investment-grade transaction, usually the borrower lends directly from a lender or a group of lenders.

For a leveraged transaction, very often an *ad hoc* company (generally under the legal form of a simplified joint-stock company) is created. This company is dedicated to the transaction and its sole activity is to purchase the target company and carry the related indebtedness. The responsibility of the shareholders of the *ad hoc* company is limited to the invested amounts.

We note that the current market practice is direct lending, and double-Luxco structures (under which the acquisition vehicle is wholly owned by a Luxembourg company, which is itself wholly owned by a second Luxembourg company) are not

---

[2] The list of non-cooperative states or territories is amended on a yearly basis. At the date of writing, the list consists of the following: Botswana, Brunei, Guatemala, Marshall Islands, Nauru and Niue.

being used any more. The double-Luxco structure is not being accepted by borrowers because of the abundance of liquidity in the market and is not even being proposed by French lenders anymore.

2.1 Key legal issues to be considered when structuring a direct lending deal

In structuring a direct lending deal in France, besides considerations related to the French banking monopoly, consideration should also be given by investors to:
- the financial assistance rules;
- upstream and cross-stream guarantees; and
- French corporate law.

(a) Acquisition of shares of a French target: financial assistance

In transactions involving the acquisition of shares in a French target, the French financial assistance rules (Article L.225-216 of the Commercial Code) prohibit the target granting either a guarantee or other security over its assets as security for the repayment of the loan granted for the acquisition of its shares. The same prohibition would apply should the guarantee or the security interest be granted by a French company in order to secure borrowings incurred for the purchase of shares in its holding company.

The above does not apply to French companies which have the corporate form of a limited liability company (*société à responsabilité limitée*).

(b) Upstream and cross-stream guarantees

As a general condition of validity and according to the rule of specialty (*principe de specialité*) under French law, an obligation contracted by a company must fall within the scope of its corporate purpose and social interest.

As a consequence, a company may not guarantee its parent's or sister's obligations unless in either case the guarantee meets each of the following tests which have been set out by case-law (*Rosenblum* case law, Cass Crim, February 4 1985):
- The company whose obligations are guaranteed must belong to the same group as the guarantor;
- Granting the guarantee must have been undertaken in consideration of an economic, corporate or financial interest impacting at the level of the corporate group;
- The company granting the guarantee must receive some benefit as a result of granting the guarantee; and
- The guarantee must not exceed the financial capacity of the company granting the guarantee.

If any of those conditions are not met, a French court would consider the guarantee or security interest to be null and void (and in addition there may be criminal liability on the part of the directors).

In order to overcome this risk, the current market practice in France is, in the context of the financing of the parent company, to set up an intercompany loan granted by the parent company to the French subsidiary. The French subsidiary will then grant guarantees to secure the obligations of the parent company up to the amount of the intercompany loan.

(c) *French corporate law*

Depending on the type of company and on the specific provisions mentioned in the bylaws and articles of association, a guarantee or security to be granted by a company may have to be approved in advance by a special resolution of a meeting of the competent corporate body, and it must not result in the maximum amount, set by the board annually for all guarantees, being exceeded, or exceed the individual limit set by the board. Investors that wish to lend money to a French company should therefore each time require a copy of the resolution of the competent corporate body of the borrower which approved the transaction.

2.2 Governing law of the transaction documents

Leaving aside smaller transactions where French law is typically used, larger deals with international lending syndicates use either French or English law-governed finance documents, depending mostly on the sponsor's precedents and composition of the syndicate. When a majority of North American investors are lending money to a French company, transactions may also be financed using New York law-governed high-yield bonds and term loan debt. The use of English or New York law is often requested by foreign credit institutions and foreign funds that wish to participate in a syndicated loan as they are more familiar with such law.

3. Lending activity in France: insolvency issues

The French legal system is considered to be debtor-friendly, even if recent reforms have tended to change it in order to give more comfort to the creditors (for instance through the introduction of mandatory debt-for-equity swaps).

3.1 Debt-for-equity swaps and cram-down of holdouts

In a safeguard or a judicial reorganisation proceeding, Article 626-30-2 of the Commercial Code provides that creditors' committees and the general meeting of the bondholders may vote in favour of a conversion of their debts into securities giving access, immediately or in the future, to the share capital of the company.

A new law which came into force on August 8 2015 (the 'Macron Law'), now allows this debt-for-equity swap to be forced on shareholders in certain judicial reorganisation proceedings. This new law only applies to companies placed into reorganisation proceedings after August 8 2015.

The law introduces two mechanisms to force out shareholders: the forced dilution of shareholders and the forced sale of the shares and other interests in the share capital held by opposing shareholders.

Under the new Article L 631-19-2 of the Commercial Code, both mechanisms require that the four following conditions be met:
- The company must have at least 150 employees or constitute, under the Labour Code, a 'dominant company';

- The cessation of business of the company could have a materially adverse effect on the national or regional economy and on employment in this area;
- The change in the company's share capital appears to be the only serious solution to avoid causing such an adverse effect and to enable the continuation of the business; and
- The change in the share capital provided for in the reorganisation plan is not approved during the shareholders' meeting.

The two mechanisms are as follows.

(a) **Dilution of shareholders**
An opposing shareholder's interest can be diluted following a capital increase (by means of an infusion of new capital or a debt-for-equity swap) approved at a shareholders' meeting called by a court-appointed judicial administrator, who will exercise the voting rights of the opposing shareholder. The capital increase must be carried out within a period of 30 days following the holding of the general meeting.

(b) **Forced sale of the shareholders' interests in the share capital**
Where a shareholder who holds a majority of the voting rights or a blocking stake refuses to vote in favour of the changes to the capital structure, the court may order that shareholder to sell all or part of its shares to those who are committed to implementing the reorganisation plan.

If no agreement is reached between the selling shareholder(s) and the purchaser(s) on the value of the shares and other capital interests to be sold, the value is then determined by an expert appointed by the court.

The new shareholders may be compelled by the court to hold the shares for a duration that may not exceed the term of the plan. The court may also require that a guarantee be issued by a credit institution to secure the new shareholders' commitments. The law also provides some procedural protections, such as the hearing of all parties by the court and the presence of the public prosecutor during the debates.

Existing shareholders, other than those that are targeted by the eviction process, have the right to obtain redemption of their shares by the new shareholders (a drag-along mechanism). For that purpose, any statutory clauses of the company requiring formal approval by a new shareholder shall be disregarded.

3.2 French law restrictions

Under Article L 622-13 of the Commercial Code, all clauses that provide for the early termination of a contract due to the opening of an amicable proceeding or a judicial insolvency proceeding are deemed void under French law.

French case law is consistent in ignoring such termination clauses, as well as clauses that would merely have the effect of triggering stricter financial conditions resulting from the opening of an insolvency proceeding.

3.3 Enforcement actions

The opening of an insolvency proceeding triggers an automatic stay of payments.

Concurrently, it prohibits the creditors from initiating any legal action related to those debts against the company aimed at enforcing the borrower's obligation to reimburse the creditor.

With respect to loan debt, French case law treats the repayment of principal and interest under a loan agreement entered into prior to the opening of an insolvency proceeding as a pre-petition debt, the repayment of which is prohibited under the automatic stay principle even if the repayment dates fall within the observation period of the insolvency proceeding. As a result, payment of principal, interest and accessories is frozen during the observation period.

3.4 Privilege of new money

The privilege of new money is awarded to any money lent to a company within a conciliation proceeding or through a conciliation agreement, provided the conciliation agreement is approved by the court.

Under Article L 611-11 of the Commercial Code whenever a new creditor agrees to lend new money or assets to ease the restructuring of a company during the conciliation proceeding, he will be awarded priority as regards reimbursement in the event of a subsequent insolvency proceeding (a safeguard proceeding, a judicial reorganisation, or judicial liquidation).

This privilege allows the lender of the new money to be repaid before all other creditors, except for court costs and a portion of pre-insolvency wages benefiting from a super-priority ranking.

If the subsequent procedure is a safeguard or rehabilitation procedure, an Ordinance dated March 12 2014 provides that conciliation financings cannot be rescheduled or written off unless the new money lenders agree to it.

This priority does not apply to shareholders providing new equity.

Legal structuring of direct lending deals: Germany

Sacha Lürken
Wolfgang Nardi
Oded Schein
Kirkland & Ellis LLP

1. **Lending activity in Germany**

    The applicable regulations under the German Banking Act distinguish between buying fully funded loans, on the one hand, and the origination of loans or the acquisition of unfunded commitments, on the other.

    While buying, holding and collecting fully funded loans is not subject to any regulatory restrictions on the buyer, the origination of loans or buying of unfunded loan commitments (subject to certain minimum thresholds) is considered a banking activity under German law and requires the lender to be licensed as a credit institution in Germany or (if eligible for the passporting regime) the European Economic Area (EEA).

    Furthermore, on March 18 2016, the 'UCITS V Implementation Act' became effective, which exempts alternative investment funds (AIFs) and alternative investment fund managers (AIFMs) from the EEA from the need for a banking licence. In anticipation of this new legislation the BaFin (the German federal regulatory agency) had announced exemptions from the requirement of being licensed for lending business in May 2015. However, the following restrictions, among others, apply: leverage may not exceed 30% of the capital of the AIF or AIFM, no loans may be granted to consumers, and there are requirements as to risk diversification. In light of this legislation being very recent, there is little certainty about several details and whether the exemptions apply to non-German AIFs and AIFMs.

2. **Investment vehicles and structures**

    Many inward investments in Germany in the form of loans are provided through the formation of a Luxembourg special purpose vehicle structure (or even multiple layers of Luxembourg entities) to allow debt funds (indirectly) to invest and hold claims against German debtors. Luxembourg is often chosen because it has a reliable and flexible legal environment which also allows a tax-efficient repatriation of profits earned from German claims. This is the case in particular for debt investors who are tax-resident in the United States. Certain debt investors (in particular domestic debt investors or debt investors who are tax resident in other EU jurisdictions) may prefer to invest directly or through holding vehicles in other jurisdictions, depending on their own tax status and taking into account taxation at their own level. Hence, there is generally no standard approach that would apply to all, or even most, of the debt investors.

3. Key legal structuring issues

The key issue for lenders is not to run foul of any regulatory restrictions. Other considerations include access to asset security, which may be restricted due to corporate limitations, and any relevant restrictions on enforcement relevant to such corporate limitations.

The choice of whether or not to use English law in a direct lending transaction will generally depend on the preferences of the borrower and the lender. German law is generally considered to be more borrower-friendly. Even loan documents entered into between merchants are subject to judicial review if and to the extent that their terms qualify as general terms and conditions (see below). In addition, where a loan has a definite term, the exercise of remedies by the lenders in the event of a default on the part of the borrower is rather restricted, as there must be a sufficiently important cause for the lenders to be allowed to terminate. German courts have held, despite criticism by several voices in the legal literature, that parties are not free to agree what constitutes a sufficiently important cause without having regard to the materiality of the underlying default and in particular to the ability of the borrower to repay all its obligations under the loan, taking into account any security provided for it.

Another aspect to consider is that for certain transaction volumes the secondary market for loans governed by English law is considered to be more liquid. English law is often chosen to govern provisions concerning payment in kind (PIK) interest (see below).

4. Enforcement considerations

The following issues need to be taken into consideration when considering a German direct lending transaction.

4.1 Interest rates

Interest rates can be held to be unenforceable because they are contrary to good morals if they grossly exceed market rates. Courts have held in the past that with regard to bank loans interest rates were unenforceable where they exceeded the effective market rate by 100% or were 120 basis points above the effective market rate;[1] but any individual rate will have to be considered on a case-by-case basis.

German law (Section 289 of the Civil Code) does not allow compound interest (ie, PIK interest). The German market addresses this restriction in several ways, one of which envisages the borrower electing for compound interest to be added to the principal at the end of the relevant interest period. In cases where parties are located in two separate EU jurisdictions, they can agree that in a credit agreement generally governed by German law, the clauses dealing with compound interest are subject to English law.

Pay-if-you-can interest is generally permissible under German law.

---

1 Permanent practice of the German courts; see, for instance, *Bundesgerichtshof* (Federal Court of Justice; 'BGH'), judgment of March 13 1990 (case XI ZR 252/89).

4.2 Fairness

German courts will generally scrutinise the terms of a credit agreement for fairness, even if the contract is made between merchant parties, if it finds that relevant terms qualify as general terms and conditions of the lender. There are several tests that may be applied by a court, including whether the relevant clause is surprising or has multiple meanings. Courts will have regard to trade practice and custom. So far, German courts have not had to apply these tests with regard to loan documentation based on international standard terms such as the form proposed by the Loan Market Association.

5. Insolvency risks

5.1 Automatic stay

The onset of an insolvency proceeding has no automatic effect on enforcement, there is no statutory automatic stay. However, the court can order a preliminary stay on enforcement actions under Section 21 of the Insolvency Code. It is in the court's discretion which orders to issue, but with respect to stay on enforcement, the law lists in particular:

- a stay of court-led enforcement procedures brought by individual creditors in respect of the debtor's non-real estate assets; and
- a stay on the realisation of certain collateral (see below) by secured creditors outside a court process, or by suppliers under retention of title, if the assets serving as collateral are of material relevance to continuing the company's business during the preliminary proceedings.

Such a preliminary stay can only affect certain assets serving as collateral. The law refers expressly to moveable assets (Section 166(1) of the Insolvency Code) and receivables assigned for security (Section 166(2) of the Insolvency Code). It is highly controversial in German law whether security over shares in subsidiaries can be made subject to a stay order. A recent judgment from the German Federal Court of Justice dealing with pledges over shares in a German listed company certificated under a global note[2] did not comment on this question generally.[3] In practice, most share pledges are taken over non-listed limited liability companies or limited partnerships with uncertificated shares. For these share pledges, however, a court might still issue a preliminary order to stay enforcement as part of the general discretion granted to it under Section 21 of the Insolvency Code.

Following the opening of the proceedings, no individual court-led creditor

---

2 BGH, judgment of September 24 2015 (case IX ZR 272/13).
3 The court held that German law shares certificated in a global note held in a securities deposit account subject to the German Securities Deposit Account Act, due to the specific *in rem* property rights that a holder of global notes has under the German Securities Deposit Account Act, part of the debtor's moveable assets. The court added though that only shares of sufficient number to amount to a 'commercial holding' were to be excluded from a secured creditor's individual enforcement rights. The court did not set a threshold for when a commercial holding has to be assumed, but referred to the presumption generally accepted in German accounting principles under Section 271(1)3 of the Commercial code, which sets a threshold of 20% of the company's equity.

enforcement actions can be taken. Any floating collateral (typically, collateral over inventory and receivables) will crystallise on the day of the opening of insolvency proceedings; in other words, assets produced or acquired and receivables generated by the debtor company after that date will not be captured by any security agreements, but will become available for distribution.

However, German law has neither a concept of priming existing security, nor a general stay on the realisation of collateral. Secured creditors generally retain their individual right to realise their collateral (including collateral over real estate) except for moveable assets[4] and receivables assigned for security, which can only be realised by the insolvency administrator (or, in debtor-in-possession proceedings, the debtor) (see Section 166 of the Insolvency Code). The secured creditors will still receive the proceeds of the realisation in this collateral after deduction of a 4% handling fee and a realisation fee, which has a default rate of 5% that can be adjusted if actual costs are substantially higher or lower (see Section 171 of the Insolvency Code).

As the secured creditors' general right to realise their collateral is value-destructive for any form of merger or acquisition process or insolvency plan (for which see the chapter on restructuring in Germany), secured creditors in practice do not usually exercise their enforcement rights, in return for a share in the proceeds negotiated with the administrator. If proceeds are sufficient to cover the fees involved in the process and administrative expenses, the share accruing to secured creditors can be up to 100% of their secured claims, including interest, minus the 9% handling and realisation fees.

5.2 Claw-back

Certain transactions entered into before insolvency proceedings are commenced (in particular, repayment of debt or transfers of assets, but also entering into agreements) that disadvantage the creditors generally can, depending on the time they were made before the commencement of proceedings, be subject to a claw-back action.

The administrator (or, in a debtor-in-possession proceeding, the trustee) has the exclusive right to pursue such an avoidance action. The insolvency administrator might even seek to avoid a transaction performed in his capacity as preliminary insolvency administrator.

(a) Detriment to creditors generally

A requirement for any claw-back action is that the transaction against which it is directed must have caused detriment to the insolvency creditors generally. A transaction is detrimental to creditors generally if it either increased the liabilities or reduced the assets of the debtor. No detriment to creditors arises when the counterparty benefiting from the transaction had an enforceable security interest over the asset transferred to it by the debtor.

(b) Fair and contemporaneous consideration defence

The creditor against whom an avoidance action is brought has a defence to all

---

4 See above for discussion of whether shares in subsidiaries are moveable assets.

avoidance actions except fraudulent preferential transfers if it provided the debtor with 'contemporaneous and fair new value'. This defence has generally been found to apply in respect of collateral granted by a borrower to secure its own[5] obligations under newly funded[6] loans where it was provided at the latest between two and four weeks after funding.

(c) *Types of avoidable transactions and claw-back periods:*
All of the actions listed below can be pursued cumulatively; that is to say, they are not mutually exclusive:
- 'congruent satisfaction' (Section 130 of the Insolvency Code) – this type of action applies in respect of any satisfaction received by a creditor (eg, repayment of debt) or granting of collateral made within three months prior to filing for insolvency, if at that time the debtor was cash-flow insolvent and the creditor was aware of it;
- 'incongruent satisfaction' (Section 131 of the Insolvency Code) – this action covers any satisfaction received by a creditor (eg, repayment of debt) or granting of collateral made to which the creditor did not have an enforceable right, if it was made:
  - within one month prior to filing for insolvency; or
  - within three months, if the debtor was cash-flow insolvent; or
  - within three months, if the creditor was aware that it was detrimental to other creditors generally;
- directly detrimental transactions made within three months prior to filing for insolvency (Section 132 of the Insolvency Code) – this type of action is generally not relevant in lending transactions;
- fraudulent preferential transactions (Section 133(1) of the Insolvency Code) – this form of action applies to any transaction made within 10 years prior to filing where the debtor has the intent to cause detriment to its creditors generally, and the receiving creditor was aware of that intent. The receiving creditor's awareness is (rebuttably) presumed if the debtor was facing imminent illiquidity and the creditor was aware of this and that the transaction generally disenfranchised other creditors.

This type of claw-back is highly relevant for any payments and other benefits (such as collateral) received from a borrower in distress, and is also the type of claw-back asserted most often in litigation due to its long look-back period. As a result of the interpretation of Section 133(1) of the Insolvency Code by the Federal Court of Justice, a lender who is aware of the financial distress of its borrower will have to demonstrate that it relied on the borrower being capable of being successfully restructured, which will in most cases be done by relying on the opinion of a restructuring expert. If the borrower's restructuring is predicated on stakeholders

---

5   The defence does not apply in respect of collateral securing another person's (eg, a parent company's) obligations.
6   The defence does not apply in respect of new collateral granted for existing indebtedness.

agreeing to certain transactions (such as debt waivers or an injection of new money), the lender will have to apply due diligence to ascertain that the borrower has a reasonable prospect of gathering the requisite support;
- contracts with related persons entered into within two years prior to filing for insolvency (Section 133(2) of the Insolvency Code) – this is generally not relevant in lending transactions;
- transactions for no consideration within four years prior to filing (Section 134 of the Insolvency Code) – this is, in particular, relevant for collateral granted by non-borrower entities to secure debt owed by a different borrower (such as a parent company);
- repayment of equitably subordinated loans entered into within one year or granting of collateral within 10 years prior to filing (Section 135 of the Insolvency Code; see below under "5.3 Equitable subordination").

5.3 Equitable subordination

Debt owed by a company to its direct or indirect shareholders holding (directly or indirectly) more than 10% of the company's share capital, or any of their affiliates or any 'quasi-shareholder', is subordinated to debt owed to all general unsecured creditors and certain other subordinated creditors in insolvency proceedings over the borrower (Section 39 of the Insolvency Code). The same applies if the lender has acquired the debt from a shareholder or quasi-shareholder within one year of the borrower's insolvency petition, or has been a shareholder or quasi-shareholder within that period.

In determining whether a lender will be considered to be a 'quasi-shareholder', courts will scrutinise the facts in each individual case. This is an extremely complex and case-law-heavy area of insolvency law. One relevant factor is whether common control is directly or indirectly exercised over the borrower and the lender. For instance, restrictive business covenants and shareholder-like instruction and profit rights, in combination with a share pledge, imposed on the borrower have been held to be enough to lead to equitable subordination of the loans made to that borrower.

Any payments made within one year prior to the borrower's filing for insolvency to:
- direct or indirect shareholders holding more than 10% of the borrower's shares, or any of their affiliates, or to a quasi-shareholder, or a person which is an assignee of any of the preceding; or
- a lender, if and to the extent that a direct or indirect shareholder, or any of their affiliates or a quasi-shareholder, has secured such debt;

can be clawed backed in an insolvency from that direct or indirect (quasi-)shareholder.

Any collateral granted to direct or indirect (quasi-) shareholders within 10 years prior to the borrower's filing for insolvency can be clawed backed in an insolvency from that direct or indirect (quasi-) shareholder.

An exemption from equitable subordination (called the 'restructuring privilege') applies to:

- loans (both existing and new loans);
- granted by persons who acquire shares in the borrower company for the first time (ie, they are not for existing shareholders or quasi-shareholders) as part of a restructuring (such as a debt for equity swap);
- at a time when the borrower is insolvent, over-indebted or is in imminent danger of becoming insolvent;
- for as long as the borrower has not been sustainably restructured (ie, the restructuring privilege falls away after the recovery of the borrower's financial situation).

In practice, the restructuring privilege is only of limited value protecting lenders from the risk of equitable subordination following a debt-for-equity swap or on their taking over the shares in a business following enforcement.

6. New money priorities

6.1 New money arising from an out-of-court agreement

There are no privileges for new money providers. On the contrary, lending to distressed borrowers creates the risk of liability on the part of the lender. Such liability could arise under Section 826 of the Civil Code if the lender is found to have intentionally damaged the creditors of the distressed borrower in a way that is contrary to good morals. The Federal Court of Justice has consistently held that this would be the case if a lender of new money that already is a creditor of the distressed borrower provides the additional financing with the intention of enhancing its own position at the expense of other creditors.[7] In such circumstances, a creditor could also be found to be aiding and abetting the borrower in delaying its filing for insolvency (which is a criminal offence), and the loan agreement and any collateral provided for it could be void.

To protect itself from such liability, a lender must be able to prove that its new loan served the purpose of pursuing a serious attempt to restructure the business and the balance sheet of the distressed borrower.[8] Whether such an attempt is indeed serious is tested from the perspective of the lender at the time of granting the loan: if the restructuring fails and causes losses for third-party creditors of the borrower, but the lender is able to prove that there were positive prospects that the borrower could be restructured, it will not be held liable.[9] The Federal Court of Justice requires a lender to base its financing on a conclusive restructuring concept that is based on the present facts, the implementation of which has already started, and which justifies serious and reasonable prospects of success.[10] In practice, lenders to a distressed borrower therefore require an opinion from an unprejudiced expert who is

---

7 Permanent practice of the German courts; see, for example, BGH, judgment of March 26 1984 (case II ZR 196/83).
8 Long-standing and permanent practice of the German courts; see, for example, BGH, judgment of July 9 1953 (case IV ZR 242/52).
9 *Oberlandesgericht* (Higher Regional Court) Düsseldorf, judgment of July 14 1981 (case 6 U 259/80).
10 Permanent practice of the German courts; see, for example, BGH, judgment of July 9 1979 (case II ZR 118/77).

familiar with the business sector in which the borrower operates, confirming that the restructuring of the borrower is possible. The new money made available must fit into the proposed restructuring as set out in that opinion and there needs to be sufficient likelihood that any conditions that the expert identifies for the success of the restructuring are achievable. In the loan agreement, the new money lender customarily includes provisions that underpin its intention to provide financing in line with the restructuring opinion and that ensure that he is provided with information on the progress and success of the restructuring.

6.2 New money arising from in-court proceedings

Loans taken out by an administrator or a debtor-in-possession can have the status of administrative expenses. However, no priming of existing liens is possible: collateral can only be provided from previously unencumbered assets or from assets acquired after the opening of the insolvency proceedings. However, since administrative expenses rank senior to debts owed to general unsecured creditors (and junior only to court and administrator's fees), in large company insolvencies they will typically be fully repaid.

An insolvency plan can provide that loans taken out after it has been approved, or loans provided during the administration, take priority over debts owed to existing unsecured creditors in a subsequent insolvency proceeding, if this is agreed between the lender and the administrator (Section 264 of the Insolvency Code). The amount of such privileged loans is capped at the value of the borrower's assets as set out in the insolvency plan.

Legal structuring of direct lending deals: Italy

Giorgio Cappelli
Andrea Martino
Giovanna Randazzo
Chiomenti Studio Legale

1. Lending activity

Lending, in whatever form, to the public in Italy has been an activity traditionally reserved to Italian, EU or non-EU authorised and to Italian, EU or non-EU authorised financial intermediaries enrolled in a register held by the Bank of Italy in accordance with Article 106 of the Italian Consolidated Banking Law, and subject to regulatory and prudential provisions reflecting those applicable to banks but modified for proportionality.

According to Ministerial Decree 53/2015, lending activity 'in whatever form' means the extension of credits, including issuance of guarantees or guarantee commitments and purchase of receivables; and it is considered as being directed at the public when it is provided:

- towards 'third parties', that is to say entities with whom a financial intermediary can enter into a business relationship (other than companies belonging to the same group under Article 2359 of the Italian Civil Code); and
- 'on a professional basis', which means on a steady, permanent and systematic basis, through an organisation allowing interaction with a multiplicity of subjects, regardless of the number of (natural or legal) entities with which transactions are actually executed or of the number of transactions executed overall (even one loan granted through a single purchase of receivables may constitute a restricted financial activity).

During recent years, certain measures have been introduced by Law Decrees 83/2012[1] and 179/2012[2] to facilitate companies' access to non-bank debt financing, aimed at incentivising the markets for corporate bonds, financial bills and subordinated hybrid debt instruments.

In particular, certain limitations applicable to non-listed companies have been removed, allowing such companies (other than banks and micro-enterprises) to issue bonds – derogating to the quantitative limit set out in Article 2412 of the Civil Code (according to which corporate bonds may be issued up to a value equivalent to twice the relevant company's share capital plus legal or available reserves) – if the corporate

---

1 Amended and converted into law by Law 134/2012.
2 Amended and converted into law by Law 221/2012.

bonds are listed on a regulated market or any other multilateral trading facility, or are structured so to allow the investors to convert them into equity.[3]

Furthermore, if certain conditions are met, such bonds issued by non-listed companies may benefit from the more favourable tax regime applicable to 'relevant taxpayers' (banks and listed companies) under Legislative Decree 239/1996.

In particular, relevant categories of investors, such as those resident or established in countries providing the Italian tax authorities' with an adequate exchange of information ('white-listed countries') and as Italian investment funds, are entitled to receive interest free of any withholding tax.

More recently,[4] Law Decree 91/2014,[5] with the purpose of allowing several entities, other than banks and financial intermediaries, to grant loans in Italy, has introduced the following provisions, among others:

- Lending activities (not in the form of the issuance of guarantees) provided by Italian insurance companies to borrowers other than individuals and micro-enterprises do not qualify as lending activities to the public (and are therefore not subject to the Consolidated Banking Law's restricted activity regime), provided that:
  - borrowers are selected by a bank or financial intermediary, retaining a significant economic interest in the transaction equal to 5% of the amount of the facility granted; and
  - the insurance company is adequately capitalised, with internal control and risk management systems allowing it to manage the lending activity risks;
- Special purpose vehicles incorporated under Italian securitisation law may advance loans (not in the form of the issuance of guarantees) in favour of borrowers other than individuals and micro-enterprises, provided that:
  - the borrowers are selected by a bank or financial intermediary, retaining a significant economic interest in the transaction;[6] and
  - the securities issued to finance such lending may be purchased only by qualified investors;
- According to Law Decree 18/2016,[7] Italian alternative investment funds[8] set

---

[3] Moreover, the quantitative limit can also be derogated from if:
- the bonds issued in excess of the specified ceiling are destined to be subscribed by professional investors subject to prudential supervision in accordance with specific legal provisions (Article 2412(2) of the Civil Code); or
- the bond issuance is secured by a first degree mortgage over immovable assets of the company for an amount no great than two-thirds of the value of those same (Article 2412(3) of the Civil Code).

[4] In particular, after Law Decree 145/2013 (amended and converted into law by Law 9/2014) providing for further measures aimed at incentivising the bond market.

[5] Amended and converted into law by Law 116/2014.

[6] As clarified by the Bank of Italy's implementing regulation of March 8 2016, the requirement to maintain a significant economic interest is complied with by retaining an interest in the transaction not lower than 5% in accordance with the provisions set out under Article 405 of EU Regulation 575/2013 (the Capital Requirements Regulation). Under Article 405 of the Capital Requirements Regulation, this 5% economic interest can be calculated, among other ways and as the case may be, in relation to:
- the nominal value of each asset transferred to investors; or
- the nominal value of the relevant securitised asset (if any).

[7] Amended and converted into law by Law 49/2016.

[8] Being collective investment schemes falling within the scope of application of Directive 2011/61/EU (the Alternative Investment Fund Managers' Directive).

up in closed-end form and with limited recourse to leverage, may extend loans, to be granted out of their relevant capital,[9] in favour of entities other than consumers. Furthermore, non-Italian EU alternative investment funds may advance loans out of their assets if:
- the relevant home country authority has authorised the fund to carry out such activity;
- the fund is established in closed-end form, and the relevant participation and operating requirements are similar to those applicable to Italian alternative investment funds advancing loans;
- the fund's home country laws on risk containment/diversification and leverage are equivalent to those applicable to Italian alternative investment funds providing loans (equivalence may be verified on the basis of the fund's articles or bylaws alone, if the relevant home country authority ensures its compliance); and
- the fund files the necessary notice with the Bank of Italy.

Any lending activity carried out in breach of the restrictions set out by the law constitutes a criminal offence under Articles 131 and 132 of the Consolidated Banking Law, and is punishable by imprisonment and fines. Although there is no consolidated case law on the matter, there is a risk that any activity performed without the relevant authorisation will be classified as 'lending activity', even where it consists of no more than a single loan granted in breach of the applicable provisions. Moreover, financing contracts concluded in breach of the regime outlined above may be declared null and void.

From a tax perspective:
- Under Article 15 onwards of Presidential Decree 601/1973, mid- to long-term loans (those having a maturity exceeding 18 months) granted by:
  - authorised Italian, EU or non-EU banks;
  - special purpose vehicles;
  - authorised insurance companies established in an EU state; or
  - alternative investment funds established in an EU state or in an EEA white-listed country (ie, a country engaging in an adequate information exchange with the Italian tax authorities),

may benefit, on an optional basis, from the 'substitutive tax' regime, providing for the payment of 0.25% on the amounts made available as loans *in lieu* of all indirect taxes due and payable on the loans and related deeds and securities;
- under Article 26(5)-*bis*, of Presidential Decree 600/1973 (introduced by Law Decree 91/2014) the 26% final withholding tax ordinarily applicable to interest payments (and other proceeds) paid by an Italian resident entity to foreign lenders is not applicable on mid- to long-term loans granted to an Italian enterprise by:
  - banks established in an EU state;

---

9   In other words, an alternative investment fund meeting the requirements set out above may advance loans using its own capital.

- authorised insurance companies incorporated in an EU state;
- entities listed under Article 2(5)(4)-(23) of Directive 2013/36/EU; and
- institutional foreign investors which, irrespective of their taxable status, are established in a white-listed country where they are subject to regulatory surveillance,

if all the Consolidated Banking Law's provisions applicable to lending activity are duly satisfied.

An alternative method for implementing lending deals is to structure them in the form of intragroup loans between a foreign parent company, as lender, and the relevant Italian subsidiary, as borrower, provided that the relevant form of control falls within Article 2359 of the Civil Code. The parent company may borrow from an authorised entity of its own country and push down the relevant loan amount to its Italian subsidiary, which may grant security interests (in accordance with its bylaws, which will in most cases be governed by Italian law) in favour of the foreign lender, to secure its parent company's obligations.

In regard to such arrangements, it is worth mentioning the following:
- The parent company must have a corporate interest in granting the loan at issue;
- The deal must comply with the general prohibition on financial assistance provided by Article 2358 of the Civil Code (under which a company cannot provide any form of loans and/or security interests in favour of another company to support the latter's purchase of or subscription to its own shares); and
- Under Article 2467 of the Civil Code, the reimbursement of a shareholder loan is subordinated to the satisfaction of the borrower's other creditors (see further below).

Such intragroup loans are usually subject to the law governing the financing granted to the parent company (typically being the latter's local law or English law), while loan agreements executed among Italian parties only are generally governed by Italian law.

More generally, finance agreements involving non-Italian parties may be (and typically are) subject – in accordance with EU Regulation 593/2008 – to a foreign law chosen by the parties (most often English law), except for documents concerning security interests granted over movable or immovable assets (which are governed by the law of the jurisdiction where the relevant asset is located).

However, under Law 218/1995, the choice of a foreign law as the governing law of a contract shall not prevent the application of those provisions of Italian law whose application is mandatory (irrespective of the law otherwise applicable to the contract); these being provisions crucial for the safeguarding of the political, social and economic organisation of the state. Moreover, a foreign law shall not be applied if its effects are contrary to Italian public policy.

2. Enforcement of finance agreements

Italian law provisions will also govern any enforcement actions to be commenced in Italy upon the occurrence of an event of default.

As a general principle, under Article 1455 of the Civil Code, an agreement may be terminated only upon the occurrence of a breach deemed material, considering the interest of the other party. However, under Article 1456 of the Civil Code, the parties to a contract may agree that, should an obligation not be performed in accordance with the relevant terms and conditions, the agreement is terminated by law upon the interested party's declaration, without any further evaluation (expressed in advance in the contract) as to the materiality of the breach. For such a clause to be effective, however, in accordance with consolidated case law,[10] the obligation must be specifically determined: a general contractual provision under which any breach of obligations under the contract would be deemed material is ineffective.[11]

The enforcement of any finance contract is subject, among other provisions, to Article 2744 of the Civil Code, providing that any arrangement under which, upon failure to pay a debt within the agreed terms, title to the secured property is transferred to the relevant creditor is null and void. However, in accordance with consolidated case law, the parties may agree that, in the same circumstances, title to the secured property is transferred to the creditor if the difference between the amount owed and the relevant asset value (as determined by a third-party expert) is paid to the debtor.

The prohibition in Article 2744 does not apply to:
- a pledge over credit deposits, goods and securities granted to secure an overdraft facility in accordance with Article 1851 of the Civil Code (an 'irregular pledge'); or
- security interests over financial collateral in accordance with Legislative Decree 170/2004.

3. Insolvency provisions

The satisfaction of creditors' claims in the context of insolvency procedures is subject to the rules and restrictions of the Italian Bankruptcy Law (Royal Decree 267/1942, as amended).[12]

3.1 Automatic stay

Under Article 51 of the Bankruptcy Law, individual enforcement or precautionary measures against a company cannot be commenced or continued as from the date on which that company makes a declaration of bankruptcy, or on which another insolvency procedure is opened against the same company, and in particular:

---

10 Among the others, Supreme Court, July 26 2002, ruling 11055.
11 Certain limitations are provided for with respect to agreements entered into with consumers.
12 Without prejudice for the rules discussed herein which are currently in place, it is worth mentioning that, as at the time of writing, the Italian legislature has approved a draft law entitled "Authorisation to the government for a comprehensive reform of the law relating to distressed companies and insolvency" which was submitted by the Rordorf Commission and is aimed at providing a new comprehensive framework for rescuing and restructuring companies.

- from the publication in the companies' register of the petition for admission into a composition with creditors until the relevant approval decree becomes final and cannot be appealed;
- for a 60-day period, starting from publication in the companies' register of a restructuring agreement in accordance with Article 182-*bis* of the Bankruptcy Law; and
- to the extent that certain conditions are met, during the negotiation phase preceding the publication of a restructuring agreement.

3.2 Claw-back actions

In terms of enforcement, Article 67 of the Bankruptcy Law provides for certain claw-back actions which may be carried out to revoke security interests granted (and other deeds and/or payments executed) during a 'suspect' period of between six months and a year before the bankruptcy declaration. With specific reference to security interests, the following may be clawed-back:

- unless the counterparty proves that it had no knowledge of the insolvency of the bankrupted party, any pledge, antichresis and/or mortgage voluntarily created in the year preceding the insolvency declaration in respect of pre-existing debts that were not due and payable, and any pledge, antichresis and/or mortgage judicially imposed or voluntarily created in the six-month period preceding the insolvency declaration in respect of debts due and payable; and
- should the receiver give evidence that the counterparty was aware of the bankrupt party's insolvency, any transaction whereby priority rights are granted in respect of debts (including third-party debts) created in the six-month period preceding the insolvency declaration.

Claw-back actions cannot be carried out with respect to security interests granted over assets of the debtor:

- under a restructuring plan according to Article 67(3)(d) of the Bankruptcy Law;[13]
- under a restructuring agreement according to Article 182-*bis* of the Bankruptcy Law;[14]

---

[13] A restructuring plan under Article 67(3)(d) of the Bankruptcy Law is an out-of-court plan aimed at permitting the restructuring of the debtor's debt exposure and ensuring the rebalancing of the relevant financial conditions, formulated by the debtor outside a formal insolvency procedure and, therefore, outside any form of judicial control. As a transaction of private nature, the plan is binding only for the creditors who directly agree to it (the parties to the transactions contemplated by it), and may include all types of provisions such as rescheduling or partial waiver of the debts, conversion of credits into equity and/or refinancing of the company with the purpose of permitting a restructuring and the continuation of the debtor's business, provided in any case that such transactions are aimed at the restructuring of the business.

[14] Restructuring agreements under Article 182-*bis* of the Bankruptcy Law are agreements that may be entered into by and between an entrepreneur in a state of distress and a number of creditors representing at least 60% of all the relevant claims. These agreements require approval by the competent bankruptcy court to be effective and, in order to be approved, must be accompanied by an opinion of an expert, appointed by the entrepreneur, evaluating the feasibility of the agreement, with particular reference to the regular payment of the claims of those creditors who are not a party to the agreement itself.

- following the filing of a 'blank petition' for a composition with creditors under Article 161(6) of the Bankruptcy Law; and
- in the context of a composition with creditors.

3.3 New money privilege

In the context of a bankruptcy liquidation, creditors' rights are satisfied in accordance with Article 111 of the Bankruptcy Law, which provides that amounts arising from the liquidation are distributed to the creditors in accordance with the following order:
- payment of pre-deductible claims;
- payment of claims secured by special liens over assets sold in compliance with the order provided by law; and
- payment of unsecured claims.

With specific reference to pre-deductible claims, Articles 182-*quater* and 182-*quinquies* of the Bankruptcy Law provide, among other things, that:
- claims arising from loans granted in performance of a composition with creditors or a restructuring agreement approved by the relevant court are fully (100%) pre-deductible; and
- the debtor filing a petition for composition with creditors or approval of a restructuring agreement, may request the court to authorise it to take out loans, to be repaid as pre-deductible claims, to finance its ongoing operations and the restructuring process, or to support its financial needs before the opening of the relevant proceeding (the court may also authorise the debtor to grant pledges, mortgages and assignments of receivables by way of security, as guarantees thereof).

The provisions relating to pre-deductibility of claims arising from loans granted in the context of a composition with creditors or a restructuring agreement are also applicable to shareholders' loans (up to 80% of the overall amount), as an exception to the provisions of Articles 2467 and 2497-*quinquies* of the Civil Code. In the absence of an equitable subordination principle, Article 2467 (expressly applying to limited liability companies only) provides that claims arising from shareholders' loans are subordinated to the payment of the company's other creditors (to the extent that they have to be repaid, where the debt was incurred in the year immediately preceding the bankruptcy declaration) if, at the time the shareholders' loan was made, it resulted in an excessive imbalance in the company's indebtedness compared to its relevant net worth, or in a financial condition in which it would have been reasonable to carry out an equity contribution. Article 2497-*quinquies* provides for the application of Article 2467 to intra-group financings, executed either by the controlling entity or between entities subject to the latter's direction and coordination.

Finally, it is worth mentioning that, according to certain case law, directors' liability for a company's bankruptcy may also arise in respect of any entity exercising *de facto* administration of that company, a circumstance which has been deemed to occur where strict conditions were imposed by the lender in the context of a loan agreement, thereby substantially limiting the borrower's independent management.

Legal structuring of direct lending deals: Spain

Iñigo de Luisa
Iñigo Rubio
Cuatrecasas, Gonçalves Pereira

1. Introduction

The Spanish banking sector has experienced a radical transformation in recent years due to the financial crisis and the latest regulation at local and EU level, which has introduced a new framework and several measures to improve their control and supervision and eventually, if required, to deal with their dissolution. As a result, after a consolidation process involving several Spanish financial entities and the disappearance of the savings banks (*cajas de ahorros*), the Spanish banking sector has been reduced to few financial institutions (mainly, banks and credit financial entities – *establecimientos financieros de crédito* or 'EFCs').

This situation has provided an opportunity to new players, non-traditional lenders or debt funds, to come to Spain to provide loans and alternative financing. Lending is not a reserved banking activity in Spain. As a result, there is significant flexibility, since neither a licence nor an authorisation is required to grant loans and credit (and consequently to become a beneficiary of any related security or guarantee). This flexibility extends to both origination of loans and those becoming secondaries by assignment. As a result, shadow banking is increasingly becoming an alternative source of financing alongside the traditional banking system in Spain.

For the past five years these new financial players have been very active in direct lending and secondary debt trading, in particular for short-term financing. Normally, such direct lending in Spain is focused on small and medium-sized enterprises rather than individuals, since consumer loans are subject to special and more restrictive regulation. In addition to debt funds and alternative lenders, asset managers and loans servicers have also emerged as new actors in Spanish financial transactions. Until a few years ago, the arranger or the leading lender would be willing to undertake these tasks and to become an agent under the loan due to its commercial relationship with the debtor, but now this role has been adopted by more specialised entities.

With this flexible set-up for lending activities in Spain, there have only been a few specific pieces of legislation which have regulated new financing alternatives. For instance, Law 5/1015 on Promoting Business Financing, deals with crowdfunding, requiring that this activity only be rendered through a platform that complies with certain legal requirements and that should have been previously authorised and registered in the special registers of the Spanish National Securities Market Commission (the CNMV). Law 5/2015 also introduces certain measures to facilitate access to funding for small and medium-sized enterprises and to promote alternative sources of financing and corporate financing mechanisms.

In addition, new opportunities for non-traditional lenders at attractive returns have opened up because of new limitations, levels of provision, the cost of capital and controls affecting traditional banks; all of which have served to act as disincentives for traditional lending transactions in certain sectors or for certain players.

Despite the flexibility outlined above, any individual or entity entering into financial transactions or providing financial services in Spain could eventually be required by the Ministry of Economy periodically to disclose any information in connection with its activities, or be subject to inspections by Bank of Spain to evidence whether the activity performed is subject to supervision.

In general, Spanish law contemplates a number of legal limitations in connection with lending transactions. We will elaborate further in other parts of this chapter, but by way of introduction, at this stage, we will mention the following:

- anti-money laundering regulations and 'know your customer' requirements;
- forms of security available (in particular, mortgages) and associated costs (especially, stamp duty, notarisation fees and, if applicable, registration fees);
- withholding tax on interest paid (normally solved by having a Spanish or EU entity as the lender);
- the requirement for non-Spanish entities to have a Spanish tax identification number for statistical purposes; and
- other general limitations on financial assistance, corporate benefits and insolvency law, which may be applicable to the deal.

2. Structuring direct lending transactions

As we have previously noted, Spanish law does not require any specific licence or authorisation for lending activities, and therefore there is no need to have a regulated entity for these purposes. Only in the case of entities lending to consumers does Law 2/2009 require lenders to be registered in the consumer registry of any autonomous community where it provides lending activities.

Therefore, the investment vehicle can be selected by the lender on the basis of considerations of tax efficiency.

From a Spanish tax perspective, when considering the structure to be adopted in this type of transaction, it is important to take into account the general tax consequences arising from the payment of interest, the running of the business and the potential withdrawal of investment.

In this regard, when funding is granted by an entity that is non-resident in Spain for tax purposes (the lender) for the benefit of an entity resident in Spain for tax purposes (the borrower), the common structure is for the lender to be resident for tax purposes in another EU member state in order to benefit from the exemption on Spanish domestic withholding tax on interest. According to the relevant Spanish legislation, interest would be exempted in Spain and, therefore, no withholding tax would arise, provided that:

- the lender is resident for tax purposes in an EU member state;
- it is the beneficial owner of the interest payment; and
- it does not obtain the interest through a permanent establishment in Spain,

nor through a permanent establishment located outside the European Union, nor through a tax haven.

In any case, in order to apply this exemption, the lender should provide the corresponding tax residency certificate issued by the relevant tax authorities prior to the payment of interest.

Ireland and Luxemburg are the countries most frequently chosen to incorporate vehicles that would act as lender to a Spanish entity, as the legislation of these countries contains favourable tax regimes for the day-to-day business of the vehicle and for its potential exit from the investment. Borrowers are usually companies, either *sociedades anónimas* (SAs) or *sociedades limitadas* (SLs). There are differences between these two forms of entity (minimum share capital level, shares versus units representing the capital, etc). However, for the lenders' perspective both entities are suitable borrowers.

The structure of a loan transaction will primarily depend on the capital structure of the company. Generally, small and medium-sized Spanish companies are mainly financed by banks with which they have a long-standing relationship, and, depending on the level of indebtedness, these banks may have security over a substantial part of the assets of the company. There is therefore a need to ensure that the borrower can offer the lender security in the form of unencumbered assets, and ideally to structure the financing in such a way that there is no need for recourse to other assets.

The 'double luxco' structure has become relatively common in Spain, especially when the lender is a foreign entity, as they are generally more comfortable with a structure that has been tested and proved to work in terms of allowing effective enforcement of security over shares. The enforcement of security rights over shares is not really a form of proceeding that could work efficiently in Spain, with the exception of pledges of shares granted in accordance to the Royal Decree Law 5/2005, which implements the EU Directive on financial collateral arrangements (Directive 2002/47/EC) and which has proved to work efficiently in several cases, particularly with regard to pledges over shares of listed companies.

In those cases where the financing is secured by real estate assets, lenders will generally be comfortable with the asset itself as collateral altogether with the cash-flow generated by the project.

Additionally, we have recently seen a substantial number of transactions secured with the rights over the invoices of the debtor companies and their other receivables, either directly or indirectly. Where this happens in a direct manner, the borrower pledges the rights over the amounts to be paid under invoices issued to its debtors. Such pledges of credit rights, unlike pledges of shares, do work efficiently in Spain and allow the creditor to receive payment under the pledged invoice by way of a set-off against the amounts due from the borrower or by assignment of promissory notes (*pagarés*) issued by the debtor.

Indirect factoring transactions have been implemented by the issuance of commercial paper instruments by the borrower. The commercial paper is issued on the Spanish Alternative Fixed-Income Market (MARF) and subscribed to by the lender, who at the same time can obtain liquidity by selling the bonds on the market. MARF has been a great tool for small and medium-sized undertakings seeking to access financing for SMEs, and even for large companies such as El Corte Inglés, which, as publicly reported, recently issued a €300 million promissory notes programme on MARF.

3. Key Spanish legal issues

3.1 Security

From a security perspective, any *in rem* security over Spanish assets (mainly mortgages and pledges) and personal guarantees provided by Spanish obligors would be governed by Spanish law. When structuring the Spanish security package, either on origination or on secondary trading by means of subrogation, it is critical to analyse the assets available and how to mitigate potential costs when granting and executing the security in Spain (ie, stamp duty, registration and notarisation fees, etc). Also note that non-credit institutions cannot benefit from certain types of security such as floating mortgages (Article 153-*bis* of the Spanish Mortgage Law). Finally, note that lenders should be recorded as direct beneficiaries of the security in the applicable registers (ie, land register or moveable asset register), and that it is not possible to appoint a security agent or trustee as beneficiary on behalf of the lenders in the applicable public register.

3.2 Enforcement

From an enforcement perspective, it is critical, in order to be entitled to enforce in Spain through straightforward executive summary judicial proceedings (*procedimiento ejecutivo*), that the finance documents are notarised as public documents. Appropriate Spanish language on enforcement in Spain should also be included in the facility agreement. In particular, reference to enforcement through the mechanisms provided under Royal Decree Law 5/2005 which implements in Spain the EU Directive on Financial Collateral Arrangements, is a must for enforcement of pledges of credit rights and of shares, even provided all other requirements are fulfilled. Notarial enforcement proceedings are also available, but are not the usual route selected by the creditor due to timing and formality constraints. Finally, as we will explain in detail below under heading 4, not all breaches and defaults under a facility agreement will lead to an event of default which Spanish courts would admit for enforcement purposes. Traditionally, only essential, continuous and severe breaches will allow the lenders to enforce the security. Other limitations and restrictions to enforcement apply when the obligor is an individual person according to consumer protection legislation (ie, when the mortgaged property is the debtor's main domicile).

3.3 Tax

From a tax perspective, the lender is normally a Spanish limited company (SL) or an EU entity, in order to avoid withholding tax on interest paid.

As regards stamp duty, applying for certain tax exemptions (for instance, under

Law 2/1994 in the case of subrogation or amendment of mortgage loans) or executing certain security before the Spanish notary by means of a *póliza* document as opposed to a public deed, may avoid triggering stamp duty while allowing the instrument to enjoy the same benefits as public documents.

3.4 Insolvency

From an insolvency perspective, if the borrower is declared insolvent, a two-year claw back period applies, and all transactions entered into by the debtor will be scrutinised. Any act or agreement which is deemed to be detrimental for the debtor's estate will be null and void. If the loan provides new money, in general, it will be presumed that it is not detrimental. However, if the new loan merely replaces a previous obligation and enjoys additional new security it will be avoided. On the other hand, security subject to Royal Decree Law 5/2005 could be enforced and no insolvency rules would apply since it would be ring-fenced. Restructuring agreements at pre-insolvency stages which comply with certain requirements and majorities would also be ring-fenced and would not be rescinded.

3.5 Corporate law

From a corporate perspective, it should be noted that some specific rules will apply in certain cases. For instance, Spanish entities are required to approve the transaction at shareholder level when selling, contributing or charging their 'essential assets', meaning assets of a value of more than 25% of the company's balance sheet (Article 160(f) of the Spanish Law on Corporations). It may be the case in certain situations that the Spanish borrower cannot be restricted from making distributions to shareholders. Finally, be aware of financial assistance prohibitions which could also be applicable to Spanish obligors in the context of share purchase deals.

3.6 Governing law

Regarding the governing law of the finance documentation, although Spanish law provides a creditor-friendly environment and offers a reliable judicial enforcement procedure, English law is often used as an alternative applicable law in the finance documentation in Spanish lending transactions. Loan Market Association templates, either on origination or trading, are often used since international debt providers are more familiar with such documentation. However, in any case, Spanish security will be subject to Spanish law. Notarisation in Spain of the finance documentation, even if it is subject to English law, would also be advisable for eventual enforcement purposes.

When English law is the governing law of the finance documentation, this also allows access to restructuring tools such as the English scheme of arrangement. However, now Spanish insolvency law provides several similar tools, such as the court-sanctioned restructuring agreement (*homologación del acuerdo de refinanciación*), and this advantage is not so important anymore. In most cases, the choice of English law has a purely commercial motive, since the debt at issue will be more easily transferable to potential international buyers.

However, Brexit may impact the use of English law in the near future, due to the uncertainties that may result in connection with the recognition of English law in some foreign jurisdictions.

4. Enforcement considerations

Under Spanish law, not all the events of default listed under a standard loan agreement will be admissible for enforcement purposes before Spanish courts. In any case, it is also usual to grant to the borrower a rectification period to solve the default situation. Only essential, continuous and severe defaults will be admissible at Spanish courts for enforcement purposes. Therefore, non-payment, breaches of financial ratios or undertakings granting additional security are typical situations which Spanish courts would accept when enforcing security. Cross-default and cross-acceleration provisions might not be enough. On the other hand, a mere breach of an information covenant will not lead to an enforcement proceeding before Spanish courts.

Individual enforcement is usually available in Spanish loan documentation if the majority level for enforcement has not been reached. However, in general, individual enforcement will not allow enforcement of security, only of personal guarantees, if applicable.

Intercreditor agreements are usually part of the finance documents in Spanish loan transactions; in particular when dealing with different layers of debt. These agreements regulate the relationship between different creditors and are critical due to the sharing and turnover provisions, waterfall clauses, limitations to enforcement and the process of making decisions requiring majority levels among creditors. Insolvency courts will not have regard to the intercreditor arrangements, but only to insolvency law, in order to determine the classification of credit claims, distributions and privileges. However, each creditor may claim under the intercreditor agreement against the other creditors, forcing them to honour the terms agreed.

5. Key insolvency issues

Insolvency proceedings against the borrower will preclude enforcement of the lender's security rights (or would stay or suspend any proceedings already initiated). A declaration of bankruptcy triggers an automatic stay of all the enforcement actions (with certain exceptions, such as security interests over collateral that is not necessary to continue the ordinary course of business).

In addition, according to Article 61.3 of the Spanish Insolvency Act, any clause establishing the right to terminate an agreement, based only on the borrower or obligor's declaration of insolvency, will be held not to have effect and become null.

Where a Spanish borrower or obligor claims pre-insolvency status following the filing before the Spanish courts of Article 5-*bis* notice, this will, in general, stay or suspend any enforcement proceeding already initiated. During the insolvency proceedings this stay on enforcement will continue for a maximum period of one year.

Equitable subordination is regulated in Article 93.2.1º of the Spanish Insolvency Act. Creditors holding a stake of at least 5% in the debtor (if the shares are listed) or 10% (if the debtor is not a listed company) at the time of granting the loan (ie, when the credit arises), will qualify as a specially related party, with its claim being subordinated (and its security avoided).

Should the lender act as a *de facto* administrator (shadow director), this would also mean that the lender will qualify as a specially related creditor and its claim, even if it is deemed to be privileged, will be subordinated (Article 93.2.2º of the Spanish Insolvency Act) and any security will be declared void. For instance, forcing the debtor to take certain business decisions at board level due to covenants under the finance documents, or controlling the debtor's bank accounts, or exercising voting rights at a shareholders' meeting would lead the courts to consider the creditor to be a *de facto* administrator or shadow director and its claim will be subordinated.

According to Article 93.3 of the Spanish Insolvency Act, it is presumed that assignments of credits from specially related parties would be classed as subordinated, provided that the acquisition occurred within the two-year period before the declaration of insolvency.

As mentioned, claw-back actions or stays of proceedings would not apply to security granted under Royal Decree Law 5/2005, which implements in Spain the EU Directive on Financial Collateral Arrangements, since such security will be ring-fenced and Spanish insolvency law will not apply.

Spanish insolvency law also provides that a director may be personally liable for the debtor's credit claims under certain circumstances.

6. Rescue financing

Spanish insolvency law provides for different treatment for out-of-court and in-court rescue financing. Out-of-court financing is also treated differently depending on whether or not it is granted within the scope of a refinancing agreement.

6.1 Rescue financing granted in connection with a refinancing agreement

Financing granted under a refinancing agreement which meets all the relevant statutory requirements, is considered in its entirety as an administrative expense (*crédito contra la masa*) with priority over any other insolvency claims (except privileged secured claims), and is paid as it becomes due (a waterfall privilege).

This privilege will only apply within two years from the date that new money was granted. Additionally the new money would have to be granted under a refinancing agreement executed before October 1 2016. After this two-year transitional period, the 'old' new money regime applies (meaning, 50% will be considered as an administrative expense, and the other 50% as a general privileged claim).

The main limitations are that:
- this new money does not have a super-priority, and therefore in a liquidation scenario, the new money ranks junior to any other administrative expenses; and
- there are no priming liens available in Spain over previously encumbered assets.

Additionally, there is a possibility for the insolvency administrator to modify the ordinary payment schedule established by the new money agreements and to extend the terms of payment. This circumstance results in heightened uncertainty for the rescue lenders and does not encourage this type of deal, due to the fact that a third party (the insolvency administrator) may affect the amortisation schedule that has been negotiated and contractually agreed by the new money lender.

The new money privilege applies even when funding is provided by the debtor or an inside party, except for new money resulting from increases in share capital. Interest payments will be deemed to be subordinated claims, however.

With a new money transaction structured in the context of a court-sanctioned scheme the claw-back risk is mitigated. Indeed, in the context of a court-sanctioned scheme the claw-back risk, according to the letter of the law, is eliminated.

In any event, and from a practical perspective, it is key to include contractual mechanisms within the credit facilities to allow the lenders of rescue funding to benefit from the new money privilege on an ongoing basis within the insolvency proceedings. These mechanisms could consist of an acceleration of the maturity schedule, or prepayments within the insolvency proceeding, or other contractual provisions which allow the new money lender to capture the insolvency cash flows.

6.2 Rescue financing granted outside a refinancing agreement

Rescue financing granted outside a refinancing agreement does not benefit from any privilege or senior ranking against other creditors of the debtor and, therefore, the general rules regarding claim classification within an insolvency proceeding will apply. In the case of rescue financing granted outside a refinancing agreement, it is key for the new money lender to structure a security package which may provide a satisfactory loan-to-value ratio. In those instances where no security package can be implemented, the new money lender's claim will be classed as an unsecured claim in the context of the debtor's insolvency proceeding, ranking equally with other unsecured claims and being junior to secured claims.

The risk of claw-back cannot be ruled out as such loans are not protected by statute. However, there are strong arguments (based on existing case law) to justify the view that claw-back would not apply if the refinancing involves new money and an extension of maturity, where security is in place and the level of security is reasonable for the amount of new money provided.

With regard to such transactions, it is always advisable to obtain the opinion of independent experts, particularly as to fairness, in order to protect them from future claw-back actions, and to build up a comprehensive record of the negotiation, the risks involved at the time of granting the new money and the transaction documentation, in case any challenges are brought against the transaction in the context of a claw-back action.

6.3 Rescue financing within insolvency proceedings

The absence of provision for debtor-in-possession financing is probably one of the main omissions from the various reforms of insolvency law that have been enacted in Spain during recent years. This is one of the reasons, albeit not the sole reason, for liquidation being the default outcome when a company files for insolvency (the liquidation rate in Spain is still around 90% of insolvencies filed, with very low creditor recovery levels). This is likely a result of the Spanish Insolvency Act ignoring the fact that, when filing for insolvency, companies unable to meet their financial obligations often need further financing to pay for the administration expenses of the case and to continue operating. Without this financing, the only outcome is liquidation. There is no incentive for post-petition financing at the initial stage of the insolvency process such as is provided for in other jurisdictions (such as, for example, Section 364 of the US Bankruptcy Code), and there is no statutory framework for the debtors promptly to access during the initial phase of any financing mechanisms which is not too burdensome and is subject to the general rules applicable to the administration of the debtor's estate and does not benefit from specific incentives or privileges. On the contrary, the entirety of the new money claim will have the status of an administrative expense, but with no super-priority over other administrative expenses and, on the contrary, ranking junior to other administrative expenses, such as labour law claims. As mentioned above, unfortunately, Spanish insolvency law does not provide for priming liens over previously encumbered assets.

New financing within an insolvency proceeding will require the approval of the insolvency administrator and, in some instances, the insolvency judge (when the financing transaction entails the granting of liens or encumbrances over any of the debtors' free or unencumbered assets). The risk of claw-back will not be applicable since the financing is authorised within the insolvency process.

Further, Spanish insolvency law has clarified the regime applicable to the financing of viability plans that support reorganisation (ie, exit financing). Under the Spanish Insolvency Act, claims resulting from exit financing granted in connection with composition agreements (*convenio*) are considered an administrative expense in their entirety, benefiting from the privileges of this type of claim.

Spanish insolvency law's failure to establish a statutory scheme to promote debtor-in-possession financing is made all the more clear by the total absence of a debtor-in-possession market in Spain (while in other countries, it is a very active and significant market) and the lack of liquidity that characterises Spanish insolvency proceedings, where debtors find themselves with no liquidity available to fund their ongoing operations unless they have been able to stockpile cash.

7. New money strategies

Of great relevance for new money lenders is consideration of how to structure and plan their exit strategy when entering into a new money transaction. In this regard, special attention should be paid to the mechanisms available under Spanish insolvency law to disenfranchise shareholders.

Debt-for-equity swaps are technically structured under Spanish law as capital increases by means of set-off (debt being set off against a certain number of shares of the debtor) or contribution in kind (the contribution being transfer of the debt, which is automatically extinguished by confusion). In both cases shareholders' support (up to certain relevant majorities) is necessary.

Under Spanish law there are no mechanisms which facilitate the takeover of distressed companies by creditors by way of a debt-for-equity swap. The cram-down of the equity, even in those cases where shareholders may be 'underwater' and they may have no economic interest in their equity, always requires the approval of shareholders. This provides shareholders with leverage in these situations, despite the fact that the real value at stake is zero or close to zero.

To tackle this issue, and perhaps as a middle ground, Spanish insolvency law includes a rebuttable presumption as to the liability of the debtor's shareholders when they reject, without a reasonable cause, a debt-for-equity swap, another capitalisation process or the issue of convertible obligations, where the result is frustration of a collective refinancing or a court-sanctioned scheme. As a result, should the debtor finally file for insolvency, the shareholders could be held liable for any shortfall for creditors within the insolvency.

Despite this, it is still the case that , unless a consensual deal is reached, it is very difficult for a new money lender to take control of the equity of an undertaking in a distressed situation, unless it opts for other more cumbersome strategies such as the enforcement of a pledge over the shares (if such a pledge was included within the security package) or it can force a strategy within the insolvency proceeding aimed at taking control of the assets through, for example, liquidation.

Recent trends in European cross-border restructurings

Arturo Gayoso
Deloitte Financial Advisory

1. Introduction

During 2014 and 2015, we have seen the beginning of the recovery of the economy in Europe due to measures carried out by European governments and the European Central Bank (with its stimulus liquidity policies), the positive macroeconomic effects from the continuing drop in oil prices, significant equilibrium in the prices of commodities and a strengthening of domestic consumption. With this positive environment, financial markets have retained enough liquidity to facilitate refinancings, amend and extend transactions and mergers and acquisitions deals, thereby avoiding a marked increase in restructuring activity. The obvious focuses for 2016 in Europe's restructuring market remain:
- high-yield bond financing that originated two or three years ago due to the special situation of some companies (oil and gas, transport, etc) and their markets;
- final refinancing for those amend and extend deals closed in the past – the positive environment should allow the search for a final solution;
- improvements in European insolvency regimes to facilitate solutions and to avoid liquidations.

The European leveraged market has seen significant growth since Lehman's bankruptcy, and high-yield bonds have become an alternative for the traditional loan sector. As an important part of financing of European companies, high-yield bonds have been affected by the downturn, and, as a consequence, the number of high-yield bonds trading at distressed levels has been progressively higher.

Now, there are a plenty of signs that the expectation that the number of high-yield restructurings should pick up significantly from the low levels of previous years, may translate into a reality. So, in this environment, companies with high-yield restructuring processes need to know how to navigate their way through them and to be aware of the main differences from 'normal' restructurings, so as to achieve a successful result.

Since the financial crisis we have realised that low interest rates and fairly open capital markets allowed companies in distress to refinance their outstanding debt at reasonable interest rates. When the credit crunch came, some of those companies were (and currently still are) what the European financial market participants began to call 'unfinished deals': companies maintaining non-sustainable levels of debt, postponing real restructuring for the coming years and delaying definitive solutions.

Although there was a sense that these unfinished deals would be resolved once European banks had finished their deleveraging processes (and alternative lenders had capitalised on this opportunity), the reality is that some large-scale European restructuring deals are still pending, and they will, undoubtedly, play a key role in the future of the restructuring market.

Alongside this situation, the effects of lower commodity prices in some sectors, geopolitical risks and the digital economy jeopardising former business models will continue to precipitate restructuring activity, especially in the oil and gas, mining, commodities and retail sectors. In some of them, the timeframe for restructuring may be accelerated due to the anxiety of lenders and bondholders to find quick solutions for their outstanding debt.

At the same time, a number of jurisdictions in Europe (especially Spain, Italy, France and Germany), have gradually begun to implement amendments to their restructuring laws (including some reforms borrowed from the US and UK restructuring schemes to facilitate solutions for restructuring deals). Some of those reforms have already started to bear fruit in a number of areas, while in others there is work to do. More importantly, these changes are steps to building a progressive (and common) European environment for cross-border restructurings.

2. Trends in the European leveraged finance market

2.1 High-yield bonds

The European financial debt market has seen huge growth since Lehman's bankruptcy. Progressive capital requirements to meet Basel III, evolution of interest rates at historic lows and the injections of monetary stimulus by the European Central Bank (to encourage economic recovery), created the perfect environment to reduce corporate lending and to open the traditional financial market for new ways of financing, like high-yield bonds. As a result of this trend, the European high-yield market has grown considerably, reflecting the appetite of investors to accept risky investments, in their continuous objective to achieve the yield. Although this evolution (from a traditional loan market to a complex capital structures market) allowed European companies to find resources and financial solutions during the downturn, it is also true that it has caused a reasonable degree of uncertainty about how such debt would be restructured in the future, if it becomes necessary.

During the last few years, we have had the opportunity to see how to manage credit risks in this new financial market, and how the different players react when faced with restructuring situations. In this context, high-yield bond restructurings present remarkable differences from normal loan restructurings.

(a) Bondholder representatives

One big difference between an ordinary loan restructuring and a high-yield bond restructuring, is the number of bondholders that the company has to negotiate with:
- Initially, it can be difficult just to identify them individually or to try to organise them for a meeting to explore an agreement;
- In addition, bondholders tend to have, naturally, different agendas or

Leverage Finance Volumes By Year (mil. €)

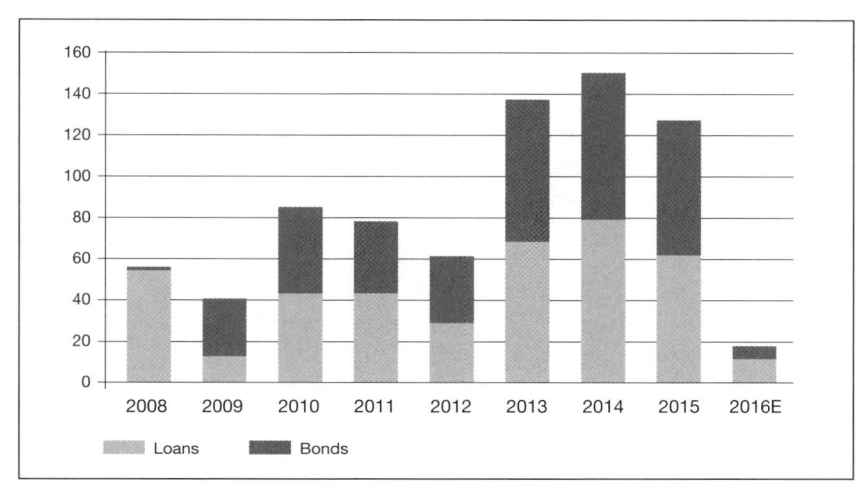

*Source: S&P Capital IQ LCD. * To March 25, 2016*

European High-Yield Bond Issuance (€B)

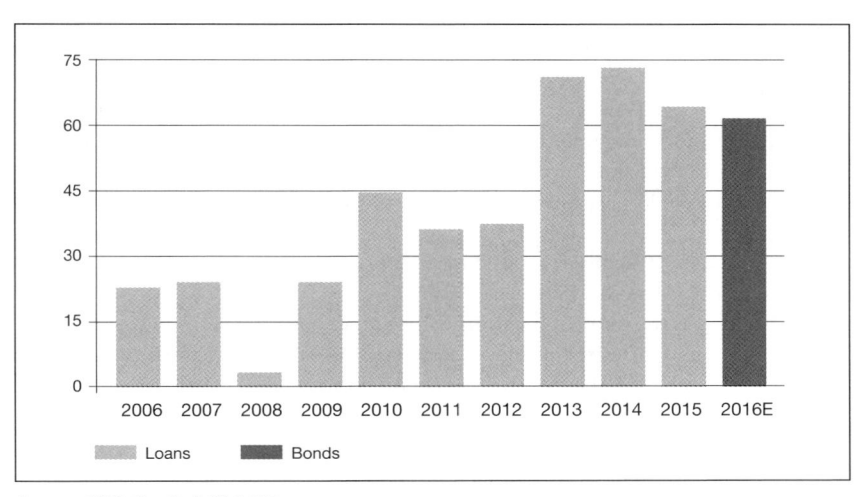

Source: S&P Capital IQ LCD.

    interests that need to be reconciled (beforehand) to maximise the benefits of the restructuring;
- Issues of precedence tend to be of greater importance due the fact that, usually, there are multiple issuances outstanding. So, in some processes, getting a bondholder agreement is extremely difficult, outside a formal insolvency proceeding.

(b) ***Protection of bondholders***
In contrast with senior loans which have maintenance covenants (under which a company needs to maintain compliance with financial metrics in order to avoid defaulting on its debt), high-yield bond deals usually have incurrence covenants (which kick in only when a company incurs additional debt or makes restricted payments to the detriment of bondholders), meaning that it is quite difficult to anticipate an event that will trigger a need for restructuring until a default situation has happened or is impending. Given the limits of this type of covenant and the evolution of the market since the Lehman's crisis, bondholders have gradually incorporated more and more protections into their investments, allowing them to play a significate role in restructuring processes. These include:

- the development of senior secured notes allowing bondholders to lead restructuring negotiations;
- the design of structures where all creditors of a specific class vote with equal weight on enforcement; and
- setting the level of consent required for key economic amendments at 90% (or more) of the issuers.

(c) ***Restrictions on bondholders***
Bondholders are usually reluctant to participate in restructuring negotiations from the beginning, as the possession of non-public information will restrict them from trading in the bonds. Consequently, management of the information divulged in conversations and potential agreements becomes a major task, until all the information gets into the public domain. Time consumption and the participants' asymmetric access to information (for a period of time) are important issues to overcome in the process. Company, legal and financial advisers perform a crucial role in ensuring the feasibility of the deal, during the restricted information period.

When a high-yield bond restructuring commences, investors have different approaches and outlooks:

- Distressed debt investors will begin to build positions in the company as soon as the restructuring process starts, usually at big discounts to the nominal value of the bonds. They tend to assume a haircut (or postponement of recovery of their debt) with new terms and conditions including:
    - taking first or second lien secured debt;
    - exchanging unsecured notes or new secured debt at a discount;
    - buying back-notes at a discount;
    - taking equity issued during the refinancing process.
- Par investors usually desire to avoid such situations. For them, haircuts or limitations on their capacity to recover the full face value of their bonds are, from the very beginning, outcomes that they are reluctant to accept.

Usually, both positions are represented in the many high-yield bond restructurings in the current European market, requiring:

- big efforts to align such divergent interests; and

- economic capacity on the part of the company to maintain business feasibility during the restructuring process.

2.2 Loans

During recent years, there have been a large number of amend and extend deals in Europe, postponing definitive solutions for ongoing debt. There have been a number of reasons behind this phenomenon:
- less developed insolvency markets, unable to provide restructuring solutions in a short period of time;
- the heterogeneous composition of bank syndicates, with divergent interests favouring different methods to carry out restructuring processes;
- the presence of enough liquidity in the market to solve short-term issues, thereby postponing discussion about the feasibility of companies in the medium-to-long term.

The hope that time (and recovery of the economy) would allow the companies to improve their capacity to repay their debt encouraged lenders to extend the maturity of the loans and to provide more favourable conditions in the meantime. The reality of the European economy's performance showed that amend and extend arrangements could only offer a temporary solution. Now those cases (often referred to as 'unfinished deals') are progressively coming back in search of a definitive solution.

The definitive solution is arriving, as certain actions and decisions have created a positive environment to provide a complete and final restructuring process for those companies:
- First, during the last two years insolvency laws in Europe (mainly in France, Italy, Spain and Germany) have evolved in terms of providing more control and predictability and increased effectiveness of the restructuring processes. Increased legal certainty in the process (in the treatment for dissenting groups, protection for new money provided, etc) has been crucial in order to ensure effective solutions (which are protected by law);
- Secondly, the strength of capital market liquidity in some countries has allowed the provision of solutions for weak companies through sales or mergers (supported by new capital providers);
- Thirdly, progressive consolidation of the financial sector (and the special capital requirements of Basel III), has established standards for provisions and has facilitated solutions for non-sustainable debt;
- Fourthly, the asset quality review carried out in 2014 for the European Central Bank (with immediate action and revision of relevant rules in 2015) required banks to report any amend and extend deals where the borrower was in a financial difficulty, forcing them to make the necessary provisions much earlier. That review's stress test has been key in terms of changing the perspective of some processes, ensuring a complete restructuring solution.
- Fifthly, of the presence of alternative lenders in the market, providing new money, has accelerated refinancing procedures and ensured monitoring of operational restructuring of certain companies.

2.3 What we can expect for the future?

(a) High-yield bonds

High-yield bonds are progressively showing a distressed profile due to macroeconomic factors (economic slowdown in China; rate rises in the United States and their impact on European Central Bank and Bank of England decisions; the reverse in Brazil's growth; the uncertain future of economies in emerging markets; commodity price declines, etc). In spite of this, European defaults are not expected to be dramatic. Depending on how the economy performs in the immediate future (and the expectations at this moment are relatively optimistic) the market will have to face either a 'rapid impairment' or an 'under control' situation in the high-yield bonds sector. It is clear that a potential rapid increase in interest rates would cause a drop in prices in security markets, causing potential losses in the market value of bonds, and increasing the number of distress situations rapidly.

(b) Loans

The number of loans in the European market with a leverage ratio of more than 6:1 dropped in 2015 from more than 20% in 2014 to close to 15% in 2015 (according to S&P Capital IQ's Leveraged Commentary and Data). Although this circumstance would indicate a more conservative profile being adopted in the loan sector, there is no consensus that this is an accurate reflection of the market. In any case, a conservative approach would be more than welcome for the future if, at the end of the day, slower than expected economic growth in Europe results in credit troubles in the coming years

3. Restructuring outlook

According to market expectations, interest rate increases will not begin (at the earliest) before the middle of this year (2016) and, if capital markets remain as open as in 2015, an increase in restructuring activity is not anticipated. However, some sectors do present challenges and, for them there are opportunities to take advantage of a restructuring process.

3.1 Energy and commodities sector (oil and gas, mining, metals)

(a) Oil and gas

Oil and gas prices have been in decline since mid-2014 and this trend will continue to disrupt the sector in 2016. Many oil and gas companies with enormous capital expenditures are starting to have severe liquidity problems due to the current pricing pressure. In the immediate future, the 'lower for longer' oil and gas prices situation (and the expiry of many financial hedge agreements coupled with high leverage) may push a large proportion of the industry into restructuring.

(b) Mining and minerals

Natural resources are also under pressure, because prices for most raw materials are low. Many businesses have developed their production capacity based on continued growth in China and other emerging markets. Now, the slowdown in those economies is affecting producers of steel, metal and minerals, resulting in levels of debt that are non-sustainable and that need to be restructured.

These industries will (most likely) account for the majority of activity in restructuring and insolvency this year.

3.2 Transport and shipping

The sector has undergone significant change in recent years. Changes in regulation, the growth of alliances and intensive competition in prices are all impacting the market. In addition to this, the need for lenders to reduce their exposure in the sector (as a part of their strategies for meeting the Basel III requirements, coupled with the European Central Bank's current focus on shipping) and the potential difficulties of some companies when it comes to repaying their debt, will likely increase the restructuring activity in the industry.

3.3 Financial services

Restructuring activity in the European financial services sector continues under government regulations that are looking for robust bank capitalisation. Regulations have required banks to sell non-core assets to increase reserves and this process will continue. In addition, changes in banks' business models (moving into the digital era) could mean a new era in the sector.

The experience of recent years has shown that restructuring activities remain slow while there is easy access to capital. While no dramatic change is expected as regards access to capital, opportunities for restructuring will still remain available in various industries.

4. Conclusion

Since 2008, the credit markets have seen an increase in the complexity of capital structures, with intensive development of financial markets (through high-yield bonds) to complement the traditional loan sector. Historically, European companies were funded by corporate loans, syndicated to a number of banks that managed any situation with the borrower (as a restructuring process) in a reliable environment. Now, new capital structures have made restructuring processes more complex due to:

- the number of debt holders (a very large number who are not all identified clearly);
- the multiple agendas and interests of the various debt holders (distressed investors and par investors);
- the protections that have been introduced into debt holders' positions in order to enforce satisfactory restructuring conditions for them.

The outcomes of traditional corporate financial restructurings carried out in recent years have been influenced by various factors:

- the situation of the debt held by the various banks and their specific interests going into the restructuring process;
- the strength of the business plan of the company involved;

- the volatility of the surrounding economic conditions; and
- the need of additional liquidity.

During the downturn, banks have sometimes been reluctant to force a definitive restructuring solution on companies so long as they can afford to keep up interest payments to the bank. This type of decision has created a number of 'unfinished deals', whereby refinancing was effected through amend and extend transactions while awaiting better times for the provision of a definitive restructuring solution.

Now, favourable conditions and regulatory decisions (the evolution of insolvency laws in Europe, the strength of liquidity of the markets, the presence of alternative lenders providing operational and financial solutions, the stress testing of European banks and its implication in their provisions statements) are encouraging companies to face up to definitive restructuring solutions, and decreasing the number of unfinished deals.

During recent years, Europe's insolvency and restructuring regimes have attempted to move away from liquidation schemes towards arrangements that support business recovery. In this context, recent evolution in the French, Italian, German and Spanish regimes could be considered steps towards a progressive European approach to insolvency, within a complete and homogeneous legal framework. In the meantime, cross-border restructurings are being developed on a consensual basis, meaning more complex and longer restructurings due to the need to achieve unanimity before finalising an agreement.

Schemes of arrangement: theory and practice

Graham Lane
Iben Madsen
Willkie Farr & Gallagher LLP

1. Introduction

The scheme of arrangement has developed into an extremely useful and powerful pre-insolvency restructuring tool under English law.[1] A scheme is a court-sanctioned cram-in procedure under Part 26 of the Companies Act 2006 that can be used by a company to compromise its obligations, including to its secured creditors. The scheme is very flexible, as it can be used to propose pretty much any kind of compromise with a company's creditors (or some of them) provided it is fair. Schemes have typically been used to implement, amend and extend arrangements, debt write-downs and debt-for-equity swaps, including in respect of foreign companies. This chapter explores the strengths of schemes of arrangement, their key characteristics, and some common issues encountered when implementing a scheme. It also outlines the procedural requirements for a scheme.

In addition to its utility as a pre-insolvency restructuring tool, distressed debt investors should be aware of the implications of a scheme from a slightly different perspective. Because a scheme enables the cram-in of a dissenting minority within a class of creditors, even for companies incorporated and located in jurisdictions other than England and with debt not governed by English law, the use of a scheme can potentially negate an otherwise effective hold-out position or strategy.

A scheme of arrangement must be sanctioned by the court, and the court has lately exhibited a tendency to scrutinise the merits and procedural compliance of schemes closely, particularly in respect of foreign companies. The final section of this chapter examines the lessons from some of the latest scheme case law.[2]

2. What is a scheme of arrangement?

A scheme of arrangement is a statutory, court-approved process which allows a company to implement a compromise or arrangement with its creditors, or any class of them (including secured creditors).[3] A scheme of arrangement is available to a company under Part 26 of the Companies Act and is not a formal insolvency process.

---

1   Although the relevant legislation applies (with certain exceptions and/or amendments) throughout the United Kingdom, England is the UK jurisdiction in which the scheme has been most utilised and which has therefore developed the most significant body of case law. As a result, this chapter focuses on English schemes.
2   As at September 8 2016.
3   Although a scheme can also compromise the rights of a company's members, that is to say its shareholders, this chapter only considers schemes affecting creditors' rights as they are more pertinent in distressed debt investment scenarios.

Creditors affected by the scheme vote in classes according to their rights against the scheme company. A scheme permits the cram-in of a dissenting minority within a class of creditors, provided that the proposed arrangement or compromise receives the consent of at least 75% in value, representing a majority in number (the latter limb being sometimes referred to as the numerosity test), of creditors in such class who vote on the scheme. If the court sanctions a scheme which has been approved by the statutory majorities of each class of creditors compromised by it, the scheme will bind all such creditors, even those who vote against the scheme or abstain.

Because a scheme is a cram-in procedure which will bind the dissenting minority, it is subject to the approval of the court (discussed in further detail under heading 4.3 below). It is also open to challenge, including on grounds of unfair prejudice, by any affected person (not only a scheme creditor).

3. Purpose

In the context of distressed debt investments, the overriding purpose of a scheme of arrangement is to implement a pre-insolvency restructuring, by imposing a compromise or arrangement between a company and its creditors on a dissenting minority of creditors. Note that, in contrast to the cram-down mechanism that is available under the US Bankruptcy Code and which permits creditors in one class to impose a restructuring on another impaired class of creditors, a scheme of arrangement only enables a cram-in: that is, the statutory majorities of creditors in a class may impose the terms of a scheme on any dissenting minority within the same class, but an entire class of affected creditors cannot be forced to accept a scheme without the consent of the statutory majorities in that class. However, not all of a company's creditors must be included in a scheme, which can help provide a workaround solution in certain circumstances (discussed in further detail under heading 4.7 below).

The key advantages and disadvantages of a scheme of arrangement are summarised in Figure 1 below.

3.1 Pre-insolvency restructuring

One of the major strengths of a scheme of arrangement is that it is not a formal insolvency procedure, such as those available in Great Britain under the Insolvency Act 1986. Instead, a scheme is available to all eligible companies under the Companies Act.[4] Although the court must have jurisdiction in respect of a proposed scheme (discussed in further detail under heading 5.2 below), there is no insolvency test or measure that determines whether or when a scheme will be available to a company. Even more importantly, formal insolvency procedures are often value-destructive due to the associated stigma, whereas the scheme is a Companies Act procedure which is available pre-insolvency.[5]

---

[4] A company in a formal insolvency procedure can also utilise a scheme, for example as a mechanism to distribute the assets of the estate among the company's creditors. This chapter focuses solely on the scheme as a tool in a pre-insolvency restructuring.

[5] This is despite the fact that a pre-insolvency scheme will nevertheless often trigger insolvency termination provisions in a company's contracts, by virtue of being a 'composition or arrangement with creditors'.

3.2 Cram-in of dissenting minority

Section 899 of the Companies Act provides that, if a majority in number representing 75% in value of a company's creditors, or class of creditors, voting on a scheme at the creditors' meeting agree the proposed compromise or arrangement, the court may sanction such compromise or arrangement. This ability to cram-in a dissenting minority of creditors within each class is one of the major advantages of a scheme. It means that the compromise proposed pursuant to a scheme can be implemented without the consent of a 25% minority in each class of creditors and imposed on that minority.

A scheme is accordingly useful in lowering any consent threshold(s) that might otherwise be required in order to amend, or take certain actions under, a company's finance documents in connection with a restructuring. In circumstances where unanimous or super-majority consent is required under the finance documents, for example to write off debt or release security, a scheme will lower the approval threshold to the statutory majorities.

3.3 Binding on secured creditors

The Companies Act does not impose any limitation on the type of creditor that can be subject to a scheme. As a result, the rights of secured creditors (as well as unsecured creditors), including contingent creditors, can be compromised by a scheme. However, only creditors (in the sense of a person with a pecuniary claim) can be compromised: a scheme of arrangement cannot be used to affect a person's proprietary rights, such as the rights of a beneficial owner to trust property held by a company.[6]

4. Key characteristics

4.1 Flexibility

A key advantage of a scheme of arrangement is its flexibility. Part 26 of the Companies Act is not prescriptive, in that it allows a company to propose any kind of compromise or arrangement, provided that it is fair. Although schemes have for many years followed a fairly well-trodden path, effecting compromises such as releases of debt, debt-for-equity swaps, and amendments to the terms of or extensions of the maturity of debt, there is no limitation on the type of scheme of arrangement that can be proposed. This makes the scheme a very adaptable tool in restructurings.

4.2 Company involvement

The Companies Act allows the company itself, as well as any creditor or shareholder of the company, to propose a scheme of arrangement.[7] In practice, because the company itself must be party to the scheme and because the cooperation of the company's management is vital to the successful implementation of the scheme, the company must be fully on board. It is therefore usually the company itself that proposes the scheme.[8]

---

[6] *Re Lehman Brothers International (Europe) (in administration)* [2009] EWCA Civ 1161.
[7] In addition, an administrator or liquidator of the company may also propose a scheme.
[8] Although there have been exceptions, such as the Countrywide scheme (*In the matter of Castle Holdco 4 Limited and others* [2009] EWHC 3919 (Ch)).

Figure 1: Key advantages and disadvantages of a scheme of arrangement

Advantages	Disadvantages
Cram-in: A majority in number representing 75% in value of creditors within a class can bind the dissenting minority in that class.	**Court-driven process:** Court involvement brings attendant scrutiny and publicity. There is the opportunity for creditors to present a challenge.
Flexible: A company can propose pretty much any kind of compromise with its creditors (or some of them) provided it is fair. Schemes can be combined with other restructuring tools, such as company voluntary arrangements and pre-pack sales.	**Publicity:** A detailed explanatory statement of the background to and the terms of the scheme must be drawn up – similar to an offering circular. This must be sent to scheme creditors and filed at court, and is in effect a public document.
No insolvency: A scheme is not a formal insolvency process (although it can be utilised in an insolvency), making it a valuable restructuring tool that avoids stigma and value destruction.	**Execution risk:** Time and cost makes it preferable to have certainty that the requisite majorities will be achieved – for this reason, lock-up agreements are used and a 'Plan B' alternative is necessary.
Global: The courts can accept jurisdiction over foreign companies with a sufficient connection to England – such as English law-governed finance documents and/or the centre of main interests being in England.	**No automatic stay or recognition:** As a scheme is not an insolvency proceeding, there is no automatic moratorium (although this can be included in a waiver/lock-up agreement) or recognition under the EU Insolvency Regulation.[9]
Primary obligors only: It is only necessary to apply the scheme to each primary obligor (ie, direct borrower) – in general, guarantor companies' obligations are considered so closely connected that they will be varied in accordance with the compromise of the primary obligors without being separately covered by the scheme. Third-party guarantees can also be fully released, provided there is some give and take (ie, there is some benefit to the creditors).	**No cram-down:** A scheme cannot bind out-of-the-money creditors without the consent of a majority in number representing 75% in value of each class of such creditors. If their consent cannot be obtained, out-of-the-money creditors can be left behind using a pre-pack, provided their claims can be released under the intercreditor agreement. This approach requires robust valuation evidence.
Availability: There are no formal requirements or tests, such as solvency or insolvency, needed in order for a company to propose a scheme.	**Cost:** Schemes can be expensive, depending on complexity. Schemes of foreign companies with English law debt require expert opinions on recognition. Schemes of foreign companies with non-English law debt require a prior shift of the centre of main interests or a change in governing law.
Tax: With careful structuring, a scheme can be used to release debt in a tax-neutral manner.	**Potential for challenge:** A scheme can be challenged by affected creditors (including out-of-the-money creditors who have been left behind).

4.3 Court approval and fairness

Court approval is required at two stages of the scheme process. At the beginning of the process, the court's leave is necessary in order to convene meetings of the scheme creditors, pursuant to Section 896 of the Companies Act. Once the creditor meetings have taken place and the scheme has been approved by the statutory majorities, the court's approval is again needed; this time to sanction the scheme, pursuant to Section 899 of the Companies Act. The convening and sanction hearings are discussed in further detail under heading 6 on procedure below.

The scheme must be in a form that the court can approve: a scheme must be fair and reasonable and represent a genuine attempt to reach agreement between a company and its creditors. The court does not merely verify that the majority are acting in good faith and thereupon register the decision of the meeting; but at the same time the court will be slow to differ from the meeting, unless either the class has not been properly consulted, or the meeting has not considered the matter with a view to the interests of the class which it is empowered to bind, or some blot is found on the scheme.[10] The court must be satisfied that the scheme is a fair scheme, although it need not be the only fair scheme, or even (in the court's view) the best scheme.[11] In addition, it is recognised that in commercial matters, creditors are much better judges of their own interests than the courts.[12]

4.4 Compromise, consideration, and consent payments

A scheme cannot be an expropriation; it must be a genuine and effective arrangement or compromise. It must therefore involve some give and take, so that creditors must obtain some benefit that compensates them for the alteration of their rights under the scheme, although this does not mean that there cannot be any disadvantage to the scheme creditors.[13] Typical forms of consideration include shares, warrants and/or cash, but consideration can take any form provided it is reasonable. The test for reasonableness is whether the compromise represented by the alteration of rights under the scheme in exchange for the consideration is a compromise that can, by reasonable people conversant with the subject, be regarded as beneficial to those on both sides who are making it.[14] All scheme creditors must be provided with some consideration, whether they vote for or against the scheme or do not vote at all, otherwise the scheme will likely be deemed unfair.

Care should be taken in apportioning consideration between scheme creditors: because classes are determined by reference to creditors' rights both coming into and out of the scheme, a disparity of treatment between creditors within the same class

---

9   Note that, depending on the terms of Brexit that are negotiated with the European Union, formal insolvency proceedings such as administration may no longer benefit from automatic recognition within the European Union in future.
10 *Re National Bank Ltd* [1966] 1 All ER 1006 at [1021], citing a passage from *Buckley On The Companies Acts* (13th edition, 1957), p409.
11 *Re Van Gansewinkel Groep BV* [2015] EWHC 2151 (Ch) at [21].
12 *Re English, Scottish and Australian Chartered Bank* [1891-94] All ER Rep 775 at [778]-[779]; *Re Van Gansewinkel Groep BV* [2015] EWHC 2151 (Ch) at [22].
13 *Re NFU Development Trust Ltd* [1973] 1 All ER 153; *Re Osiris Insurance Ltd* [1999] 1 BCLC 182.
14 *Re Alabama, New Orleans, Texas and Pacific Junction Railway Co* [1886-90] All ER Rep Ext 1143 at [1152].

has the potential to fracture a class. Classes are discussed in further detail under heading 5.1 below.

It has become common practice to pay a consent fee (also known as an early-bird fee or a lock-up fee) only to certain scheme creditors, namely to those who agree to vote in favour of a scheme in advance of its launch by entering into a lock-up agreement prior to a certain date. The consent fee must be available to all scheme creditors who enter into the lock-up agreement prior to a reasonable deadline. In addition, the consent fee must only constitute compensation for the scheme creditors' efforts in assessing whether to support the scheme, as opposed to an inducement that would convince scheme creditors who would otherwise have voted against the scheme to enter into it. To avoid creating a class issue, the consent fee must therefore be relatively minimal in size[15] when compared with the overall value of the claims being schemed. If any debt was acquired by a scheme creditor at a discount, this should also be taken into account when determining the materiality of the fee.[16]

Although class questions are very fact-specific, in past cases, consent fees of up to 3% of the value of the claims being included in the scheme have been paid without causing class issues. However, in the Global Garden Products scheme, Snowden J looked closely at fees of 0.5% paid under a lock-up agreement. In the evidence, the fees were described as being designed to recognise the resource commitment required on the part of the scheme creditors to consider and evaluate the transaction.[17] The judge was not persuaded that the description would sustain close examination: there was no requirement to demonstrate that any work had actually been done; the fees would not be paid to scheme creditors who carried out the work but decided not to support the scheme; and nor would the fees be paid to scheme creditors who had carried out the work and supported the scheme if it was not approved or sanctioned.[18] Snowden J ultimately accepted that the fees were very unlikely to have a material effect on the decision of a creditor to support the scheme, on the basis that they were available to all scheme creditors and of relatively low value, and therefore that they did not give rise to a class issue. Nevertheless, this scrutiny highlights that it is vital to provide proper justification as regards any fees paid in connection with a scheme, as well as ensuring that the size of the fees cannot be said to have a material effect on a decision to support a scheme.

4.5 Rights against third parties

It is well established by case law that a scheme can vary or release creditors' rights against third parties where necessary in order to give effect to the arrangement that is proposed by the company.[19] This is particularly the case for guarantee obligations relating to the principal debt which is the subject of the scheme. In general,

---

15 *Re DX Holdings Ltd* [2010] EWHC 1513 (Ch) at [6]-[7]; *Re Primacom Holding GmbH* [2011] EWHC 3746 (Ch) at [55]-[57]; *Re Seat Pagine Gialle SPA* [2012] EWHC 3686 (Ch) at [14]-[22].
16 *Re Public Joint-Stock Company Commercial Bank "Privatbank"* [2015] EWHC 3299 (Ch) at [26].
17 *Re Global Garden Products Italy SpA* [2016] EWHC 1884 (Ch) at [15].
18 *Re Global Garden Products Italy SpA* [2016] EWHC 1884 (Ch) at [15] and [53].
19 *Re Lehman Brothers (Europe) International* [2009] EWCA Civ 1161 at [65]; *Re La Seda de Barcelona SA* [2010] EWHC 1364 (Ch) at [12]-[23]; *Re Magyar Telecom BV* [2013] EWHC 3800 (Ch) at [33]; *Re Van Gansewinkel Groep BV* [2015] EWHC 2151 (Ch) at [63]; *Re DTEK Finance BV* [2015] EWHC 1164 (Ch) at [18].

guarantor companies' obligations are considered so closely connected with those of the primary obligors (borrower companies) that they will automatically be varied in accordance with the compromise of the primary obligors without the need for a separate scheme.[20]

Third-party guarantees can also be fully released by a scheme without the guarantor company proposing a scheme itself, provided there is some give and take, that is to say some benefit accruing to the creditors.[21] In practice, the release of a third party, such as a guarantor which is not itself a scheme company or otherwise party to the scheme, is usually effected by a provision in the scheme which authorises an attorney to execute a deed of release in favour of the guarantor on behalf of all the scheme creditors.

4.6 Combination with other processes

A scheme can be even more powerful when used in combination with other processes. It is common practice that, in a scheme compromising the debt of a group of companies with multiple borrowers, the scheme proposed by each borrower company is made conditional on the approval of the scheme proposed by each other borrower company within that group. This is so that an effective overall restructuring can be achieved in respect of a group, rather than an unsatisfactory hotchpotch.

The DTEK arrangement[22] showcased the adaptability of the scheme in tandem with another process. DTEK involved a twin-track process of an exchange offer and consent solicitation with a fall-back to a scheme of arrangement if the requisite consent level for the consensual exchange offer was not achieved. The company sought the consent of at least 98% of the noteholders to the exchange offer, failing which it would implement the exchange of existing notes for new notes (with extended maturities) via a scheme. The process was simplified considerably in the DTEK case by providing that noteholders who had consented to participate in the exchange offer were also automatically deemed both to have approved the change in the governing law of the notes from New York to England (in order to achieve a sufficient connection with England so that the English court could exercise jurisdiction to approve the scheme, as to which see further detail under heading 5.2 below), and to have voted in favour of the scheme.

It is possible to make the scheme of a company inter-conditional with a procedure such as a company voluntary arrangement under the Insolvency Act, in order to achieve both a financial and an operational restructuring, as was the case with the restructuring of the Travelodge hotel group in 2012. In that case, a scheme of arrangement was used to write down debt and restructure the group's financial indebtedness, and a company voluntary arrangement was used to compromise its ailing hotel leasehold portfolio. The effectiveness of the scheme was conditional on the effectiveness of the company voluntary arrangement and vice versa, and this

---

20   However, security and guarantees granted by companies based in non-UK jurisdictions may be required to be re-taken immediately following a scheme in order to ensure effectiveness under local laws.
21   *Re La Seda de Barcelona SA* [2010] EWHC 1364 (Ch) at [12]-[23].
22   *Re DTEK Finance BV* [2015] EWHC 1164 (Ch).

approach assisted in achieving a balanced restructuring, in which the burden was shared and losses were imposed on the group's landlords as well as on its lenders.

Although Section 900 of the Companies Act provides that a court may approve a scheme where the whole or part of the undertaking or property of one company is transferred to another company, it is only permitted to do so in the context of the reconstruction or amalgamation of companies. Reconstruction has been held to mean that the shareholders of both the transferor and transferee companies must be substantially the same persons.[23] Section 900 therefore does not assist where a change of control is contemplated; for example to disenfranchise the sponsor in favour of one or more of the company's creditors. However, when combined with a pre-packaged sale carried out by an administrator appointed under the Insolvency Act (a 'pre-pack'), a scheme of arrangement under the remaining sections of Part 26 of the Companies Act can be used to implement an enforcement of security and change of ownership in favour of secured lenders.

When a scheme is combined with a pre-pack, a contractual transfer of the company's business and/or assets to a new corporate structure controlled by the secured creditors (a 'newco') can take place. The transfer itself is carried out by means of the pre-pack, which is effected by the appointed administrators (typically with the cooperation of the security agent), and is pre-arranged to occur immediately on the opening of the administration. As administration is a formal insolvency process currently subject to Council Regulation (EC) 1346/2000 of May 29 2000 (the 'EU Insolvency Regulation'),[24] the company's centre of main interests must be in Great Britain to use a pre-pack. Alternatively, depending on the terms of the underlying security documents, a receiver may be able to carry out the transfer in place of an administrator, avoiding the need for a formal insolvency process altogether.

The consideration for the pre-pack sale by the scheme company to the secured creditor-controlled newco is usually discharged by way of a credit bid of the debt held by such creditors, reducing the scheme company's indebtedness in part or in whole. The scheme comes into play in order to lower the consent threshold required to transfer debt claims to the newco to permit it to credit-bid, to transfer some or all of the outstanding debt obligations of the company to newco, and/or to write off or exchange the company's debt for newco equity/debt instruments.

The effect is to leave any out-of-the-money junior creditors behind. However, it is vital that the intercreditor agreement contains an effective mechanism that can be used to release any security granted in favour of the junior creditors (who will not be bound by the scheme) over the assets being transferred to the newco without any requirement for their consent. Otherwise the pre-pack transfer scheme will not be viable, as a scheme only lowers a consent threshold but does not obviate it entirely. In addition, even if they are not party to the scheme, disgruntled creditors may challenge it, and therefore valuation evidence is crucial to demonstrate that they have no economic interest and are therefore not entitled to participate in the scheme in any event (see under heading 4.7 below for further discussion on this point).

---

23 *Re Mytravel Group Plc* [2004] EWHC 2741 (Ch).
24 It is unlikely to be in future, depending on the terms that are negotiated with the EU in respect of Brexit.

4.7 Potential to leave behind out-of-the-money creditors

There is no requirement for a scheme to be proposed in respect of each and every class of a company's creditors; a company is free to select the creditors with whom it wishes to enter into an arrangement and need not include creditors whose rights are not altered by the scheme.[25] Typically, when used in a restructuring context, a scheme leaves a company's ordinary unsecured creditors, such as trade creditors and employees, unaffected. Instead, the scheme is often tailored to only affect the classes of financial creditors that are required to be compromised to implement a balance sheet restructuring.

The IMO Carwash schemes[26] compromised only those creditors who were senior lenders, in order to implement a debt-for-equity-and-debt swap into a new corporate structure owned principally by the senior lenders (the business was transferred to the new group by way of a pre-pack). The group's mezzanine lenders were left behind with claims against the old group which had no assets. This treatment was justified by reference to valuation evidence on the basis that the value of the IMO Carwash group was significantly less than the amount of the debt owed to the senior lenders, and that the mezzanine lenders therefore had no economic interest in the group. Although the schemes were challenged (unsuccessfully) by one of the group's mezzanine lenders, the challenge was to the valuation itself, rather than to the established principle that it is not necessary to consult any class of creditors who are not affected by the scheme, either because their rights are untouched or because they have no economic interest in the company.[27]

4.8 Duration

Schemes can be implemented with relative speed. Much of the preparation for a scheme, including negotiation with the relevant creditors (or groups or committees thereof), structuring and drafting of documentation will take place prior to the launch of the scheme itself. Provided that the support of the requisite number of creditors necessary to approve the scheme has been secured in advance (for example, under a lock-up agreement), the scheme can typically be implemented in a matter of between six and eight weeks. See the simplified scheme timetable and steps in Figure 3 below.

4.9 Jurisdictional requirements

Because a scheme of arrangement is a procedure under the Companies Act and not a formal insolvency procedure under the Insolvency Act, it is not subject to the EU Insolvency Regulation or its replacement, the recast EU Insolvency Regulation.[28] This means that a scheme of arrangement is not subject to the jurisdictional hurdle that

---

25   *Sea Assets Ltd v Pereroan etc Garuda Indonesia* [2001] EWCA Civ 1869; *In re British & Commonwealth Holdings plc* [1992] 1 WLR 672; *Re Bluebrook Ltd* [2009] EWHC 2114 (Ch) at [24].
26   *Re Bluebrook Ltd* [2009] EWHC 2114 (Ch).
27   *Re Bluebrook Ltd* [2009] EWHC 2114 (Ch) at [25]; *In re Tea Corporation Ltd* [1904] 1 Ch 12.
28   Regulation (EU) 2015/848 of May 20 2015, which will begin to take effect from June 26 2017, although it may not be effective in England for long given the Brexit decision in the UK referendum on membership of the European Union of June 23 2016. The regulation is discussed further in a separate chapter: "The recast EU Insolvency Regulation and its impact on distressed investing."

it may only be proposed by a company which has its centre of main interests in England. Instead, the courts exercise a less rigorous 'sufficient connection' test. This permits a company incorporated and carrying on business in a jurisdiction other than England to take advantage of a scheme of arrangement, provided that it can demonstrate a sufficiently strong link with England (which can be established on a number of grounds, see further discussion under heading 5.2 below).

5. Key issues

5.1 Classes

Creditors compromised under the scheme are divided into classes, based on their rights, for the purposes of voting on the scheme. It is for the company proposing the scheme to make an initial determination of the classes, which determination is then scrutinised by the court at the convening hearing (the procedure is discussed in further detail under heading 6.3 below). The company must also notify the scheme creditors of its determination of the composition of classes in advance of the convening hearing, so that creditors have the opportunity to raise any objections at that hearing.

The starting position is that there is one class of creditors. The test as to whether more than one class of creditors is necessary is whether the rights of the creditors are so dissimilar as to make it impossible for them to consult together with a view to their common interest.[29] This test is assessed by reference to an analysis of:

- the existing rights which are to be released or varied under the scheme of arrangement; and
- the new rights (if any) which the scheme of arrangement gives, by way of compromise or arrangement, to those creditors whose rights are to be released or varied.[30]

When determining classes, the appropriate comparator – the realistic alternative to the proposed scheme – must also be taken into account. In the context of investments in distressed debt and schemes proposed as part of a pre-insolvency restructuring to deal with a company's financial difficulties, the appropriate comparator will usually be formal insolvency proceedings. In such a situation, the correct approach is to consider the rights which are to be released or varied under the scheme as compared to the rights which the creditors would have in the insolvency.[31] In practice, the company will need to consider carefully and to provide detailed material to the creditors and the court in order to justify the comparator it has selected, including detail as to the basis for any predicted outcome on an insolvency (such as a liquidation analysis conducted by financial advisers), and such information is likely to be key in the event of a challenge to the scheme.[32]

---

29 *Re Sovereign Life Assurance v Dodd* [1892] 2 QB 573 at [583]; *Re Hawk Insurance Co Ltd* [2001] EWCA Civ 241.
30 *Re Hawk Insurance Co Ltd* [2001] EWCA Civ 241 at [30].
31 *Re Hawk Insurance Co Ltd* [2001] EWCA Civ 241 at [42].
32 *Re Van Gansewinkel Groep BV* [2015] EWHC 2151 (Ch) at [22] – [24].

Figure 2: Summary of selected recent schemes of arrangement

Debtor	Jurisdiction of incorporation	Size of debt subject to scheme	Compromise	Governing law
Magyar (2013)	The Netherlands†	€345 million	Debt-for-debt and equity swap	New York
Zlomrex (2013)	France†	€118 million	Amend and extend (via notes exchange)	New York
Vietnam Shipbuilding Industries (2013)	Vietnam	$600 million	Amend and extend (via substitution of senior facilities for government guaranteed notes)	England
Zodiac (2014)	USA, France, Finland	€1.1 billion	Amend and extend	England
Hibu (2014)	UK, USA, Spain	£2.3 billion	Debt-for-equity swap; amend and extend	England
Tele Columbus (2014)	Germany	€630 million	Amend and extend	England
Apcoa (2014)	Germany, Austria, Belgium, Denmark, UK, Norway	€730 million	Amend and extend (first scheme); repayment of super senior bridge loan, partial hive-up of senior debt to new lender-owned holdco, exchange of second lien debt for cash or warrants (second scheme)	England (originally Germany)*
Stemcor (2014)	UK, Singapore	$2.2 billion	Partial repayment; amend and extend; new money facility	England
DTEK (2015)	The Netherlands	$200 million	Amend and extend (via notes exchange)	England (originally New York)*
Van Gansewinkel Groep (2015)	The Netherlands, Belgium	€800 million	Debt-for-equity swap; amend and extend; reinstatement/transfer of debt	England
Codere (2015)	UK	€1.2 billion	Debt-for-debt and equity swap; new money injection; hive-down of assets	New York
Global Garden Products (2016)	Italy	€224 million	Amend and extend; collapse of fronting bank structure	England

† The centre of main interests of the company was shifted to England prior to the launch of the scheme.
* The governing law of the debt subject to the scheme was changed to England prior to the launch of the scheme.

In deciding the composition of classes, it is the creditors' legal rights against the scheme company, as opposed to their interests or motives in voting on the scheme, which are determinative.[33] Therefore, separate interests of scheme creditors, such as claims against the scheme company which fall within another class or outside the scheme (for example, the interests of a lender who has cross-holdings as both a senior and a junior lender) do not of themselves mean that a separate class is required. However, interests will not be entirely disregarded: if the court is satisfied that a class meeting was unrepresentative, or that those voting at the meeting had voted to promote a special interest which differed from the interests of the ordinary independent and objective creditors, the court will refuse to sanction the scheme.[34]

Although the court will generally take a broad approach to classes to avoid creating any hold-out rights for minorities (which goes against the purpose of a scheme),[35] the constitution of classes requires careful consideration and structuring to avoid creating any potential hold-out and/or numerosity issues.

In general, for schemes that are an alternative to insolvency, classes will follow the priority structure for ranking and enforcement in the intercreditor agreement. For example, senior creditors who benefit from the ability to lead an acceleration or enforcement and rank higher in the post-enforcement waterfall would be in a different class to junior creditors who are subject to standstill or similar restrictions on enforcement and rank lower in the waterfall for post-enforcement distributions.

The class test is formulated such that only differences in rights that are sufficiently material to make consultation by the creditors in the proposed class with a view to their common interest impossible will fracture the class, meaning that there can be some differences in rights between creditors within one class, which can be material and more than minimal.[36] Notably, differences in rights such as variations in interest rates, currencies and maturity dates across different loan tranches in a facilities agreement will not generally fracture a class of themselves.[37] (See also the discussion under heading 4.4 above in relation to the payment of consideration under the scheme, payment of minimal consent fees in connection with lock-up agreements, and the potential effect on classes.)

5.2 Jurisdiction

English courts have jurisdiction to sanction a scheme of arrangement in respect of a 'company', as that term is defined in the Companies Act. The definition of a company for the purposes of a scheme[38] is any company liable to be wound up under the Insolvency Act. A company that is not registered under the Companies Act in any part of the United Kingdom may nevertheless be wound up under Section 221

---

33 UDL Argos Engineering & Heavy Industries Co Ltd v Lin [2001] HKCFA 19; Re Telewest Communications plc (No 1) [2004] EWHC 924 (Ch) at [19]; Re Zodiac Pool Solutions SAS [2014] EWHC 2365 (Ch).
34 Re BTR plc [2000] 1 BCLC 740.
35 Re Hawk Insurance Co Ltd [2001] EWCA Civ 241 at [33]; Re Telewest Communications plc (No 1) [2004] EWHC 924 (Ch) at [37].
36 Re Telewest Communications plc (No 1) [2004] EWHC 924 (Ch) at [37]; Re DX Holdings Ltd [2010] EWHC 1513 (Ch) at [5].
37 McCarthy & Stone plc [2009] EWHC 712 (Ch); Re Primacom Holding GmbH [2011] EWHC 3746 (Ch).
38 Other than a reconstruction or amalgamation scheme under Section 900 of the Companies Act.

of the Insolvency Act. Accordingly, and importantly, a scheme can therefore be used to compromise the obligations of foreign companies.

It has been established in a significant body of case law that there are a number of requirements which must be met in order for an English court to exercise its discretion to approve a scheme in respect of a foreign company. It is also clear that the court will not simply act as a rubber stamp, even where the scheme has the support of an overwhelming majority of creditors: whether or not the scheme is opposed, the court requires those presenting the scheme to bring to its attention all relevant matters so that the court can determine whether it has jurisdiction, and whether it is appropriate to exercise such jurisdiction. That is particularly the case for a scheme of an overseas company which does not have its centre of main interests or an establishment in England, where jurisdictional issues necessarily arise, and where recognition of the scheme in other countries will be crucial.[39]

The first requirement is that there is a 'sufficient connection' with England.[40] The second requirement is that it is likely that the scheme will achieve its purpose, because the court will not generally make any order which has no substantial effect.[41] In considering the Magyar Telecom scheme, David Richards J expressed the view that these two requirements are not wholly separate questions but (if not aspects of the same question) at least closely related.[42]

The sufficient connection that a foreign company has with England will vary with the circumstances. It has been held that where the governing law of the debt instruments to be compromised in the scheme is English law and it is stipulated that the English courts have exclusive or non-exclusive jurisdiction in respect of disputes, a sufficient connection exists for the purposes of establishing jurisdiction.[43] The reasoning is that, under generally accepted principles of private international law, a variation or discharge of contractual rights in accordance with the governing law of the contract will usually be given effect to in other countries.[44]

In addition, it has been held that where the governing law has been amended from a foreign law to English law by creditor consent in accordance with the terms of the underlying documents, and provided that the relevant creditors were made aware that the primary purpose of the change of law was to establish a sufficient connection with England in order to implement a scheme, there will be a sufficient connection with England to establish the jurisdiction of the English court.[45] However, the new choice of law should not be a law which appears entirely alien to the parties' previous arrangements or with which the parties had no previous connection.[46]

---

39 *Re Van Gansewinkel Groep BV* [2015] EWHC 2151 (Ch) at [6].
40 *Re Drax Holdings Ltd* [2003] EWHC 2743 (Ch).
41 *Sompo Japan Insurance Inc v Transfercom Ltd* [2007] EWHC 146 (Ch).
42 *Re Magyar Telecom BV* [2013] EWHC 3800 (Ch) at [21].
43 *Re Rodenstock GmbH* [2011] EWHC 1104 (Ch); *Re Primacom Holding GmbH* [2011] EWHC 3746 (Ch); *In Re Vietnam Shipbuilding Industry Group* [2013] EWHC 2476 (Ch); *Re Hibu Finance (UK) Ltd* [2014] EWHC 370 (Ch); *Re Tele Columbus GmbH* [2014] EWHC 249 (Ch); *Re Van Gansewinkel Groep BV* [2015] EWHC 2151 (Ch).
44 *Re Magyar Telecom BV* [2013] EWHC 3800 (Ch) at [15].
45 *Re Apcoa Parking Holdings GmbH* [2014] EWHC 1867 (Ch); *Re Apcoa Parking Holdings GmbH* [2014] EWHC 3849 (Ch); *Re DTEK Finance BV* [2015] EWHC 1164 (Ch).
46 *Re Apcoa Parking Holdings GmbH* [2014] EWHC 3849 (Ch) at [251].

A sufficient connection has also been found to exist where a foreign company's centre of main interests is located in England, including in circumstances where its centre of main interests has deliberately been shifted to England in order to take advantage of the ability to propose a scheme of arrangement.[47] In practice, a shift of the centre of main interests is only really an option for a holding company, rather than an operating company, and may be unworkable due to adverse tax implications.

In the *Codere* scheme, it was not possible to establish a sufficient connection with England by conducting a shift of the centre of main interests or by other means. Instead, a new English special purpose vehicle was incorporated to accede as co-issuer of the notes to be compromised, in order to propose a scheme to compromise not only its liabilities, but also those of the Luxembourg-incorporated co-issuer and the guarantors. Although the judge at the convening hearing commented that this seemed to be "quite an extreme form of forum shopping", he granted leave to convene the meetings of creditors. At the sanction hearing the court acknowledged that such deliberate actions to give the English court jurisdiction can constitute "good forum shopping", if what is being attempted is to have recourse to the law of a particular jurisdiction not in order to evade debts, but with a view to achieving the best possible outcome for creditors.[48]

As to the requirement that the scheme must be likely to achieve its purpose, the central questions are:

- what effect the scheme would have in any relevant foreign jurisdiction (such as that where the company is incorporated and any jurisdiction in which it has assets); and
- whether the scheme would be recognised in any relevant foreign jurisdiction in order to give effect to it.

If a creditor could frustrate the scheme by asserting that its foreign-law governed rights had not been compromised by the scheme, and by exercising remedies in a foreign jurisdiction in which the company has assets or operations, the scheme could not generally be said to achieve its purpose. Although it does not need certainty as to the position under foreign law,[49] the court will require credible expert evidence on the question of whether the scheme would be recognised as having compromised creditor rights in such a foreign jurisdiction, and that it would not be acting in vain in sanctioning the scheme of a foreign company.[50] Such expert evidence should be provided by independent experts because the expert evidence is an important feature of independence, particularly where there is no opposition to the scheme application.[51]

---

47   *Re Zlomrex International Finance SA* [2013] EWHC 3866 (Ch); *Re Magyar Telecom BV* [2013] EWHC 3800 (Ch); *Re New World Resources NV* [2015] BCC 47.
48   *Re Codere Finance (UK) Ltd* [2015] EWHC 3778 (Ch) at [13]-[18].
49   *Sompo Japan Insurance Inc v Transfercom Ltd* [2007] EWHC 146 (Ch); *Re Hibu Finance (UK) Ltd* [2014] EWHC 370 (Ch).
50   *Re Van Gansewinkel Groep BV* [2015] EWHC 2151 (Ch) at [71].
51   *Re Magyar Telecom BV* [2013] EWHC 3800 (Ch) at [27].

Another factor that will be relevant to the court's considerations as to whether a scheme will achieve its purpose is what level of support the scheme has received. If a large majority of scheme creditors have voted in favour of the scheme, the court can take comfort that the chances of frustrating action being taken by a dissenting creditor are relatively low and unlikely to negate the beneficial effect of the scheme for the scheme company and the majority of the scheme creditors.[52]

A somewhat thorny issue has arisen in relation to the application of Chapter II of the recast EU Regulation on jurisdiction and the recognition and enforcement of judgments in civil and commercial matters (Regulation (EU) 1215/2012 of December 12 2012; the 'recast Brussels Regulation') to schemes of arrangement. A full discussion of the issue is beyond the scope of this chapter.[53] In practice, in order to avoid requiring a decision on the question, many schemes are proposed on the basis that if Chapter II of the recast Brussels Regulation does apply, jurisdiction exists under it.

In order for such jurisdiction to exist under Article 8(1) of the recast Brussels Regulation, there should be at least one scheme creditor domiciled in England, and it must also be expedient for the 'claims' against all the other scheme creditors to be heard before the English court.[54] There are two main arguments as to expediency: first, that it is expedient because all the scheme creditors should be bound to the same restructuring to avoid inconsistent judgments from separate proceedings;[55] second, that it is expedient because of the number and value of scheme creditors domiciled in the United Kingdom.[56]

Alternatively, jurisdiction may exist under Article 25 of the recast Brussels Regulation, if the parties (regardless of their domicile) have agreed that the courts of an EU member state are to have jurisdiction to settle any disputes in connection with their particular legal relationship. Although the point has not been finally decided, it appears that where a jurisdiction clause is expressed to be for the benefit only of certain and not all parties (as is commonly the case with facility agreements, where the jurisdiction clause is stated to be for the finance parties only and therefore cannot be relied upon by the scheme company) Article 25 would not be satisfied.[57]

---

52 See, for example, *Re Van Gansewinkel Groep BV* [2015] EWHC 2151 (Ch) at [76].
53 It is summarised by Snowden J in *Re Van Gansewinkel Groep BV* [2015] EWHC 2151 (Ch) at [41]-[52]. See also Snowden J's consideration of the point in *Re Global Garden Products Italy SpA* [2016] EWHC 1884 (Ch) at [21]-[33].
54 Depending on the nature of the agreement that is reached with the European Union on the terms of Brexit, the recast Brussels Regulation (or a substantially similar instrument, such as the Lugano Convention) may or may not apply to schemes in future. Although this may in effect render moot the unresolved recast Brussels Regulation jurisdiction issue, the recast Brussels Regulation is currently also often relied on to demonstrate that the scheme will be recognised in another EU member state and will therefore achieve its purpose. Other recognition principles such as those available under private international law may have to be relied on in future.
55 *Re Metinvest BV* [2016] EWHC 79 (Ch) at [33].
56 *Re Van Gansewinkel Groep BV* [2015] EWHC 2151 (Ch) at [41]-[45]. Note that it is not yet established how many scheme creditors must be domiciled in the United Kingdom to demonstrate expediency. In *Re Rodenstock GmbH* [2011] EWHC 1104 (Ch) at [62], more than 50% by value were domiciled in England; in contrast, in *Re Public Joint-Stock Company Commercial Bank "Privatbank"* [2015] EWHC 3299 (Ch) at [21] only 12% by value were domiciled in the United Kingdom and in *Re Global Garden Products Italy SpA* [2016] EWHC 1884 (Ch) at [26], 28.37% by value were domiciled in the United Kingdom.
57 *Re Global Garden Products Italy SpA* [2016] EWHC 1884 (Ch) at [30]-[33].

5.3 Challenge

Various issues – including the composition of creditor classes, fairness and any unfair prejudice caused to any person affected by a scheme, material irregularities, and the jurisdiction of the court – may give rise to a challenge to a scheme of arrangement. An objection to a matter notified to scheme creditors in advance in the practice statement letter, such as a class issue, should be raised at the convening hearing, in order to ensure that fundamental issues are flushed out early on (see under heading 6.2 below regarding the implementation phase of a scheme and the practice statement letter). However, any person affected by a scheme, and not just a scheme creditor, may appear at the sanction hearing and raise a challenge, and it is at the sanction hearing (rather than at the convening hearing) that the court will consider the overall merits and fairness of the scheme.[58]

Challenges on the basis of unfair prejudice arising from valuations purporting to demonstrate that certain creditors have no economic interest and therefore do not need to be included in a scheme have been considered in a number of cases.[59] Although a liquidation valuation was approved in the *MyTravel* scheme, it was restricted to the facts of the case, and it is now generally accepted that a going concern valuation as approved in the *IMO Carwash* scheme should be used to demonstrate that certain creditors have no economic interest in the underlying business and assets.

The court has struck down a number of other challenges, including challenges to the proposed class composition of a scheme on the basis that scheme creditors who:
- were 'connected with' or held equity in the scheme company's group;
- were lenders of a revolving facility advanced to fund the scheme; and
- had sub-participated their loans,

in each case could not be placed in the same class as other scheme creditors.[60] The court considered that each of those objections went to creditors' interests and motivations, rather than rights, and did therefore not constitute grounds for creating separate classes. Another scheme which involved the provision of a new loan facility incentivised scheme creditors to participate in the new facility by giving their rights that were compromised by the scheme higher priority relative to scheme creditors that did not participate. A scheme creditor objected but the court held that the scheme was fair, because it was open to all the relevant scheme creditors to participate and it was reasonable to give priority to those prepared to fund the new facility.[61]

In the Apcoa schemes, various objections were raised at both the convening and sanction hearings. These included objections as to class composition, on the basis that the scheme creditors who had entered into a lock-up agreement or a turnover agreement (the latter entered into in connection with new emergency super-senior

---

[58] *Re Telewest Communications plc (No 1)* [2004] EWHC 924 (Ch); *Re Icopal AS* [2013] EWHC 3469 (Ch).
[59] *In re Tea Corporation Ltd* [1904] 1 Ch 12; *Re MyTravel Group plc* [2004] EWHC 2741 (Ch); *Re Bluebrook Ltd* [2009] EWHC 2114 (Ch).
[60] *Re Zodiac Pool Solutions SAS* [2014] EWHC 2365 (Ch).
[61] *In the matters of Stemcor (SEA) PTE Ltd* [2014] EWHC 1096 (Ch) at [36]-[37].

financing provided to avoid insolvency and permit the restructuring to continue) had different rights to those creditors who had not. The court rejected both of these arguments, reasoning that the turnover agreement operated behind the curtain, and did not substantively alter the rights of the scheme creditors who had entered into it; in any event, the turnover agreement had been terminated prior to the convening hearing.[62] The lock-up agreement did not justify fracturing the classes either. Although it affected the enjoyment of certain rights such as voting and enforcement by the persons who entered into it, it did not affect those rights themselves.[63] One of the objections raised at the convening hearing but considered at the sanction hearing was that the scheme imposed a new obligation on certain scheme creditors to indemnify an issuer of new guarantees in respect of the future business of the Apcoa group. Hildyard J was not persuaded that a scheme is capable of imposing new obligations, as opposed to varying creditors' rights, and was particularly uneasy in doing so in the context of a cross-border scheme and against the will of dissenting creditors.[64] In the event, the judge did not have to make a final determination on the point, as the scheme companies amended the scheme so that the affected scheme creditors could elect whether or not to enter into the indemnity provision. However, Hildyard J did comment that nothing he said should be taken to cast doubt on the ability of a scheme to implement mere extensions or the rolling over of existing facilities involving no new contract or more extensive obligations.[65]

6. Procedure and process overview

6.1 Preparation phase

A scheme is divided into a preparation phase and an implementation phase. Most of the work, including negotiating and documenting the scheme, is completed during the preparation phase. Depending upon the complexity of the scheme, and the dynamics of negotiations between the company and the scheme creditors, this phase can be relatively swift, or quite protracted. Typically, this phase involves agreeing the terms and structure of the scheme between the company and the scheme creditors (or committees thereof), assessing tax implications, and determining scheme classes.

Once these items have been settled, a lock-up agreement will be negotiated and agreed. The lock-up agreement will annex a restructuring term sheet, outlining the terms of the scheme and usually also a 'Plan B' alternative restructuring mechanism to be implemented in the event that the scheme is not approved. Creditors who enter into the lock-up agreement are bound to vote in favour of and otherwise support the scheme, although those provisions of the lock-up agreement may only become binding once the statutory majorities (75% in value representing a majority in number of each class of scheme creditor) have entered into it.

The scheme documentation will be drafted in tandem with the lock-up agreement (see Figure 3 for a summary of the key documents). The main document

---

62   *Re Apcoa Parking Holdings GmbH* [2014] EWHC 3849 (Ch) at [90]-[93].
63   *Re Apcoa Parking Holdings GmbH* [2014] EWHC 3849 (Ch) at [100].
64   *Re Apcoa Parking Holdings GmbH* [2014] EWHC 3849 (Ch) at [164]-[166].
65   *Re Apcoa Parking Holdings GmbH* [2014] EWHC 3849 (Ch) at [167].

is the scheme circular to be sent to scheme creditors once the court has given permission for the scheme meeting(s) to be convened. The scheme circular contains the terms of the scheme itself, and also typically sets out the background to and necessity of the scheme, contains a recommendation by the company or its chief executive officer that the scheme is in the best interests of the scheme creditors, sets out the expected timetable, and provides an explanatory statement of the key legal and economic implications of the scheme.

6.2 Implementation phase

Once the statutory majorities of each class of scheme creditors have become bound by the lock-up agreement and it has become effective, the implementation phase will commence. In this phase, a convening hearing takes place to obtain the court's permission to summon the meeting(s) of the scheme creditors, the meeting(s) of the scheme creditors by class are held to vote on the scheme, and a sanction hearing takes place once the scheme has been approved at the creditor meeting(s).

An indicative timetable and overview of the key steps is set out in Figure 3 below.

Advance notice of the application to convene the scheme meeting(s) must be given to the scheme creditors, in accordance with the practice statement.[66] The main purpose is to enable issues concerning the composition of classes of creditors and the summoning of meetings to be identified and resolved early in the proceedings. Although the practice statement does not prevent a challenge to the scheme being raised at the sanction hearing, it does require the person making the challenge to show good reason why they did not raise it at an earlier stage; that is, at the convening hearing. In addition, the practice statement places the burden on the applicant (usually the company) to determine the composition of creditor classes, and to provide evidence or otherwise draw the court's attention to any class or other issues that might affect the conduct of the scheme meeting(s).

The practice statement also requires the applicant to take all steps reasonably open to it to notify any person affected by the scheme of the existence of the scheme, its purpose, and the composition of the classes of creditors it considers necessary. This requirement has led to the practice of the scheme company sending a 'practice statement letter' to scheme creditors prior to the convening hearing:

- to notify them that the company is proposing the scheme and will apply to court for leave to convene the scheme meeting(s);
- to explain why the scheme is necessary, what its purpose is and how the scheme will operate;
- to explain how the scheme will affect scheme creditors, including how the company has determined the composition of classes; and
- to set out the expected scheme timetable and steps.

Creditors must be given adequate notice of the convening hearing. What is adequate will depend on all the circumstances, but the more complex or novel the scheme, and the less consultation that has taken place with creditors as a whole

---

66   *Chancery Division Practice Statement (companies: schemes of arrangement)* [2002] 3 All ER 96 (April 15 2002).

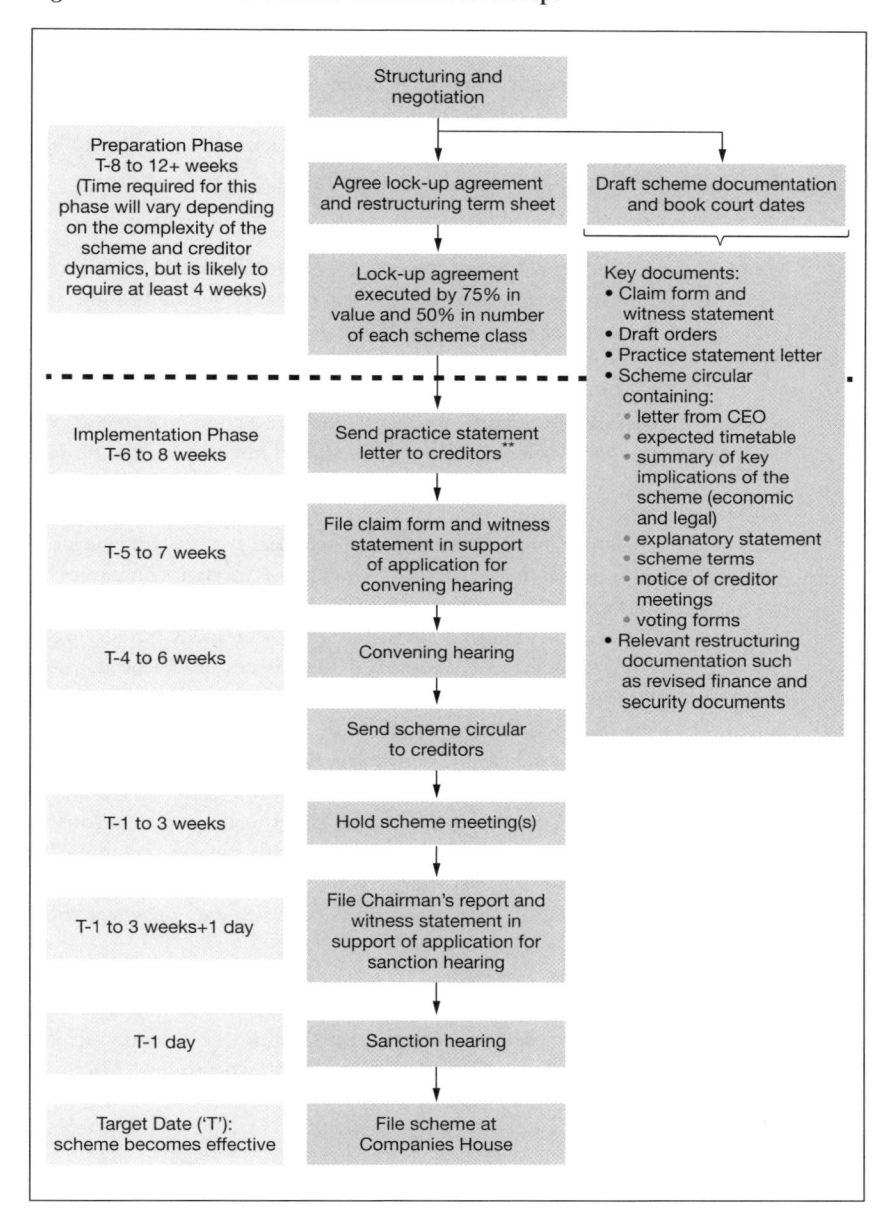

Figure 3: Overview of Scheme Timetable and Steps*

Phase / Time	Step	Details

Preparation Phase T-8 to 12+ weeks (Time required for this phase will vary depending on the complexity of the scheme and creditor dynamics, but is likely to require at least 4 weeks)	Structuring and negotiation → Agree lock-up agreement and restructuring term sheet; Draft scheme documentation and book court dates → Lock-up agreement executed by 75% in value and 50% in number of each scheme class	**Key documents:**
		• Claim form and witness statement
		• Draft orders
		• Practice statement letter
		• Scheme circular containing:
		  ○ letter from CEO
		  ○ expected timetable
		  ○ summary of key implications of the scheme (economic and legal)
		  ○ explanatory statement
		  ○ scheme terms
		  ○ notice of creditor meetings
		  ○ voting forms
		• Relevant restructuring documentation such as revised finance and security documents

Implementation Phase T-6 to 8 weeks	Send practice statement letter to creditors**	
T-5 to 7 weeks	File claim form and witness statement in support of application for convening hearing	
T-4 to 6 weeks	Convening hearing	
	Send scheme circular to creditors	
T-1 to 3 weeks	Hold scheme meeting(s)	
T-1 to 3 weeks+1 day	File Chairman's report and witness statement in support of application for sanction hearing	
T-1 day	Sanction hearing	
Target Date ('T'): scheme becomes effective	File scheme at Companies House	

* Note that this timetable is indicative and subject to potential delay/extension in the case of complex schemes or in the event of creditor challenge. It is also dependent on the court's timetable and vacation periods.

**The practice statement letter must give scheme creditors 'adequate' notice of the convening hearing. What is adequate will depend on the circumstances. At least 2 weeks' notice is usually required, although shorter or longer notice periods will be justified in some situations.

before the scheme is launched, the longer the notice period should generally be.[67] Two weeks' notice to scheme creditors has been common practice, but in the recent *Indah Kiat* scheme, Snowden J held that to be insufficient. A large supporting creditor had been involved in negotiating the scheme, but other scheme creditors had not been consulted and could not be identified from any register held by the company. These creditors could not be notified directly of the scheme, but had to be notified via clearing systems.[68]

6.3 Convening hearing

As noted under heading 6.2 above, the main aim of the practice statement is for the correct composition of classes to be determined at the convening hearing, rather than waiting until the sanction hearing. In addition, the court at the convening hearing will consider whether there are any apparent jurisdictional impediments that demonstrate that it is unlikely that the scheme could be sanctioned by the court in due course. Jurisdiction covers both whether the court has jurisdiction to exercise power, and whether there are any obvious reasons why it should not exercise that power.

The practice statement does not mention any other issues which might be considered at the convening hearing. However, a practice has developed that the court at the convening hearing can consider whether the court has jurisdiction, in the international sense, in respect of schemes of foreign companies.[69] If such international jurisdictional issues are to be raised for determination at the convening hearing, this should be indicated in the practice statement letter, together with proper details of the argument. Further, if such issues are to be considered and determined in a way that can be relied upon as a basis for persuading the judge at a sanction hearing not to revisit the question, then that must very clearly be brought to the attention of the judge at the convening hearing.[70]

In considering those issues at the convening hearing, the court does not bind itself as regards the sanction hearing, even on issues relating to class constitution or its fundamental jurisdiction. Its determination at this stage is preliminary, and not final, especially in circumstances where creditors may not have had sufficient time to consider and marshal all arguments against the scheme, or where the issues at stake are complex or novel.[71]

If the court grants permission to summon the scheme meeting(s) at the convening hearing, the scheme creditors must be given fair notice of the scheme prior to the meeting(s). This is achieved by sending the scheme circular to the scheme creditors immediately following the convening hearing. In practice, 21 days' notice of the meeting(s) is commonly given.

6.4 Scheme meeting(s)

Creditors vote on a scheme in classes, and a separate meeting will be held for each

---

67 *Re Indah Kiat International Finance Company BV* [2016] EWHC 246 (Ch) at [28].
68 *Re Indah Kiat International Finance Company BV* [2016] EWHC 246 (Ch) at [30]-[34].
69 *Re Van Gansewinkel Groep BV* [2015] EWHC 2151 (Ch) at [31].
70 *Re Van Gansewinkel Groep BV* [2015] EWHC 2151 (Ch) at [55]–[56].
71 *Re Apcoa Parking (UK) Ltd* [2014] EWHC 997 (Ch) at [16]-[17].

class to vote on the proposed scheme. A particular date will be designated as the reference date for the purpose of valuing creditors' claims for voting.

The scheme meeting(s) must be held at a time and in a place that is convenient for the majority of the scheme creditors. Although the scheme creditors may attend and vote in person, most will usually designate the chairman appointed to conduct the meeting(s) as their proxy and direct how he or she must vote in advance of the meeting date.

Importantly, the required voting thresholds only apply to creditors present and voting at the scheme meeting(s), whether in person or by proxy. Those not voting are not counted. However, the court at the sanction hearing will be interested in the level of attendance (in person or by proxy) at the meeting(s).

6.5 Sanction hearing

At the sanction hearing, the court will review the outcome of the scheme meeting(s), consider jurisdiction and fairness and (if satisfied) sanction the scheme. It is concerned primarily with determining whether the requirements of Section 899 of the Companies Act (relating to voting at the scheme meeting) have been complied with so that it has jurisdiction to sanction the scheme, and if it does have jurisdiction, whether it should exercise its discretion to sanction the scheme.

The court must be satisfied that:
- the meeting(s) of creditors have been summoned and held in accordance with the order of the court convening such meeting(s);
- the proposed scheme has been approved by the requisite majority of those present and voting at the meeting(s); and
- the creditors were treated in appropriate classes for the purpose of convening the meeting(s).[72]

The general test for the court as to whether it should exercise its discretion to sanction a scheme is to verify that:
- the provisions of the Companies Act have been complied with;
- each class was fairly represented by those who attended the meeting, and that the statutory majority are acting in good faith and are not coercing the minority in order to promote interests otherwise adverse to those of the class whom they purport to represent; and
- the arrangement is such as an intelligent and honest man, a member of the class concerned and acting in respect of his interests, might reasonably approve.[73]

In addition, the court will generally not sanction a scheme if there is a 'blot' on it, such as a material mistake or an illegality.

At the sanction hearing, the court will also hear any objection to the scheme by any affected party (even if not a scheme creditor), although challenges should

---

[72] *In the matters of Stemcor (SEA) PTE Ltd* [2014] EWHC 1096 (Ch) at [25].
[73] *Re Telewest Communications (No 2) Ltd* [2005] 1 BCLC 772 at [20]-[22].

generally be raised at the convening hearing stage and a creditor must demonstrate a good reason if it has not done so.

6.6 Effectiveness of the scheme

The court order sanctioning the scheme does not become effective until it is filed with the registrar of companies, pursuant to Section 899(4) of the Companies Act.[74] Note that Companies House will require written confirmation from Her Majesty's Revenue and Customs as to whether the scheme is liable to stamp duty or not. Obtaining such written confirmation should therefore be factored into the timetable.

7. Conclusion: increased scrutiny

As can be deduced from the recent case law referred to in this chapter, the law in relation to schemes of arrangement has been rapidly evolving, as schemes have gained renown and popularity as a pre-insolvency restructuring tool. The English court has demonstrated its willingness to accept jurisdiction over foreign companies proposing a scheme by reference to progressively less substantial links with England. The high-water mark was reached in the *Apcoa* and *Codere* schemes discussed earlier in this chapter.[75]

However, the court has sounded a note of caution in a number of recent cases. In respect of the *Van Gansewinkel* scheme, Snowden J emphasised that, in particular as regards schemes of overseas companies without their centre of main interests, an establishment or significant assets in England, the court will not act merely as a rubber stamp, even in cases where the overwhelming majority of creditors support the scheme and there is considerable commercial imperative (and pressure) on the court to approve the scheme.[76] The judge then proceeded to scrutinise the proposed scheme in depth, including jurisdiction and recognition issues, before ultimately approving it.

In the case of *Indah Kiat*,[77] the scheme was vigorously opposed by a creditor who sought, and was granted, an adjournment of the convening hearing. The scheme application was subsequently withdrawn by the company. In his judgment, Snowden J highlighted a number of deficiencies of the scheme, including lack of adequate notice to the scheme creditors, shortcomings in the evidence and disclosure provided by the company, and other procedural issues. In addition, there were concerns that the largest creditor supporting the scheme, who had been presented as independent, was in fact not, that the shift in the centre of main interests that had been undertaken to establish jurisdiction of the English court was ineffective and amounted only to window-dressing, and that the scheme would discharge a solvent and profitable parent guarantor that was not party to the scheme from its obligations. Although it acknowledged its more limited role at the

---

74 Subject to any other conditions to which the effectiveness of the scheme might be subject, such as interconditionality with schemes of other group companies and/or other restructuring processes.
75 *Re Apcoa Parking Holdings GmbH* [2014] EWHC 3849 (Ch); *Re Codere Finance (UK) Ltd* [2015] EWHC 3778 (Ch).
76 *Re Van Gansewinkel Groep BV* [2015] EWHC 2151 (Ch) at [6]; see also *Re Global Garden Products Italy SpA* [2016] EWHC 1884 (Ch) at [37]-[38].
77 *Re Indah Kiat International Finance Company BV* [2016] EWHC 246 (Ch).

convening hearing stage, the court nevertheless undertook a detailed assessment of the evidence presented in support of the class composition proposed by the company and the draft scheme circular, and concluded that there were material deficiencies. Snowden J noted that a company proposing a scheme of arrangement has a duty to make full and frank disclosure, and that: "The scheme jurisdiction can only work properly and command respect internationally if parties invoking the jurisdiction exhibit the utmost candour with the court."[78]

Snowden J took the same approach of close examination in respect of the *Global Garden Products* scheme.[79] In particular, the judge adjourned the sanction hearing so that additional evidence could be adduced as to the domicile of scheme creditors for the purposes of establishing jurisdiction (at least, in theory) under Article 8 of the recast Brussels Regulation. In addition, he required further evidence regarding a the payment of a fee to two coordinators (who were also scheme creditors) for their work in negotiating and progressing the scheme. Although the judge ultimately accepted that the fee was unlikely to affect the scheme, he held that the details and amount of it should have been disclosed in the explanatory statement and the evidence, and should have been drawn to the attention of the court at the convening hearing as a potential class issue.[80] This emphasises the duty of full and frank disclosure that Snowden J himself highlighted in respect of the *Indah Kiat* scheme.

In conclusion, these developments reinforce current indications that schemes of arrangement may face increased scrutiny by the court in future. Looking further ahead, schemes also now face a potentially prolonged period of uncertainty as to how they will be recognised and enforced in EU member states post-Brexit.

---

[78] *Re Indah Kiat International Finance Company BV* [2016] EWHC 246 (Ch) at [40].
[79] *Re Global Garden Products Italy SpA* [2016] EWHC 1884 (Ch).
[80] *Re Global Garden Products Italy SpA* [2016] EWHC 1884 (Ch) at [56].

Developments in the legal framework for restructuring: France

Jérémie Bismuth
Marie Dubarry de Lassalle
Olivia Locatelli
Caroline Texier
Gide Loyrette Nouel

1. Summary of the legal restructuring and insolvency framework in France

As a matter of general principle, French law distinguishes between amicable proceedings and judicial insolvency proceedings.

1.1 Amicable proceedings

The purpose of amicable proceedings under French law is to allow the appointment, by the president of the relevant commercial court, of a third party (either a *mandataire ad hoc* or a conciliator) who will be in charge of assisting the management of the company in its negotiations with its main partners (creditors, shareholders and so on).

Two forms of amicable proceedings (as further described below) are used by French courts, depending on whether or not the company is insolvent.

(a) Mandat ad hoc

The *mandat ad hoc* is governed by Articles L 611-3 onwards of the Commercial Code and is a proceeding open to companies which are not insolvent.

The opening of such a proceeding allows the appointment of a *mandataire ad hoc* whose mission will be to facilitate discussions between the company and its creditors in order to ensure the viability of the business of the company. The *mandataire ad hoc* does not have any coercive rights over the creditors.

Generally, at the beginning of a mandate, the *mandataire ad hoc* asks the creditors to agree to a standstill on enforcement of their claims for the period during which discussions are taking place.

Goal: to ensure the viability of the business of the company

There is no specific limit to the duration of the standstill. It can be given for a few weeks or months or for the entire period of the *mandat ad hoc*. The length of the *mandat ad hoc* is fixed by the president of the court at the opening of the proceeding, and is generally a few months, but there is no legal maximum duration.

(b) Conciliation

Conciliation is governed by Articles L 611-4 onwards of the Commercial Code and is a proceeding open to companies which have been insolvent for less than 45 days.

The opening of such a proceeding allows the appointment of a conciliator, whose mission will be to conclude a conciliation agreement between the company and its creditors. The conciliation agreement will be reviewed and either acknowledged or approved by the commercial court.

In addition, the president of the commercial court that has opened the conciliation proceeding may, at the request of the company, grant a deferral of payment to a creditor, for a maximum period of two years, if this creditor requests the payment of its claim during the conciliation.

1.2 Judicial proceedings

Three categories of judicial proceedings can be opened by French courts under French law, depending on whether or not the company is insolvent, and whether the recovery of the company is or is not possible.

(a) Safeguard proceedings

Under Article L 620-1 onwards of the Commercial Code, safeguard proceedings are open to companies which are not yet insolvent, but which face financial difficulties that they are not able to overcome by themselves.

The opening judgment appoints:
- a commissary judge to oversee the proceedings;
- a judicial administrator in charge of supervising or assisting the management of the company; and
- a creditors' representative to represent the creditors' interests.

The opening of a safeguard proceeding:
- launches an observation period (generally six months) which may be extended up to 18 months and during which a safeguard plan is prepared by the company and presented to its creditors; and
- triggers an automatic stay.

For companies whose annual accounts are certified by a statutory auditor or drawn up by a chartered accountant and which employ more than 150 employees or have an annual turnover of more than €20 million, creditors' committees must be established (with bondholders consulted separately in one general meeting).

The creditors' committees and bondholders group are invited to vote on the draft of safeguard plan presented by the company (which may include debt restructuring, recapitalisation of the company, debt-for-equity swaps, and so on). Such a plan will require approval by a majority of creditors representing two-thirds (by value) of debt held by the voting members.

If the committees do not vote on the safeguard plan within six months from the date of the opening judgment or if they refuse to accept the plan, the creditors must be consulted individually. The commercial court can impose deferrals of payment of up to 10 years on the creditors, but cannot impose a reduction of debt.

(b) *Accelerated safeguard and accelerated financial safeguard proceedings*
Two further specific types of safeguard proceedings exist which can come into play only in the event of an unsuccessful conciliation: accelerated safeguard proceedings and accelerated financial safeguard proceedings.

In order to facilitate the treatment of difficulties arising from financial debt owed by French companies, a law dated October 22 2010, applicable as of March 1 2011, introduced accelerated financial safeguard proceeding, a process which is mainly inspired by American Chapter 11 'prepack' proceedings.

An accelerated financial safeguard proceeding is aimed at treating financial debt only and therefore exclusively concern financial creditors, including bondholders, and do not affect other creditors, such as suppliers.

This proceeding must be preceded by a conciliation proceeding. During the conciliation, an agreement – which will then become the draft plan if an accelerated financial safeguard proceeding is opened – is negotiated between the company and its financial creditors. This agreement must be acceptable to most of the creditors, in order to prove that the adoption of a safeguard plan is likely to occur within a period of a month following the opening of the accelerated financial safeguard proceeding. If not, the court will not authorise the opening of the proceeding.

The scope of this form of proceeding has been extended through Reform Order 2014-326 dated March 12 2014, which created a new proceeding: the accelerated safeguard proceeding. This reform entered into force on July 1 2014.

As a consequence, the accelerated financial safeguard proceeding is now a sub-category of the accelerated safeguard proceeding.

Opening of proceedings: Either proceeding may only be opened in the course of a conciliation proceeding at the request of the debtor. The legal representative must file a petition with the court.

To be eligible for these proceedings, the following conditions must be fulfilled by the debtor:
- It must draw up consolidated annual accounts; or
- Its accounts must be certified, and it must:
  - employ more than 20 people; or
  - have a turnover of at least €3 million; or
  - have a balance sheet total of at least €1.5 million.

A safeguard proceeding is opened following a conciliation where unanimous consent cannot be reached but it is shown that majority agreement can be acquired.

The debtor must therefore show that it has drafted a safeguard plan which is likely to be supported by a majority of the creditors that will take part in the safeguard proceeding.

The public prosecutor is called to the hearing of the court.

The debtor must not be insolvent on the date of the request. It can however be insolvent if the accelerated safeguard proceeding or accelerated financial safeguard proceeding follows a conciliation opened when the debtor had already been insolvent for less than 45 days.

Potential actions to challenge the opening of proceedings: The judgment opening the accelerated safeguard proceeding or the accelerated financial safeguard proceeding may be challenged by third parties through the filing of a third-party objection.

This objection must be filed before the same court as the one that opened the proceeding. It must be filed within 10 days of the publication of the judgment opening the proceeding. This period is increased by two months for persons residing abroad.

In order to be admissible, an objection must satisfy the conditions of Article 583 of the Code of Civil Procedure:
- The requesting party must not be a party to the challenged judgment or have been represented at the hearing giving rise to the judgment, and must have an interest in challenging it; and
- A creditor or a person who was represented in the hearing giving rise to the judgment may none the less challenge the judgment if it can demonstrate fraud impacting its rights, or that it suffered personal and specific harm.

As a result, the possibility for a creditor to file an objection to a judgment opening a safeguard proceeding is very limited under French law.

Effects of the proceedings: The opening of an accelerated safeguard proceeding launches an observation period of three months during which a safeguard restructuring plan (the one negotiated in the conciliation proceeding) must be agreed by the creditors and submitted to the court for approval.

The opening of an accelerated financial safeguard proceeding launches an observation period of one month, which may be extended for one additional month.

(c) *Judicial reorganisation proceedings*

Under Article L 631-1 onwards of the Commercial Code, judicial reorganisation proceedings are open to companies which are insolvent, but whose recovery is possible.

The goal of the reorganisation proceeding is:
- to safeguard the company's activities and its prospect of recovery;
- to save jobs; and
- to pay creditors.

The opening judgment appoints:
- a commissary judge to oversee the proceedings;
- a judicial administrator in charge of supervising or assisting the management of the company; and
- a creditors' representative to represent the creditors' interests.

In contrast to amicable proceedings or safeguard proceedings, which are voluntary, reorganisation proceedings can also be asked for by a creditor or by the public prosecutor.

As with safeguard proceedings, the opening judgment will lead to an observation period (generally six months) that can last for a maximum of 18 months provided that the financing of the company is assured. During this period, the company is forbidden to proceed with payment of any pre-petition claims, and continues its activity. As soon as a reorganisation proceeding is opened, third parties are invited to bid on all or part of the going concern.

As regards ongoing contracts, the judicial administrator can chose whether to terminate them or not, and can require the contracting party to continue its performance in exchange for the performance of the company's post-petition obligations.

The same committees of creditors are set up with the same majority requirements as under safeguard proceedings to approve the reorganisation plan. If the court decides that no proposed plan is viable, it can approve the sale of part or all of the business to reimburse creditors.

A reorganisation plan can combine debt restructuring, recapitalisation of the company, a debt-for-equity swap and the sale of some assets of the company.

(d) *Judicial liquidation proceedings*

Under Article L 640-1 onwards of the Commercial Code, liquidation proceedings apply to all companies which are insolvent and whose restructuring is clearly impossible.

A liquidator will be appointed by the commercial court to dispose of the company's assets and to repay its debts.

The opening of liquidation proceedings has the following consequences:
- the opening judgment renders the creditors' claims immediately due;
- the company's activity stops, and the liquidator proceeds to the sale of its assets to cover the company' debts; and
- creditors are paid according to their rank as determined by the nature of their claim and the date on which it arose.

2. Summary of key elements of insolvency proceedings under French law

2.1 Automatic stay

The opening of judicial proceedings triggers an automatic stay in accordance with Article L 622-7 of the Commercial Code.

The automatic stay leads to the suspension of all pre-petition claims.

The company must, however, continue to pay its wages and any debts that fall due during the observation period, if they are necessary for the continuation of the business (such as payment for new supplies).

French case law treats the repayment of principal and interest under a loan agreement or bond documentation entered into prior to the opening of an insolvency proceeding as a pre-petition debt, the repayment of which is therefore

Amicable proceedings	
• Appointment of a third party (mandataire ad hoc/conciliator) by the president of the relevant commercial court • Mission: assisting the management of the company in its negotiations with its main partners (creditors, shareholders etc)	
Mandat ad hoc Available to companies that are not insolvent Opened at request of debtor (Articles L 611-3 onwards of Commercial Code)	*Conciliation* (i) Available to companies that are not insolvent or those that have been insolvent for less than 45 days (ii) Opened at request of debtor (Articles L 611-4 onwards of Commercial Code)
Appointment of a mandataire ad hoc Mission: to facilitate discussions between the company and its creditors Goal: to ensure the viability of the business of the company No coercive rights over the creditors	Appointment of a conciliator Mission: to facilitate discussions between the company and its creditors and to conclude a conciliation agreement between the company and its creditors The conciliation agreement will be reviewed and either acknowledged or approved by the commercial court Goal: to ensure the viability of the business of the company Deferral of payment: possibility to request, from the president of the commercial court that has opened the conciliation proceeding, a two-year postponement of payment to a creditcr if this creditor requests payment of its claim during the conciliation (upon petition of the company)

Judicial proceedings Three different categories depending on whether or not the company is insolvent and whether its recovery is or is not possible		
Safeguard proceedings Available to companies that are not yet insolvent but facing difficulties that they cannot cope with by themselves (iii) Opened at request of debtor (Articles L 620-1 onwards of Commercial Code)	**Judicial reorganisation proceedings** (iv) Available to insolvent companies with a possibility of recovery (v) Opened at the request of debtor, creditor or public prosecutor (Articles L 631-1 onwards of Commercial Code)	**Judicial liquidation proceedings** (vi) Available to insolvent companies with no chance of recovery (vii) Opened at request of debtor, creditor or public prosecutor (Articles L 640-1 onwards of Commercial Code)
The opening judgment appoints: • a commissary judge to oversee the proceedings; • a judicial administrator in charge of supervising or assisting the company's management; and • a creditors' representative to represent the creditors' interests Observation period: six months extendable to 18 months during which a safeguard plan is prepared by the company and presented to its creditors Creditors' committees and bondholders: • committee compulsory for companies with a statutory auditor or with more than 150 employees or with an annual turnover of more than €20 million; • invited to vote on the draft of safeguard plan presented by the company with the required majority being two-thirds of debt (by value) held by the voting members; • in the event of a refusal or of a	The opening judgment appoints: • a commissary judge to oversee the proceedings; • a judicial administrator in charge of supervising or assisting the company's management; and • a creditors' representative to represent the creditors' interests Goals: • safeguard the company's activities and prospect of recovery; • save jobs; and • pay creditors Observation period: six months extendable to 18 months during which the company is forbidden to proceed	Appointment of a liquidator by the commercial court Mission: to dispose of the company's assets and repay the debts Opening of liquidation proceedings has the following consequences: • the opening judgment renders the creditors' claims immediately due; • business activity stops and the liquidator proceeds to sale of the company's assets to cover its debts; and • the creditors are paid according to their rank as determined by the nature of their claim and the date on which it arose

continued on next page

failure to vote within six months, the consultation is done individually Deferral of payment: possible up to 10 years' maximum; granted by the commercial court Reduction of payment: not possible In case of an unsuccessful conciliation: Accelerated safeguard proceedings Two forms: • accelerated safeguard proceedings allow the company to be restructured in a very short time frame, with a two-thirds majority within creditors' committees, including trade creditors; and • accelerated financial safeguard proceedings (SFA) aim at treating financial debt only and therefore exclusively concern financial creditors including bondholders, and do not affect other creditors such as suppliers Legal regime: Law of October 22 2010 applicable as of March 1 2011 inspired by the American Chapter 11; and Reform Order 2014-326 dated March 12 2014 entered into force on July 1 2014, which extended the scope of this proceeding and created the accelerated safeguard proceeding. SFA is now a sub-category of the accelerated safeguard proceeding Opening of SFA: preceded by a conciliation proceeding. The agreement negotiated between the company and its financial creditors must be acceptable by	with payment of any pre-petition claim, and continues its business activity Reorganisation period: third parties are invited to bid on all or part of the going concern The judicial administrator can chose whether to terminate ongoing contracts or not, and can require the contracting party to continue its performance in exchange for the performance of the company's post-petition obligations Creditors' committee and bondholders: • committee compulsory for companies with a statutory auditor or with more than 150 employees or with an annual turnover of more than €20 million; • invited to vote on the draft of safeguard plan presented by the company, with the required majority being two-thirds of debt (by value) held by the voting members; • in the event of a refusal or of a failure to vote within six months, the consultation is done individually	

continued on next page

most of the creditors to prove that the adoption of a safeguard plan in a SFA is likely to occur within a period of a month (the agreement will then become the draft plan). If not, the court shall not authorise the opening of the SFA	Reorganisation plan: can combine debt restructuring, recapitalisation of the company, a debt-for-equity swap and the sale of some assets of the company	
Opening conditions: either form of proceedings may only be opened in the course of a conciliation proceeding at the request of the debtor. The legal representative must file a petition with the court. The following eligibility conditions must be fulfilled by the debtor who cannot be insolvent on the date of the request unless the proceeding follows a conciliation opened where the debtor was already insolvent for less than 45 days: • the debtor draws up consolidated annual accounts; or • the debtor's accounts are certified and the debtor employs more than 20 people, or has a turnover of at least €3 million, or has a balance sheet total of at least €1.5 million	If the court decides that no proposed plan is viable, it can approve the sale of part or all of the business to reimburse creditors	
Safeguard proceeding: opened following a conciliation where unanimous consent cannot be reached but it is shown that a majority one can be acquired. The debtor must therefore show that it has drafted a safeguard plan which is likely to be supported by a majority of the creditors that will take part in the safeguard proceeding. The public prosecutor is called to the hearing of the court.		
Potential actions to challenge the opening of the proceeding: the judgment opening the proceeding may be challenged		

continued on next page

by third parties through the filing of a third-party objection before the same court as the one that opened the proceeding within 10 days of the publication of the opening judgment (two months for persons residing abroad). In order to be admissible, it must satisfy the conditions of Article 583 of the Code of Civil procedure, which makes it very limited:
- The requesting party must not be a party to the challenged judgment or have been represented in the hearing leading to the judgment, and must have an interest in challenging it;
- A creditor or a person who was represented in the hearing leading to the judgment may none the less challenge the judgment if it can demonstrate fraud affecting its rights, or that it suffered personal and specific harm

Effects of the proceedings:
- The opening of an accelerated safeguard proceeding launches an observation period of three months during which a safeguard restructuring plan (the one negotiated in the conciliation proceeding) must be voted on by the creditors and submitted to the court for approval;
- The opening of an SFA launches an observation period of one month, which may be extended for one additional month

prohibited where there is an automatic stay, even if the repayment dates fall within the observation period of the proceeding.

If the payment of interest is prohibited during the observation period as a result of the automatic stay, interest shall however continue to accrue if it arises from a loan with an initial duration of at least one year or from a contract providing for deferred repayment of at least one year.

2.2 Appointment of a third party

In a safeguard proceeding or judicial reorganisation, a judicial administrator is appointed at the commencement of the proceeding to supervise, assist or replace the management.

In a safeguard proceeding, the management remains in place and the appointed judicial administrator generally only supervises it. Sometimes the judicial administrator can have a mandate to assist the management, which is equivalent to a co-management.

In a judicial reorganisation, the appointed judicial administrator is generally given a mandate to assist the management (co-management). Sometimes, however, the judicial administrator can be in complete charge of the management. Such a situation will arise where the judicial administrator has doubts as to the ability of the existing management to carry on the business (ie, a lack of confidence in the current management).

Some decisions are the exclusive purview of the judicial administrator, such as the decision to continue an ongoing contract.

In a judicial liquidation, the management of the company will not be in charge, and the judicial administrator will take over.

2.3 Privilege of new money

New money lenders who extend credit to the company as part of conciliation proceedings rank ahead of all pre-petition and post-petition claims, except for the arrears of wages and post-filing court costs.

In safeguard or reorganisation proceedings, post-petition claims benefit from a statutory privilege provided that they:

- arose for the purpose of funding the observation period; and
- were directly useful to the company's activities during the observation period.

Post-petition debts must be paid when they fall due, if not they rank higher than all secured or unsecured pre-petition claims.

2.4 Debt-for-equity swaps

In safeguard or judicial reorganisation proceedings, Article L 626-30-2 of the Commercial Code provides that creditors' committees and the general meeting of the bondholders may vote in favour of a conversion of their debts into securities giving access, immediately or in the future, to the share capital of the company.

A new law which came into force on August 8 2015 (the 'Macron Law') now allows such a debt-for-equity swap to be forced on shareholders in certain judicial reorganisation proceedings. The Macron Law only applies to companies placed into reorganisation proceedings after August 8 2015.

The Macron Law introduces two mechanisms to force out shareholders: the forced dilution of shareholders and the forced sale of the shares and other interests in the share capital held by opposing shareholders.

In accordance with Article L 631-19-2 of the Commercial Code, either mechanism requires that the four following conditions must be met:

- The company must have at least 150 employees or constitute, under the French Labour Code, a dominant company;
- The cessation of business by the company could have a materially adverse effect on the national or regional economy and on employment in this area;
- The change in the company's share capital appears to be the only serious solution to avoid causing such an effect and to enable the continuation of the business; and
- The change in the share capital provided for in the reorganisation plan is not approved during the shareholders' meeting.

Seen as a welcome reform, the eviction mechanism is much more complex and detailed than the eviction process that was already in place. This new regime, combined with the reforms in March 2014, should encourage creditors to propose restructuring plans involving debt-for-equity swaps. It is also likely to create a renewed interest from turnaround investment funds for loan-to-own strategies in France, as it shifts the existing balance between creditors and shareholders in favour of the former.

From a turnaround perspective, it is unfortunate that the new mechanism is only available in the context of judicial reorganisation proceedings (ie, at a time when the distressed company is already insolvent), and the triggers are considered to be too high, which severely limits the companies eligible for it.

2.5 Sale of assets

In an amicable proceeding or a safeguard proceeding there is no specific provisions under French law allowing the relevant commercial court or the judicial administrator to organise the sale of assets of the company. The assets can however be sold under a conciliation agreement or a safeguard plan.

In a judicial reorganisation, third parties are allowed to bid for all or part of the assets. The assignment plan which must be drawn up in respect of the going concern is regulated by the Commercial Code.

In a liquidation proceeding, the liquidator can try to sell the going concern through an assignment plan, or sell the assets separately.

In principle, sales of assets are supposed to be made through public auction. Nevertheless, in order to get better prices, the commissary judge may authorise a private auction or a sale by mutual agreement.

In any event, a notice of the sale of each asset must be published by the liquidator prior to the sale (through an internet website).

Certain persons related to the company (such as managers and their family members) are prevented from acquiring assets in the context of liquidation proceedings unless they obtain an authorisation from the commissary judge.

One must pay attention to the fact that the transfer of certain assets to a purchaser may trigger the automatic transfer of the employment contracts assigned to those assets if they constitute an 'autonomous economic entity' under the definition in the Labour Code, which is maintained by the purchaser under the same conditions.

When the criteria for the existence of an autonomous economic entity are met, the parties (the seller, the purchaser and the employees) may not object to the transfer, under Article L 1224-1 of the Labour Code.

3. Insolvency-related considerations that an investor should take into account when investing in France

3.1 Equitable and voluntary subordination

There is no principle of equitable subordination under French law pursuant to which a loan granted by shareholders should be treated as equity.

In insolvency proceedings, secured creditors are ranked ahead of unsecured creditors. But until recently, contractual subordination was not explicitly recognised by French statute law, although French legal scholars shared the view that contractual subordination was valid under French law: in their view, creditors, whether secured or unsecured, could subordinate their rights voluntarily. More recently, French law has formally recognised the enforceability of subordination agreements: Article L 626-30-2(2°) of the Commercial Code provides that a safeguard plan relating to a French debtor in safeguard proceedings must take into account all subordination agreements entered into by that debtor's creditors before the start of the proceedings (the same rule applies to reorganisation proceedings). In liquidation proceedings, the secured creditors are ranked ahead of unsecured creditors and paid in priority even if a subordination agreement applies.

3.2 Suspect period (claw-back)

A lender should also be aware of the existence of a suspect period, taken into consideration by French courts. This period begins on the date on which a court considers that the company became unable to pay its debts and ends on the date the insolvency proceeding is opened.

Certain acts or transactions made or entered into during the suspect period are either automatically void, or can be declared so by the court. For example, new security granted during the suspect period to secure a pre-existing debt could be declared void by the commercial court, on the request of the judicial administrator or the liquidator of the company.

If, in order to delay the opening of insolvency proceedings, the company obtained funds by overly expensive means, the company's manager(s), and possibly in certain circumstances the lender, could be held liable.

3.3 Security rights

French law allows for other protections in favour of creditors:

211

- Claims may be secured by a security conferring a retention right;
- Claims may be assigned by way of a 'Daily assignment' of receivables under which creditors can themselves seek payment of the assigned receivables. A debtor can transfer present or future debts owed to it by third parties to the creditor together with all security interests attached to them (Article L 313-23 of the Monetary and Financial Code). Such a Dailly assignment of receivables can only be used if all the following apply:
  - The creditor is a credit or banking institution licensed to carry out banking activities in France;
  - The receivables are assigned to secure facilities granted in connection with business activities; and
  - The assigned receivables arose during business or professional activities.

Claims must be assigned using a special transfer form signed by the assignor, describing the amount and type of receivables to be assigned. The assignment comes into effect from the date specified on the form. Failing any agreement to the contrary, the remittance of the transfer form results in the legal assignment to the assignee of the security interest attached to the assigned receivables. The Paris Commercial Court held, in a widely discussed decision rendered in the *Coeur Défense* Case (Commercial Court of Paris, October 19 2009), that a Dailly assignment was enforceable despite the debtor's filing for insolvency. This decision was confirmed by the Court of Appeals of Versailles on February 28 2013.

- Claims may be secured by a fiducie (trust) agreement under which the creditors can enforce their rights over the assets transferred to the trust, except where the creditor initially agreed that those assets would remain in the company's possession.

A Law of February 19 2007 introduced this concept to the French legal system. In a fiducie, one or several settlers transfer assets, rights or security interests to a trustee that manages those assets, according to the terms of the trust agreement, for the benefit of designated beneficiaries. This trust agreement must be registered with the French tax authorities within one month of signing. Compliance with this filing obligation is necessary to ensure validity and perfection of the security.

3.4 Appointment of controllers

There is a feature in French insolvency proceedings that can allow a creditor to gain access to more information concerning the proceedings.

A creditor may request to be appointed as a 'controller' by filing a request to the commissary judge (such a filing is made through the posting of a request to the relevant clerk of the commercial court). Every insolvency proceeding has between one and five controllers to represent the creditors, and to assist the creditors' representative and the commissary judge in monitoring the management of the company. For that purpose, the controllers have privileged access to information regarding the proceeding. They are entitled to review any document transmitted to the trustee or to the creditors' representative.

3.5 Insolvency of groups of companies

The French insolvency regime does not yet include specific rules tailored for corporate groups. Therefore, a separate insolvency proceeding must be opened with respect to each distressed company of the group, and conflicts of jurisdiction (even within France among different local courts) may arise as a result. Practitioners have attempted to avoid such conflicts and centralise all proceedings concerning group companies using concepts such as 'centre of main interests' (stemming from EC Regulation 1346/2000 of May 29 2000 on insolvency proceedings) or a merger of the assets and liabilities. None of these concepts are, however, ideal for the (albeit common) situation where a corporate group is affected by financial difficulties.

Developments in the legal framework for restructuring: Germany

Sacha Lürken
Kirkland & Ellis International LLP

1. German legal framework for restructuring

German law generally (with the exception of German-law governed bonds and financial institutions, discussed below under heading 4) has no restructuring procedure short of the insolvency process.[1] This has resulted in several prominent restructuring cases where German debtor companies have resorted to non-German restructuring procedures, in particular English schemes of arrangement (as in the cases of Tele Columbus, Rodenstock, Primacom, APCOA Parking and CBR Fashion) or English insolvency procedures (as with Schefenacker and ATU). Discussion on whether to introduce a general pre-insolvency restructuring procedure in German law has reemerged in the light of the European Commission's capital markets union action plan, which includes a legislative initiative to present a draft directive on pre-insolvency restructuring procedures in the fourth quarter of 2016.[2]

1.1 Duty to file

A German company's directors must (to avoid personal liability) file for insolvency (Section 15a Insolvency Code) if the company is either:

- cash-flow insolvent (Section 17 of the Insolvency Code); or
- balance-sheet insolvent (Section 19 of the Insolvency Code),

without undue delay, and in any case at the latest within three weeks.

(a) Cash-flow insolvency

Cash-flow insolvency means that the debtor is unable to pay its liabilities that are due for payment (Section 17(1) of the Insolvency Code). If the debtor has generally ceased to make payments, there is a (rebuttable) presumption that the debtor is cash-flow insolvent (Section 17(2) of the Insolvency Code).

For forward-looking purposes, based on the case law by the German Federal Supreme Court,[3] cash-flow insolvency is tested as a comparison of:

---

[1] The legal framework of the German insolvency process is set out in the Insolvency Code. Many other laws, most notably, but only, the Civil Code, the Commercial Code, the Civil Procedure Code and the Real Estate Enforcement Act, also contain provisions relevant to insolvency-related issues.
[2] See European Commission Communication of September 30 2015: *Action Plan on Building a Capital Market Union*, COM(2015) 468 final (ec.europa.eu/finance/capital-markets-union/docs/building-cmu-action-plan_en.pdf).
[3] *Bundesgerichtshof* (Federal Supreme Court; 'BGH'), judgment of May 24 2005 (case 123/04).

- cash; and
- assets that can immediately be turned into cash; against
- all liabilities due and payable at a specific date.

Where the total of the cash and relevant assets is at least 90% of due and payable liabilities, there is (generally) no cash-flow insolvency, unless it can already be anticipated that the cash and assets will not reach 100% of due and payable liabilities in the near future.

Where the total of cash and assets is less than 90% of due and payable liabilities, the question is asked whether they will become more than 90% within three weeks.
- Where the answer is yes, then (generally) there is no cash-flow insolvency, unless creditors would be unduly impaired through the three week period.
- Where the answer is no, then (generally) there is cash-flow insolvency, unless in very exceptional circumstances creditors can be expected to wait.

The Federal Supreme Court did not provide guidance on whether, where the total of cash and assets are less than 90% of liabilities, the liabilities to be taken into account need to include not only those due and payable on the date of the test, but also those becoming due and payable during the three-week period. In practice, management advisers should include these.

For retrospective purposes (eg, personal liability of management or avoidance claims), courts will often determine cash-flow insolvency based on the argument that the debtor has generally ceased to make payments to its creditors. Cessation of payments means any kind of expression of the debtor that it will not be able to satisfy all of its creditors. Whether the debtor generally has ceased to make payments will always be assessed based on each individual case, but the following indications usually can be considered as a general cessation of payments:[4]
- non-payment of salaries and social security liabilities;
- non-payment of costs essential for the continuation of the business;
- returned cheques;
- ignoring invoices and payment reminders; and
- creditors' proceedings.

If the debtor is still making payments to certain creditors, but not to others, it will depend on whether the unpaid due creditors are material compared to the creditors paid.[5]

(b) Balance-sheet insolvency

A debtor company is suffering from balance-sheet insolvency:
- if its liabilities (on a nominal value basis) are higher than its assets (on a fair value basis);
- unless it is more likely than not that the company can continue as a going concern (a positive going concern prognosis).

---

4 BGH, order of August 21 2013 (case 1 StR 665/12).
5 BGH, judgment of October 12 2006 (case IX ZR 228/03).

In practice, most emphasis is put on the going concern prognosis. A positive going concern prognosis requires that:
- the debtor will more likely than not be able to pay all its liabilities as and when they fall due; and
- will be able to do so within the forecast period.

The forecast period typically covers the current and next financial year; if it can already be anticipated that material liabilities will become due after that period (eg, maturity of substantial financial indebtedness), the forecast period also needs to extend until that time.

If liabilities are not scheduled to become due and payable during the forecast period, but the creditor has acceleration rights, it must be more likely than not that the creditor will not accelerate.[6] If a liability will become due, it can only be disregarded if the debtor can certainly expect that the creditor will agree to a standstill or extension of the liability.[7]

(c) *Imminent cash-flow insolvency*

Debtors have the right, but no duty, to file for insolvency in case of imminent cash-flow insolvency. Imminent cash-flow insolvency is broadly similar to a negative going concern prognosis (see under heading (1.1(b) above), so is given if a debtor company will more likely than not be unable to pay all its liabilities as and when they fall due, within the forecast period (see above for details).

1.2 Automatic stay

No automatic stay applies upon a filing, but the court can (and typically will) order a stay on certain enforcement actions by preliminary order under Section 21 of the Insolvency Code. It is in the court's discretion which orders to issue, but with respect to stays on enforcement, the law lists in particular:
- a stay of court-led enforcement procedures brought by individual creditors in respect of the debtor's non-real estate assets;
- a stay on the realisation of certain collateral (see below) by secured creditors outside a court process, or by suppliers under retention of title, if the assets serving as collateral are of material relevance to continuing the company's business during the preliminary proceedings.

This preliminary stay can only affect certain assets serving as collateral. The law refers expressly to moveable assets (Section 166(1) of the Insolvency Code) and receivables assigned for security (Section 166(2) of the Insolvency Code). It is highly controversial in German law whether security over shares in subsidiaries can be made subject to a stay order. A recent judgment from the German Federal Supreme Court dealing with pledges over shares in a German listed company certificated under a

---

6   BGH, judgment of December 5 2013 (case IX ZR 93/11).
7   BGH, judgment of November 22 2012 (case IX ZR 62/10).

global note[8] did not comment on this question generally.[9] In practice, most share pledges are taken over non-listed limited liability companies or limited partnerships with uncertificated shares. For these share pledges, however, a court might still issue a preliminary order to stay enforcement as part of the general discretion granted to it under Section 21 of the Insolvency Code.

Following opening of the proceedings, no individual court-led creditor enforcement actions can be taken. Any floating collateral (typically, collateral over inventory and receivables) will crystallise on the day of the opening of insolvency proceedings; in other words, assets produced or acquired, and receivables generated by the debtor company, after that date will not be captured by any security agreements, but will become available for distribution.

However, German law has neither a concept of priming existing security, nor a general stay on the realisation of collateral. Secured creditors generally retain their individual right to realise their collateral (including collateral over real estate) except for moveable assets[10] and receivables assigned for security, which can only be realised by the insolvency administrator (or, in debtor-in-possession proceedings, the debtor) (see Section 166 of the Insolvency Code). The secured creditors will still receive the proceeds of the realisation of this collateral after deduction of a 4% handling fee and a realisation fee, which has a default rate of 5% that can be adjusted if actual costs are substantially higher or lower (see Section 171 of the Insolvency Code).

As the secured creditors' general right to realise their collateral is value-destructive for any form of merger or acquisition process or insolvency plan (for which see below), secured creditors in practice do not usually exercise their enforcement rights, in return for a share in the proceeds negotiated with the administrator. If proceeds are sufficient to cover the fees involved in the process and administrative expenses, the share accruing to secured creditors can be up to 100% of their secured claims, including interest, minus the 9% handling and realisation fee.

1.3 Insolvency courts

Germany has specialised insolvency courts established within its local courts. However, in many smaller local courts, judges in insolvency courts will not only handle insolvency matters, but also other matters generally assigned to local courts. In addition, after the opening of insolvency proceedings, cases are generally deferred to court clerks, even in large company insolvencies. Local courts are the lowest courts in the German court system; judges who want to pursue a career in the judicial system will usually look to become judges in higher courts after a certain time. This

---

8   BGH, judgment of September 24 2015 (caseIX ZR 272/13).
9   The court held that German law shares certificated in a global note held in a securities deposit account subject to the German Securities Deposit Account Act were, due to the specific *in rem* property rights that a holder of global notes has under the German Securities Deposit Account Act, part of the debtor's moveable assets. The court added, though, that only shares of sufficient number to amount to a 'commercial holding' were to be excluded from a secured creditor's individual enforcement rights. The court did not set a threshold for when a commercial holding has to be assumed, but referred to the presumption in generally accepted German accounting principles under Section 271(1)3 of the Commercial Code, which sets a threshold of 20% of the company's equity.
10 See above for discussion whether shares in subsidiaries are moveable assets.

system has had the effect that, apart from a few exceptions, no insolvency judge has remained in their office for a long time.

Based on the Act on Further Facilitation of Business Restructurings (known as 'ESUG') of 2012, a few changes have been introduced:
- Insolvency judges now have to have 'demonstrable' knowledge of insolvency law and its surrounding laws, or it has to be expected that a judge will soon acquire this knowledge.
- Court decisions during the preliminary proceedings and decisions in insolvency plan procedures need to be rendered by a judge, and cannot be deferred to a court clerk (Section 22 of the Act on Court Clerks).

However, proposed reforms to have large company insolvency cases assigned to higher courts, or to concentrate large insolvency cases in certain local courts, have failed due to political resistance.

1.4 Insolvency administrators and debtor-in-possession proceedings

Unless a debtor applies for, and the court approves, debtor-in-possession status upon filing, the court will appoint a preliminary administrator.

(a) *Preliminary administrator*

If the court appoints a preliminary administrator, it has two choices:
- It can appoint a preliminary administrator with the general power to manage the debtor's assets (a so-called 'strong' preliminary administrator). This happens rarely in practice, as expenses incurred by the strong preliminary administrator as part of continuing the debtor's business will become administrative expenses and rank senior to general unsecured claims.
- It can issue specific instructions for the preliminary administrator. In most cases, the court will not appoint a strong preliminary administrator, but issue specific instructions. In most cases, one of the instructions will be that company's debtors have to make all payments to the preliminary administrator to discharge them from their liability. In practice, the court will also authorise the preliminary administrator to enter into certain, specific liabilities with administrative expenses status.

(b) *Debtor-in-possession status*

If the company has filed for debtor-in-possession status, the court has to grant it if either:
- the company's filing is part of a 'protective shield' filing (Section 270b of the Insolvency Code) and all other requirements have been complied with (in particular, the company has submitted an opinion by a restructuring expert that a restructuring is not expected to be manifestly unsuccessful); or
- it is made as a regular filing, and it is supported by a unanimous resolution of the preliminary creditors' committee, unless the court finds that debtor-in-possession status would be evidently disadvantageous to creditors.

In recent cases, debtor-in-possession status has been denied by courts based on (manifest) disadvantage to creditors for the following reasons:
- where the preliminary creditors' committee has unanimously objected to debtor-in-possession status;[11]
- where a material creditor has objected to debtor-in-possession status;[12]
- where the filing is incomplete, in particular where it does not contain all the details on the company's creditors required by law;[13]
- where the company's management is likely to face personal liability charges[14] or there is another conflict of interest;[15]
- where the costs of debtor-in-possession status (including fees for a chief restructuring officer to be appointed to the company's management) would be higher than the costs of regular insolvency proceedings;[16]
- where the company does not have a business that requires to be continued.[17]

Where debtor-in-possession status is approved, the court will appoint a (preliminary) trustee. The (preliminary) trustee's tasks are:
- to investigate the company's financial condition;
- to supervise the debtor's management of the assets;
- to notify the court and the (preliminary) creditors' committee of any facts that make it likely that the debtor-in-possession management impairs creditors;
- to consent to incurrence of out-of-ordinary course liabilities;
- after the opening of insolvency proceedings, to consent to the appointment or removal of managing directors or company directors;
- also after the opening of insolvency proceedings, if it is so ordered by the court, to consent to transactions by the company in order for them to be legally effective; and
- again after the opening of insolvency proceedings, to receive and examine filings of proof of debt by the company's creditors.

1.5 Insolvency process

The insolvency process is divided into two stages:
- first, from the initial filing until the opening of the insolvency proceedings, there are 'preliminary proceedings', which usually last up to three months, during which the business is usually continued, and typically the process of seeking new investors is initiated; and
- secondly, the formally opened insolvency proceedings, in which creditors resolve whether the debtor's business is to be sold, reorganised or liquidated.

---

11 *Landgericht* (District Court) Halle (Saale), order of November 14 2014 (case 3 T 86/14) – "MIFA".
12 *Amtsgericht* (Local Court) Köln, order of July 1 2013 (case 72 IN 211/13).
13 *Amtsgericht* Hamburg, order of February 28 2014 (case 67c IN 1/14).
14 *Amtsgericht* Hamburg, order of December 18 2013 (case 67c IN 410/13).
15 *Amtsgericht* Hamburg, order of February 28 2014 (case 67c IN 1/14)
16 *Amtsgericht* Essen, order of February 3 2015 (case 163 IN 14/15); *Amtsgericht* Mannheim, order of February 21 2014 (case 4 IN 115/14).
17 *Amtsgericht* Hamburg, order of December 18 2013 (case 67c IN 410/13).

Typically, the preliminary insolvency proceedings last for three months from the filing date, to allow calculation of the cost of state-funding of any unpaid wages and salaries during the three months prior to the opening of the insolvency proceedings. After that period, the court will open insolvency proceedings, unless the company's assets are insufficient to fund the costs of the proceedings.

Within, at the latest, three months after the opening of proceedings, a creditors' meeting has to agree on liquidation, sale or continuation of the debtor's business. The creditors' meeting can also agree an insolvency plan. The plan can only be presented by the administrator or by the debtor.

(a) *Standard insolvency procedure*

If the company's business is sold or its assets are otherwise liquidated, the administrator will distribute any proceeds less administrative expenses and fees to the general unsecured creditors and, to the extent allocated to their collateral, to secured creditors. The company debtor will be struck off the companies' register. Ranking of claims is generally as follows:

- court fees;
- fees of the preliminary and non-preliminary insolvency administrators or trustees and fees for the members or creditors' committee; and
- administrative expenses incurred by the administrator, including from electing to continue executory contracts. These expenses will typically be for advisers and certain key contracts, such as supplier and lease contracts on terms favourable to the estate.

(b) *Insolvency plan procedure*

Instead of selling or otherwise liquidating the debtor's business and striking the company off the companies register, the company can be reorganised through an 'insolvency plan'. The insolvency plan procedure is closely modelled on the Chapter 11 process under the US Bankruptcy Code.

Right to propose insolvency plan: Only the management of the debtor company or the administrator (upon instruction by the creditors' meeting) have the right to propose a plan. Creditors or investors have no rights to propose a plan. However, creditors whose consent is material for approval of the plan, such as secured creditors (see below), will typically be informally involved in the plan drafting process. The same applies for investors.

Content of insolvency plan: The insolvency plan consists of two parts:
- a declaratory part containing a description of the factual background; and
- a constructive part setting out how the legal position of each respective creditor class will be affected under the plan.

The factual part describes all information relevant for creditors to make an informed voting decision on the debtor's business, actions taken prior to and during the insolvency proceedings and so on. The constructive part sets out the different classes of creditors (see below), how the plan will affect creditors' rights and (if applicable) any necessary corporate actions, such as share capital reductions and increases, change of articles and so on.

Class formation: The insolvency plan can impair the rights of secured creditors, general unsecured creditors, subordinated creditors and shareholders. It cannot affect the rights of administrative creditors (creditors whose claims have administrative expenses status). The plan must provide for separate classes for at least secured and unsecured creditors. Generally, no class is required for subordinated creditors; their claims are deemed to be waived unless otherwise provided for in the plan. A separate class for shareholders is required if the plan impairs shareholders' rights. The plan can provide for additional classes if it is necessary to distinguish between the creditors' legal and commercial interests. It should provide for separate classes for employees and the pension protection fund if their claims are to be impaired under the plan. In practice, separate classes are created for trade creditors, financial creditors, small creditors and other unsecured creditors.

Voting on plan: A plan is accepted if, in a creditors' meeting, in each class, a majority (50%) by both amount and number of creditors present in the meeting vote in favour of the plan. In the class of shareholders, a majority of 50% of shares is sufficient. If those majorities are not reached, the court can still confirm the plan (ie, impose a cram-down) if:
- a majority of classes has voted in favour;
- the plan does not put non-consenting classes into a worse position than they would be without a plan;
- no creditor receives any value in excess of its par claim;
- no creditor ranking equally with a creditor in a non-consenting class receives more value; and
- no subordinated creditor or shareholder receives any value.

Confirmation of plan: The court will (after consultation with the creditors' committee, the administrator and the debtor company's management) confirm the plan if:
- the plan substantially complies with all legal requirements, in particular with regards to class formation;
- the plan has been accepted in the creditors' meeting with the majorities required (as set out above);
- the accepting vote was not unduly influenced (eg, through buying votes); and
- no creditor or shareholder has objected, or, if a creditor or shareholder has objected:
  - the objecting person has not provided present evidence that it would likely receive less value under the plan than without a plan; and
  - the plan provides for sufficient reserves to compensate for the difference between what the objecting person receives under the plan and what it claims it would receive without a plan.

Appeal: After confirmation of the plan by the court, creditors or shareholders who voted against the plan and filed an objection in the creditors' meeting can, within two weeks, file an appeal. The appeal is successful if they can provide present evidence that they would receive materially less value under the plan than without the plan. As long as the appeal is pending, the plan confirmation does not become effective. The proposer of the plan can, however, file a motion with the court of appeal to grant immediate execution of the plan. The court of appeal can grant the motion if it considers that its benefits outweigh the appellant's potential damage.

Effect of plan: Once the court order confirming the plan has become effective because no appeals have been filed, or the court of appeal has granted a motion to consummate the plan notwithstanding an appeal (see above), the plan will be binding on all creditors and shareholders, whether or not they were present in the creditors' meeting, or have filed a proof of debt. However, under German law claims are not time-barred by adoption of the plan. Creditors could still file proofs of debt after confirmation of the plan and are entitled to receive what other similarly situated creditors in their class receive under the plan.[18] Debtor companies therefore need to take care in identifying the amount of all potential liabilities completely before finalising the financing of the insolvency plan (which can be an issue, eg, for mass tort liabilities).

2. Recent reforms of German insolvency law

The present German Insolvency Code was enacted in 1994 and came into effect as of January 1 1999, replacing the more than 100 years old Bankruptcy Code and the 1935 Composition Code.

On October 18 2008, during the financial crisis, the definition of balance-sheet insolvency (see above) was modified to its current version (originally only until 2010, but later extended to 2013 and now without limitation).[19]

On March 1 2012, the 'ESUG' (the Act on Further Facilitation of Business Restructurings) came into effect, which aimed at facilitating in-court restructurings of going concerns and improving creditor involvement in insolvency proceedings. In only a very few large cases, such as *IVG Immobilien AG*, and a few more mid-cap cases, have there been successful restructurings since ESUG came into effect. The majority of insolvencies have not benefited, as ESUG requires careful preparation, triggering significant outlays for advisers, experienced chief restructuring officers and trustees. As many companies prepare for insolvency too late, they will not have sufficient cash reserves to meet these costs.

The key changes introduced by ESUG are discussed in the following paragraphs.

| 18 | There is a, less restrictive, concept in Section 259b of the Insolvency Code, which subjects any unfiled claims to a one year time-limit after the date of the meeting at which the plan is voted upon. |
| 19 | Under the former definition, a company was already balance-sheet insolvent if its liabilities exceeded its assets; the going concern test was only relevant for the valuation of assets. |

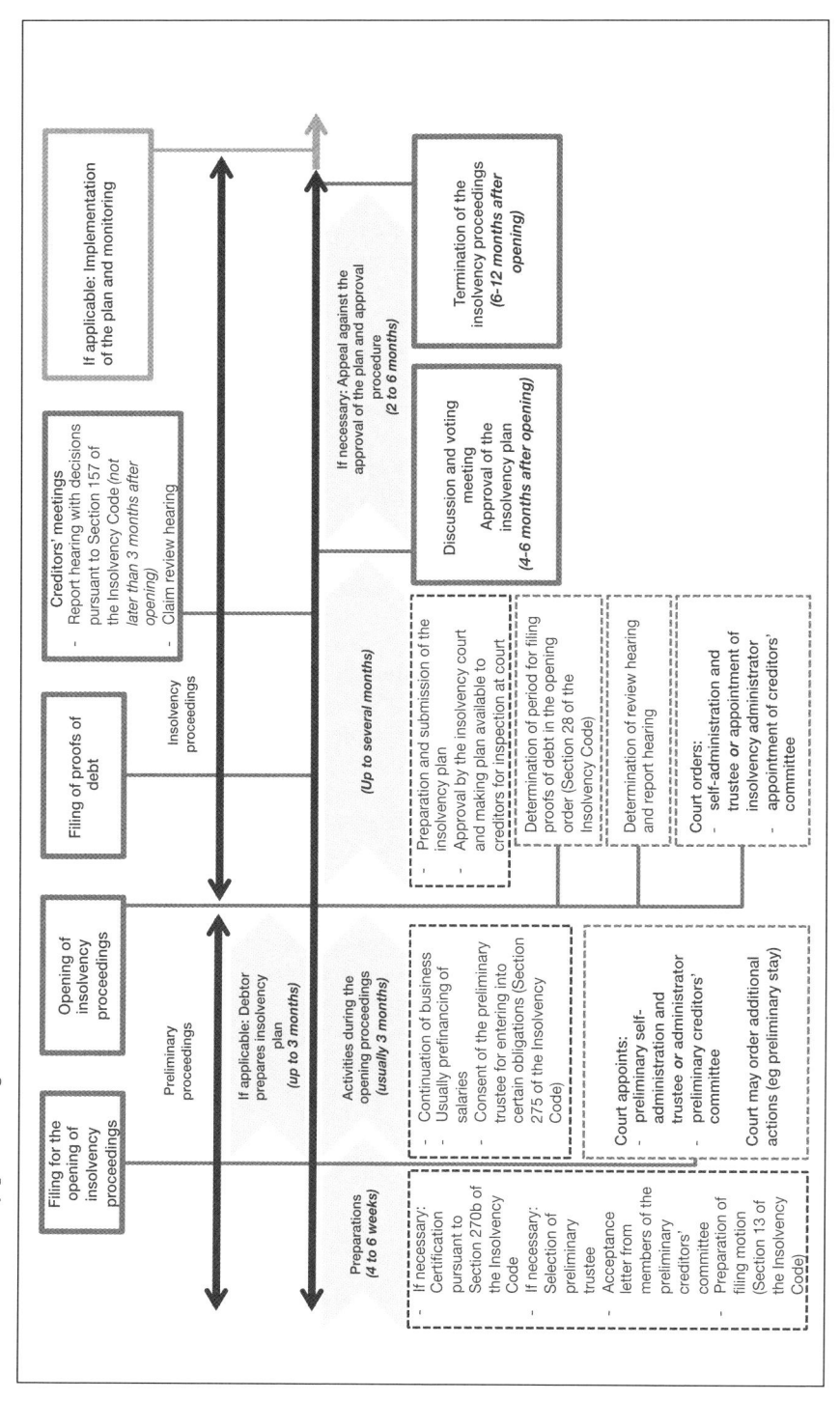

Developments in the legal framework for restructuring: Germany

In court insolvency proceedings

| Preparations (4 to 6 weeks) | Filing for the opening of insolvency proceedings | Preliminary proceedings | Activities during the opening proceedings (usually 3 months) | Opening of insolvency proceedings | If applicable: Debtor prepares insolvency plan (up to 3 months) | Filing of proofs of debt | Insolvency proceedings (Up to several months) | Creditors' meetings - Report hearing with decisions pursuant to Section 157 of the Insolvency Code (not later than 3 months after opening) - Claim review hearing | Discussion and voting meeting Approval of the insolvency plan (4-6 months after opening) | If necessary: Appeal against the approval of the plan and approval procedure (2 to 6 months) | If applicable: Implementation of the plan and monitoring | Termination of the insolvency proceedings (6-12 months after opening) |

Preparations (4 to 6 weeks):
- If necessary: Certification pursuant to Section 270b of the Insolvency Code
- If necessary: Selection of preliminary trustee
- Acceptance letter from members of the preliminary creditors' committee
- Preparation of filing motion (Section 13 of the Insolvency Code)

Activities during the opening proceedings (usually 3 months):
- Continuation of business
- Usually prefinancing of salaries
- Consent of the preliminary trustee for entering into certain obligations (Section 275 of the Insolvency Code)

Court appoints:
- preliminary self-administration and trustee or administrator
- preliminary creditors' committee

Court may order additional actions (eg preliminary stay)

- Preparation and submission of the insolvency plan
- Approval by the insolvency court and making plan available to creditors for inspection at court

Determination of period for filing proofs of debt in the opening order (Section 28 of the Insolvency Code)

Determination of review hearing and report hearing

Court orders:
- self-administration and trustee or appointment of insolvency administrator
- appointment of creditors' committee

224

2.1 Strengthening of creditor control

(a) Mandatory preliminary creditors' committee

The court now must[20] appoint a preliminary creditors' committee for companies meeting certain business thresholds,[21] and shall[22] appoint a preliminary creditors' committee if eligible members have been proposed and have accepted their appointment. This is important, as the preliminary creditors' committee has the right to be heard on certain matters, such as the appointment of an administrator or trustee (see below), and in general will also be involved in the day-to-day administration of the business.

(b) Creditors' committee's role

The court now must consult with the (preliminary) creditors' committee (which is now mandatory, see above) prior to:

- appointing a (preliminary) administrator; or
- granting (preliminary) debtor-in-possession administration and appointing a (preliminary) trustee;

unless consultation could result in a delay that affects the debtor's assets. In that case, the (preliminary) creditors' committee can, with a unanimous vote, appoint a different (preliminary) administrator or (in the case of debtor-in-possession) a different (preliminary) trustee. If the (preliminary) creditors' committee unanimously votes in favour of a particular person as (preliminary) administrator or trustee, the court generally must appoint that person.[23] It is now also expressly permitted to appoint a person who has been advising the debtor company prior to filing, to enable auditors or restructuring professionals, who often have been involved with the debtor's business for months prior to a filing, to be appointed as administrator or trustee.[24] The creditors' committee can also (in case of a 'protective shield' motion) vote to revoke the debtor-in-possession status.[25]

---

20 Under the former law, the court had unfettered discretion as to whether to establish a preliminary creditors' committee.
21 Two of the three following criteria must have been satisfied during the last financial year:
   • €6m assets;
   • €12m revenues;
   • 50 employees.
22 Unless the debtor does not have a business to continue, the costs would be inappropriate, or establishment of the preliminary creditors' committee could result in a delay that affects the debtor's assets.
23 Unless the court finds that the proposed person is not suitable to be appointed as an administrator, eg because of affiliations with the debtor or creditors.
24 It is still not possible to have firms appointed as administrators (as in the United Kingdom), only individuals. Likewise, professionals who have been in management positions at the debtor (such as a chief restructuring officer) cannot be appointed.
25 Section 270b(4)(2) of the Insolvency Code.

(c) Strengthening of debtor-in-possession and insolvency plan restructurings

Strengthening of debtor-in-possession administration: If the company files a motion for debtor-in-possession proceedings, the court will now[26] generally have to grant this. See above under heading 1.4 "Insolvency administrators and debtor-in-possession proceedings" for details.

Strengthening of insolvency plan procedures: The rights of non-consenting creditors to appeal insolvency plans have been limited.[27] See above under heading 1.5(b) "Insolvency Plan Procedure" side heading "Appeal" for details.

(d) Facilitation of debt-equity-swaps

The ESUG added shareholders as a class of persons who could be impaired under the insolvency plan.[28] In addition, any other corporate action (such as a capital reduction and increase, change of articles and so on) can now be implemented as part of an insolvency plan. Change of control clauses cannot be triggered by a change of control that occurs as part of an insolvency plan (see below under heading 3 "Debt-for-equity swaps under German insolvency law" for details).

3. Debt-for-equity swaps under German insolvency law

Debt-for-equity swaps under general German corporate law require the consent of each affected creditor, an opinion as to their fairness and a resolution from at least 75% of the shareholders present at the meeting. One of the most recent cases of a debt-for-equity swap under general corporate law was the financial restructuring of SolarWorld AG.

In an insolvency process, as part of an insolvency plan, the creditors' meeting can resolve on a debt-for-equity swap. In addition to the voting majorities for an insolvency plan (see above under heading 1.5(b) "Insolvency plan procedure" side heading "Plan voting"), each creditor who has to take equity will have to consent individually. The shareholders will vote as a separate class. At least 50% approval by share value is sufficient in the shareholders' class. If this level is not achieved, shareholders can be crammed down. The most recent case of a debt-for-equity swap in an insolvency proceeding was the *IVG Immobilien AG* case.

In either case, a debt-for-equity swap consists of two steps:
- The existing registered share capital is written down (outside insolvency, typically to between 0 and 5%; in insolvency to 0%);
- Then new shares are issued against contribution of the debt liabilities (which typically are then cancelled).

---

26 Under the former law, the court had to make a positive determination that debtor-in-possession status would not impair the creditors' interests; ie, if it was in doubt, the court would rather dismiss the motion. Now, the court has to make a positive determination that creditors' interests would be impaired in the event of debtor-in-possession status.
27 In particular, under the former law, any appeal delayed the confirmation of the plan until the court of appeal had decided, and an appellant did not have to prove that it would receive less under the plan.
28 Under the former law, debt-for-equity swaps could not be implemented as part of the insolvency process. The shareholders' consent had to be sought under general corporate German law.

Debt-for-equity swaps also typically require:
- tax waivers for the profits created from the cancellation of the indebtedness – as German companies' income is taxed with corporate income tax (which is levied by the Tax Office) and trade tax (which is levied by municipalities), it can be difficult to obtain all tax waivers within a short period of time (for instance, for the proposed insolvency plan of the German retail chain Karstadt, several dozen municipalities would have had to grant trade tax waivers);
- waivers of change-of-control clauses in commercial agreements; although this is mitigated if the debt-equity-swap is part of an insolvency plan, as contractual counterparties are not permitted to terminate the contract based on a change of control occurring as part of an insolvency plan (Section 225a(4) of the Insolvency Code).
- public offering memorandum – if the securities to be offered will be listed on a stock exchange or otherwise publicly offered, a prospectus will need to be published.

4. Restructuring of bonds and banks

German law has an out-of-court restructuring procedure only for the restructuring of bonds under the Bond Restructuring Act and the restructuring of banks under the Bank Reorganisation Act, but not generally for specific liabilities as is possible under a scheme of arrangement.

4.1 Bond Restructuring Act

(a) Applicable bonds

The Bond Restructuring Act only applies to:
- German law-governed bonds (and guarantees for such bonds);[29]
- that are not issued by a German or Eurozone sovereign or sub-sovereign;[30] and
- are issued after August 5 2009.

(b) Bondholder resolutions

If, and only if, it is provided for in the terms and conditions of the bond through a 'collective action' clause, bondholders can by majority vote in a bondholders' meeting agree to:
- any amendment (other than incurrence of liabilities to the issuer) of these terms and conditions;
- a waiver of past or future events of default;
- appointment of a common representative of the bondholders. The common representative has the right to assert the claims of all bondholders.

---

29 The jurisdiction of the issuer is irrelevant.
30 Similar rules apply for German-law governed sovereign bond issues; most notably, amendments only require a 66²/₃% majority.

(c) Bondholders' meeting[31]

A bondholders' meeting can be convened by the issuer, the common representative (if one has been appointed), or the court, if so requested by at least 5% of bondholders (by amount) who have demonstrated a need.

Notice: There must be a minimum of 14 days' public notice in the online federal gazette (*Bundesanzeiger*).

Place of meeting:[32] The meeting shall be at the registered office of the issuer.[33] If the issuer has no office in Germany, then the meeting shall be held in Frankfurt am Main.

Agenda: The convening person (ie, usually the issuer) has to publish an agenda. Bondholders have the right:
- to file countermotions to a published item on the agenda; and
- if representing at least 5% (by amount) of bondholders, to request that items be added to the agenda.

Chairman and notary: The issuer (represented by its managing director(s)) is chairman of the bondholders' meeting, unless the court (upon a motion by 5% of bondholders) has appointed a different chairman. Minutes of the meeting must be recorded by a notary.

Quorum: To amend material[34] terms and conditions, a quorum of at least[35] 50% of bondholders (by amount) is required. If that quorum is not reached, a second meeting can be convened where the quorum is reduced to 25%.[36] If the quorum is not reached in either meeting, the meeting has failed.

No quorum is required for a resolution to appoint a common representative, unless the common representative shall be authorised to amend the terms and conditions.

Majority: To amend material[37] terms and conditions, a majority of at least[38] 75% of bondholders (by amount) present at the meeting is required. A 50% majority is

---

31 Bondholder resolutions can also be passed in a non-physical ('virtual') bondholders' meeting. Unless indicated otherwise, the same provisions apply.
32 In a virtual bondholders' meeting, bondholders will be given at least 72 hours to submit their votes in text form.
33 If bonds are listed on a regulated market in Germany and have a minimum €100,000 denomination, the meeting can also take place in any other location within the European Union or the European Economic Area.
34 'Material' includes, among other things:
  • extension of maturities or interest payment dates;
  • reduction of principal or interest;
  • subordination;
  • exchange of bonds into shares, other securities or other instruments or rights;
  • release of collateral;
  • change of currency; and
  • waiver of acceleration rights.
35 The terms and conditions may stipulate a higher (but not lower) quorum.
36 The terms and conditions may stipulate a higher (but not lower) quorum.
37 See footnote 34 for details.
38 The terms and conditions may stipulate a higher (but not lower) majority.

required for any other resolution (including appointment of a common representative, unless the common representative shall be authorised to amend the terms and conditions).

(d) *Effectiveness of resolutions*

Any bondholders' resolution passed has to be made public in the online federal gazette. A copy of the minutes of the bondholders' meeting has to be submitted to the depositary bank holding the global note, so that they can be appended to the global note. The chairman has to represent to the depositary bank that no appeals have been filed, or the timeline to file appeals has expired.

(e) *Appeals*

Each bondholder can, within one month after publication, file an appeal against a bondholders' resolution with the district court. The appeal is successful if the bondholders' resolution has been passed in breach of law, including any formalities in convening or during the bondholders' meeting. As long as the appeal is pending, the bondholders' resolution does not become effective. The issuer can, however, file a motion with the court of appeal to grant effectiveness to the bondholders' resolution. The court of appeal can grant the motion if, among other things:
- the appeal is evidently inadmissible or without merits; or
- it considers that its benefits outweigh the appellant's potential damage and the breach of law is not severe.

4.2 Bank Restructuring Act

(a) *Application*

The Bank Restructuring Act applies to all credit institutions with a registered office in Germany. It applies in addition to the European bank restructuring legislation under the Single Resolution Mechanism I Regulation[39] and the Bank Recovery and Resolution Directive.[40] Although it has been in effect since 2009, it has never yet been applied.

(b) *Procedures*

Two processes exist under which a bank can propose a restructuring of its liabilities:
- a recovery procedure; and
- a reorganisation procedure.

The recovery procedure does not allow for any forced haircuts or imposition of losses on creditors. However, it does allow for granting super-seniority to new loans, senior to other unsecured creditors in any insolvency proceedings in respect of a bank's assets that are opened within three years after an order for commencement of a recovery procedure has been issued.

---

39 Regulation (EU) 806/2014 establishing uniform rules and a uniform procedure for the resolution of credit institutions and certain investment firms.
40 Directive 2014/59/EU establishing a framework for the recovery and resolution of credit institutions and investment firms.

The reorganisation procedure will be more relevant to this chapter, since it allows for impairments of all stakeholders through a reorganisation plan. The procedure draws heavily on the insolvency plan procedure under the Insolvency Code.

(c) **Requirements for initiation of reorganisation procedure**
A reorganisation procedure can only be initiated:
- upon a filing by a credit institution;
- with the consent of the German Financial Supervisory Authority (BaFin);
- if the credit institution is under an imminent threat to its existence; which is presumed to be the case if:
  - the bank's core capital ratio falls more than 10% below the required regulatory capital ratio;
  - the bank's liquidity falls more than 10% below the required regulatory liquidity; or
  - circumstances exist under which the occurrence of one of the events above can reasonably be expected, in particular, if the bank is generating losses which can result in one of these events occurring; and
- that threat results in a systemic crisis in the banking sector.

(d) **Content of reorganisation plan**
Any type of action can be suggested in a reorganisation plan, such as haircuts, a debt-for-equity-swap or a transfer of assets and liabilities to a new bank. No creditor can be forced to take equity without giving its express consent.

(e) **Class formation**
Only those creditors whose claims are to be impaired need to be put in classes. Classes are construed according to the creditors' legal position. This means that (if they are to be impaired) a reorganisation plan must at least separate out the following classes:
- secured creditors;
- general unsecured creditors;
- unsecured creditors subordinated by law; among subordinated creditors, different classes must be formed in accordance with the ranking set out at Section 39(1) of the Insolvency Code:
  - post-insolvency interest;
  - costs and expenses;
  - fines and penalties;
  - liabilities arising under contracts for no consideration;
  - shareholder loans and equivalent liabilities;
- contractually subordinated creditors.[41]

The reorganisation plan may provide for additional classes of creditors with similar legal rights, but different economic interests.

---

41   Credit institutions will often have issued debt instruments with a contractual subordination in order to comply with regulatory capital requirements.

Deposits secured by a deposit protection scheme, employee liabilities and pension liabilities cannot be impaired.

(f) Voting on plan

A plan is accepted if, in each class, a majority (50%) by amount and by number of creditors present in the meeting vote in favour of the plan. In the class of shareholders, a majority of 50% of shares is generally sufficient. However, $66^2/3\%$ is required if new shares are issued and existing shareholders are excluded from subscription rights, unless 50% of the shareholders are present. If those majorities are not reached, the court can still confirm the plan (and enforce a cram-down) if:

- a majority of classes has voted in favour;
- the plan does not put non-consenting classes into a worse position than they would be without the plan;
- no creditor receives any value in excess of its par claim;
- no creditor ranking equally with a creditor in a non-consenting class receives more value; and
- if the class of shareholders has not accepted the plan, if the plan provides for reasonable and appropriate measures to avoid any instability in the financial system.

(g) Confirmation of plan

The court will confirm the reorganisation plan if:

- the plan substantially complies with all legal requirements, in particular with regards to class formation;
- the plan has been accepted in the creditors' meeting with the majorities required, as set out above;
- the accepting vote was not subject to undue influence (eg, through buying votes); and
- no creditor has objected, or, if a creditor has objected:
  - the objecting person has not provided present evidence that it would likely receive less value under the plan than without the plan; and
  - collateral is provided to compensate the difference between what the objecting person receives under the plan and what it claims it would have received without the plan.

(h) Appeal

There are no rights of appeal against confirmation of a plan by the court.

5. Sale of assets in insolvency

If the debtor is already in an insolvency process and no insolvency plan is proposed, the administrator or the debtor-in-possession runs a competitive sales process for the debtor's business (or parts of it). Sales processes are increasingly also used to increase the competitiveness of an insolvency plan procedure (a 'dual track' procedure).

The sales process in an insolvency generally follows the typical process for mergers and acquisitions processes outside insolvency. The seller (the debtor-in-possession or

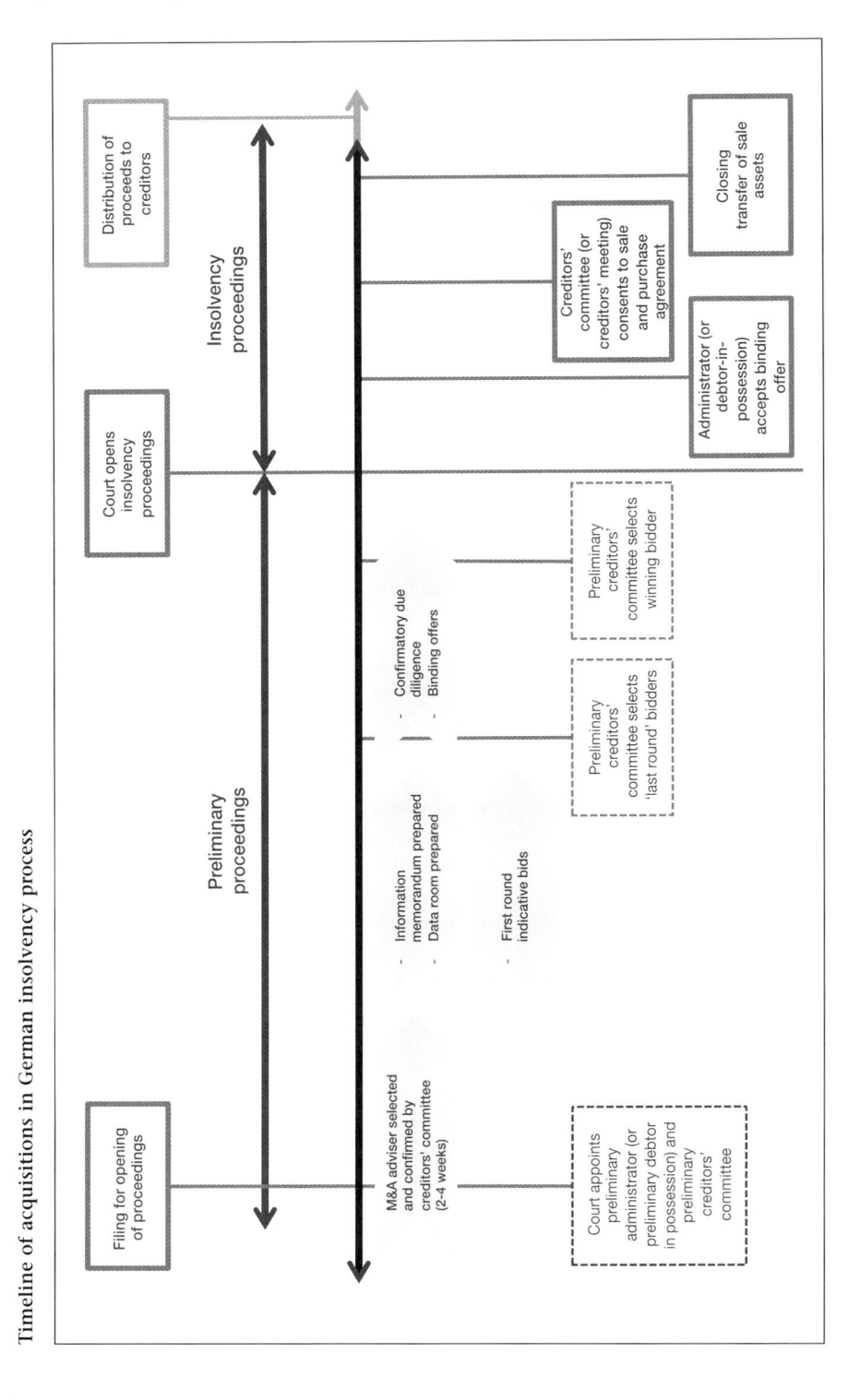

Developments in the legal framework for restructuring: Germany

Timeline of acquisitions in German insolvency process

administrator) will often engage an mergers and acquisitions adviser to send information memoranda to interested parties, then select a number (typically between five and 15) of more serious parties for confirmatory due diligence and indicative offers, then continue discussions with two or three parties for binding offers.

The following paragraphs consider some key issues relating to acquisitions in a German insolvency process.

5.1 Due diligence, timing and signing

Except for the actual signing, most of the acquisitions process (due diligence, indicative bids, negotiation of the asset purchase agreement) will occur during the preliminary proceedings. The final round bidders (usually two or three) will have to submit a (notarised) irrevocable offer to accept the (pre-negotiated) asset purchase agreement. These offers will be taken to the creditors' committee (or the creditors' meeting, if applicable, see below under heading 5.4) for selection of the successful bidder. After the formal opening of insolvency proceedings, the administrator (or debtor-in-possession) will accept the selected bidder's offer, thus making the asset purchase agreement binding.

5.2 Bank guarantee for purchase price

The final round bidders will almost always have to present a bank guarantee for the full amount of their bid.

5.3 Asset purchase agreement

The asset purchase agreement will be as short as possible, and will almost always contain these key features:
- no or very limited representations and warranties as to the business being sold;
- cash purchase price only; and
- no closing conditions or only those required by law (eg, merger and other regulatory clearances).

5.4 Consent requirements

In debtor-in-possession procedures the (preliminary) trustee will need to consent to the signing of the asset purchase agreement by the debtor (Section 275 of the Insolvency Code).

If the asset purchase agreement is signed during the preliminary proceedings, the court will need to authorise the signing in order to elevate the liabilities under the asset purchase agreement to administrative expense seniority.

The signing of the asset purchase agreement will generally require consent from the creditors' committee (Section 160 of the Insolvency Code).[42]

Sales to certain interested parties (including, among others, persons affiliated with the debtor and creditors with claims exceeding 20% of all claims) require consent from the creditors' meeting (not just the creditors' committee).[43]

---

42 However, breach of this rule does not render the asset purchase agreement invalid.
43 However, breach of this rule does not render the asset purchase agreement invalid.

5.5 Successor liability

As a general rule, if assets are acquired in an insolvency process (ie, after the opening of insolvency proceedings), liabilities that have arisen before the opening of the insolvency proceedings remain with the debtor by operation of law. This applies in particular to employee and pension liabilities. Exceptions from this rule include:

- environmental liabilities: if the assets purchased include real property, the authorities can also hold the purchaser responsible for environmental liabilities in respect of that property, even those arising before the insolvency; and
- liability for employees' untaken leave: in the case of a transfer of a business with employees, the purchaser will be liable for all the employees' untaken leave.

If assets are acquired in preliminary proceedings, the general rule does not apply. Purchasers will (in the case of a transfer of a business) be liable for employee liabilities (Section 613a of the Civil Code), tax liabilities (Section 75 of the Fiscal Code) and, if the debtor's name is also acquired, be liable for all liabilities of the debtor (Section 25 of the Commercial Code).

6. Final considerations

Financing structures are complex and so are the restructuring deals relating to them. Recent examples for restructuring deals with complex capital structures include:

- SolarWorld AG – the company restructured (partly in and partly out of court) a total of around €950 million of liabilities, comprising, among other things, several dozens of individually held and voting promissory notes with a total of around €350 million, two listed bonds with a total of around €550 million and a secured facility with a total of around €50 million.

    While the promissory notes and the secured facility lenders agreed to a deal negotiated by a group of lenders out of court, SolarWorld AG had to file (and was granted) motions with the Cologne court of appeals to grant consummation of the bondholders' resolution notwithstanding appeals filed by shareholders and bondholders.

- IVG Immobilien AG – the company restructured, through an insolvency plan, a total of around €4 billion of liabilities, comprising, among other things, two secured syndicated facilities with more than €2 billion of outstanding loans, a €400 million convertible note issued out of a subsidiary, but guaranteed by the parent, a €400 million subordinated bond and several bilateral facilities.

    The company had originally sought to restructure out of court, but had to concede that the positions between the secured lenders, the convertible bondholders, the subordinated bond and the shareholders could not be aligned. Through the insolvency plan, the subordinated bondholders and the shareholders were taken out of the equation.

- Scholz Holding – the company restructured out of court a total of around €900 million of liabilities comprising, among other things, €450 million in syndicated secured facilities, €50 million of promissory notes, a €182.5 million Austrian-law governed listed bond, several bilateral loans and trade credit insurance and receivables factoring facilities.

While the secured lenders and the promissory noteholders agreed to a deal negotiated by a steering committee of lenders out of court, the company had to deal with bondholders through an Austrian court process that was used for the first time outside an Austrian insolvency process.

The rescue culture and the restructuring profession are still in development in Germany. Out-of-court restructurings can only be achieved with all creditors' consent and if they fail, can expose the directors to material litigation risk. Many administrators will have issues with the English language or with foreign investors, and will still have a very bureaucratic approach, although this has improved in the larger cases in the past decade.

Developments in the legal framework for restructuring: Italy

Giulia Battaglia
Antonio Tavella
Chiomenti Studio Legale

1. Legal framework for restructuring in Italy

Under Italian law, a distressed company may choose among different out-of-court or court-supervised restructuring tools. The choice of the relevant restructuring tool depends on, among other things, the seriousness of the company's financial crisis, the going-concern perspective (if any) and the creditors' availability to agree upon a possible consensual restructuring. Below is a brief overview of the main restructuring tools provided for in the Italian Bankruptcy Law (Royal Decree 267/1942, as amended and supplemented from time to time), which have different features and characteristics in relation to, among other things, the involvement of the courts, the role played by creditors and the binding nature of the restructuring upon non-adhering creditors.

1.1 Out-of-court restructuring agreements

A restructuring plan certified by a third-party expert, in accordance with Article 67(3)(d) of the Bankruptcy Law does not involve any form of supervision by the courts (it is an out-of-court restructuring arrangement), and its main feature is that any act, payment and/or guarantee executed in the implementation of the plan is exempted from bankruptcy claw-back actions (although, according to the most prudent interpretation, not from general claw-back and set-aside actions which may apply under general civil law principles, nor from certain other voidance actions).

1.2 Court-supervised restructuring

A restructuring agreement under Article 182-*bis* of the Bankruptcy Law basically consists of an agreement to be executed by the debtor and creditors representing at least 60% of its indebtedness, which has to be certified by a third-party expert and then approved by the competent court. Any creditors not agreeing to the settlement have to be paid in full by the company within specific terms provided by law. Following a restructuring agreement under Article 182-*bis*, there is no dispossession and the debtor remains entitled to manage its business. For a 60-day period starting from publication of the restructuring agreement in the relevant companies' registry, the debtor will be granted with an automatic stay against existing creditors. Restructuring agreements may include a wide range of provisions such as rescheduling of debts, partial debt forgiveness, transfer of assets to creditors, conversion of credits into equity and refinancing of the company. Each creditor is free to evaluate the debtor's proposals and no cram-down applies, with the exception set out under Article 182-*septies* of the Bankruptcy Law (see under heading 3 below).

1.3 Pre-insolvency preventive agreements

A pre-insolvency compromise 'preventive agreement' with creditors in accordance with Articles 160 onwards of the Bankruptcy Law is a court-supervised proceeding quite similar to US Chapter 11, and includes the following main phases:
- filing of the petition for admission to the process;
- admission by the competent court;
- approval of the agreement by creditors representing the majority of claims admitted to vote; if there are different classes of creditors, approval of the agreement requires a favourable vote by creditors representing the majority of claims admitted to each class and approval by the majority of classes; and
- court approval of the agreement.

A major distinction can be made between preventive agreements allowing a going concern under Article 186-*bis* of the Bankruptcy Law and those not allowing for a going concern. The first of these provides for the continuation of the business activity by the debtor, the transfer of the going concern or its assignment to one or more companies, which may including Newcos. In the case of a preventive agreement without a going concern, it should be noted that, for the purposes of the admission to the process of reaching an agreement, the debtor's proposal must envisage the payment of at least 20% of unsecured claims.

During the implementation of the preventive agreement, the company is managed by the debtor but under the surveillance of an official appointed by the court, and under the supervision (and, for a number of transactions, requiring the prior authorisation) of the court itself. Moreover, starting from the date on which the petition for admission to the process is published in the companies register, the debtor cannot make any payments in respect of claims that have arisen prior to the date of that publication. On the other hand, starting from the very same date, the debtor benefits from a stay of actions in relation to claims arising prior to the date of publication.

It is difficult to estimate the duration of a preventive agreement proceeding. On average, a procedure could last between about eight months and a year from the date of filing of the full proposal to implementation (and this assumes no opposition or appeals). In addition, if, before the proposal, a simplified request (see under heading 1.4 below) is filed, an additional period of up to 120 days should be added. Even if no simplified request is filed, the same (or slightly less) period should be added to the overall length of the process to prepare the full proposal and get the expert report.

1.4 Simplified requests

In addition to the above, under Article 161(6) of the Bankruptcy Law, a distressed company may also file a 'simplified request' for admission to the pre-insolvency preventive workout agreement process, in order to benefit from the protective effects provided under the Bankruptcy Law (for instance, suspension of enforcement actions), although only for a limited time. The debtor needs to file the proposal, the plan and other necessary documents for the agreement itself, within a time limit to be established by the judge and which shall be between 60 and 120 days from the filing of the simplified request (extendable for duly justified reasons to be evaluated by the courts on a case-by-case basis).

As an alternative route (with equally protective effects), in accordance with Article 182-*bis*(6) of the Bankruptcy Law, the debtor may also file a simplified request for the approval of the restructuring agreement within a time limit of 60 days.

When distressed companies choose one of the restructuring measures provided under Articles 161 and 182-*bis* of the Bankruptcy Law, by way of a simplified request, debtors may benefit from certain protective effects, such as obtaining an automatic stay of enforcement (whose scope is quite similar to the one provided under English law). In other words, for as long as the automatic stay is in effect, creditors generally may not initiate or continue lawsuits, seek attachment orders or demand payment. However, debtors will not be able to access the early automatic stay procedure under the simplified request procedure if, during the two years prior to filing for that procedure, they had already filed for another early automatic stay procedure and, following such filing, their proposed preventive agreement or Article 182-*bis* restructuring agreement was not ratified by the court.

1.5 Similarities and differences

Restructuring agreements under Article 182-*bis* of the Bankruptcy Law and preventive agreement proceedings share a common theme: any acts, payments and securities or guarantees made by the debtor in connection with these proceedings (or with any underlying plans) are exempted from bankruptcy claw-back actions. However, it is worth noting that they also enjoy their own peculiar features that make them suitable for specific situations depending upon the needs of the company and its counterparties.

For example, a preventive agreement implies significant court involvement to control and supervise the company. This is regarded as protection for prospective buyers, but significantly lengthens the duration of the restructuring process, thus possibly adversely affecting the company's goodwill.

On the other hand, a restructuring agreement implies a lighter involvement of the court, with a shorter duration and the ability of the debtor to continue managing the business during its negotiations. However, creditors that do not sing up to the agreement and that hold claims due and payable have to be paid in full within the terms set out under the Bankruptcy Law, thus possibly increasing the needs of new financial sources.

If it proves eventually necessary, the Bankruptcy Law also provides for bankruptcy proceedings which involve the divestment of the debtor and the appointment of an insolvency administrator with the sole task of liquidating the debtor company.

With respect to court-supervised proceedings, it should be noted that there are no specialised insolvency courts in Italy, there are only different specialised divisions of the same court.

Developments in the legal framework for restructuring: Italy

1.6 Main restructuring tools and key features at a glance

	Restructuring plan pursuant to Article 67(3)(d)	**Restructuring agreement pursuant to Article 182-*bis***	**Preventive agreement**
Contents	Flexible, provided that the plan is feasible in terms of permitting the restructuring of the debtor's indebtedness and supporting the rebalancing of the debtor's financial condition.	Flexible. Restructuring agreements must provide for the full repayment of non-participating creditors. Such full repayment shall be made in accordance with the following terms: • It must be done within 120 days from the court's approval of the agreement, insofar as there are any debts already due and payable on such a date; and • In respect of any debts not yet due and payable on the aforementioned date, they must be settled within 120 days from their respective due dates.	First of all, a major distinction can be made between preventive agreements 'with a going-concern' under Article 186-*bis* of the Bankruptcy Law and those 'without a going concern'. For the purposes of the admission to the preventive agreements process, the debtor's proposal must envisage the payment of at least 20% of the unsecured claims where the preventive agreement is one without a going concern. *The preventive agreement* must be based on a compromise plan (which must be certified by a third-party independent expert pursuant to the Bankruptcy Law and in accordance with the requisites set out therein) which may include, among other things: • debt restructuring and payment of creditors by a variety of means, such as assignment of assets, assumptions of the debt and other extraordinary transactions including the granting to creditors, and to companies formed or owned (in whole or in

continued on next page

	Restructuring plan pursuant to Article 67(3)(d)	Restructuring agreement pursuant to Article 182-*bis*	Preventive agreement
			part) by creditors, of shares, bonds (including convertible bonds) or other financial and debt instruments; • the assignment of the debtor business to third parties including creditors, and companies formed or owned (in whole or in part) by creditors, or to be formed during implementation of the plan, the shares of which are to be attributed to creditors as a result of the plan; • the division of creditors into classes according to their legal position and homogenous economic interests; and/or • differential treatment of creditors belonging to different classes.
Classes of creditors	N/A	Permitted where the restructuring agreement falls within the scope of Article 182-*septies* of the Bankruptcy Law; ie, where the debtor owes at least half its debts to banks. The agreement of 75% by value of the claims of the participating creditors within each category is required in order for the agreement to become binding.	Permitted, according to the legal position and the homogenous economic interests of the creditors.

continued on next page

	Restructuring plan pursuant to Article 67(3)(d)	**Restructuring agreement pursuant to Article 182-*bis***	**Preventive agreement**
Court approval	N/A (it is a completely out-of-court proceeding/restructuring tool)	Court approval is granted after publication of the restructuring agreement in the relevant Companies' Register (and after rulings on any opposition).	The proceeding involves two different approvals by the courts: first with regard to admission to the proceeding and, secondly, after admission and a positive vote in the creditors' meeting, implementation will be approved by the court (absent any challenges).
Publicity	No mandatory publicity. The debtor can voluntarily decide whether or not to publish the restructuring plan in the Companies' Register.	Publication in the Companies' Register.	Publication in the Companies' Register.
Automatic stay	N/A	Applicable during the 60-day period following the date on which the agreement is published in the Companies' Register.	Applicable starting from the date on which the petition for admission to the agreement procedure is published in the Companies' Register and up until the decree approving implementation has become final.
Management of the procedure	Debtor.	Debtor.	Debtor under the supervision and, for a number of transactions, prior authorisation by the judicial commissioner(s) and the courts.

continued on next page

	Restructuring plan pursuant to Article 67(3)(d)	Restructuring agreement pursuant to Article 182-*bis*	Preventive agreement
Majority for creditors' approval	N/A	60% of all claims. Where the restructuring agreement provides for different classes pursuant to Article 182-*septies* of the Bankruptcy Law, agreement of 75% of claims within each category of debt is required.	Majority of claims admitted to vote. If there are different classes of creditors, approval of the agreement requires the favourable vote of creditors representing the majority of claims admitted to each class, and approval by the majority of classes.
Expert report	Required.	Required.	Required.
Claw-back in subsequent bankruptcy	Bankruptcy clawback exemptions according to Article 67 of the Bankruptcy Law.	Bankruptcy claw-back exemptions according to Article 67 of the Bankruptcy Law.	Bankruptcy claw-back exemptions according to Article 67 of the Bankruptcy Law.

2. Bankruptcy claw-back actions

Under the Italian rules on claw-back in bankruptcy, set out in Article 67 of the Bankruptcy Law, the following transactions may be declared void if they have been carried out during the year prior to the bankruptcy declaration, unless the debtor's counterparty proves that it was not aware of the debtor's insolvency at the time of the transaction:

- transactions where the consideration paid by the debtor exceeds by more than one quarter what was given or promised to it;
- payments not made in cash or other normal means of payment; and
- liens granted for pre-existing debts not yet due and payable.

While liens granted for debts due and payable may also be declared void under the same conditions, the applicable period is reduced to six months.

In addition, standard transactions made in the ordinary course of business (ie, conveyances for adequate consideration, payment of due debts, and granting of security interests upon contracting a debt) may be declared void if:

- they have been carried out during the six months prior to the bankruptcy declaration; and
- the bankruptcy receiver proves that the debtor's counterparty was aware of the debtor's insolvency at the time of the transaction.

Certain specific transactions are exempt from the claw-back and set-aside actions, including, but not limited to:
- payments for goods and services made in the ordinary course of business on customary market terms and conditions;
- payment of salaries to employees; and
- as already noted, transactions, payments and guarantees or security interests implementing a certified restructuring plan under Article 67(3)(d) of the Bankruptcy Law.

In addition to the all the above, any transactions, payments and guarantees or security interests implementing an approved preventive agreement, an approved restructuring agreement under Article 182-*bis* of the Bankruptcy Law, or transactions, payments and guarantees or security interests legally carried out after the deposit of a petition to allow a preventive agreement under Article 161 of the Bankruptcy Law are also exempt from claw-back.

There is some discussion among scholars whether the exemption from claw-back during bankruptcy proceedings also encompasses ordinary claw-back rights under Article 2901 of the Italian Civil Code. According to the most prudent approach, however, exemptions from claw-back set out under Article 67 would apply only to claw-back actions arising from the bankruptcy.

Furthermore, under Article 65 of the Bankruptcy Law (which is generally not regarded as a claw-back action and which deals with prepayments) in the event that a company is declared bankrupt, any payments made during the two-year period prior to the declaration of bankruptcy in respect of any amount which was not due and payable until on or after the date of the declaration of bankruptcy are ineffective insofar as concerns the relevant creditors.

3. Recent reforms on restructuring deals

Law Decree 83/2015, subsequently converted into law (with certain amendments) by Law 132/2015, has introduced several amendments to the restructuring procedures set out in the Bankruptcy Law, mainly aimed at encouraging the use of alternative methods for reaching resolution in cases of corporate distress, promoting the competitiveness of companies in Chapter 11-type procedures in Italy and encouraging 'virtuous behaviour' from Italian debtors in financial difficulty.

Law 132/2015 has among other things introduced Article 182-*septies* of the Bankruptcy Law which is intended to encourage consensual settlement agreements by distressed companies heavily indebted to banks. The new provision allows a debtor that owes at least half its total debts by value to financial institutions to enter into a specific debt-restructuring agreement with those financial institutions, subject to the rights and claims of non-financial creditors. In particular, Article 182-*septies* has introduced – in certain specific circumstances – a mechanism allowing a cram-down of the minority of dissenting lenders in the context of new restructuring agreements and in preventive agreement proceedings. In this way, the restructuring agreement mechanism under Article 182-*bis* is supplemented by the cram-down mechanism provided under Article 182-*septies*, paragraphs 2, 3 and 4, representing a significant step in bringing Italian restructuring tools closer to the English model.

Another innovative feature introduced by Law 132/2015 is the new Article 163 of the Bankruptcy Law which has introduced the 'competing offers' regime in the context of preventive agreement proceedings. According to this provision, one or more creditors, representing at least 10% of the company's creditors by value, are entitled to file with the court competing offers to the debtor's compromise proposal in the event that the debtor's proposal does not provide for the discharge of at least 40% by value of its unsecured claims (or, in case of a pre-insolvency agreement on a going concern basis, 30%).

In other words, creditors of an Italian company subject to a proposed preventive agreement may become active participants in pre-insolvency proceedings by making alternative proposals themselves. This constitutes a very important step aimed at facilitating the acquisition by qualified investors of a distressed company's debts.

A third novelty worthy of note is the abolition of the 'you snooze, you lose' mechanism, which could be regarded as a disincentive for the preventive agreement proceedings on one hand, but on the other is fully in line with those provisions which intend to encourage creditors' participation in the resolution of a debtor's financial problems. Before this reform any creditor (entitled to vote) who had not voted in the creditors' meeting within the terms set out under the Bankruptcy Law was considered as a participating creditor consenting to the agreement, but now this rule does not apply anymore. The reform is aimed at ensuring a higher degree of participation by creditors in the context of the preventive agreement, but from a practical perspective, it would most likely render approval by creditors of the agreement more difficult.

The new rules will certainly have a positive impact on the operation of preventive agreement proceedings, even though several questions are still to be answered; for instance in relation to the construction and interpretation of the new rules and their consistency with the existing rules. For this reason, the Bankruptcy Law is currently in the legislative spotlight and the Italian legislature, aware of uncertainties over the newly introduced provisions, has approved a draft law providing for an authorisation to the government for a comprehensive reform of the law relating to distressed companies and insolvency, which was submitted by the Rordorf Commission. The draft law is still under discussion and has not yet been enacted. The draft law envisages a general, comprehensive and thorough reform of the Bankruptcy Law and of any relevant restructuring and bankruptcy tools. The draft law provides for, among other things, the introduction of a judicial liquidation procedure to replace the bankruptcy procedure currently in force. In addition, the draft reform deals with group insolvency issues and provides for alert procedures aimed at preventing financial crisis, which are both concepts new to Italian legislation. Finally, the draft law provides for reform of the preventive agreements where there are no going concern considerations.

With regard to security packages, certain measures have been introduced over the last few years to increase the likelihood of distressed companies returning to financial health. The introduction of the exemption from claw-back actions of security interests granted as part of the implementation of a restructuring plan, restructuring agreement or preventive agreement proceedings undoubtedly represents a decisive step in the promotion of alternative methods in the bankruptcy arena. As to the 2015 reforms, the only amendment of note relates to interim financing under Article 182-*quinquies* of the Bankruptcy Law, aimed at clarifying that new financing under that provision may be secured by liens, mortgages and asset-backed lending structures.

4. Equity instruments and intercreditor agreements

Under Italian law, a debtor may convert the relevant debt into equity or quasi-equity instruments. From a practical perspective, there is a strong and growing preference for conversion of the debt into quasi-equity instruments, by means of which:
- the lenders will have administrative and economic rights, without becoming shareholders of the distressed company; and
- a compromise might be more easily reached among lenders with different interests.

As far as shareholder loans are concerned, note that in a distressed scenario, both according to the applicable statute law and prevailing case law, they have to be treated and considered as fully subordinated to any other claims (save for very few exceptions by operation of law, including, for instance, shareholder loans granted in the implementation of a preventive agreement or a restructuring agreement under Article 182-*bis* of the Bankruptcy Law).

In the implementation of court-supervised proceedings, intercreditor agreements are generally considered as no longer in force or are formally terminated by the relevant parties. This raises complex issues in relation to 'IBLOR' (Italian bank lender of record) financings, where only one bank (the agent) is the lender of record and all other lenders are sub-participants. From an Italian legal standpoint, the sub-participants are not considered as direct creditors of the borrower and, therefore, may not be entitled to file proof of their claims. It follows that sub-participants' voting rights in a preventive agreement might be limited. In light of the above, arrangements among the sub-participants and the agent should contain provisions regarding how, and upon the instruction of whom, the agent will vote in any potential court-supervised proceedings should the sub-participants not be recognised as creditors of the distressed company.

5. Asset disposals

Disposals of distressed assets are usually carried out through a competitive sales mechanism and under the supervision of the competent monitoring bodies, with a disclosure regime which would allow the widest possible participation of third parties interested in the transaction.

During recent years, one of the most significant trends has been the use of 'pre-pack' transactions in the context of preventive agreement proceedings, which usually involves:
- the execution with a third party (prior to the commencement of the proceedings) of a lease agreement in relation to the company as a going

concern, providing for the subsequent sale of the company to this same third party; and
- the sale of the company as a going concern to this third party, subject to the approval by the courts.

This kind of transaction does not seem fully permissible due to the recent amendments to the Bankruptcy Law which effectively impose a competitive sales process. However, market participants and the courts are currently exploring how to implement the mandatory competitive sale mechanism introduced by Law Decree 83/2015.

Many restructuring plans that have already been implemented provide for disposal of the assets or the business of the company. This circumstance will create a number of business opportunities for acquisitions. Moreover, many Italian banks have publicly announced their willingness to sell distressed debt portfolios or individual claims. The latter would also constitute an opportunity to be taken by investors specialising in distressed debt, especially if the new changes in the law allow the development in Italy of loan-to-own strategies.

Another interesting strategy currently being used is the assignment of distressed claims to funds specialising in distressed assets, which are becoming significant players in the restructuring market.

6. Group insolvency

The Bankruptcy Law does not provide for specific rules on insolvency proceedings involving a group of distressed companies. With specific reference to the preventive agreement proceedings, the most recent Italian case law (Supreme Court, October 13 2015, ruling 20559) has expressly excluded the admission of a proposal for an agreement aimed at regulating and restructuring the financial indebtedness of a group of companies given that, among other things:

- rules relating to the territorial jurisdiction of the special chambers of the court have mandatory and binding nature;
- in the event of a preventive agreement relating to different entities controlled by a single entity, or subject to direction and coordination as provided for in the Civil Code, the insolvency assets maintain their legal autonomy, and therefore they have to be kept separate for each company; and
- the preventive agreement proceedings have to be approved by the majority of creditors of each company of the group individually.

The only insolvency proceeding dealing, in some sense, with the group concept is the 'extraordinary administration' of large companies facing insolvency under Legislative Decree 270 of 1999.[1] In fact, according to Article 81 of this legislative

---

1   The purpose of the administration proceedings is to rehabilitate a company in financial distress in light of the significance of the company's technical, commercial and productive value. Under Legislative Decree 270 of 1999, the prerequisites for admission to extraordinary administration are:
• at least 200 employees in the year before the procedure was commenced; and

continued overleaf

decree, once the parent company has been admitted to the extraordinary administration, while that proceeding is ongoing, any group company becoming insolvent can be admitted to the extraordinary administration proceeding even if it does not itself fulfil the requirements for admission set out in the legislative decree.

- debt equal to at least two-thirds of its total assets and two-thirds of its total income generated by sales and services for the last fiscal year.

The effects of the procedure consist of:
- the adoption of a rehabilitation programme which might be either a programme of corporate restructuring (lasting a maximum of two years) or a programme of asset disposals (lasting a maximum of one year);
- a stay of actions by creditors; and
- appointment by the government of one or three receivers to replace the existing management in the company's operation.

The court must assess the prospects of the plan's success in the light of reports submitted by the receiver(s). The court then either issues a decree to place the enterprise under the administration procedure or orders judicial liquidation.

Developments in the legal framework for restructuring: Spain

Cristóbal Cotta
Andrea Perelló
Fedra Valencia
Cuatrecasas, Gonçalves Pereira

1. Introduction

There have been several reforms of the Spanish Insolvency Act in the last two years.

These reforms began in March 2014[1] with changes in out-of-court settlements. Among other things, there were changes to the effects of '5 bis' proceedings in order to stop enforcement actions against the debtor, to the majorities required to reach a refinancing agreement and to the effects of a cram-down of dissenting creditors.

In September 2014,[2] changes were also made to the agreement with creditors of reorganisation plans within bankruptcy proceedings (questions such as permissible contents and the requisite majorities were modified). At the same time, the reform introduced important changes on the sale of business units (some of them improve this solution, such as the automatic subrogation of all the contracts, while others will make it worse for investors, such as the subrogation of salary claims).

Second chance proceedings for individual persons were changed in February 2015.[3]

Finally, a small but very important change was introduced in October 2015[4] regarding pledges over credits.

In order to understand the importance of these changes, we must remember that under the Insolvency Act, bankruptcy is the compulsory process in which to handle financial distress, although the act does also contemplate alternative mechanisms to handle insolvency out of court in order to avoid a full-blown bankruptcy proceeding.

2. Pre-bankruptcy restructuring tools

Out-of-court settlements can be individual agreements, collective agreements or court-sanctioned arrangements (also known as a 'Spanish scheme of arrangement').

2.1 Refinancing agreements

An individual refinancing agreement is a notarised agreement that satisfies the following conditions:
- It improves the ratio of assets over liabilities;

---

[1] Royal Decree Law 4/2014, March 7 2014, together with Law 17/14, September 30 2014.
[2] Royal Decree Law 11/2014, September 5 2014, together with Law 9/2015, May 25 2015.
[3] Royal Decree Law 1/2015, February 27 2015, together with Law 25/15, July 28 2015.
[4] Law 40/15, October 1 2015.

- It ensures that the current assets are no less than the current liabilities;
- The value of the security interest[5] is not a greater proportion of the outstanding debt owed to the creditors than it was prior to the refinancing, and does not exceed 90% of the value of the outstanding debt owed to the creditors; and
- It does not increase the interest rate applicable to the debt prior to the refinancing.

A collective refinancing agreement is a notarised agreement, which satisfies the following conditions:
- It has the support of creditors holding at least 60% of debtor's liabilities (as shown by an auditor's certificate);
- It extends maturity dates and/or grants new credit and/or amends financial obligations; and
- It is based on a business plan that allows business activity to continue in the short and medium term.

2.2 Spanish scheme of arrangement

A court-sanctioned settlement, or 'Spanish Scheme of arrangement', is a collective agreement that has the support of creditors holding at least 51% of the total of financial claims against the debtor and is ratified by a judge.

Under a Spanish scheme of arrangement, dissenting creditors holding financial claims (including absentees) may also be dragged along. The required majorities depend on the content of the agreement and whether it refers to secured or only unsecured claims. In the case of unsecured financial claims (which include deficiency claims), creditors representing a majority of 60% of such claims may drag along dissidents in respect of stays of payments of up to five years and conversion of the claims into subordinated debt with a term up to five years. Furthermore, a majority representing 75% of financial claims can drag along dissenters as to stays of payments up to 10 years, conversion of the claims into subordinated debt with a term up to 10 years, haircuts, debt-for-equity swaps, debt-to-asset swaps and conversions of claims into new debt instruments.

With regard to secured financial claims, the requisite majorities are 65% and 80% respectively to achieve the same results.

---

[5] Defined according to Royal Decree 4/2014 as the result of deducting the outstanding debts covered by the pre-emptive security on a given asset from nine-tenths of the reasonable value of that asset, while that value must not be less than zero or greater than the value of the claim held by the creditor or the value of the maximum secured liability agreed. Depending on the type of asset, 'reasonable value' is defined as follows:
- for listed securities, the weighted average selling price obtained in one or more regulated markets for the last quarter for the refinancing agreement, as certified by the management board of the relevant capital market;
- for real estate assets, the value established in the valuation report issued by an authorised appraisal firm; and
- for other assets, the value established in the report issued by an independent expert in accordance with local generally accepted accounting principles (GAAP). Such reports are not required if the value has been determined by an independent expert within six months before starting the negotiations for the refinancing scheme.

A special rule applies in the case of syndicated loan agreements. As a result, all syndicated lenders will be considered to be in support of the refinancing scheme if creditors representing at least 75% of the syndicated loan debt (or a lower percentage if that is agreed in the syndication rules set out in the loan agreement) vote in favour of the refinancing scheme. Therefore, in those cases where a 75% majority is achieved, the remaining 25% will be crammed down and the lenders holding the entirety of that debt will be deemed to have accepted the refinancing.

A dissenting creditor may challenge a court-sanctioned agreement if the relevant required majority has not been obtained or the agreement imposes a disproportionate sacrifice on the creditor. The lack of a legal definition of 'disproportionate sacrifice' makes it necessary to ascertain the extent of the dissenting entity's suffered sacrifice. An EU Commission Recommendation of March 12 2014, on a new approach to business failure and insolvency, states that sacrifices imposed on dissenting creditors cannot reduce the rights of dissenting creditors below what they would reasonably be expected to receive in the absence of the restructuring; that is, if the debtor's business was liquidated or sold as a going concern.

	Which corporate debtor	Majority	Which creditors?	Secured creditors cram-down?	Effects
Collective refinancing agreement	All corporate debtors	60%	All creditors	N/A	Claw-back protection (only as regards creditors)
Individual refinancing agreement	All corporate debtors	N/A	All creditors	N/A	Claw-back protection (only as regards creditors)
Spanish Scheme of arrange-ment – basic majority	Holders of financial debt	51% of financial debt	All creditors	No	Claw-back protection

continued on next page

	Which corporate debtor	Majority	Which creditors?	Secured creditors cram-down?	Effects
Spanish Scheme of arrange-ment – reinforced majority	Holders of financial debt	60% to 75% of financial debt	Holders of financial debt	No	Stays/con-version into particip-ative loans/write-offs/etc
	Holders of secured financial debt	65% to 80% of secured financial debt by value of security	Holders of secured financial debt	Yes	Stays/con-version into particip-ative loans/write-offs/etc
Payment scheme	Only if: • less than €5 million in assets • less than €5 million in liabilities; • less than 50 creditors; and • other requirements	60% or 75% if transfer of assets *in lieu* of payment	All creditors (except public creditors)	No Write off (up to 25%)	Extension of term (up to three years)

Finally, it must be noted that credits held by specifically related parties to the debtor (that is, shareholders) are excluded and do not have the right to vote, but the effects of the scheme can be extended to them and they will be bound by the court's approval of it. Non-financial creditors, in turn, can also adhere to the scheme.

3. Special rules on debt-for-equity swaps

Certain measures to enhance debt-for-equity swaps have been introduced in the Insolvency Act (and other legislation) which tackle areas that range from limitations on equitable subordination, through introduction of insolvency liability for shareholders unreasonably withholding their consent to debt-for-equity swaps in the context of a refinancing transaction, to reducing required corporate majorities, as well as tax advantages and exemptions in order for these transactions to be tax neutral for both the debtor and creditors as regards corporation tax.

Some of these measures are:
- Debt-for-equity swaps can now be included within the content of a court-sanctioned refinancing agreement (Spanish scheme of arrangement) and can be crammed-down on dissenters. However, dissenters are allowed to choose

between the proposed debt-for-equity swap or a write-off in an amount equivalent to the par value of the shares.
- The Insolvency Act has excluded from the definition of 'specially related parties' for purposes of equitable subordination, those creditors who become shareholders of the debtor as a result of a debt-for-equity swap implemented in the context of a statutory refinancing agreement (either an out-of-court refinancing agreement or a court-sanctioned refinancing agreement).
- The majority required for a shareholders' meeting to approve a debt-for-equity swap in the context of a refinancing have been lowered to a simple (ordinary) majority, instead of a reinforced majority.
- The Takeover Bid Royal Decree 2007 was amended with respect to those transactions consisting in debt-for-equity swaps where the target company is subject to serious financial distress. These transactions, as long as their goal is to restore the financial viability of the companies in the long term, are, in principle, exempt from the obligation to launch a takeover bid subject to an authorisation confirming this exemption from the Spanish Securities Market Authority (the CNMV). This authorisation from the CNMV is not necessary where the debt-for-equity swap is performed in the context of a court-sanctioned Spanish scheme of arrangement backed by the favourable opinion of an independent expert.
- The Insolvency Act provides that creditors entering into a refinancing agreement shall not be considered *de facto* directors of the debtor as a result of any obligations undertaken in the agreement in connection with the viability plan (divestments, monitoring and previous consent of creditors for certain material business actions, etc). As a result, it is made clear that these creditors would not be equitably subordinated on the grounds of being *de facto* directors.
- The Insolvency Act has been amended to include a new rebuttable presumption as to the liability of shareholders of the debtor when they reject, without a reasonable cause, debt-for-equity swaps, capitalisation processes or the issue of convertible obligations, thereby frustrating a collective refinancing or a court sanctioned scheme. As a result of this, should the debtor finally file for insolvency, shareholders can be affected by the classification of the insolvency proceeding and, among other things, could be held liable for any shortfall for creditors within the insolvency.

This has been perhaps one of the major changes under Spanish law with respect to debt-for-equity swaps, and has tried to address one of the key challenges that many Spanish restructurings face: the inability to force a cram-down of the equity, contrary to what happens in other jurisdictions. In this regard, under Spanish law, a cram-down of the equity always requires the approval of shareholders, even if they have no interest. This has jeopardised many Spanish restructurings and provides shareholders leverage in these situations, despite the fact that the real value at stake is zero or close to zero. However, as we can see the Insolvency Act has still not taken a firm step towards aligning the shareholders' rights within a refinancing process to their real economic rights. In fact, as the Insolvency Act has not introduced restrictions to the rights of existing shareholders in the context of the refinancing of distressed debtors, the result in practice is that debt-for-equity swaps in Spanish restructurings only take place when a consensual deal is put in place (and, therefore, blockades mounted by existing shareholders are prevented). Lenders can still have recourse to other strategies such as the enforcement of pledges over the shares of the debtor (if they were included within the security package of the original financing transaction) or forcing the liquidation of the debtor in bankruptcy proceedings, which can be less attractive to lenders and which may not be as effective from a time and cost perspective.

4. Bankruptcy proceedings

4.1 Duty to file for insolvency and '5 bis notice'

The directors of a company are obliged to file for bankruptcy upon actual insolvency, within two months following the date on which the debtor knew or should have known that it was not able to meet regularly its payment obligations as they become due (cash-flow insolvency). In a case of imminent insolvency, when the debtor foresees that it will be unable to pay obligations regularly within the short or medium term, directors have the right to file for insolvency.

Companies can obtain an additional four-month period to tackle insolvency out of court, if they serve notice (the so-called '5 bis notice') with the court that would have jurisdiction over the bankruptcy proceeding. For this purpose, companies must state that they are engaged in negotiations aimed at reaching either an out-of-court agreement – which is what happens in the vast majority of the cases – or a pre-packaged plan of reorganisation ahead of a subsequent bankruptcy proceeding.

The 5 bis notice stays petitions for involuntary bankruptcy, the duty to file for bankruptcy (providing a safe harbour for directors) and certain enforcement actions. With regard to enforcement actions, the stay could also affect secured financial creditors if the debtor files written evidence that more than 51% of financial creditors support negotiations aimed at reaching an out-of-court agreement.

In addition to the debtor having standing to file for bankruptcy, any creditor (even those who hold contingent or future claims) can petition for involuntary bankruptcy. When filing such a petition a creditor should give evidence of its claim and some facts providing proof of the insolvency, such as a general default on payments by the debtor, the occurrence of generalised attachments on the debtor's assets, hasty or loss-making liquidation of assets, or a general default on tax, social security and employment obligations during the applicable statutory period (three months).

4.2 Management powers and insolvency trustee

Whether bankruptcy is voluntary or involuntary is relevant as regards the limitation on the debtor's (or its directors') ability to run the business. In voluntary cases, the default position is that the debtor (through its directors) retains the power to manage the business, although supervised by the bankruptcy officer. There is no debtor-in-possession status, as there is always a supervising bankruptcy officer. In involuntary cases, on the other hand, the default position is that the bankruptcy officer steps into the shoes of the directors.

The insolvency trustee controls the process and is in charge of:
- the classification of creditors' claims; and
- the valuation of the assets (with no clear statutory guidance as to how this valuation is to be performed).

He also will bring claw-back actions and report on directors' liability.

The insolvency trustee must report to the court all the debtor's liabilities. These are divided into privileged claims, ordinary claims and subordinated claims.

Privileged claims can have a special or general privilege, depending on whether they are secured with specifically identified collateral (granting a special privilege – although the privilege will only cover the claim to the extent that it does not exceed the value of the respective guarantee), or generally over the whole of the estate (granting a general privilege, which will be the base with certain tax, social security, labour law and tort claims, etc). Ordinary claims are those not classified as either privileged or subordinated. Subordinated claims do not vest creditors with voting rights in the composition phase (although they get the same treatment as ordinary claims, albeit deferred). Such claims embrace, for instance, late proofs of claim, interest, sanctions or equitable subordination (which will apply to 'specially related persons').

Additionally, there are four classes of credits: labour, public, financial and other, which cannot cram down each other.

4.3 Automatic stay; accrual of interest

Once bankruptcy is declared, accrual of interest on debts is suspended as of the date of the declaration except for secured claims up to the maximum covered by the security. Furthermore, the declaration of bankruptcy triggers an automatic stay on payment, declaratory and enforcement actions (with the exception of certain actions conducted by public authorities that do not concern assets necessary for the business). The enforcement of security interests over collateral that is necessary to pursue the ordinary course of business, through repossession or auction, are also stayed upon the declaration of bankruptcy, for a maximum period of one year, unless a reorganisation plan is approved or the liquidation phase starts first.

The moratorium does not apply to secured claims over assets that are not related to the business or to certain financial collateral (pledges over shares or holding companies quotas). The determination as to whether particular assets are necessary for the business is made by the commercial court in charge of the bankruptcy proceeding.

In addition, creditors maintain their ability to seek payment in full from guarantors, so long as they do not vote in favour of the reorganisation plan (unless it has been agreed otherwise). Normally, the guarantee will be affected by any change in the secured credit (such as write-off or rescheduling of due dates). However, if the creditor does not accept the change (by voting in favour of the reorganisation plan), the guarantee will not be affected by the agreement.

4.4 Procedural rules

From a procedural perspective, bankruptcy gets started with the 'common phase', where the bankruptcy officer appointed by the court puts together a report on the debtor's estate and claims. Also in this phase, the bankruptcy officer can file claw-back actions and actions seeking to establish director's liability.

Claw-back may apply to any acts or transactions beyond the ordinary course of business, entered into within two years prior to the declaration of insolvency, where:
- the debtor did not receive reasonable fair value in exchange; or
- certain creditors were favoured over others when the company was already insolvent (ie, unable to pay its debts as they came due).

The hardening period in either case is two years. Unless certain the presumptions provided by law apply, the burden of the proof will be on the insolvency trustee (although in some cases creditors can bring an action when the trustee fails to do so).

A successful claw-back action will mean the act is declared void, and the benefit will be returned (even if the defendant acted in good faith, otherwise he will have a subordinated claim).

The common phase is followed by the 'composition phase', aimed at agreeing a reorganisation plan, or the liquidation phase, in which the business unit is sold as a going concern or assets are sold off piecemeal. In addition, there is a 'qualification phase'. This is aimed at investigating the potential liability of directors and accomplices to the directors.

It is not always mandatory to start the process of categorisation of the insolvency at this stage, as it depends on the outcome of the insolvency proceedings. When the liquidation phase starts, the insolvency must be categorised. However, in the event of a composition, the categorisation process will only start in some cases, unless the agreement is breached.

Insolvency may be categorised as 'fortuitous' or 'culpable'. Fortuitous insolvency refers to a case where the insolvency or its aggravation is not attributable to a particular person, so there is no reproach.

Insolvency is categorised as culpable when the insolvency situation is created or aggravated by the wilful misconduct or gross negligence of the formal or *de facto* directors, or of any person who had that status within the two years before the declaration of insolvency.

A ruling that categorises an insolvency as culpable gives rise to important effects for the directors as persons (potentially) affected by the categorisation, so the ruling must specify:
- the reasons for the insolvency being categorised as culpable;
- the identity of the directors affected; and
- the effects of the categorisation.

Those effects for directors may include:
- a ban on holding office for between two and 15 years;
- loss of any claims those directors might have as creditors in the insolvency or against the insolvency estate, and the requirement to return any assets or

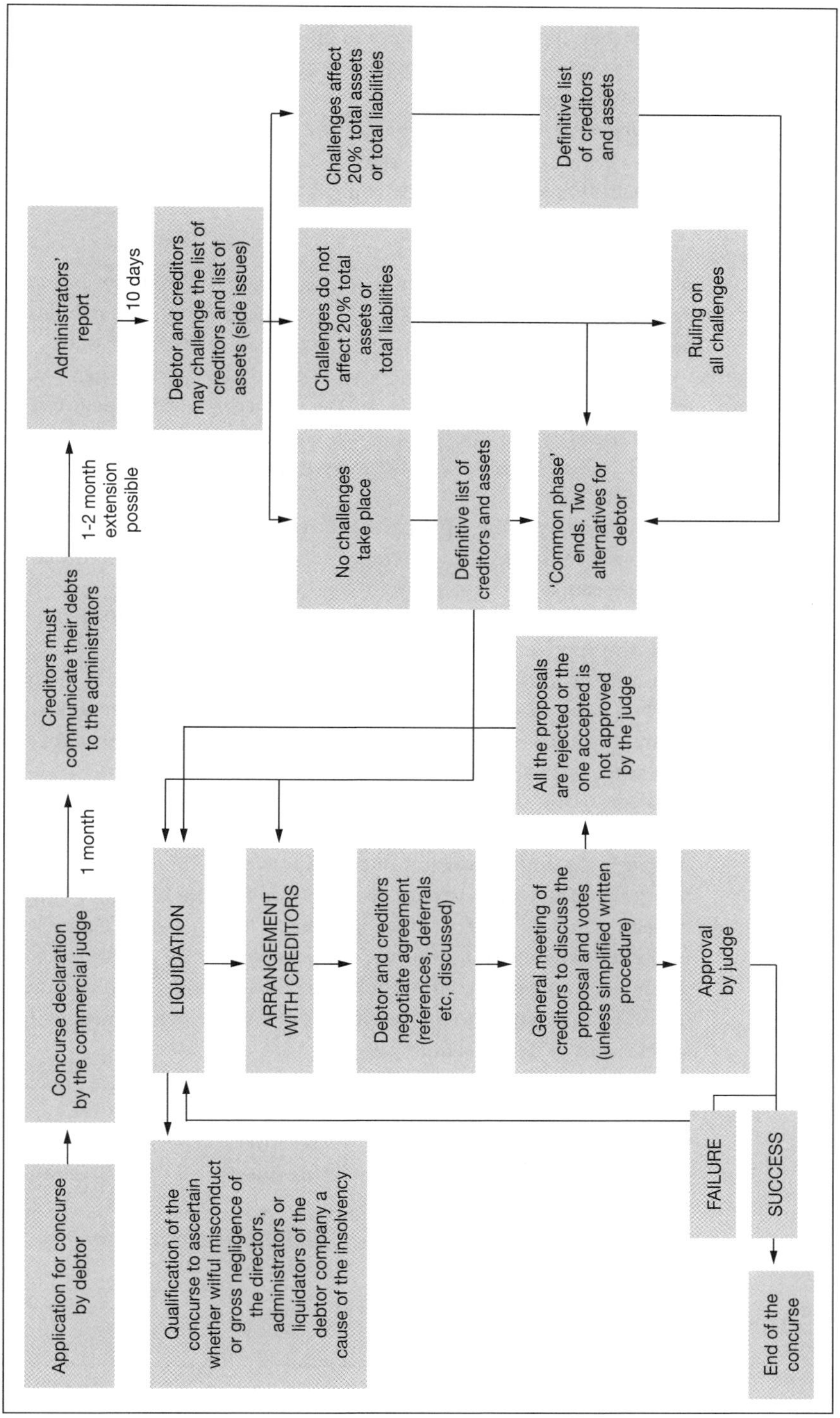
Application for concurse by debtor
Concurse declaration by the commercial judge
1 month
Creditors must communicate their debts to the administrators
1-2 month extension possible
Administrators' report
10 days
Debtor and creditors may challenge the list of creditors and list of assets (side issues)
No challenges take place
Challenges do not affect 20% total assets or total liabilities
Challenges affect 20% total assets or total liabilities
Definitive list of creditors and assets
Definitive list of creditors and assets
Ruling on all challenges
'Common phase' ends. Two alternatives for debtor
All the proposals are rejected or the one accepted is not approved by the judge
LIQUIDATION
ARRANGEMENT WITH CREDITORS
Debtor and creditors negotiate agreement (references, deferrals etc, discussed)
General meeting of creditors to discuss the proposal and votes (unless simplified written procedure)
Approval by judge
FAILURE
SUCCESS
End of the concurse
Qualification of the concurse to ascertain whether wilful misconduct or gross negligence of the directors, administrators or liquidators of the debtor company a cause of the insolvency

rights they have obtained improperly from the debtor's assets or received from the insolvency estate, together with an obligation to provide indemnity for the damage caused; and
- an obligation to cover all or part of the deficit (an obligation that can also be imposed on partners that have rejected without reasonable cause the capitalisation of credits or the issue of convertible securities or instruments).

(a) *Reorganisation plans*

Reorganisation plans may be filed by the debtor or by the creditors and may consist of a deferral of payment and/or haircuts. In addition, the plan may also contain alternative proposals for all or any of the creditors (except for public creditors), consisting of debt-to-equity swaps, convertible bonds, subordinated claims, loans with payment-in-kind (PIK) interests, or the conversion of claims into other debt instruments. The plan may also include structural changes (mergers, spin-offs, etc) or the sale of the business unit to a third party in exchange for the assumption of the restructured debt.

The debtor may only file a pre-packaged reorganisation with the court.

Any proposal must include a payment schedule and, if the continuation of the business is foreseen, a business plan.

Following an amendment made by Royal Decree-Law 11/2014 the majorities required for the approval of reorganisation plans are as follows:
- a simple majority of ordinary claims by value participating in the vote (or 60% of secured claims), if the plan proposes payment in full of ordinary claims within a maximum term of three years, or a haircut of less than 20% of the face value;
- at least 50% of ordinary claims by value (60% of secured claims), when the plan proposes haircuts up to 50% of the face value, stays of payments of up to five years and conversion of claims into subordinated debt for a term no longer than five years (except for public and labour claims);
- at least 65% of ordinary claims by value (75% of secured claims) if the plan proposes haircuts over 50%, stays of payments of up to 10 years and, except for public and labour claims, the conversion of claims into subordinated debt for a term no longer than 10 years, or other new debt instruments, debt-to-asset swaps or debt-to-equity swaps.

Proposed content of plan	Unsecured creditors threshold	Privileged creditors threshold
No write-off and < three years moratorium or Write-off < 20% no moratorium	Simple majority of those voting	>60% each class

continued on next page

Proposed content of plan	Unsecured creditors threshold	Privileged creditors threshold
Write-off < 50% Moratorium < five years Participative loan < five years	>50%	>60% each class
Write-off > 50% Moratorium > five < 10 years Participative loan > five < 10 years Debt-for-equity swaps PIK loans Other financial instruments Sale of business or assets	>65%	>75% each class
Singular treatment for some creditors	Plus the same majority of those creditors unaffected by the singular treatment	Same, but keeping previous guarantee is not a singular treatment

The rules as to syndicated voting and valuation of collateral, explained under heading 2.2 on schemes of arrangement, apply in the same way here.

(b) *Sale of assets*

A declaration of bankruptcy does not trigger suspension of the commercial activities of the debtor. Moreover, the bankruptcy officer may provide directors with a general authorisation to enter into certain transactions, notwithstanding their obligation to report to the bankruptcy officer upon transactions entered into by the debtor. The debtor or the bankruptcy officer are able to sell assets if this is within the debtor's ordinary commercial activities, or, otherwise, where the court authorises such sales.

During bankruptcy, and before approval of a reorganisation plan, the debtor's assets cannot be sold without court authorisation.

4.5 **Liquidation**

If no reorganisation plan is agreed, the liquidation phase will commence and the bankruptcy officer will liquidate all the debtor's assets. The bankruptcy officer must attempt the sale of the business unit as a going concern (as the best way to protect creditors' interests). Within the framework for the sale of the business unit (preferably by auction), the law enables, among other things:

- assumption or rejection of executory contracts, licences and administrative permits;

- release of debts, aside from certain social security and labour claims; and
- the cancellation of security interests, so long as 75% of secured creditors consent.

Secured creditors who fail to enforce their security interest prior to liquidation lose control over the collateral, although they are entitled to a percentage of the price achieved for the entire estate equivalent to that represented by the value of the collateral.

In order to facilitate the sale of a distressed debtor's business, the Insolvency Act envisages an abbreviated bankruptcy procedure if the debtor files a pre-packaged plan or a reorganisation plan that includes the transfer of all its assets and liabilities through a structural change in the company. Additionally, abbreviated procedures also apply when the debtor files, along with the petition for bankruptcy, a liquidation plan containing a binding written offer to purchase an existing business unit, or when the debtor has ceased carrying out its activity and has no employment contracts in force.

5. Conclusion

The reforms introduced in the last two years have changed the challenges those investing in distressed debt encounter every day. The legislative reforms over the last couple of years have focused on eliminating problems arising in relation to refinancing agreements.

The most recent reforms clearly seek to offer better solutions to debtors that, despite being operating companies, have a debt so high that it has limited their growth, and to investors that want to help these companies, either by financing them or by acquiring assets or business units.

Unlike other jurisdictions, Spain does not have an insolvency procedure for groups of companies, although there are some rules which seek coordination between individual proceedings concerning each company within a group (one court, appointment of one trustee or a group of trustees, coordinated reorganisation or liquidation plans, etc).

Restructuring high-yield bonds in Europe

Paul Durban
Grégoire Hansen
Brown Rudnick LLP

1. Introduction: evolution of the European high-yield bond market

The size of the European high-yield bond market has grown significantly since the 2008 financial crisis, as the reluctance of banks to lend and low interest rates have pushed corporates to issue bonds.

In particular, banks' appetite for risk has been suppressed by both internal caution following the losses incurred during the economic downturn and more stringent global regulatory and capital constraints, meaning banks have reduced their risk-weighted assets and cut lending significantly. In fact, much of the new high-yield debt has been issued to refinance maturing bank debt as the high-yield bond market supplants the banking sector as the finance source of choice for European debtors.

Although high-yield bond issuance in Europe has decreased compared to roughly the same period last year – up to the end of July 2016, there has been €27.5 billion of issuance in 2016, compared to €54.4 billion during the same period in 2015[1] – the European high-yield market has grown exponentially from approximately €80 billion in 2008 to an expected €600 billion by the end of 2016. But why has this been the case?

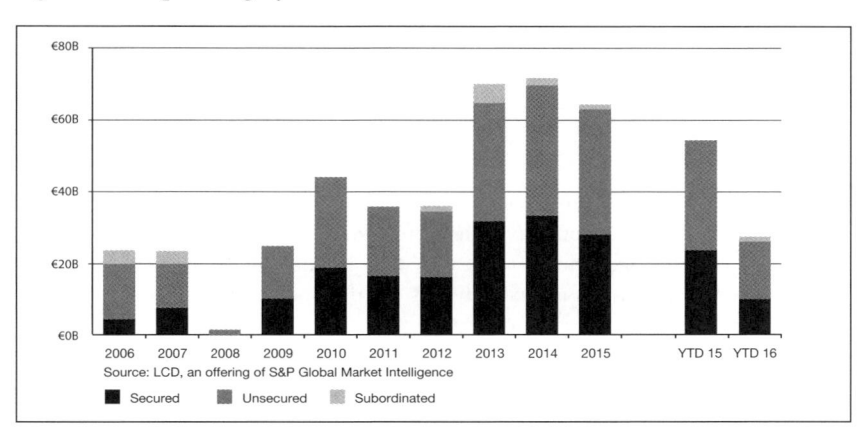

Figure 1: European high yield bond issue

1   Source: *Leveraged Commentary & Data (LCD)*, an offering of S&P Global Market Intelligence.

There are various reasons why European debtors are attracted by high-yield bond debt. Bond indentures tend to contain only incurrence covenants and not the financial maintenance covenants typically seen in loan agreements. In addition, the terms and structure of bond issuances tend not to be negotiated as vigorously as bank debt. Finally, the search for yield has allowed some lower-rated credits to gain market access at volumes and rates which would have not have been the case in the past.

From the investors' perspective, high-yield bonds offer potentially higher income than more conservative fixed-income investments. The yield spread between high-yield bonds and investment-grade bonds has traditionally been between two and five percentage points, depending on the issuer and market conditions. However, market conditions and volatility have caused spreads to expand significantly outside this typical range.

The explosion of bond issuances presents its own challenges when a debtor defaults and the time comes to restructure the bond debt.

On the debtor side, complex capital structures, combined with globalised operations, pose a test for companies and their restructuring professionals seeking to implement solutions that minimise disruption of the business while maximizing the benefits from the restructuring.

In relation to bondholders, publicly traded high-yield issues typically have hundreds, and in certain cases thousands, of holders, including banks, distressed-debt institutions, investment funds, hedge funds, private equity firms and individual investors, all with varying motives and incentives in relation to their investment. In the pre-restructuring phase, it can be difficult just to locate these holders, let alone organise, negotiate and execute a transaction with them. This becomes particularly problematic if there is not a concentration of large holders, and debtors can spend considerable time and resources carrying out bondholder identification exercises to locate holders.

Obtaining the necessary bondholder consents (often requiring unanimous consent to change payment terms, or 75% consent thresholds in a UK scheme of arrangement) from widely held high-yield bond issuances can be extremely difficult outside a formal insolvency proceeding. The high thresholds also allow opportunistic bondholders to pursue hold-out strategies. Any bondholder who can successfully hold out of an out-of-court restructuring may end up retaining the original payment terms in a company that is often substantially deleveraged – increasing the value of a bondholder's bonds at the expense of participating bondholders.

The presence of high-yield bonds in the capital structures of European companies and the above factors have therefore forced investors to start looking at possible restructuring scenarios at an early stage in their investment planning, and have forced financial and legal advisers to develop new methods for rescuing and restructuring distressed companies.

This chapter will focus on the various issues in navigating high-yield restructuring transactions, including discussion of the structures of high-yield bond issuances, creditor dynamics, bond restructuring techniques and other implementation and reorganisation options, including US Chapter 11 and whether Chapter 11 is a realistic option for European debtors.

2. Key differences between loans and high-yield bonds

Historically, a company that issued high-yield bonds was unlikely to do so without first accessing funding through secured and unsecured bank lending, which would usually rank in priority of repayment before all other types of debt in the debtor's insolvency. Although various credits in the market such as Phones 4u Finance Plc and Avanti Communications Group plc have capital structures without bank debt, meaning that bonds rank at or near the top of the repayment waterfall on the debtor's insolvency, a bond restructuring still may end up being part of a wholesale restructuring of the company's entire debt structure which could include its term loans.

The main characteristics of, and distinctions between, loans and high-yield bonds are set out below.

	Credit facility (bilateral or syndicated term loan)	High-yield bonds
Investors	Typically banks and investment funds.	Banks, distressed-debt institutions, investment funds, hedge funds, pension funds, insurance companies, private equity firms and individual investors.
Ranking	Senior, usually secured and guaranteed.	Traditionally subordinated to senior and mezzanine debt but can be equal with senior debt.
Term	Generally five years or less, with interim payments.	Between five and 10 years, with bullet repayment upon maturity.
Interest rate	Typically variable.	Fixed or variable.
Payment	Committed facility with availability period.	Upon issuance of the bonds.
Early repayments	Permitted at any time; potential prepayment restrictions.	Non-call period and prepayment premiums often included.
Covenants	Maintenance (periodical or permanent compliance). Examples include: • information covenants (audited accounts, events of default and material litigation); • non-financial covenants (restrictions on unauthorised borrowing, acquisitions or disposals of assets, investments, dividends, expenditure, and additional security and guarantees); • financial covenants (leverage, liquidity and interest cover ratios, restriction on capital expenditure).	Incurrence (compliance at the time of a specific event). Examples include: • limitations on incurrence of indebtedness (other than permitted indebtedness such as refinancing of existing senior bank debt, intra-group indebtedness and subordinated debt); • limitation on the payment of dividends and other distributions to shareholders; • limitations on security in respect of debt which is subordinated to or ranks equally with the high-yield bonds; • limitations on asset sales and sale and leaseback transactions.

continued on next page

	Credit facility (bilateral or syndicated term loan)	**High-yield bonds**
Amendments	Relatively frequent and easy.	Consent of the relevant majorities of bondholders required.
Credit agency rating	Not necessarily required.	Required.

3. Structures in high-yield bond issuances

3.1 Traditional European structure

A financing vehicle (often incorporated for the sole purpose of issuing the high-yield debt) issues the high-yield bonds. The holding company and/or the group's main operating companies are the borrowers under the senior credit facility. The proceeds from the high-yield bond issue are either loaned to the holding company or contributed as equity. The operating companies give a financial support package (which usually includes security over the assets of the operating companies and guarantees from them) to the senior lenders and any mezzanine lenders. Bondholders are sometimes given guarantees from the holding companies with respect to the high-yield debt. The structure traditionally takes the following form:

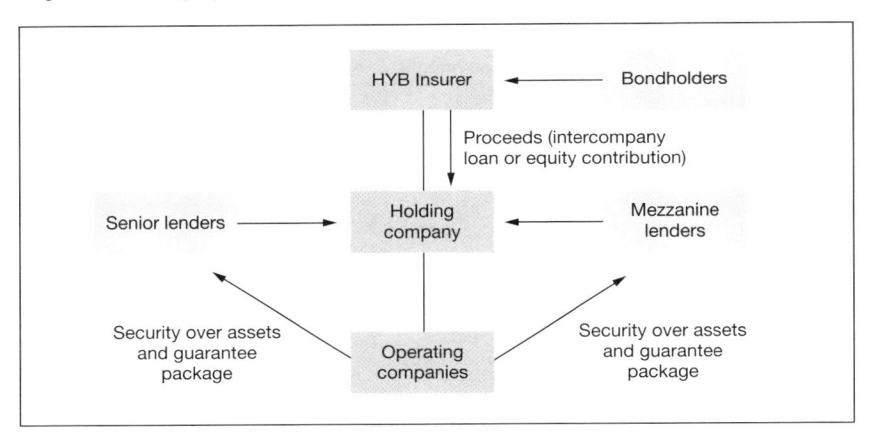

3.2 Super-senior secured revolving credit facility (SSRCF) structure

Issuers will typically need one or more loan facilities alongside high-yield bonds, either to provide a portion of their term debt or a revolving facility for working capital and other purposes. To accommodate this, European senior secured loan and high-yield bond structures have emerged. Two common structures are:
- SSRCF: super-senior secured revolving credit facilities with senior secured bonds;
- *pari passu*: senior secured revolving credit and term loan facilities with senior secured bonds.

Currently the SSRCF structure is the most prevalent of the senior secured loan and high-yield bond structures and commonly takes the following form:

4. Dynamics in high-yield bond restructurings

4.1 Bondholder recovery strategies and valuation

There are a number of different tactics that bondholders can employ in a restructuring to make a return on their investment. The first is known as 'loan to own', in which investors purchase distressed bonds at a discount in the secondary market, with the aim of converting these debts into shares in a restructuring of the issuer's debt.

A second strategy, sometimes referred to as 'pay to shut', occurs when distressed-debt investors seek to encourage other bondholders to group together to block a restructuring agreement. The aim of this is to induce payment of a higher dividend to the blocking bondholders by the senior creditors, who may have more to lose if the company collapses, and therefore a greater economic interest in clearing the way to a successful restructuring.

The valuation of the issuer's assets prior to the corporate restructuring will play a very significant part in dictating bondholders' recovery strategies and the degree to which the bondholders have power to negotiate. If the issuer clearly has insufficient assets to pay bondholders if it were to go into liquidation, then often the bondholders will not be given the right to participate in any new equity or debt created by the issuer as part of the restructuring, and in some cases can be excluded from the restructuring process entirely.

As a result, the hypothetical question of whether the different scenarios the issuer faces could generate any return for the bondholders can be contentious from the outset.

4.2 The impact of credit default swaps (CDS)

While it is normally assumed that creditors are interested in keeping a solvent but financially distressed company out of insolvency and are therefore willing to negotiate a consensual solution, restructuring companies in respect of which there exists a significant CDS market adds an additional level of complexity.

Where junior creditors with CDS protection also have cross-holdings in the senior debt, these creditors may have sufficient bargaining power to dictate the manner in which a restructuring will proceed. Acting as a group, they may be capable of blocking any proposal that does not also trigger a credit event on the CDS, thus ensuring par recovery on their junior debt even where the restructuring proposal envisages a compromise and/or release of that debt.

Carrying out a restructuring of high-yield obligations against which CDS has been issued can be extremely challenging. For example, in the restructuring of Truvo, (formerly World Directories), a European yellow pages business operating in the search and advertising market (*Re Truvo Belgium Comm V* [2009] EWHC 325 (Ch)), the initial restructuring proposal failed to achieve sufficient bondholder support as a large number of bondholders had CDS protection. Not until the company intentionally triggered a credit event (in this case a bankruptcy event as a result of Truvo's Chapter 11 filing), and only after the CDS auction settled, was it able to obtain the required level of support from its creditors to proceed with the restructuring.

4.3 Enforcement and the trustee

Under a trust deed, the bond trustee plays an important role in the enforcement process. For example, the trustee will typically have discretion to determine whether a breach of covenant is 'materially prejudicial' to the interests of the bondholders and can therefore be characterised as an event of default under the trust deed. The trustee will also have an almost exclusive right to accelerate the bonds: the trustee must accelerate the bonds when instructed by at least 25% of the bondholders to do so, but bondholders have no power to do so themselves. In addition, the trustee does not have to accelerate the bonds unless provided with an unlimited and unqualified indemnity against all costs and damages by bondholders. By contrast, under New York law indentures, 25% of bondholders can themselves usually accelerate the bonds following an event of default without the need to involve the trustee.

5. Involvement of bondholders and their negotiating position

Bondholders tend to take a proactive role in the debt restructuring of a financially distressed issuer, particularly where the value of the issuer, or the willingness of senior lenders to negotiate the terms of a restructuring, is perceived to make it more likely that the high-yield bonds will be paid a return, or where distressed-debt investors that purchase senior secured high-yield bonds may have a commercial position that differs from the holders of the company's senior bank debt.

In fact, it could be said that since the economic downturn, the balance of power in restructurings has shifted gradually towards bondholders. Many intercreditor agreements in the post-Lehman era now incorporate an enhanced set of protections for bondholders, including the more recent move to 'one dollar, one vote' structures, where all creditors of a specific class vote with equal weight on enforcement and other matters. Furthermore, with greater volumes of high-yield debt, more recent financings often provide that if there are loan facilities involved, lenders will only have control over enforcement if the loans represent a significant part of the capital structure. This has shifted the traditional dynamic in restructuring talks, where banks exercised near-exclusive control over the process and outcome, meaning that bondholders and their advisers now play a much more active role.

6. **Organising the bondholders and bond restructuring techniques**

There has long been a set of guiding principles in European restructurings, starting with the 'London approach'. One of the cornerstones of those principles is coordination among stakeholders. Regardless of whether the debt consists of senior bank or high-yield bonds, the largest and most high-profile European restructurings tend to be negotiated between the debtor and committees of its creditors (several committees in multiple-layered capital structures). In the case of bond debt, such committees tend to be formed on an *ad hoc* basis, usually with no formal agreement between committee members and the debtor or committee members and other bondholders.

Unlike formal creditor committees in a US Chapter 11 process, an *ad hoc* committee is not a separate legal entity, and it is not mandatory for the debtor to engage with a committee absent commercial necessity. But the primary reasons for forming *ad hoc* committees are self-evident.

First, debtors are far more willing to negotiate with a group of creditors who hold substantial claims in the aggregate rather than with a series of individual creditors. For this reason, it tends to be critical for the committee to represent at the minimum an amount of the bonds which is able to block any transaction proposed by the debtor (so, if 75% bondholder consent is required to implement a deal, the debtor will be forced to deal with a bondholder group that represents more than 25% of the bonds, assuming there is no way to implement the deal around them).

While there are certainly no guarantees that a settlement negotiated by an *ad hoc* committee will be accepted by the requisite number of bondholders generally in a consent solicitation, exchange offer or a restructuring plan vote, it is certainly beneficial to know whether a critical mass of bondholders is willing to support a proposed solution.

Secondly, teaming up with like-minded bondholders enables cost-sharing of legal and financial adviser fees, and a committee representing a blocking stake will also be better positioned to negotiate the payment of its advisers' fees. It should be noted that unlike Loan Market Association form banking documents, bond documents do not tend to provide for the restructuring costs and expenses of creditors to be paid – the committee will need to negotiate this with the debtor on an informal basis. Advisers will therefore often need to be prepared to align themselves economically with the committee members (by back-ending some part of fees on the condition of a successful transaction).

6.1 Disclosure and confidentiality agreements

Once a group of bondholders has been organised, disclosure and confidentiality become sensitive issues.

There is a natural tension in any bond restructuring between the bondholders' desire to preserve their ability to trade the bonds and the need for committee members to have sufficient information to consider restructuring proposals put forward by the debtor and its advisers. Moreover, if an insolvency officeholder has been appointed to the debtor, there can be similar pressure between the bondholders' desire to remain unrestricted on the one hand, and their desire to obtain information from the insolvency officeholder on the condition of company and how it intends to manage the business on the other.

There may be some limited ability to preserve the interests of bondholders if the debtor or an insolvency officeholder discloses certain information to the committee's advisers only, on the understanding that it will not be circulated to the committee members themselves unless and until they sign confidentiality agreements. At some point, however, the committee members will need to become 'insiders' in order properly to engage in negotiations.

In such circumstances, a robust confidentiality agreement is critically important as a way to balance the competing interests of the parties. From the committee's perspective a confidentiality agreement will allow committee members to receive confidential information with the certainty that they can ultimately be 'cleansed' of it. Cleansing is achieved by the debtor's disclosure of all non-public information that is still material on completion of the restructuring or earlier termination of negotiations. It is usual for the confidentiality agreement to include an obligation on the debtor to confirm that all such information has been disclosed following cleansing, and for it to permit committee members or their advisers to disclose information if the debtor fails to comply with the cleansing obligation.

6.2 Standstill and lock-up agreements

In certain circumstances, bondholders may be bound to more than just confidentiality agreements.

If the bonds are in default, or if a default is imminent, a standstill agreement is likely to be appropriate. A standstill agreement is a temporary arrangement entered into between the company and its creditors. The agreement will usually prevent bondholders from taking any enforcement action against the company for a sufficient period of time to allow a more formal restructuring agreement to be entered into, and will fix the amount of the debts owed to bondholders as at a particular date. In return, bondholders may request certain benefits, such as information access rights or an agreement that the company will pay their expenses.

In other circumstances, the company may wish to insist that the bondholders with which it is negotiating support a restructuring proposal for the company and agree not to sell their holdings for a certain period of time.

A 'lock-up agreement' is a contractual agreement between an insolvent company and certain of its creditors, or shareholders, to support a restructuring proposal for the company. Lock-up agreements are designed to give the company certainty earlier in the restructuring process that it has enough votes and, accordingly, that the restructuring proposal is worth pursuing. The use of a lock-up agreement was a key aspect in obtaining requisite bondholder support during the 2014 restructuring of New World Resources, the central European hard coal producer (*Re New World Resources NV* [2014] EWHC 3143 (Ch)), and such an agreement has been used as recently as October 2016 in the initial stages of the restructuring of the oil and gas development and production company Enquest Plc, in which bondholders have locked up to support the restructuring proposal and the proposed amendments to the terms of the bonds.

Without an adequate lock-up agreement, the company may negotiate a bond restructuring agreement only to find that the parties with whom they have been negotiating have traded to a new group of bondholders with completely different goals and objectives, so that negotiations must begin all over again. A lock-up agreement can therefore often be accompanied by the payment of a small consent fee to each party who agrees to be 'locked up'. Note that it is unusual for creditors who have accepted the consent fee to be treated differently, unless the court considers that due to the payment of the fee, such creditors are unfairly advantaged or have different interests.

Lock-up agreement	
What is it?	Contractual agreement between an insolvent company and certain of its creditors or shareholders to support a restructuring proposal for the company.
Effects?	To commit creditors and/or shareholders to vote in favour of the restructuring proposal, and so give the company certainty earlier in the restructuring process that it has enough votes and, accordingly, that the restructuring proposal is worth pursuing.
Special features?	Payment of a small consent fee to each party who agrees to be locked up, although bigger fees may be challenged as a bribe.
When is it used?	It is common for a company proposing a scheme of arrangement to enter into lock-up agreements with individual creditors in advance of the voting process, under which the creditor contractually agrees to vote in favour of the scheme.

7. Implementing a restructuring

The debtor has a choice of several mechanisms for implementing its restructuring plan. However, in the context of a European high-yield bond restructuring, the following are the most common methods of restructuring debt.

7.1 Waivers and supplemental trust deeds

If a debtor is facing short-term financial difficulty but appears capable of an imminent turnaround on an operational level, such that it will ultimately be able to repay the principal and interest on the bonds, the optimum solution may be a short-term waiver or amendment of the issuing documents (such as the trust deed) that can be quickly accomplished out of court.

Most bond issuances (including US law indentures) require the unanimous consent of every bondholder in order to amend or modify the monetary terms of the bonds (such as the principal amount, interest rate and term). However, the non-monetary covenants that restrict various activities of the issuer can be amended by a vote of a controlling majority.

Similarly, it is often possible for a controlling block of bondholders to agree to refrain from declaring an event of default or taking collection action over certain covenant defaults. If such a modification is sufficient to solve the company's financial difficulties (for example by allowing new borrowing, eliminating troublesome financial covenants or allowing disposals of assets), the company can often negotiate to pay a consent fee to a controlling block of the bondholders in exchange for their agreement to the proposed amendment.

7.2 Cash tender offer

A cash tender offer involves a buy-back by the issuer of all or some of its bonds. It is typically used where the bonds are not callable by their terms, and is normally extended to all bondholders. The offer price will normally include either a fixed price or a fixed spread reflecting a premium over the then trading price of the bonds to entice bondholders to sell. The offer will be open for a set period of time and may have various conditions attached to it (such as withdrawal rights or a price increase).

The tender offer can also be run in tandem with exit consent solicitations, enabling the issuer to amend certain terms of the bond such as removal of restrictive covenants from the trust deed. An exit solicitation is usually structured so that if the required proportion of bondholders accept the tender offer, there will be a modification of terms applying to the entire bond series. This is designed to encourage a higher proportion of bondholders to take up the offer or be left holding bonds which have been amended and which consequently may be less liquid.

A variation of the cash tender offer is a 'Dutch auction' which entails the issuer offering to repurchase a certain number of bonds within a fixed price range. Bondholders tender their bonds indicating the lowest price they would be willing to accept. The issuer aggregates all tender offers and buys back bonds up to its specified limit at the lowest price.

7.3 Exchange offers

An exchange offer is effectively a tender offer where the consideration offered for the bonds includes new debt or equity securities as well as, or instead of, cash.

It is usual for exchange offers to be made conditional on high minimum acceptance levels, often 90% or 95%, as an exchange offer will tend not to bind non-consenting bondholders to the exchange. This will mean that some existing bonds are likely to remain outstanding following the exchange offer. and in theory holders of such bonds may continue to be paid on the terms of the existing bonds and not the new bonds. Therefore, to incentivise all bondholders to participate, an exchange offer is usually accompanied by a consent solicitation to make amendments to the non-payment covenants set out in the trust deed, additional security in exchange for concessions on other terms or, depending on the exact exchange mechanism, a small cash payment to consenting bondholders.

7.4 Exit consents

Exit consents are commonly used in bond exchange offers where a debtor wants to alter its debt maturity profile, retire debt, or replace expensive debt with cheaper debt.

The debtor invites bondholders to exchange their bonds on condition that they commit to vote at the bondholder meeting in favour of extraordinary resolutions to amend the terms of the existing bonds. The incentive to exchange or tender is that, ultimately, if the resolutions are passed, the minority bondholders who do not accept the exchange offer will be left with illiquid bonds of lesser financial and/or legal value.

However, the landmark decision in *Assenagon Asset Management SA v Irish Bank Resolution Corporation Ltd (formerly Anglo Irish Bank Corporation (Anglo Irish))* [2012] EWHC 2090 cast doubt on the legality of coercive exit consents under English law.

Anglo Irish launched a distressed exchange offer pursuant to which bondholders could exchange their notes for new senior notes and an exit consent commitment to vote in favour of a resolution introducing an amendment that would allow Anglo Irish to redeem all outstanding subordinated notes for 1% per €1,000.

Although the resolution was passed at a bondholder meeting, there was a substantial disparity between the value offered to those who accepted the exchange offer and voted in favour of the resolution, and those who did not. As the judge emphasised:

The exit consent is, quite simply, a coercive threat. Its only function is the intimidation of a potential minority based upon the fear of any individual member of the class that, by rejecting the exchange ... he (or it) will be left out in the cold.

The court therefore found that the resolution was an abuse of the majority's power to bind the minority, and that the exit consent was unlawful.

The key is therefore to establish whether there is an acceptable level of coercion using the exit consent mechanism. This would fall well short of the nature of the coercion adopted by Anglo Irish, but still provide a real financial or legal incentive for bondholders to come into the exchange offer.

7.5 Debt-for-equity swaps

A debt-for-equity swap takes place where bondholders (and possibly other creditors) exchange bonds (or other debt) and any other claims they have against the issuer for new shares of the issuer. Debt-for-equity swaps can also include a partial swap of the bond debt for the payment of cash and/or the issue of a new debt instrument (such as a convertible bond or warrant instrument), or a combination of these.

Bondholders that swap their debt for equity may be particularly keen to obtain equity that has certain debt-like characteristics, such as the right to payment in priority to ordinary shareholders in the event of insolvency. Similarly, convertible bonds and warrants offer bondholders the chance to retain their status as creditors until the bondholders are more certain that the issuer is on a sounder footing, and then convert their bonds into shares once the rising share price makes this profitable.

To the extent that the senior creditors are adequately secured, they are unlikely to participate in a debt-for-equity swap. As a result, high-yield bondholders are likely to become the issuer's main shareholders following a debt-for-equity swap.

However, given that much of the recent issuance of high-yield debt has been by private rather than public companies, any debt-for-equity swap is likely to require a shareholders' agreement to regulate the post-restructuring governance of the company. The greater the number of potential equity holders, the more complex this document will be.

7.6 Open market bond buy-backs

This tool involves the issuer repurchasing some or all or of its outstanding bonds in one or more open market transactions. Bond buy-backs will be particularly attractive where bonds are trading at a significant discount to their face value.

The ability of a company to effect a bond repurchase will depend on whether it has the necessary cash resources or the ability to obtain affordable financing to fund a bond repurchase programme. In the context of a possible restructuring, a company will often seek to reduce its ratio of debt to share capital through debt repurchases to avoid the need to implement a full restructuring.

However, market repurchases of high-yield bonds are usually only an interim measure until a full restructuring is implemented that addresses the company's underlying problems. Moreover, they must be structured correctly to avoid crossing mandatory thresholds which may trigger disclosure requirements.

Restructuring tools

Mechanism	What is it?	Advantages	Disadvantages
Waiver and supplemental trust deeds	Short-term waiver or amendment of the issuing documents.	• Useful for when debtor is facing short-term financial difficulty. • Non-monetary restrictive covenants can be amended by a vote of a controlling majority.	• Often short-term solution pending full restructuring.

contuinued on next page

Restructuring tools

Mechanism	What is it?	Advantages	Disadvantages
Cash tender offer	Buy-back by the issuer of all or some of its bonds	• Offer price will normally include either a fixed price or a fixed spread reflecting a premium over the trading price of the bonds to entice bondholders to sell. • Tender offer can be run in tandem with exit consent solicitations enabling the issuer to amend certain terms of the bond.	• Issuer may be required to comply with the rules under the US securities laws which, among other things, require that a tender offer be held open for a minimum of 20 business days. • Cash tender offer will not compel investors to sell, even if a certain percentage of investors agree to sell.
Exchange offer	Tender offer where the consideration includes new debt or equity securities as well as, or instead of, cash.	• Diverse instruments offered as part of restructuring tool. • Can be used as an alternative to a scheme of arrangement.	• Issuer will need to comply with applicable securities laws as it entails issuing a new security. • May not bind non-consenting bondholders, so some existing bonds may remain outstanding following the offer.
Debt-for-equity swap	Exchange of bonds (or other debt) for new shares of the issuer.	• Bonds may be exchanged for a meaningful equity interest in the issuer that will eventually yield a substantial profit. • Can include a total or partial swap of the bond debt.	• Certain distressed investors may be precluded from participating if they are unable to hold equity. • Likely to require a shareholders' agreement to regulate the post-restructuring governance of the company.
Open market bond buy-back	Issuer repurchases some or all or of its outstanding bonds in one or more open market transactions.	• Attractive where bonds are trading at distressed levels.	• Usually only an interim measure until a full restructuring is implemented. • Need to ensure the repurchase does not constitute a 'tender offer' obliging the issuer to comply with US securities laws. • Can be adverse tax consequences for issuers.

8. UK statutory restructuring frameworks

The commercial, or mechanistic, aspects of a bond restructuring described above may be completed by consensual agreement, particularly where the issuer is able to obtain funding to purchase the relevant bonds under a buy-back or tender offer. However, where the issuer needs the agreement of a large proportion of the relevant creditors and possibly also of its shareholders (for example, in the case of a debt-for-equity swap), a legally binding statutory framework is often needed. The most commonly used frameworks are set out below.

8.1 Schemes of arrangement

A scheme of arrangement under Part 26 of the Companies Act 2006 is a compromise or other arrangement between a company and its creditors. A scheme of arrangement is approved if 75% in value of each class of creditors (such as bondholders) and shareholders voting at a meeting of the company, and representing a majority in number of each class, vote in favour of the scheme. If the shareholders are not affected by the scheme (for example, if the company's shares are effectively worthless and no debt-for-equity swap is proposed), then the shareholders are not required to vote on the scheme. The same principle applies to any class of creditors that has no prospect of recovery.

The determination of the correct creditor voting classes can give rise to the some of the biggest difficulties when implementing a scheme of arrangement. Creditor rights, not interests or motives, are the governing factor in class composition (*Re BTR plc* [1999] 2 BCLC 675). Further, whether members or creditors form one or more classes depends on the circumstances of each case. For example, whether bondholders with claims under sterling-denominated bonds formed a separate class of creditors from bondholders with claims denominated in US dollars, depends on the similarity or dissimilarity of the bondholders' rights against the company, not on any interest deriving from such rights (*Re Telewest Communications plc* (No 2) [2004] EWHC 924 (Ch)).

Despite these hurdles, English court-sanctioned schemes of arrangement have been a key cram-down tool for restructuring a company's liabilities and binding all bondholders into a transaction and have been used in many high-profile cases, including to complete the liability management exercise carried out by the Co-operative Bank in 2013 which included a scheme of arrangement of its subordinated securities (*Re Co-operative Bank plc* [2013] EWHC 4072 (Ch)). Whether a scheme can be used in a given situation will depend on the facts and, in particular, jurisdictional considerations which are beyond the scope of this chapter.

Although it is clear that the English court will not blindly accept a company's proposal relating to a scheme and will assess the facts of each case, recent cases appear to demonstrate the court's readiness to facilitate financial restructurings by way of scheme of arrangement.

By way of example, in the recent case of *DTEK Finance BV* [2015] EWHC 1164 (Ch), a change in the governing law of loan notes from New York law to English law was sufficient to found jurisdiction for the English court to sanction a scheme of arrangement between a Dutch company and holders of loan notes issued by DTEK despite the issuer not having a substantial connection to England.

The threat which a scheme poses for bondholders (and other creditors) should therefore not be underestimated. Schemes have also been used to alter the fundamental terms of a bond or to facilitate debt-for-equity swaps, both of which would usually require higher consent thresholds. Importantly, there is no requirement of insolvency or impending insolvency for a company to use a scheme. Schemes therefore can be used to avoid insolvency. Where cram-down procedures are available in other countries, this is often only within insolvency or other formal procedures.

Although the prevalence of schemes of arrangement as a restructuring tool and the threat they pose has led to some negative press from high-yield investors, structured correctly, a scheme can also work in bondholders' favour:

- Flexibility – a scheme can be used for implementing almost any compromise or arrangement a company or its creditors and members may agree among themselves (including an exchange offer, debt-for-equity swap or amendments to existing agreements);
- Out-of-the-money creditors – when proposing a scheme there is no need to consult creditors who can be shown to have no economic interest in the company, for example where the valuation evidence clearly establishes subordinated claims are out of the money;
- Injecting new liquidity – a scheme may provide a mechanism which allows bondholders to take equity interests in the business by overriding any provisions contained in intercreditor agreements which would otherwise have blocked the proposed investment;
- Contingent liabilities – schemes can allow a company whose business is being impaired by the existence of significant contingent claims (such as litigation) to reach a binding, court-approved, compromise with those potential claimants, effectively ring-fencing the problem;
- Distribution of assets – finally, in appropriate cases, schemes can offer a more flexible restructuring alternative, particularly where there are questions about identifying assets which, in a formal insolvency process, could delay distributions to creditors.

8.2 Pre-packaged administrations

The other tool that has drawn a number of companies to restructure in the United Kingdom is the 'pre-pack'. The sale of a distressed company's business is negotiated before it enters a UK administration process and executed shortly after an administrator is appointed. The aim is to minimise the delay, costs and destruction of value often associated with entry into an insolvency process.

However, for bondholders, the pre-pack is one of the most controversial procedures available. Although it reduces the transaction costs of the insolvency, meaning that, in theory, there should be more funds available for distribution to bondholders, in reality, debts owing to out-of-the-money bondholders can be left behind in the insolvent company. Moreover, there is often a tension between the bondholders' desire to preserve their ability to trade the bonds and their desire to obtain information from the administrator on the terms of the business sale and be involved in that process.

When used in combination, the scheme and the pre-pack become an even more powerful restructuring tool, which can be used to isolate bondholders in an insolvent company and transfer its business to a Newco, sometimes owned by the senior lenders.

For example, in late 2009, the English High Court granted administration orders for Hellas Telecommunications II, a company in the WIND Hellas group (*Re Hellas Telecommunications (Luxembourg)* II SCA [2009] EWHC 3199 (Ch)). This enabled, among other things, a pre-pack administration sale of its main asset, the shares of WIND Hellas Telecommunications SA, the third largest integrated telecommunications operator in Greece, to a newly incorporated group.

A year later, during a second restructuring involving the WIND Hellas group, an English-law scheme of arrangement between Hellas Telecommunications (Luxembourg) V, one of the group companies, and the senior secured noteholders (*Re Hellas Telecommunications (Luxembourg) V* [2010] EWHC 3295 (Ch)) was used to transfer 100% ownership of approximately €1.2 billion of senior secured notes to an entity within the newly incorporated group in order to facilitate a broader restructuring, including a further pre-pack sale of various assets of the group companies to the newly incorporated group.

9. US Chapter 11

Despite the prevalence of these restructuring tools, European companies needing to restructure bond debt face some significant practical challenges from the growth in European high-yield issuances mainly, as described above, related to obtaining the necessary bondholder consents from widely held high-yield bond issuances. It is therefore paramount that a company develop a potential backstop option for use in the event that it cannot lock up the consents required to execute a consensual restructuring or a light-touch process such as a scheme of arrangement.

For years, the Chapter 11 procedure in the US has been viewed as the model restructuring regime. Much weight is attached to its wide moratorium and cram-down provisions, the predictability of the courts based upon case law, the flexibility provided by allowing companies to treat similarly situated creditors differently and the effectiveness created by being able to obtain liquidity and discharge financial creditors on a worldwide basis. These factors are discussed in more detail below.

9.1 Control

One of the key features of a US Chapter 11 proceeding is that a company's board of directors and management can maintain absolute control of the day-to-day operations of the business after an insolvency procedure commences. This feature, known as 'debtor in possession', constitutes a major difference between the United States and many key European jurisdictions that replace management with an administrator or other insolvency officeholder.

9.2 Debtor-in-possession financing and other liquidity enhancement

Unlike many insolvency regimes, the US Chapter 11 process permits a company to raise additional liquidity through debtor-in-possession financing that may 'prime' unsecured creditors. This financing can be particularly effective when the fulcrum securities are unsecured obligations, which is common in high-yield bond restructurings. Furthermore, the US Bankruptcy Code allows debtors to stop paying interest on unsecured obligations, further enhancing a company's liquidity during a restructuring of unsecured high-yield obligations.

9.3 Worldwide automatic stays

Unlike in most insolvency regimes, the automatic stay, under US law, has worldwide effectiveness. This comes from a provision in the US Bankruptcy Code that defines a bankruptcy estate as comprised of the debtor's property, wherever located. However, in order for the court to enforce this provision effectively, a company's creditors must have some nexus with the United States. In the case of financial institutions, being the likely holders of high-yield bonds, it is likely that they will have a US connection given the United States' place as a worldwide financial centre. On the other hand, if a number of creditors do not have a connection to the United States, it is possible for a company to file for a complementary or secondary insolvency proceeding to enforce the stay in other territories.

10. US Chapter 11 or UK/European restructuring mechanisms?

It is clear that in restructurings where the fulcrum security consists of European high-yield bonds, the US Chapter 11 reorganisation process possesses certain key attributes. The popularity of Chapter 11 is also partly due to the increasing diversity among the bondholder community as more US participants invest in distressed European companies.

Growing pressure for national regimes to incorporate certain of its key features has therefore reignited the debate as to what constitutes an effective insolvency and restructuring regime. There has long been a debate in Europe as to whether the ideal process should be a 'full service' insolvency procedure which allows the debtor to stay in possession, with a wide moratorium, protection for new financing and the ability to cram down creditors in the manner of a US Chapter 11.

However, the current state of the UK restructuring market suggests that it is still some way off from implementing a regime such as this.

Although more unwieldy than Chapter 11 because it requires actual creditor meetings and, if they still have an economic interest, shareholder meetings, a key advantage to European issuers of schemes of arrangement over Chapter 11 is that it is better suited to move directly and quickly into the protections of administration if the company's business begins to collapse, in a way that Chapter 11 cannot achieve. As the *DTEK Finance Case* demonstrates, the flexibility of a scheme also gives European issuers who issue New York law-governed notes much better access to English rescue procedures, and is a less costly and quicker route out of distress.

Moreover, Chapter 11, while clearly an effective restructuring tool, also involves a debtor filing for bankruptcy. From a reputational perspective, European debtors need to ensure that any such strategy is carefully managed, given that many European jurisdictions typically associate bankruptcy with liquidation. One method of potentially minimising any fallout is to enter into a pre-packaged Chapter 11 where the reorganisation plan is negotiated prior to the filing and there is a bankruptcy exit plan in hand, although this is not always a viable option for European debtors with complex capital structures.

Over time, innovative restructuring and insolvency practitioners, supported by a highly regarded judiciary, have managed to attract many overseas companies to restructure in Europe, and above all in the United Kingdom, where there is an active distressed-debt market and levels of corporate insolvency are relatively low. This indicates that the United Kingdom currently has a relatively efficient restructuring regime in place, which is able to meet the market's demands for speedy, cost-effective, fair and predictable outcomes, without those key features which are enshrined in US statute and Chapter 11. Having said this, other contributors to this book have highlighted how a number of European jurisdictions are developing rescue procedures that they hope will rival those in the United States and the United Kingdom. As a result, and as the legal and economic impact of Brexit becomes more discernible, it will be interesting to see whether the United Kingdom remains the jurisdiction of choice for high-yield European bond restructurings in the future.

The recast EU Insolvency Regulation and its impact on distressed investing

James Bell
Douglas Hawthorn
Jeremy Walsh
Travers Smith LLP

1. **Key concepts**

In this chapter, 'EIR' (or '2000 EIR') refers to Council Regulation (EC) 1346/2000 of May 29 2000 on insolvency proceedings. The term 'recast EIR' refers to Regulation (EU) 2015/848 of May 20 2015 on insolvency proceedings (recast). At the time of writing, the EIR is due to be replaced by the recast EIR (as further detailed under headings 3 and 4 below). As both regulations contain similar terms, the 'EIRs' is a reference to both the 2000 EIR and the recast EIR.

The 2000 EIR introduced a regime governing the administration of insolvent corporates or individuals which operate in more than one member state of the European Union. The EIRs ensure recognition, without further formality, of insolvency proceedings throughout the European Union (except Denmark) and determine the law applicable to such proceedings. They apply only where the debtor's centre of main interests is situated in a member state (other than Denmark)[1] and do not apply to insolvency proceedings on foot in other jurisdictions. The EIRs are only binding on participating member states and so will be of limited practical use where assets are situated outside the European Union.[2] The EIRs envisage there being one set of main insolvency proceedings, with the possibility of multiple territorial (or secondary) insolvency proceedings. Currently (under the 2000 EIR), secondary insolvency proceedings must be winding-up proceedings (as listed in Annex B to the EIR). Broadly speaking (and with certain exceptions), the EIRs follow the general principle that the applicable law shall be that of the member state in which the proceedings (main, territorial or secondary) have been opened. This law determines, in particular, the ranking of claims and the procedural rights of creditors.[3] Under the 2000 EIR there is no process for the coordination of (or

---

1   In the interests of brevity, the term 'member states' is used throughout this chapter to refer to participating member states for the purposes of the EIRs. Note however that Denmark is not bound by the EIRs and the EIRs do not apply to debtors in Denmark or to establishments in Denmark of debtors from elsewhere in the European Union. Similarly, given the direct effect of the EIRs, if a current participating member state were to leave the European Union, the EIRs would cease to apply following that departure.
2   For instance, if an insolvent Italian company has granted security over assets in New York, the New York court will not be required by the EIRs to recognise insolvency proceedings opened in Italy. It might be necessary to take steps to open separate US proceedings or to apply to the New York court to recognise the Italian proceedings based on US rules for recognition of foreign insolvency proceedings.
3   See EIR, Article 4; recast EIR, Article 7.

cooperation between) different insolvency proceedings affecting a group of companies.

2. Relevance of the insolvency regulations to distressed-debt investing

It is important to highlight at the outset that many investor claims in the context of distressed-debt investing may either fall outside the scope of the EIRs or fall to be determined by a law other than the law of the main insolvency proceedings. Such matters include rights *in rem* (security), set-off and claims in respect of securities held in a settlement system (see under headings 7 and 8 below). Insurance undertakings, banks and other credit institutions, and collective and other investment undertakings are excluded from the scope of the EIRs (see under heading 9 below). Furthermore, despite recent enlargement in the scope of proceedings covered by the recast EIR, some tools commonly used for the solvent restructuring of a debtor will continue to fall outside the scope of the EIRs. These include the English law scheme of arrangement procedure (a commonly used option for the restructuring in the United Kingdom of overseas companies, as explained under heading 12 below), discussed in detail in a separate chapter.[4]

Distressed claims will take many forms, and the correct categorisation of the claim will determine whether the EIRs are relevant. For instance, the treatment of debt claims acquired under syndicated loans could amount to a claim against the borrower (for instance, if a loan is acquired through a transfer or assignment) and the EIRs would apply to the insolvency proceedings of that borrower. Alternatively, where the investor has entered into a risk participation with an existing lender, while the investor will clearly be interested to receive timely and accurate information regarding any insolvency proceedings relating to the borrower, it may have no direct claim in the borrower's insolvency; rather, a separate contract with the lender of record. Investments may be made through capital market instruments, which are frequently held in a settlement system where the investor's direct counterparty is not the issuer. If the issuer becomes insolvent, the EIRs will not be relevant to determine the claim of the investor against its immediate counterparty. Investors will often take synthetic positions in debt through contracts for difference (or they may participate in hedging documentation in relation to a company's debt obligations to third parties), in which case the EIRs will have no bearing on the investor's claim against its counterparty. In cases where the investor is exposed to the credit risk of a credit institution, note that the eventual insolvency of that counterparty would also be outside the scope of the EIRs (see under heading 9 below). Claims against a debtor purchased by an investor which itself owes money to that debtor (ie, an attempt to use set-off) also fall outside the scope of the EIRs (see under heading 8 below).

Distressed-debt investors will commonly adopt a multi-strategy approach, investing in instruments at different levels of the capital structure (potentially including direct or synthetic equity stakes, for instance). As a result, an investor may be faced with multiple exposures, some being within the scope of the EIRs and some outside their scope. It should be noted that the EIRs do not, of themselves, regulate

---

4   See "Schemes of arrangement" chapter.

mergers and acquisitions processes for the acquisition of equity, or conversion of debt into equity; these are matters for local law procedures. However, to the extent that such local law process is an 'Annex A' procedure (further explained under heading 6 below), the recognition of the procedure, and of any moratorium which accompanies it, may provide more stability and certainty of outcome for a loan-to-own investor.

3. **A brief history of the 2000 EIR and recast EIR**

After 40 years of successive aborted projects for pan-European conventions on insolvency proceedings led by various committees of the European Economic Community, the Council of Europe and the European Council of Ministers, the EIR came into force as a regulation on May 31 2002. It sets out insolvency recognition and conflict of law rules for the European Union, except Denmark. As a regulation, the EIR has direct effect in participating member states and its interpretation is a matter of European Union law. The EIR's objectives (set out in Recitals 2 and 4) were:
- that cross-border insolvency proceedings should operate efficiently and effectively so as to encourage the proper functioning of the internal market; and
- to avoid incentives for the parties to transfer assets or judicial proceedings from one member state to another, seeking to obtain a more favourable legal position, commonly referred to as 'forum shopping'.

The EIR is generally regarded as a success. Case law of the Court of Justice of the European Union has clarified interpretation on a number of points, leading to more uniform application across participating member states. However, the financial crisis of 2008 and ensuing Eurozone crisis put growth firmly back on the Commission's agenda, and it was concluded that revision of the EIR would link in with the European Union's political priorities to promote economic recovery and sustainable growth, to encourage investment and to promote the survival of businesses. Consultation of stakeholders and legal and empirical studies commissioned by the Commission identified five main shortcomings with the 2000 EIR:[5]
- The EIR does not cover national procedures which provide for a restructuring of the company at a pre-insolvency stage or proceedings which leave the existing management in place.
- There can be difficulties in determining which member state is competent to open insolvency proceedings.
- The opening of secondary insolvency proceedings can hamper the efficient administration of the company's estate.
- It is difficult to obtain reliable information on proceedings in other jurisdictions, in the absence of effective rules on publicity of insolvency proceedings and the lodging of claims.
- The EIR does not contain specific rules dealing with the insolvency of a multinational enterprise group, despite a large number of cross-border insolvencies involving groups of companies.

---

[5] Proposal for a regulation of the European Parliament and of the Council amending Council Regulation (EC) No 1346/2000 on insolvency proceedings (COM(2012) 744 final) (2012/0360 (COD)).

Negotiations between the European Parliament, the Council and the Commission culminated with the regulation recasting the EIR being adopted on May 20 2015. The stated objectives of the recast EIR are to improve efficiency of the European framework for resolving cross-border insolvency cases, to ensure a smooth functioning of the internal market and its resilience in economic crisis. This objective, the Commission[6] says, links in with the European Union's current political priorities to promote economic recovery and sustainable growth, a higher investment rate and preservation of employment as set out in the 'Europe 2020' strategy.

4. Implementation timetable for the recast EIR

The recast EIR will apply to insolvency proceedings commenced on or after June 26 2017 (Articles 84(1) and 92).[7] The 2000 EIR will continue to apply to any proceedings opened before that date (Article 84(2)). Note however that the obligation for member states to establish national registers (discussed under heading 15 below) will apply from June 26 2018, and the interconnection of national insolvency registers will apply from June 26 2019. The recast EIR effects various fundamental changes to the scope and operation of the 2000 EIR.

In view of the imminent implementation of the recast EIR, the remainder of this chapter focuses on the rules as amended by the recast EIR.

5. Brexit

This chapter was, for the most part, written before the outcome of the referendum on the United Kingdom's membership of the European Union became known on June 24 2016. At the time of publication, the exit model and the legislative changes that will result from Brexit (assuming that the procedure under Article 50 of the Treaty on European Union is invoked) remain wholly unclear. The formalities for the United Kingdom to leave the European Union are unlikely to be completed before 2019 at the earliest. At that point the recast EIR (being an EU regulation) will cease to apply automatically between the United Kingdom and the remaining EU member states (rEU). It is the authors' hope, given the success of the EIRs, that there will be a collective desire, both in the United Kingdom and in the rEU, to retain the effects of the recast EIR regime as far as possible. This could be achieved as part of a withdrawal treaty between the United Kingdom and the rEU. Alternatively, it could be achieved through a series of bilateral agreements between the United Kingdom and as many of the rEU member states as possible to achieve broadly the same effect; though potentially resulting in inconsistent and unpredictable outcomes for pan-European insolvencies. A less attractive outcome still is that the United Kingdom is forced to rely on the vagaries of private international law in each rEU member state.

---

6   Commission staff working document – Impact assessment – Accompanying the document Revision of Regulation (EC) No 1346/2000 on insolvency proceedings (SWD (2012) 416 final).

7   Article 84 is (oddly) silent as to how to treat proceedings opened on June 26 2017! *Moss, Fletcher and Isaacs on the EU Regulation on Insolvency Proceedings* (3rd edition 2016, at 8.808) suggests the recast EIR should apply to proceedings opened on June 26 2017 because Article 92 (entry into force) states that the recast EIR applies from June 26 2017.

From the United Kingdom's perspective, any such halfway solutions to the gap left by the EIRs would increase the risk of competing insolvency proceedings between the United Kingdom and the rEU, due to the removal of the rule requiring automatic recognition of insolvency proceedings. There could also be increased uncertainty for UK insolvency practitioners seeking the assistance of the rEU courts (and vice versa).

6. Main, territorial and secondary proceedings

The recast EIR places a greater emphasis on rescue and rehabilitation, and is extended to proceedings which provide for restructuring of a debtor at a stage where there is only a likelihood of insolvency, proceedings which leave the debtor fully or partially in control of its assets and affairs, and proceedings providing for a debt discharge or a debt adjustment. Consistent with this approach, the term "liquidator" has been replaced with the term "insolvency practitioner" throughout. Annex A sets out, for each member state, an exhaustive list of proceedings which are within the regulation's scope. In the case of the United Kingdom, for instance, this includes a court-supervised winding-up, a creditors' voluntary winding-up (with confirmation by the court), administration, voluntary arrangements under insolvency legislation (such as company and individual voluntary arrangements) and bankruptcy or sequestration. However, none of the types of receivership available under English law fall within the scope of the EIRs. Receiverships are not collective regimes and do not have an equivalent in most other member states. Although it is no longer a procedure of wide application, note that this includes administrative receivership, which can apply where a floating charge has been granted by specific entities defined by statute (including project finance and utility companies). An administrative receiver has wide powers to take custody of the charged assets, run a company's business and dispose of its assets, either piecemeal or as part of the sale of the business as a going concern, to satisfy the secured debt.

The concept of a debtor's centre of main interests ('COMI') is an essential element of the recast EIR. The debtor's COMI is defined as "the place where the debtor conducts the administration of its interests on a regular basis and is ascertainable by third parties" (Article 3(1)). It has been common for debtors to move (or purport to move) their COMI in order to utilise insolvency proceedings available in other member states and the recast EIR attempts to curb this trend (see under heading 13 below).

If a debtor's COMI is within the European Union (with the exception of Denmark) then the courts of the member state where the debtor's COMI is situated have the jurisdiction to open "main insolvency proceedings" (recast EIR, Article 3(1)). There can only be one set of main insolvency proceedings in respect of a debtor. If a debtor's COMI is within a member state, but the debtor has an establishment in another member state, the courts of the member state where that debtor has an establishment have jurisdiction to open territorial insolvency proceedings (Article 3(2)). Territorial insolvency proceedings are restricted to the assets in the relevant member state (Article 3(2)). For rules determining where assets are situated for these purposes, see under heading 10 below. Once main insolvency proceedings are opened, any territorial insolvency proceedings already in progress or opened subsequently will be classed as secondary insolvency proceedings (Article 3(3) and (4)). There can be multiple territorial/secondary insolvency proceedings.

A welcome change effected in the recast EIR is that secondary insolvency proceedings are no longer required to be winding-up proceedings (as were listed in Annex B of the 2000 EIR). The former position had been widely criticised as frustrating efforts to rescue group companies or divisions in other member states.

The recast EIR has an enlarged scope. Article 1 states that it will apply to public collective proceedings, including interim proceedings, which are based on a law relating to insolvency and in which, for the purpose of rescue, adjustment of debt, reorganisation or liquidation:

- the debtor is totally or partially divested of his assets and an insolvency practitioner is appointed;
- the assets and affairs of the debtor are subject to control or supervision by a court (this is to include a situation where the court only intervenes on appeal by a creditor; see Recital 10); or
- a temporary stay of individual enforcement proceedings is granted by a court or by operation of law to allow for negotiations between the debtor and creditors, provided sufficient safeguards are in place for creditors during this time (which includes *sauvegarde financière accélérée* in France; *procedimiento de homologación de acuerdos de refinanciación* in Spain; and *accordi di ristrutturazione* in Italy).

The recast EIR will not apply to confidential procedures. A new Recital 12 explains that while confidential proceedings may play an important role in some member states, their confidential nature makes it impossible for a creditor or a court located in a different member state to know that such proceedings have been opened, thereby making it difficult to provide for recognition on an EU-wide level. French mandataire ad hoc and conciliation proceedings will therefore remain outside the scope of the recast EIR.

In order to avoid the delay and expense of opening secondary insolvency proceedings, Article 36 allows the insolvency practitioner in the main insolvency proceedings to give a unilateral undertaking, in respect of assets located in any member state in which secondary insolvency proceedings could be opened, to the effect that when distributing those assets or the proceeds received as a result of their realisation, it will comply with the distribution and priority rights that creditors would have under national law if secondary insolvency proceedings were opened in that member state. These are colloquially referred to as 'synthetic' (or 'virtual') proceedings. Secondary insolvency proceedings, it is broadly accepted, can frustrate entirely or disrupt a rescue or better realisation of a group's assets, and lead to duplicated and/or wasted costs. Article 36 follows the template established in *Collins & Aikman* [2007] 1 BCLC 182 and *Nortel* [2009] BCC 343; cases where an administrator in United Kingdom insolvency proceedings undertook to respect local priorities of distribution in order to avoid a plethora of secondary insolvency proceedings being opened.

7. **Cross-border recognition of insolvency proceedings – scope**

The recast EIR provides that any judgment opening insolvency proceedings shall be recognised in all other member states (Article 19). Article 7 lists all the matters to be determined by the law applicable to such proceedings. The aim is to achieve certainty of outcome by replacing the various national conflict of laws rules which might otherwise apply in relation to insolvency proceedings. There are several exceptions to the general rule that the law applicable to insolvency proceedings is that of the state where proceedings are commenced. These are contained in Article 8 (third parties' rights *in rem*), Article 9 (set-off), Article 10 (reservation of title), Article 11 (contracts relating to immovable property), Article 12 (payment systems and financial markets), Article 13 (contracts of employment), Article 14 (effects on rights subject to registration), Article 15 (European patents with unitary effect and Community trademarks), Article 16 (detrimental acts), Article 17 (protection of third-party purchasers) and Article 18 (effects of insolvency proceedings on pending lawsuits or arbitral proceedings). We will now examine the exceptions of most relevance to distressed-debt investors.

8. **Exceptions to the basic choice of law rule – rights *in rem*, set-off and securities held in a payment or settlement system**

Investors with the benefit of security for the debt or obligation of a distressed debtor will be keen to ensure that they have direct recourse to the relevant collateral in the event of default by the debtor, regardless of the onset of the debtor's insolvency. A prerequisite for this result (as stated in Recital 68, which highlights that "such rights are of considerable importance for the granting of credit") is that the laws of every relevant jurisdiction should respect the continued validity and enforceability of such rights *in rem* despite the debtor's insolvency. Otherwise, where the collateral is situated in a different member state from that in which the main insolvency proceedings are opened, a secured creditor could be vulnerable to variations between national laws relating to the impact of insolvency on security arrangements, the resulting uncertainty impacting negatively on the value of secured debt.

Article 8[8] protects secured creditors and states:

The opening of insolvency proceedings shall not affect the rights in rem of creditors or third parties in respect of tangible or intangible, moveable or immoveable assets, both specific assets and collections of indefinite assets as a whole which change from time to time, belonging to the debtor which are situated within the territory of another Member State at the time of the opening of proceedings.

This means that, to the extent that the law where the assets are situated protects the rights of a secured creditor and permits enforcement (notwithstanding the debtor's insolvency), these rights will trump any contrary provisions in the law of the main insolvency proceedings. While the use of "such a negative and vague phrase"[9] as "shall not affect" could lead to various interpretations, it is generally accepted to

---

8   See also Recitals 22, 39 and 68.
9   McCormack, "Security rights and the European Insolvency Regulation: a legal quagmire" (2016) 4 JIBFL 224.

be more than simply a choice of law rule, and to mean that a creditor may seek to enforce its security interest in the member state where the charged assets are situated despite the opening of insolvency proceedings. Investors may also take comfort from the wide drafting of Article 8, which covers future assets, monetary claims and other receivables. The reference in Article 8(1) to "collections of indefinite assets as a whole which change from time to time" gives comfort that a floating charge (a key concept in the United Kingdom and Ireland, but with no equivalent in most civil law jurisdictions) falls within the scope of the exemption.

Nevertheless the Article 8 exemption will not always be available. For instance, if assets are not situated in a member state, Article 8 will not apply and so the law of the main insolvency proceedings will determine the extent to which local law is to be followed. In this context the revised and improved *situs* rules contained in the recast EIR (considered under heading 10 below) are relevant. Note also the importance of the distinction between the local assets and the rights *in rem* over them; any surplus remaining after the exercise of such rights are subject to the law of the main insolvency proceedings. Furthermore the exemption in Article 8 is not applicable to security granted after the opening of the main insolvency proceedings; such rights will be subject to the law of the main insolvency proceedings. This is significant in view of the expansion, under the recast EIR, of proceedings which fall within its scope (some of which are early stage or interim proceedings). Fresh security granted in the context of such proceedings would not therefore benefit from the Article 8 exemption.

Despite the importance of the rights *in rem* exemption, some significant concerns remain about its scope.[10] Article 8 states that insolvency proceedings "shall not affect" secured creditors. However it is unclear how this principle sits alongside either the possibility of an insolvency practitioner making a payment to a secured creditor to extinguish its security right (especially in situations where the creditor is undersecured), or an obligation on a secured creditor to contribute to the general costs of the insolvency proceedings (eg, to pay the expenses of an administrator). An investor in secured debt might also be concerned as to the potential application of moratoria on enforcement, which could reduce the value of the collateral. This is particularly relevant as the recast EIR includes several provisions for a court to order a stay of opening proceedings or of enforcement proceedings. Although a new Recital 69 states that "any such stay should not affect the rights in rem of creditors," recitals are not binding, and so it is unclear how this principle might be respected alongside the overriding objective of business rescue (often facilitated by moratoria on security enforcement).

Article 9[11] provides that:

The opening of insolvency proceedings shall not affect the right of creditors to demand the set-off of their claims against the claims of a debtor, where such a set-off is permitted by the law applicable to the insolvent debtor's claim.

---

10   For further analysis of the uncertainties surrounding the application of the rights *in rem* exemption, see McCormack, "Security rights and the European Insolvency Regulation: a legal quagmire" (2016) 4 JIBFL 224.
11   See also Recital 70.

As a consequence, set-off rights potentially remain available to an investor, whether or not the law of the relevant insolvency proceedings permits set-off in the circumstances. Set-off receives very different treatment from one jurisdiction to another. For instance, most civil law systems apply a restrictive approach to insolvency set-off. When read together, Article 7 (applicable law) and Article 9 (set-off) potentially allow an investor to elect to take advantage of set-off rights where this is permitted under either the law of the contract (assuming the investor's claim derives from a contract incorporating an express and valid choice of law), or the law where proceedings are opened. There is some debate as to whether the 'law applicable' (for the purposes of Article 9) is restricted to the law of a member state (which is not an express requirement of Article 9, despite being an express requirement of other articles containing exemptions) and also whether 'law' for these purposes means the generally applicable civil or common law, or whether it could also encompass that member state's insolvency law. In some scenarios this may be a crucial question because set-off is commonly applied differently in insolvency. In the United Kingdom for instance, set-off is treated as a mandatory process which applies (as a matter of public policy) where requirements of mutuality are satisfied. Investors may be able to indulge in forum shopping in the application of available set-off rights, something which the recast EIR has attempted to restrict in other areas (for instance in its restrictions on COMI-shifting).[12] The wording of the Article 9 exemption also means that creditors likely to benefit from set-off will be best advised to ensure that the debtor's claim against them is expressly governed by a law which allows the broadest possible set-off rights.

Distressed investing will often relate to securities held in a payment or settlement system. The impact of counterparty insolvency on contracts between parties operating in such systems is therefore of significant commercial importance, crucial for the market to retain confidence in the binding nature of such transactions. Article 12 provides that:

> ... the effects of insolvency proceedings on the rights and obligations of the parties to a payment or settlement system or to a financial market shall be governed solely by the law of the Member State applicable to that system or market.

This rule is bolstered by Article 12(2), which states that actions for voidness, voidability or unenforceability of payments or transactions carried out under the relevant system (potentially detrimental to creditors) will be subject to the law applicable to the relevant system. A special proviso in Article 12(1) subjects the protection of rights *in rem* over assets belonging to the debtor to the law of the *situs* (as envisaged by Article 8, discussed above). As highlighted by Recital 71, Article 9 potentially overlaps with Directive 98/26/EC on settlement finality in payments and securities settlement systems (the 'Finality Directive'). Since the recast EIR does not include any express provisions on formal netting arrangements (beyond the comment in Recital 71 as to the "need for special protection in the case of ... netting agreements to be found in such systems"), there is some uncertainty as to whether

---

12 Recital 29 to the recast EIR states: "This Regulation should contain a number of safeguards aimed at preventing fraudulent or abusive forum shopping."

the recast EIR may have a wider scope than the Finality Directive with regard to netting, and also whether netting arrangements are covered by Article 9 (set-off) or by Article 12 (payment systems and financial markets).

9. Debtors outside the scope of the recast EIR

A 'debtor' for the purposes of the recast EIR includes companies, legal persons and individuals. Recital 25 states that the recast EIR "applies only to proceedings in respect of a debtor whose centre of main interests is located in the Union". This potentially includes a debtor which is registered outside the European Union but which is found to have its COMI within it. The correct ascertainment of the debtor's COMI (as further discussed under heading 13 below) is therefore critical to determine whether a debtor is subject to the recast EIR. Debtors that do not have their COMI in a member state are out of the EIRs' scope. This is significant because even if a debtor has substantial connections with the European Union and assets located in member states, the EIRs will be of no assistance in achieving certainty of outcome for creditors. Where the EIRs do not apply, the pre-existing laws of each member state will apply to determine the conduct of proceedings and matters of cross-border recognition. Applicable rules will vary significantly depending on the location of relevant assets or counterparties. English courts, for instance, might instead have to apply the rules contained in the common law, the Cross-Border Insolvency Regulations 2006 (SI 2006/1030), Section 426 of the Insolvency Act 1986 or bilateral treaties with other non-EU states.

Article 1(2) of the recast EIR expressly excludes proceedings that concern specified entity types. Of particular reference to distressed-debt investing (depending on the nature of the investor's counterparty on any given trade), note that insolvency proceedings relating to credit institutions are outside the scope and reference should instead be made to the Credit Institutions Directive,[13] Bank Recovery and Resolution Directive (2014/59/EU) and implementing legislation such as (in the United Kingdom) the Credit Institutions (Reorganisation and Winding Up) Regulations 2004 (SI 2004/1045). Article 1(2) also excludes insolvency proceedings relating to insurance undertakings, investment undertakings and collective investment undertakings.

10. Where are distressed assets situated for the purposes of the recast EIR?

Article 2(9) contains rules determining where assets are situated for the purposes of the recast EIR. These rules are significantly more detailed than corresponding provisions in the 2000 EIR, reducing the scope for uncertainty. For example, registered shares in companies (unless they are held via an intermediary and constitute 'book entry securities') are deemed to be situated in the member state where the company that issued the shares has its registered office. Financial instruments, the title to which is evidenced by entries in a register or account maintained on behalf of an intermediary ('book entry securities') are deemed to be

---

[13] Directive of the European Parliament and of the Council of 4 April 2001 on the reorganisation and winding up of credit institutions (2001/24/EC).

situated in the member state in which the register or account in which the entries are made is maintained. For instance, this includes bonds held through a clearing house such as Euroclear or Clearstream. Cash held in a bank account is deemed to be situated in the member state indicated on the account's international bank account number (IBAN). Clarification is also included as to the *situs* of other assets, such as intellectual property.

11. Related actions and recognition of judgments – which rules to apply?

Article 6 provides that the courts of the member state where insolvency proceedings have been opened will have jurisdiction for any action deriving directly from the insolvency proceedings and closely linked with them, such as avoidance actions. Recital 35 explains the purpose of Article 6 and states that:

> Such actions should include avoidance actions against defendants in other Member States and actions concerning obligations that arise in the course of the insolvency proceedings, such as advance payment for costs of the proceedings. In contrast, actions for the performance of the obligations under a contract concluded by the debtor prior to the opening of proceedings do not derive directly from the proceedings. Where such an action is related to another action based on general civil and commercial law, the insolvency practitioner should be able to bring both actions in the courts of the defendant's domicile if he considers it more efficient to bring the action in that forum. This could, for example, be the case where the insolvency practitioner wishes to combine an action for director's liability on the basis of insolvency law with an action based on company law or general tort law.

The EIRs and the recast Brussels Regulation[14] (the 'Judgments Regulation') are intended to be mutually exclusive and to "dovetail almost completely with each other".[15] However, confusion has often arisen as to how the two regimes should interact, and as to which proceedings, judgments and other actions derived therefrom fall within their scope.[16] Article 6 of the recast EIR is intended to codify existing principles governing the relationship between the Judgments Regulation and the EIRs.

Article 32 (recognition and enforceability of other judgments) provides for automatic recognition, without further formalities, of judgments given by competent courts concerning "the course and closure of insolvency proceedings, and compositions approved by the court". This rule applies to judgments deriving directly from the insolvency proceedings and closely linked with them, even if they were handed down by another court, and also to judgments relating to preservation measures taken after the request for the opening of insolvency proceedings or in connection with it. Article 32(2) provides that the recognition and enforcement of judgments that do not fall within the scope of the recast EIR will be governed by the Judgments Regulation.

---

14 Council Regulation (EU) 1215/2012 on jurisdiction and the recognition and enforcement of judgments in civil and commercial matters.
15 Schlosser Report on the Brussels Convention [1979] OJ C59/91, [53]. See also *Re Rodenstock GMBH* [2011] BUS LR 1245 [47].
16 See, for example, C-295/13 *H (Liquidator of GT GmbH v HK* and C-111/08 *SCT Industri v Alpenblume; Polymer Vision R&D Ltd v Van Dooren* [2012] ILPr 14 and *Fondazione Enasarco v Lehman Brothers Finance SA* [2014] EWHC 34 (Ch).

12. Schemes of arrangement

Schemes of arrangement under Part 26 of the UK Companies Act 2006 allow a company to reach an arrangement or compromise with its members and/or creditors. With particular regard to distressed investing, it should be noted that the scheme of arrangement procedure is not included in Annex A (as it is not a "voluntary arrangement under insolvency legislation") and so falls outside the scope of the recast EIR. The English courts have, for many years, asserted a jurisdiction to sanction (ie, approve) schemes of arrangement in respect of foreign companies, including those domiciled in other member states and further afield. As a result English law schemes of arrangement have become an attractive option for the solvent restructuring of overseas companies. Recent case law has made it easier for an overseas company to establish a sufficiently close connection with England for the court to sanction a scheme of arrangement (for instance, on the basis of the company simply being party to finance documents governed by English law). Insolvency is not a prerequisite and the scheme of arrangement is a powerful restructuring tool: it will bind each class of members and/or creditors irrespective of whether they voted in favour of the scheme of arrangement, provided the requisite majority of that class of members or creditors approves the scheme of arrangement and it is sanctioned by the court. A scheme of arrangement is the only procedure available under English law that enables secured creditor claims to be compromised without their consent (ie, a cram down) if such approval and sanction are obtained. The English courts' extensive jurisdiction to sanction schemes of arrangement in respect of overseas companies would have been significantly restricted if schemes of arrangement had been included in Annex A. The impact of schemes of arrangement on distressed investing are covered in more detail in the "Schemes of arrangement" chapter of this book.

In *Re Rodenstock GmbH* [2011] EWHC 1104, Briggs J (as he then was) concluded that a scheme of arrangement, at least in respect of a solvent company, is a proceeding within the ordinary scope of the Judgments Regulation and should therefore be recognised in each other member state. Briggs J did, however, leave open the question of whether a scheme of arrangement in respect of an insolvent company could be said to be within the scope of the Judgments Regulation. The Judgments Regulation expressly states that it does not apply to "proceedings relating to the winding-up of insolvent companies or other legal persons, judicial arrangements, compositions and analogous proceedings."[17] In *In re Magyar Telecom BV* [2014] BCC 448, Richards J referred to *Rodenstock*, and suggested that a scheme of arrangement between an insolvent company and its creditors would fall within the Judgments Regulation, at least unless the company was subject to any insolvency proceeding failing within the EIR.

A foreign company proposing a scheme of arrangement and wishing to ensure that the English court is willing to assume jurisdiction under the Judgments Regulation might be well advised to ensure that at least one (preferably more, both in terms of number and in value) of its scheme creditors is domiciled in England

---

17 Judgments Regulation, Article 1(2)(b).

prior to launching the process. Article 8(1) of the Judgments Regulation provides that a person domiciled in a member state may be sued:

> ... where he is one of a number of defendants, in the courts for the place where any one of them is domiciled, provided that the claims are so closely connected that it is expedient to hear and determine them together.

In *Rodenstock*, Briggs J suggested that if the Judgments Regulation applied, schemes could fall within the scope of this article, as scheme creditors, being entitled to appear and oppose the scheme, could be regarded as 'defendants' for this purpose. In *Re Van Gansewinkel Groep BV and others* [2015] EWHC 2151 (Ch) Snowdon J, and in *Re Codere Finance (UK) Ltd* [2015] EWHC 3778 (Ch) Newey J, reached the same conclusion.

If the Judgments Regulation ceases to apply to the United Kingdom following its exit from the European Union this could affect the recognition of schemes of arrangement in the rEU. Those seeking to promulgate schemes in the United Kingdom would be required to establish recognition in the rEU via the application of rules of private international law, which could produce uneven results across rEU member states.

If the Judgments Regulation does not apply to a scheme of arrangement for an insolvent company, Article 32 of the recast EIR should ensure recognition of the scheme if it is proposed as part of a compromise through a main insolvency proceeding. However if the recast EIR is no longer applicable to the United Kingdom post-Brexit, this could result in continued uncertainty (see under heading 5 above).

13. Restrictions on moving a debtor's COMI to achieve a favourable outcome

The recast EIR contains various new provisions which are designed to curb abusive COMI-shifting. Companies commonly engineer an artificial shift in their COMI in order to make use of proceedings not available in their home jurisdiction, often to the disadvantage of unsecured creditors. English courts, for instance, have jurisdiction to appoint an administrator to a foreign company if it can be shown that the insolvent company's COMI is in the United Kingdom. This has led to overseas companies becoming subject to 'pre-packaged administrations' in the United Kingdom – an expedited sale process whereby an 'administrator in waiting', having concluded that the purposes of the administration are best served by selling some or all of the business and assets of a distressed company, negotiates with potential buyers and agrees a sale prior to the company going into administration. Once the company goes into administration, the sale assets are purchased by the buyer immediately thereafter. Pre-packs avoid an administrator having to deal with unsecured creditors, and the practice has received criticism for a perceived lack of transparency and accountability; see for example the case of *Re Damovo Group SA* (unreported, April 25 2007) and *Re Hellas Telecommunications (Luxembourg) II SCA* [2009] EWHC 3199 (Ch).

One of the core objectives of the recast EIR is "preventing fraudulent or abusive forum shopping". Recital 28 states:

> When determining whether the centre of the debtor's main interests is ascertainable by third parties, special consideration should be given to creditors and to their perception

as to where a debtor conducts the administration of its interests. This may require, in the event of a shift of centre of main interests, informing creditors of the new location from which the debtor is carrying out its activities in due course.

Article 3(1) provides that, in the absence of evidence to the contrary, the COMI of a company is presumed to be the place of its registered office, and the COMI of an individual exercising an independent business or business activity, is presumed to be his principal place of business, while that of an individual not exercising an independent business or business activity, is presumed to be the place of his habitual residence.

Recital 30 of the recast EIR identifies the circumstances in which this presumption may be rebutted. These are, in relation to a company:

… where the company's central administration is located in a Member State other than that of its registered office, and where a comprehensive assessment of all the relevant factors establishes, in a manner that is ascertainable by third parties, that the company's actual centre of management and supervision and of the management of its interests is located in that other Member State.

A common hallmark of abusive forum shopping over the years has been an artificial COMI shift achieved shortly before entry into insolvency proceedings. Article 3(1) establishes a new look-back test, whereby the registered office presumption will only apply if the registered office has not been moved to another member state within the three-month period prior to the request for the opening of insolvency proceedings. Although this mechanism will make it harder to demonstrate an effective COMI migration (and is intended to prevent abuses), it will not necessarily frustrate a COMI shift required to complete an expedited debt restructuring using the EU procedure likely to achieve the most favourable outcome for creditors. A similar three-month look-back test applies to the definition of 'establishment', relevant to the facility to open territorial (or secondary) proceedings. This rule aims to prevent a debtor from impeding territorial proceedings by closing an establishment shortly before the onset of insolvency.

The Commission is keen to prevent abuses and the recast EIR requires it to submit a study on abusive forum shopping by June 27 2020.[18] The effectiveness of the new rules on COMI-shifting is promoted by additional safeguards designed to ensure that insolvency proceedings are opened in the appropriate jurisdiction. Under (new) Article 4, a court seised of a request to open insolvency proceedings (or, where insolvency proceedings are opened in accordance with national law without a decision of the court, the insolvency practitioner appointed in such proceedings) must of its own motion examine whether it has jurisdiction under Article 3, specifying the grounds on which jurisdiction is based. Under (new) Article 5, the debtor or any creditor may challenge the decision opening main insolvency proceedings. These new articles are intended to address the suspicion that the courts of some member states were not examining their jurisdiction with sufficient rigour. It will be interesting to see how the courts apply the COMI test where a migration occurs during the look-back period; for instance when faced with a challenge by a debtor or creditor under Article 5.

---

18   Recast EIR, Article 90.

14. Groups of companies

Groups of companies are addressed in a new Chapter V (insolvency proceedings of members of a group of companies) of the recast EIR, introducing procedural rules on the coordination of the insolvency proceedings of members of a group of companies. These include rules providing for coordination and cooperation between courts and insolvency practitioners, and the new possibility of synthetic (or virtual) secondary insolvency proceedings. The requirement in the EIR whereby territorial insolvency proceedings and secondary insolvency proceedings had to be liquidation proceedings has been removed. Where one company controls (directly or indirectly) another company, there will be a group of companies for the purposes of the recast EIR.

The recast EIR imposes duties on insolvency office-holders and courts seised of insolvency proceedings to cooperate ("to facilitate the effective administration of proceedings") and communicate with one another in respect of insolvency proceedings of group companies. Article 56 requires an insolvency practitioner, in implementing the required cooperation, to consider whether possibilities exist for coordinating the administration and supervision of the affairs of group members, and for restructuring group members, and if so to coordinate the proposal and negotiation of a coordinated restructuring plan. Article 60 confers various rights on an insolvency practitioner in respect of a group of companies, being:

- a right to be heard in any of the proceedings opened in respect of any other member of the same group;
- a right to request a stay of the realisation of assets in insolvency proceedings relating to any other member of the same group; and
- a right to apply for the opening of group coordination proceedings.

Of these, the right to apply for the opening of group coordination proceedings is perhaps the most significant. Such proceedings will involve the appointment of a 'group coordinator' to oversee the various insolvency proceedings and/or the restructuring of the group to facilitate a group coordination plan. Any court having jurisdiction over the insolvency proceedings of any member of the group may consider a request to open group coordination proceedings. Any insolvency practitioner appointed in respect of any member of the group may object to the inclusion of that member of the group in group coordination proceedings, but flexibility is given to that insolvency practitioner to opt back in later. Under Article 70, insolvency practitioners must "consider the recommendations of the coordinator and the content of the group coordination plan". The procedures for coordination of groups of companies are elaborate and it remains to be seen whether extensive collaboration between insolvency practitioners in different jurisdictions will prove to be workable in practice.[19]

---

19 See for instance Fletcher, "The European Insolvency Regulation Recast: the main features of the new law" 2015 (28) *Insolvency Intelligence* 97. Ian Fletcher QC expresses the view that the coordination procedures are so complex that it "cause[s] one to doubt whether this elaborate compromise will prove to be workable in practice."

15. Improved access to information for creditor and more user-friendly procedures for submitting claims

The recast EIR sets out a requirement for member states to establish national registers of insolvency proceedings by June 26 2018.[20] These are to display core information about the proceedings (listed in Article 24(2)) which will include practical details to inform creditors and enable them to file claims. Registers must be updated as soon as possible after the opening of any relevant proceedings. A second phase (applicable from June 26 2019) will entail the creation of a system for the interconnection of national registers. Core information on insolvency proceedings must be made available free of charge, but member states will be permitted to charge a reasonable fee for access to underlying documentation. Recital 76 states that the aim is to improve the provision of information to relevant creditors and courts and to prevent the opening of parallel insolvency proceedings.

The recast EIR includes provisions for the Commission to adopt further legislation to introduce standardised forms both for the notification of known foreign creditors when proceedings are opened and for the subsequent filing of claims by creditors. Article 53 (right to lodge claims) states that legal representation is not necessary for a creditor to lodge a claim, and that a foreign creditor may lodge claims "by any means of communication, which are accepted by the law of the State of the opening of proceedings". Article 54 (duty to inform creditors) potentially allows notices to "known foreign creditors" to be transmitted in another language, "if it can be assumed that that language is easier to understand for the foreign creditors". Article 55 (procedure to lodge claims) allows a creditor to lodge a claim in any official language of the European Union (although the creditor may still be required to provide an official translation). These changes should make communication easier for distressed investors, but it remains to be seen to what extent they will facilitate the prompt and cost-effective exchange of information and filing of claims across the European Union.

16. Conclusion

It is the authors' hope that the recast EIR will encourage greater investment (including distressed investment) in Europe, due to its greater emphasis on rescue and rehabilitation, by imposing mandatory obligations of cooperation and coordination between office-holders and courts, by facilitating group insolvency processes, and by creating interconnected insolvency registers to share information. Investors, it is submitted, want information, legal certainty, predictability of outcome and the ability and opportunity to participate in a rescue and/or restructuring which will recover value. The recast EIR should, at least in some part, help investors to meet those objectives. However some commentators have expressed concern that the new group coordination procedures are complex and may prove difficult to put into practice.[21]

---

20   Recast EIR, Article 24.
21   See, for instance, Lane & Madsen, "Procedural law implications in the European Union under the Insolvency Regulation" in Olivares-Caminal (ed), *Expedited Corporate Debt Restructuring* (OUP, 2015): "Arguably, group coordination proceedings could increase restructuring costs in circumstances where little benefit is returned, and cross-border coordination is already separately provided for in the revised ECIR."

Structuring the acquisition and disposal of distressed debt

Rebeca Rodríguez
Cuatrecasas, Gonçalves Pereira
Luke Vassay
Milbank, Tweed, Hadley & McCloy LLP

1. **Introduction**

This chapter aims to provide an overview of some of the tax issues affecting investments in distressed debt of borrowers resident in the European Union. References are made throughout the chapter to the tax laws of certain EU jurisdictions, though space does not allow for an examination of any one EU jurisdiction's tax laws in detail.

Investments in distressed debt can take various forms. This chapter, therefore, looks at tax issues arising in the context of some of the more common forms of distressed debt investment.

Under heading 2 we discuss tax issues arising in relation to investments in distressed loans, while the discussion under heading 3 focuses on investments in distressed bonds. Under heading 4 we look at some of the additional tax considerations relevant to investors investing in a portfolio of non-performing loans. Under heading 5 we then deal with debt restructuring and the particular tax concerns of investors and borrowers that participate in those restructurings. Under heading 6 we look at the potential impact of the Organisation for Economic Cooperation and Development (OECD)'s base erosion and profit-shifting (BEPS) project, including some of the BEPS 'actions' that may be of particular relevance to investors in distressed debt. Finally, under heading 7 we discuss some potential consequences of the UK's Brexit vote of June 23 2016.

2. **Distressed lending**

This part of the chapter considers some of the common tax issues which arise in relation to what might be termed 'plain vanilla' loans to distressed EU borrowers. The tax issues discussed are of general relevance to typical lending transactions involving EU borrowers and may, therefore, also be relevant to the other forms of distressed debt investment which are the focus of the following sections.

As well as discussing some of the technical tax issues, this part also considers how those tax risks are typically allocated between the parties in the relevant loan documentation.

2.1 **Withholding tax**

A common tax concern of any investor in cross-border debt is whether withholding tax will be imposed on interest payments made by the borrower to that investor.

The scope and application of withholding taxes differ in each member state of the European Union. For example, some member states, such as the United Kingdom and Spain, generally impose withholding tax on interest payments. Others, such as Luxembourg, France and Germany, generally do not. Other payments which a borrower might make as part of a lending transaction, such as the payment of arrangement fees, are ordinarily not subject to withholding taxes.

However, even in those jurisdictions which do impose withholding tax, it is often possible for an investor to take advantage of an exemption or relief from such withholding taxes.

2.2 Reliefs and exemptions from withholding tax

(a) **EU domestic laws**

The domestic laws of the Member States typically provide for various reliefs and exemptions from withholding tax.

A particularly important domestic exemption for UK and Irish borrowers is the so-called quoted Eurobond exemption. Under this exemption, no UK or Irish withholding tax is applied to interest payments on securities issued by a company and listed on a recognised stock exchange.

This exemption is widely used in the context of bond issues (see under heading 3 below), but may also be used in bilateral lending scenarios, particularly in the case of a UK borrower where the loan may be listed on a smaller exchange, such as the Channel Islands Securities Exchange.

Certain EU jurisdictions, such as Italy and Spain, offer exemptions from local withholding tax to lenders resident in the European Union, provided certain conditions are met.

(b) **EU directive**

Where an investor in distressed debt owns shares in the relevant debtor (for example, following a debt-for-equity swap), interest payments by the relevant EU borrower may also be exempt from withholding tax under the EU directive on interest and royalties (the 'IR Directive').[1]

The IR Directive broadly provides for interest payments by associated EU companies (or EU permanent establishments of associated EU companies) to be exempt from tax in the payer's jurisdiction. Companies will be 'associated' under the IR Directive where one of them owns directly at least 25% of the capital in the other, or a third company owns directly at least 25% in the capital of them both (member states may opt to replace references to capital with voting rights). However, the benefit of the IR Directive will not be available where arrangements have been put in place for which a principal motive is tax evasion, avoidance or abuse.

---

1   Council Directive 2003/49/EC of June 3 2003 on a common system of taxation applicable to interest and royalty payments made between associated companies of different member states.

(c) Double taxation agreements

Relief or exemption from withholding taxes may also be available under an applicable double taxation agreement between the investor and borrower jurisdictions.

A usual requirement for relief from interest withholding tax under double taxation agreements is that the recipient of the interest payment be the 'beneficial owner' of that interest payment.

This issue was examined by the UK Court of Appeal in the *Indofood Case*.[2] The court applied an international fiscal meaning to the concept of beneficial ownership under the double taxation agreement between the Netherlands and Indonesia and found that the relevant Dutch company needed "the full privilege to directly benefit from the income" to have the necessary beneficial ownership.

This requirement will often exclude conduit entities that pass on the interest payments they receive to underlying investors under a back-to-back arrangement. This point may be of relevance to distressed debt structures under which investors in tax havens channel funds through intermediate financing entities established in treaty jurisdictions, such as Luxembourg, to the distressed borrower (see Diagram 1 on the next page). Such entities may also be denied benefits under a double taxation agreement under specific anti-conduit provisions (as in the double taxation agreement between the United States and the United Kingdom).

Furthermore, Action 6 of the OECD's BEPS project (which is discussed under heading 6 below) has recommended certain measures to restrict this kind of treaty shopping.

Subject to the foregoing comments, therefore, an investor in EU distressed debt should generally be able to structure investments appropriately to take advantage of one or more reliefs or exemptions from withholding tax.

2.3 Other tax issues: tax on disposal, VAT and transfer taxes

An investor will be concerned to minimise any other tax exposures in the borrower's jurisdiction.

Provided the investor is not lending through a branch or permanent establishment in the borrower's jurisdiction, the investor would not generally expect to incur corporate income taxes on any gain arising from the disposal of the distressed debt in the borrower's jurisdiction. In any event, it may be possible to shelter any such taxes that do arise under an applicable double taxation agreement.

In broad terms, EU value added tax (VAT) is charged on supplies (other than exempt supplies) of goods and services made by businesses and which take place in the European Union. Supplies of finance and financial services are generally exempt supplies for VAT purposes.[3]

An investor will wish to avoid the cost of any stamp duties or other transfer taxes applying on its acquisition of distressed debt, and will usually expect the relevant borrower to bear any such costs (although see under heading 2.4 below). The

---

2   *Indofood International Finance Ltd v JP Morgan Chase Bank NA, London Branch* [2006] EWCA Civ 158.
3   Article 135(1) of Directive 2006/112/EC.

Conduit Financing Structure

Diagram: Borrower (UK) ↔ Finance Co (Luxembourg) (Inter-loan company; Interest and principal) ↔ Investor (Cayman Islands) (Loan; Interest and principal)

(1) A loan directly from a Cayman Islands Investor to a UK borrower would generally be subject to UK interest withholding tax. There is no double taxation agreement between the UK and the Cayman Islands and the Investor may also not be permitted (eg, due to its investment criteria) to hold listed debt securities and so the UK "quoted Eurobond" exemption would not be available. Therefore, Investor may look to structure its investment through a third jurisdiction (eg, Luxembourg).

(2) Finance Co pays interest on the loan from Investor free from withholding tax since Luxembourg does not generally impose withholding tax on such payments.

(2) Interest payments by the UK Borrower to Finance Co would be subject to UK withholding tax unless an exemption applies.

(3) Relief from UK withholding tax under the Luxembourg-UK double tax treaty may be available provided Finance Co is the "beneficial owner" of the interest it receives from UK Borrower. If Finance Co is obliged to use interest received from UK Borrower to pay interest on the loan from Investor (ie, Finance Co is a mere conduit), Finance Co will likely fail the "beneficial ownership" test and not be eligible for treaty relief.

(3) However, the inter-company loan may be listed on a recognised stock exchange (such as the Channel Islands Securities Exchange), in which case the UK "quoted Eurobond" exemption would apply to exempt from UK withholding tax the interest payments from UK Borrower.

triggering of stamp duties or other transfer taxes may depend on whether the loan is secured on real estate or other property that is located in the jurisdiction in question.

2.4 EU loan documentation

Further protection from withholding taxes imposed in the borrower's jurisdiction is often obtained under the relevant loan documentation. This will usually provide for the relevant borrower, and guarantor (if applicable), to gross up a lender for any withholding tax the investor suffers on payments made under the loan documentation.

However, such a grossing-up provision is generally only intended to protect investors from future changes of law in the borrower's jurisdiction which result in withholding taxes being imposed on payments to the investor. Accordingly, it is not generally designed to protect investors from any withholding taxes which exist on the date the investor makes its investment.

Indeed, an investor will usually have to be able to receive interest free from withholding tax on the date it makes its investment in order to be a 'qualifying lender' under the loan documentation. The loan documentation will then limit the borrower's grossing-up obligation to such qualifying lenders (who, by definition, will not require a grossing-up since payments to qualifying lenders should not be subject to withholding tax) and lenders who are not, or have ceased to be, qualifying lenders solely because of a change of law occurring after the date on which the lender became a lender. The effect of these provisions is to allocate to the borrower the risk of a future change of law which imposes withholding tax on interest payments to investors.

Accordingly, an investor will be expected to structure its investment in a way that avoids any day-one withholding taxes.

The relevant loan documentation governing the loan to an EU borrower will usually include a provision dealing with VAT, notwithstanding that VAT will not generally be an issue in lending transactions (see under heading 2.3 above).

Under the relevant VAT provision, any supplies made under the documents are made on a VAT-exclusive basis, requiring the recipient to pay over any such VAT to the supplier (if the supplier is liable to account for the VAT) in addition to any other consideration for such supply. To the extent a party is required to indemnify another party for any costs or expenses incurred, the indemnifying party is also generally required to reimburse any VAT charged on those costs or expenses, but only to the extent the recipient cannot otherwise recover the VAT.

The loan documentation will also usually provide for the borrower to indemnify the investor for any stamp duties or other transfer taxes, although a borrower will often exclude any such taxes which arise as a result of the investor's voluntary assignment or transfer of its loan investment.

3. Bonds

This part of the chapter focuses on tax issues arising in relation to investments in bonds (or notes) of distressed EU issuers. As another form of lending transaction, many of the more general tax issues discussed under heading 2 will also be relevant to distressed bond investments.

3.1 Withholding tax

Withholding tax on interest payments made by the bond issuer, and any available reliefs or exemptions from such withholding tax, will be just as important a factor for a bond investor as for an investor in a distressed loan.

The bond markets generally expect issuers to be able to pay interest free from local withholding taxes, or otherwise to bear the cost of any withholding tax under an applicable grossing-up clause in the bond documentation. Accordingly, a concern of the issuer will be to ensure that no withholding tax will be due in respect of interest payments under the bonds.

In contrast to a bilateral lending transaction, bond issues in the capital markets will often target a large pool of disparate bondholders. These bondholders may comprise a mixture of corporate bodies, tax-transparent funds or individuals that are located in a variety of jurisdictions. Accordingly, it will not generally be possible to draft the tax provisions in the relevant bond documentation in the same way as for bilateral or syndicated loan facilities where there is usually a greater awareness of the identity of the specific lenders.

Furthermore, bond issues are very often listed on securities exchanges, and EU jurisdictions often accommodate this practice by offering exemptions from local withholding tax for listed bonds.

As mentioned under heading 2.2(a) above, issuers based in Ireland and the United Kingdom can benefit from quoted Eurobond exemptions available in both jurisdictions. Provided the bond is issued by a company, carries a right to interest and is listed on a recognised stock exchange (all conditions that a standard bond issuance would usually meet), no withholding tax is imposed on the relevant interest payments.

Spain offers a broad exemption from taxation on income received by all bond investors that are not tax resident in Spain, to the extent that those investors do not obtain the income through a permanent establishment located in Spain and certain other conditions are met (in particular, among others, that the bonds are listed on a regulated market, a multilateral trading facility or other organised market).

However, exceptions for unlisted bonds may also be available. An exemption from Italian withholding tax is available for bonds which are not listed and which are held by certain 'qualified investors' (broadly, entities which are authorised or regulated to operate in the financial markets) provided that they are resident in countries that allow for an adequate exchange of information with Italy.

Similarly, a UK withholding tax exemption is available for certain unlisted securities where (among other conditions) the issuer and investor are not connected and both parties are acting for genuinely commercial reasons.

3.2 VAT and transfer taxes

Under the EU VAT Directive, the issuance and disposal of bonds is exempt from VAT.[4]

Additionally, according to Council Directive 2008/7/EC concerning indirect taxes on the raising of capital (the 'Capital Duties Directive'), member states shall not impose any form of indirect tax (such as transfer tax or stamp duty) on the creation or issue of negotiable bonds.

4. NPL portfolios

While the discussion under headings 2 and 3 has focused on the tax treatment of

---

4   Article 135(1) of Directive 2006/112/EC.

standalone distressed loans or bonds, an investor in distressed debt may choose to acquire a portfolio of non-performing loans (an 'NPL portfolio'). This part of the chapter, therefore, considers some of the specific tax issues which can arise in relation to such acquisitions where the underlying borrowers in the NPL portfolio are EU-resident companies.

Many of the general tax comments discussed in the previous sections may also apply to acquisitions of NPL portfolios. Accordingly, this section focuses on the tax issues pertaining to the structure of the acquisition and the management of an NPL portfolio.

Simplified NPL Portfolio Structure

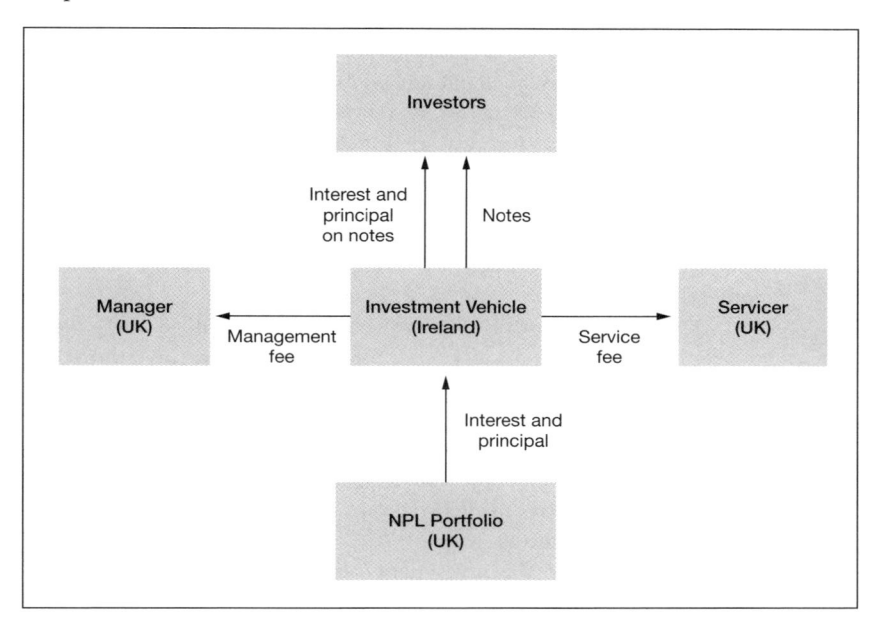

4.1 Structuring the acquisition of NPL portfolios

An investor of a NPL portfolio will typically structure its acquisition through an appropriate investment vehicle in a jurisdiction with a tax regime that makes the acquisition economically viable.

The choice of jurisdiction for the investment vehicle will be influenced by the location of the underlying borrowers. An investor will be concerned to ensure that the investment vehicle will be able to receive payments from the underlying borrowers free from withholding taxes imposed in the local jurisdictions of the borrowers (or that there is an appropriate grossing-up for any such withholding taxes in the underlying loan documentation).

Traditionally, Ireland and Luxembourg have proven to be popular jurisdictions for investors in NPL portfolios to locate their investment vehicles. The following discussion therefore looks at some of the tax benefits offered by Ireland and

Luxembourg, but also discusses more generally the importance of establishing the investment vehicle with sufficient substance in the chosen jurisdiction and ensuring that the investment vehicle meets the requisite beneficial ownership test, topics which are becoming increasingly important in Europe, not least as a result of the OECD's BEPS project (see under heading 6 below).

(a) **Substance**

While the investment vehicle will usually automatically be tax resident in its jurisdiction of incorporation, it will also be important to ensure that its tax residency is not inadvertently displaced as a result of the effective management of the investment vehicle in another jurisdiction. Where the investment vehicle is effectively managed from another jurisdiction, it may be regarded as resident in that other jurisdiction under the domestic law of that other jurisdiction as well as under the 'tie-breaker' article of an applicable double taxation agreement.

Accordingly, it will be necessary to ensure that the investment vehicle has sufficient substance in its jurisdiction of incorporation.

There is no uniform definition of economic substance in the European Union, and different EU jurisdictions may specify their own requirements. However, establishing substance in a jurisdiction will generally require evidence that the investment vehicle has a sufficiently strong tie to that jurisdiction and may include, among other things, that:

- the investment vehicle employs sufficiently qualified employees with in-country resources to carry out the daily duties of the investment vehicle;
- a majority of the directors of the investment vehicle are resident in its jurisdiction and attend regular board meetings in that jurisdiction;
- the directors of the investment vehicle carry out their duties on its behalf with due consideration and independence (that is, not simply rubber-stamping decisions made by an outsider, such as an investment manager in another jurisdiction);
- the directors of the investment vehicle are sufficiently experienced and knowledgeable to perform their duties; and
- the bank accounts of the investment vehicle are maintained in the investment vehicle's jurisdiction.

(b) **Beneficial ownership**

Where the investment vehicle is seeking to rely on a relief or exemption from withholding tax imposed in an underlying borrower's jurisdiction, it will often be a requirement of that relief that the investment vehicle be the beneficial owner of the relevant payment made by the borrower (see under heading 2.2(c) above in relation to the requirement in double taxation agreements).

It will generally be a requirement, therefore, that the investment vehicle has the right to use and enjoy the interest paid on the underlying loans in the NPL portfolio. This test may be failed where the investment vehicle is bound by a contractual obligation to pass on the payments received to another person (that is, where it is acting as a mere conduit – see Diagram 1 above).

The method by which the investment vehicle is funded is, therefore, important for the purposes of the beneficial ownership test. Where the investment vehicle is funded by way of a bond or note issue in the capital markets, interest payments on those notes will generally be funded by interest payments received by the investment vehicle from the NPL portfolio.

As mentioned above, this arrangement may jeopardise the investment vehicle's ability to claim relief from withholding tax imposed in the underlying borrower jurisdictions, depending on the terms and conditions of the financing.

However, this may not be fatal under an applicable double taxation agreement with the United Kingdom. For example, an Irish investment vehicle holding a portfolio of UK loans (see Diagram 2 above), the acquisition of which was funded from the issue proceeds of listed bonds, should be able to claim relief under the double taxation agreement between the United Kingdom and Ireland from UK interest withholding tax. This is because, in such circumstances, the UK tax authority (HMRC) recognises that there is no treaty shopping taking place via the investment vehicle, since the relevant bondholders would have been able to receive interest payments on their bonds free from UK withholding tax in any event under the UK quoted Eurobond exemption.[5]

(c) *Ireland and Luxembourg*

As mentioned above, Ireland and Luxembourg are popular European jurisdictions for structuring the acquisition of NPL portfolios, owing to the attractive legal, regulatory and tax environment in those jurisdictions. The paragraphs below examine certain of the tax advantages offered by each jurisdiction.

Ireland: Traditionally, an Irish Section 110 company has been an attractive option for international investors. It is a well-known investment entity, having been in existence for over 20 years.

A Section 110 company is an Irish resident special purpose vehicle which holds and/or manages qualifying assets (including, among other things, a wide range of financial assets such as shares, bonds, receivables and commercial paper). This regime allows for a neutral corporation tax treatment provided certain conditions are met.

In general, a Section 110 company qualifies for the benefits of Ireland's network of double taxation agreements, which reduce or eliminate withholding taxes on income flows and capital gains in jurisdictions with which Ireland has such an agreement.

Ireland is also one of the leading European jurisdictions for regulated investment funds (UCITS and non-UCITS). Regulated funds can be structured in several ways and in certain circumstances they can be combined with a Section 110 company as part of a structure for the investment in an NPL portfolio.

In addition, the new Irish collective asset-management vehicle (ICAV) can be used to establish both UCITS and alternative investment funds. The ICAV will constitute an investment undertaking for Irish tax purposes and, therefore, subject

---

5   See Example 1 in HMRC's International Manual at INTM 332080.

to certain conditions, any profits and gains of the ICAV will broadly be exempt from tax in Ireland.

Luxembourg: Luxembourg is a leading jurisdiction for the establishment of international investment vehicles. This status has arisen from a combination of several factors:
- the flexibility of its company law (including the creation and perfection of security and its enforceability);
- the availability of certain tax-efficient intra-group corporate financial instruments;
- its significant network of double taxation agreements; and
- its position as an EU member state.

While Luxembourg investment vehicles are generally fully taxable, it is usually possible to ensure that such tax is payable on a relatively modest sum in Luxembourg, with tax deductions generally available to the Luxembourg investment vehicle for onward payments to investors.

Luxembourg generally does not impose withholding tax on interest payments, and otherwise offers a flexible regime for returning profits to investors in a tax-efficient manner.

However, it should be noted that certain traditional tax planning arrangements involving Luxembourg may be targeted by the BEPS project (see under heading 6 below).

4.2 Relationship with manager of the NPL portfolio

Investments in NPL portfolios will often be managed on the investment vehicle's behalf by a separate entity acting as the investment manager. While the investment vehicle itself may be resident in a jurisdiction such as Ireland or Luxembourg, the manager will typically be located in a large financial centre, such as London.

An important tax consideration, therefore, will be to ensure that the activities of the manager do not give rise to a taxable permanent establishment of the investment vehicle in the manager's jurisdiction.

The manager will usually be resident in a jurisdiction which has a double taxation agreement in force with the investment vehicle's jurisdiction. The relevant test of permanent establishment will be that set out in the applicable double taxation agreement, which will itself usually be based on the OECD's Model Tax Convention on Income and on Capital 2014 (the 'OECD Model Tax Treaty').

(a) *Dependant agents*

Under the usual double taxation agreement definition of permanent establishment, a manager will constitute a permanent establishment of the investment vehicle if the manager: "has, and habitually exercises, an authority to conclude contracts in the name of the [investment vehicle]." A manager will often exercise such authority on behalf of an investment vehicle and so will constitute a permanent establishment, unless the manager is acting as an independent agent.

(b) **Independent agents**

Under Article 5(6) of the OECD Model Tax Treaty:

An enterprise shall not be deemed to have a permanent establishment in a Contracting State merely because it carries on business in that State through a broker, general commission agent, or any other agent of an independent status, provided that such persons are acting in the ordinary course of their business.

The term 'agent of independent status' is not defined in the OECD Model Tax Treaty, but guidance is given on the term in the Commentary on Article 5 in the OECD's *Commentaries on the Articles of the Model Tax Convention.*

Under Paragraph 37 of the Commentary on Article 5, a person will not constitute a permanent establishment of an enterprise on whose behalf he acts provided:

- he is independent of the enterprise both legally and economically; and
- he acts in the ordinary course of his business when acting on behalf of the enterprise.

Paragraph 38.3 of the commentary states that: "The fact that the principal is relying on the special skill and knowledge of the agent is an indication of independence."

Paragraph 38.6 of the commentary further states that:

Another factor to be considered in determining independent status is the number of principals represented by the agent. Independent status is less likely if the activities of the agent are performed wholly or almost wholly on behalf of only one enterprise over the lifetime of the business or a long period of time. However, this fact is not by itself determinative.

The commentary provides other considerations relevant to the determination of independence. In particular, it stresses that all the facts and circumstances must be taken into account when making the determination.

However, it will often be the case that the manager's specialist skill and knowledge is being relied upon by the investment vehicle, and the manager may often act for more than one investment vehicle. In addition, the relationship between the manager and investment vehicle will typically be on arm's length terms. Accordingly, the manager should often be acting as an independent agent in the ordinary course of its business with the investment vehicle.

Furthermore, where a manager carries out 'investment transactions' in the United Kingdom on behalf of a non-UK resident investment vehicle and certain other conditions of the UK investment manager exemption are satisfied, the manager will be deemed to be an agent of independent status acting in the ordinary course of its business for UK tax purposes, such that the manager will not constitute a UK permanent establishment of the investment vehicle.

4.3 Relationship with servicer of the NPL portfolio

The investment vehicle will also generally need to engage a separate service provider (the 'servicer') to carry out various administrative functions on behalf of the investment vehicle, including the collection of payments received from the underlying borrowers in the NPL portfolio.

Where the servicer is based in a different jurisdiction from the investment vehicle, it will again be important to ensure that the servicer does not constitute a permanent establishment of the investment vehicle in the servicer's jurisdiction. Given its generally administrative role, the servicer is less likely to constitute a permanent establishment of the investment vehicle than the manager. Moreover, the servicer's relationship with the investment vehicle may in any event be that of an independent agent acting in the ordinary course of its business (see under heading 4.2(b) above).

4.4 Secured NPL portfolios: tax considerations on enforcement

Given the heightened risk of default of a distressed borrower, security over the relevant investment will be a key concern for an investor, as will any tax issues arising on enforcement of such security.

The tax issues arising will depend on the type of security interest enforced. Where the relevant security interest granted to the investor (or investment vehicle) includes real estate, it is sometimes prudent for the enforcing investor to establish a real estate owning company ('REOCO') in the jurisdiction in which the real estate is located. This can ensure that a taxable permanent establishment of the enforcing lender is not created in that jurisdiction.

The procedure for assigning real estate to a REOCO upon enforcement will depend on the rules governing the enforcement in each jurisdiction. In some jurisdictions, such as Spain, it is possible for the enforcing lender to assign its rights to receive the relevant real estate on enforcement to the REOCO.

The assignment of real estate assets to the REOCO may be achieved by the shareholder of the REOCO (that is, the enforcing investor entity) contributing its rights on enforcement to the REOCO, or otherwise by the REOCO purchasing those rights for cash. The assignment would generally need to be structured on arm's length terms to ensure that there are no adverse tax implications.

The tax treatment applicable to REOCOs may depend on whether the REOCO is able to benefit from a special tax regime for real estate owning companies in the jurisdiction of the REOCO's residence. Other taxes (such as VAT, transfer tax and stamp duty) should also be borne in mind when considering whether a REOCO is an appropriate vehicle through which to enforce security on real estate.

Any profit distributions made by the REOCO to the investment vehicle may be exempt from any applicable withholding tax under the EU Parent-Subsidiary Directive.[6] In some cases, the special beneficial tax regime afforded to a REOCO in its home jurisdiction can have knock-on effects in the recipient's jurisdiction. For example, where a REOCO benefits from a general tax exemption in its home jurisdiction, dividends of the REOCO received by a Luxembourg investment vehicle may not be eligible for the Luxembourg participation exemption.

---

[6] Council Directive 2011/96/EU of November 30 2011 on the common system of taxation applicable in the case of parent companies and subsidiaries of different member states.

5. Restructuring of distressed debt

This part of the chapter examines tax issues arising in relation to the restructuring of the debt of EU company borrowers.

A restructuring of the distressed borrower will often play a key part in the strategic thinking of an investor in distressed debt, and complex tax issues can arise for any such investor. In particular, an investor may wish to preserve valuable tax reliefs in the borrower and maximise the tax deductibility of interest accruing on any new or remaining debt in the company. Moreover, efficient tax structuring can be employed to minimise tax costs arising on a subsequent exit from the investment.

An investor intending to participate in the restructuring of the distressed company will often look to invest across the entire capital structure of the company. For example, a loan-to-own investor may look to acquire part of a company's distressed debt with a view to converting that debt into an equity interest in the company, hoping that by doing so it will share in the upside associated with a recovery of the underlying business.

To the extent such a strategy results in the investor acquiring control of the borrower, additional tax complications may arise.

5.1 Impairment and releases of distressed debt

An important tax consideration in a restructuring context is whether the investor will be entitled to recognise a loss for tax purposes when it recognises an impairment or releases a debt. A further concern will be whether a taxable profit arises in the debtor on the release of its debt.

(a) The investor's position

For accounting purposes, impairments and releases of debt are typically recognised as expenses of the investor. Investors using a fair value method of accounting will obtain such accounting relief as the debt goes bad and its fair value decreases. Investors using an amortised cost basis of accounting will generally have to consider at each balance sheet date whether there is any objective evidence that a loan is impaired (see, for example, International Accounting Standard IAS 39.58). If there is such evidence, the loan has to be revalued accordingly.

The accounting treatment may form the basis for determining the tax treatment of impairments and releases of debt. However, such accounting treatment is often subject to a complex overlay of tax provisions which override the accounting treatment.

This may most clearly be seen in a restructuring context where the investor and borrower company are, or become, connected. For example, in a pre-pack sale, an existing distressed group may be sold to a newly formed holding company incorporated and owned by enforcing lenders. The resulting connection between investor and borrower can give rise to specific tax issues for both investor and borrower.

For example, a UK investor holding debt in a connected company will not generally be able to claim a tax deduction for any loss arising on an impairment or release of that debt. Limited exceptions apply where such a loss arises while the UK investor is insolvent, or where the loss is incurred as part of a debt-for-equity swap and the UK investor only becomes connected to the debtor as a result of that swap.

(b) ***The borrower's position***

The recognition of an impairment loss by the investor should not affect the borrower. The debt remains outstanding and so no taxable profit arises in the borrower.

A concern of the borrower's will be whether it has to recognise a taxable profit if and when the investor releases all or part of its debt. This will also concern an investor participating in a debt-for-equity swap since a taxable profit in the borrower may affect the value of the investor's equity holding following the swap.

Reliefs may be available to shelter any taxable profit where a borrower is in distressed circumstances. For example, corporate rescue exemptions may be available where the borrower is insolvent, or might soon become insolvent if its debt is not restructured. Relief may also be available to a borrower where the release of its debt forms part of a debt-for-equity swap.

If a UK investor and borrower are connected, however, a corollary of the restriction on the investor's ability to claim tax deductions for impairments or releases (see under heading 5.1(a) above) may be that the borrower also does not have to recognise any corresponding taxable profit. However, for a UK borrower this rule is subject to exceptions where the relevant debt is deemed to be (rather than actually is) released.

For a UK borrower, a deemed release can arise where, broadly, the debt of a UK company is bought in at a discount by a connected party from an unconnected lender or, conversely, an unconnected lender subsequently becomes connected with the borrower (for example, by acquiring voting control of the borrower). In each case, subject to limited exceptions, an amount of the debt broadly equivalent to the discount is deemed to be released, giving rise to a taxable profit in the UK borrower. Certain methods of structuring around such deemed releases might be available, though care must be taken that such structuring does not trigger widely-drawn anti-avoidance rules.

In certain circumstances, a taxable profit can also arise in a UK borrower where debt is 'substantially modified' for accounting purposes, requiring the debt to be re-recognised at fair value. Again, reliefs may be available for distressed borrowers.

In Spain, there are specific rules governing debt-for-equity swaps and debt restructurings that, in certain circumstances, can prevent or defer a taxable profit arising in the borrower.

5.2 Tax deductions

A natural concern for a taxpaying borrower will be whether it can deduct its interest expense for tax purposes. An investor is also likely to take this into account when assessing the risks of an investment. To date, there has been no uniform code in the European Union governing the deductibility of interest expense, though this is one of the focuses of the OECD's BEPS project and the EU anti-tax avoidance package (see under heading 6 below).

For example, UK borrowers have traditionally enjoyed a generous regime for interest deductions under which third-party interest expense is generally deductible in full for UK tax purposes (though this is set to change – see under heading 6.1 below). By contrast, other jurisdictions, such as Germany, Italy and Spain, have operated so-called interest barrier rules, which typically limit a local company's interest deductions to a percentage of the company's earnings before interest, taxation, depreciation and amortisation (EBITDA), subject to exceptions.

Additionally, under transfer pricing rules, it is a requirement that connected party debt be on arm's length terms; otherwise, an adjustment by a tax authority might reduce or deny a deduction for the affected interest expense.

5.3 Tax losses

A distressed company may have potentially valuable tax attributes, such as carried forward trading losses and historic interest deductions, which an investor will often wish to preserve in the restructured group. These may be immediately useful if a release of debt in the course of the restructuring triggers a taxable profit in the borrower (see under heading 5.1(b) above).

While general restrictions on the use of such losses may apply, complex tax planning will often need to be employed in a restructuring context to ensure that such tax attributes are not lost on any change of control resulting from the restructuring (as in loan-to-own or pre-pack sales circumstances).

It is common for jurisdictions to impose restrictions on the use of a target company's or group's tax attributes following a change of control, and it may be necessary to put in place strict control mechanisms to ensure that these rules are not inadvertently triggered.

5.4 VAT

As mentioned above under heading 2.3, financial services are generally VAT-exempt supplies, while share issues (as in debt-for-equity swaps) are not supplies for VAT purposes, and so not within the scope of VAT.[7]

However, in a restructuring context, there may be other supplies for which VAT is chargeable, such as professional fees charged by advisers. The question, therefore, will be whether any VAT charged on such supplies can be reclaimed. Where the recipient is based in the European Union and makes taxable supplies for VAT purposes, such VAT should be recoverable in full.

In the context of a leveraged acquisition, a new company will often be established to acquire the target group. In this context, it will often make sense for the relevant new company to enter into management services agreements with the target group, so that it can thereby make the requisite taxable supplies for VAT purposes and recover any VAT charged on professional services charged to it.

5.5 Transfer taxes

Stamp duty and other transfer taxes may feature more prominently in a restructuring

---

7   *Kretztechnik AG v Finanzamt Linz* (Case C-465/03).

situation, particularly where shares in the borrower are acquired by the investor. In certain EU jurisdictions, for example, Germany and Spain, the acquisition of shares in groups owning real estate may trigger real estate transfer tax. However, under the Capital Duties Directive, no stamp tax should be payable on the issue of shares by an EU company in a debt-for-equity swap.

5.6 Taxes on exit

Where the group holding company of the restructured group is incorporated and resident in a non-taxing jurisdiction, a sale by the company might be achieved on a tax-free basis.

However, a similar result may also be achieved where the holding company is situated in a jurisdiction which provides for a participation exemption on such sales, such as the United Kingdom, Spain, the Netherlands or Luxembourg. Broadly, provided that, among other conditions, a minimum shareholding is held for a minimum time period, gains may be exempt from tax in the holding company jurisdiction. Tax levied on any gain in the target company jurisdiction (if any) may often be effectively excluded under a double taxation agreement or a domestic exemption if specific requirements are met (for example, in Spain, capital gains obtained through a tax haven country are not exempted).

Degrouping charges may arise where assets (which may include capital and loan assets) have previously been transferred to a target company on a tax-neutral basis (for example, within a fiscal unity or local tax group) by a group company which is not being disposed of as part of the target group. The effect of the degrouping charge is effectively to recapture any tax that did not fall into charge as a result of the earlier tax-neutral transfer. Such charges may be mitigated, either by available losses in the target group or because the charge is deemed (or elected) to accrue to the seller, where it may be sheltered by a participation exemption.

A sale of shares of an EU company may trigger stamp duties. In some cases, UK groups have incorporated the target holding company in a low-tax jurisdiction, such as Jersey. The Jersey company is nevertheless UK tax-resident, by reason of central management and control being exercised in the United Kingdom, but a sale of the company may be made without triggering UK stamp taxes (provided certain conditions are met).

Where the selling holding company belongs outside the European Union for VAT purposes, any supplies (such as professional services) made to the company should fall outside the scope of VAT. Where the company is based in the European Union, then it may be necessary to structure the sale appropriately to maximise VAT recovery on such supplies (see, for example, under heading 5.4 above).

6. The BEPS project

The BEPS project is a reference to the ongoing project to reform various domestic and treaty-based tax rules undertaken by the OECD. The project seeks to counteract so-called base erosion and profit shifting (BEPS) practices, which broadly refers to practices designed to reduce taxable income in particular jurisdictions through the exploitation or other use of these rules.

Underpinning the BEPS project are 15 'actions' which the OECD has identified to counteract the BEPS problem. Final reports covering each of these 15 actions were published on October 5 2015 and were subsequently endorsed by the G20 finance ministers.

It should be noted that, at this stage, the final outcome of the BEPS project is uncertain, and will depend on the willingness of participating states to implement the various recommendations into their domestic law or their double taxation agreements with other states.

The EU Commission published its own package of measures aimed at countering corporate tax avoidance on January 28 2016 (the 'EU anti-tax avoidance package').[8] On June 21 2016, as part of the EU anti-tax avoidance package, the EU Council agreed the text of a directive laying down rules against certain tax avoidance practices. Member states will generally have until December 31 2018 to transpose the directive into domestic law. Certain measures in the EU anti-tax avoidance package overlap with recommendations made by the BEPS project (including those BEPS actions discussed below).

The wide ambit of the BEPS proposals and recommendations could affect a wide range of commercial structures. Some of the BEPS actions which may be of particular relevance to an investor in the distressed debt market are discussed briefly below.

6.1 Tax deductions for interest

The ability of a borrower to deduct interest payments may be affected by both Actions 2 and 4.

Action 2 makes various recommendations to counteract the tax advantages associated with the use of so-called hybrid financial instruments or hybrid entities. Broadly, these are financial instruments or entities which receive a different tax treatment in different countries.

In the context of structuring an investment in distressed debt, these rules could deny interest deductions in the borrower's jurisdiction where no tax is included in the recipient investor's jurisdiction, or possibly where a deduction is obtained for the same payment in two different countries. These rules could affect the viability of common investment structures which make use of Luxembourg preferred equity certificates or convertible preferred equity certificates or which include corporate entities for which a US check-the-box election has been made (see Diagram 3 for an example of the latter).

Action 4 contains recommendations to restrict the amount of a company's deductible net interest (and interest equivalent payments) to a percentage (between 10% and 30%) of the relevant company's (or local group's) tax-adjusted EBITDA (the fixed ratio rule). Countries may allow an additional deduction to the extent the consolidated group's net external interest expense/EBITDA ratio is higher than under the fixed ratio rule.

The UK government plans to enact rules based on Action 2 with effect from January 1 2017 and, on May 12 2016, published a detailed consultation on the

---

8   ec.europa.eu/taxation_customs/taxation/company_tax/anti_tax_avoidance/index_en.htm.

Hybrid Entity Tax Advantage

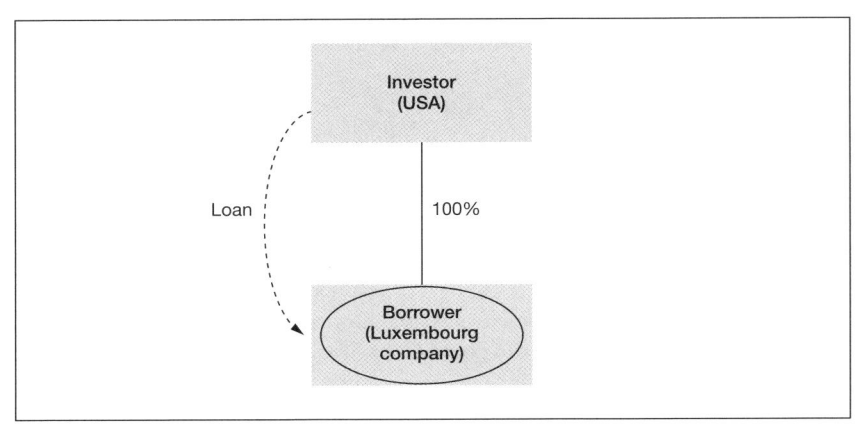

Current Treatment
1. Borrower is a separate legal entity for Luxembourg tax purposes, paying deductible interest on a loan.
2. A US "check-the-box" election is made to treat Borrower as a disregarded entity for US tax purposes.
3. A hybrid tax advantage arises since a tax deduction is claimed in Luxembourg for interest payments on the loan while, due to the "check-the-box" election, the Investor does not pay tax on the receipt of the interest in the US.

Potential Anti-Hybrid Counteraction
1. Luxembourg denies the interest deduction of Borrower; or
2. US taxes the interest payments in US.

design of rules based on Action 4 with a view to enacting those rules with effect from April 1 2017. The Spanish government has also included some of the Action 2 recommendations within recent tax reforms that came into force for tax periods starting as of January 1 2015. As mentioned above, Spain (among other EU jurisdictions) already operates interest barrier rules of the kind recommended by Action 4.

6.2 Access to double taxation agreements

The purpose of Action 6 is, among other things, to stop the practice of treaty shopping, whereby entities that would not otherwise be entitled to treaty benefits structure their investments through conduit entities in treaty jurisdictions (see Diagram 1).

The final report on Action 6 recommends the insertion into countries' bilateral double taxation agreements of a US-style limitation on benefits provision and/or a principle purposes test, which may make it harder for certain entities to obtain the benefit of a double taxation agreement.

To the extent that an investor in distressed debt needs to rely upon a double taxation agreement – for example, in order to receive interest from a borrower free from withholding tax – these changes (if implemented) may be of direct relevance. In addition, certain investment vehicles may find it difficult to satisfy any limitation on benefits provision in a double taxation agreement (although further work is being carried out by the OECD in this respect).

The EU anti-tax avoidance package does not, however, recommend that member states adopt a limitation on benefits rule in applicable double taxation agreements, viewing such rules as detrimental to the functioning of the EU single market.

6.3 NPL portfolio managers

Action 7 targets certain strategies which artificially avoid the creation of a permanent establishment under an applicable double taxation agreement. Action 7 recommends a number of amendments to Article 5 (the permanent establishment article) of the OECD Model Tax Treaty, with a recommendation that these changes be reflected in new and existing double taxation agreements.

Of particular relevance to investors in NPL portfolios are the changes which broaden the circumstances in which a person may be viewed as a dependent agent of another person, thereby creating a permanent establishment for that other person.

In particular, under changes to the definition of 'independent agent' (as discussed under heading 4.2(b)), a manager who acts exclusively or almost exclusively on behalf of one or more investment vehicles to which it is closely related would not be considered to be an independent agent with respect to those investment vehicles.

The OECD envisages that the treaty-based recommendations of Action 6 and 7 be implemented into existing double taxation agreements by way of a multilateral instrument signed by the participating states.

7. The Brexit vote

In a referendum held on June 23 2016, the UK public voted to leave the European Union. While the result of the referendum put the United Kingdom on the path to leaving the European Union, an event popularly known as Brexit, the result itself has no legal effect.

The legal process by which the United Kingdom will formally leave the European Union will commence once the United Kingdom gives notice to the European Council under Article 50 of the Treaty on European Union,[9] which, at the time of writing, the United Kingdom has not yet done. The United Kingdom would then formally cease to be part of the European Union upon reaching an agreement with the European Union setting out the terms of Brexit (a withdrawal agreement) or, failing that, two years after the date on which the notice under Article 50 is given (unless an extension is agreed between the United Kingdom and the European Council).

---

9   The current form of the Treaty of European Union results from the amendments introduced by the Treaty of Lisbon, which was signed on December 13 2007 in Lisbon and which entered into force on December 1 2009.

Accordingly, the result of the referendum has no immediate impact on UK direct or indirect taxes. The ultimate effect of Brexit on the tax treatment of investors in the distressed debt of UK companies, or UK investors in the distressed debt of EU companies, will depend on the terms of any withdrawal agreement the United Kingdom is able to reach with the European Union. Until those terms are known, it is difficult to predict what impact Brexit will have on those investors. Nevertheless, some potential effects of Brexit on the tax treatment of investors are discussed below.

7.1 Withholding tax

Brexit should have no direct effect on the withholding tax rules of the United Kingdom or the other EU member states, since withholding taxes are imposed under domestic tax laws rather than at the EU level.

However, a notable exception is the exemptions afforded to EU groups under the IR Directive (see under heading 2.2(b)) and the EU Parent-Subsidiary Directive (see under heading 4.4). As a result of Brexit, UK group companies may no longer qualify under these directives to receive free from local withholding taxes payments of dividends and interest from subsidiaries in the member states.

Furthermore, certain EU member states provide domestic exemptions from withholding tax where, among other conditions, the relevant recipient is a resident of another member state (see under heading 2.2(a) above).

Groups that are particularly adversely affected by the loss of these exemptions may consider restructuring, including by re-locating their European holding company to another EU member state, provided that they can ensure sufficient substance in that other member state (see under heading 4.1(a)). It may, however, be premature for groups to take such action at this stage, before the terms of any withdrawal agreement are known.

Brexit would not, however, have any direct effect on the availability of relief or exemption from withholding taxes under an applicable double taxation agreement (see under heading 2.2(c)). The United Kingdom has agreed double taxation agreements with every EU member state. However, many such double taxation agreements (for example, the double taxation agreement with Italy) do not provide a full exemption from local withholding tax, but rather only provide for a reduced rate of withholding tax.

It may also be the case that a worldwide group can match any incremental withholding taxes suffered in its European group as a result of Brexit with an increased foreign tax credit in the ultimate parent's jurisdiction, potentially eliminating or reducing the effect of such withholding taxes on the group as a whole.

The question of whether UK companies will be able to continue to benefit from the exemptions provided by the IR Directive and the Parent-Subsidiary Directive may feature prominently in the United Kingdom's Brexit negotiations with the European Union, particularly given the United Kingdom's role as a gateway into the European Union for foreign direct investment.

7.2 VAT

While VAT derives from an EU directive,[10] it has been thoroughly enacted into UK domestic law. VAT is also a valuable source of revenue for the UK exchequer. Accordingly, it is anticipated that the United Kingdom will retain VAT in UK law following Brexit.

Outside the European Union, the United Kingdom will have greater freedom to diverge from EU VAT law. However, it may be more beneficial to UK business to keep UK VAT and EU VAT largely aligned, though the United Kingdom may consider broadening the scope of supplies subject to zero and reduced rates of VAT. Over time, the two VAT systems may gradually diverge to a greater extent.

7.3 Capital duties

As mentioned under heading 3.2, the Capital Duties Directive prohibits EU member states from charging indirect taxes, such as stamp duties, on the issue of securities.

UK stamp duty reserve tax is chargeable at 1.5% on the issue of UK securities into a clearance service. However, this charge has been found to contravene the Capital Duties Directive by both the European Court of Justice[11] and the UK First-tier Tribunal.[12]

As result of those judgments, HMRC no longer seeks to collect the 1.5% charge. Following Brexit, however, the United Kingdom would be free to reinstate the charge immediately.

7.4 UK tax policy

It remains to be seen what effect Brexit will have on the UK domestic tax landscape. The United Kingdom may choose to adopt a highly competitive fiscal policy in a bid to attract and retain business, stimulate the UK economy and increase the competitive edge of UK businesses.

An early indication of this approach was seen soon after the referendum vote when George Osborne, then UK Chancellor of the Exchequer, in an interview with the *Financial Times*, mentioned a plan to lower the rate of UK corporation tax to below 15%. However, Philip Hammond, the current incumbent, has not confirmed this.

Furthermore, the economic uncertainty caused by the referendum vote may encourage the UK government to rethink or delay existing tax policy. The United Kingdom has already received calls to delay its planned implementation of new rules restricting the deductibility of UK net interest expense, as recommended by Action 4 of the BEPS project (see under heading 6.1 above), to beyond the scheduled date of April 1 2017.

The prospect of a new and improved UK tax landscape may be one of the reasons that dissuades investors from eschewing the United Kingdom as an attractive investment proposition.

---

10 Council Directive of November 28 2006 on the common system of value added tax (EC Directive 2006/112).
11 *HSBC Holdings plc and Vidacos Nominees Ltd v HMRC* (Case C-569/07).
12 *HSBC Holdings plc and The Bank of New York Mellon Corp v HMRC* [2012] UKFTT 163 (TC).

About the authors

Giulia Battaglia
Partner, Chiomenti Studio Legale, Milan
giulia.battaglia@chiomenti.net

Giulia Battaglia joined the firm in 1992 and became partner in 2003. She has extensive experience in the structured finance field and in debt restructuring. In 1994 she was visiting lawyer at Slaughter and May in London.

Giulia Battaglia specialises in providing assistance to Italian and foreign clients in finance, insolvency and restructuring and in infrastructure and public tenders (energy infrastructure projects, infrastructure concessions and contracts).

She graduated with a degree in economics from the University of Rome, La Sapienza, in 1991 and was admitted to practise before the Taxation Courts (in Italy) in 1992. Giulia Battaglia also obtained a degree in Law from the University of Rome, La Sapienza, in 1999 and was admitted to the Bar in 2003 (Italy).

She is admitted to practise before the Taxation Courts in Milan and is also a member of the Milan Bar. Giulia Battaglia speaks Italian and English.

James Bell
Senior professional support lawyer, Travers Smith LLP
james.bell@traverssmith.com

James is a senior professional support lawyer in the finance and restructuring department at Travers Smith LLP. He advises on developments in law and practice of relevance to English finance lawyers, develops training and prepares the firm's standard form manuals and precedents. James has a maîtrise in French law from the University of Paris I: Panthéon-Sorbonne and an LLB in English and French law from King's College London.

James trained and practised at Linklaters in London and Paris and previously worked for 10 years in the London finance group of Shearman & Sterling.

Elizabeth Bilbao
Partner, Mandel, Katz & Brosnan LLP
ebilbao@mkbllp.com

Elizabeth Bilbao has been a partner of Mandel, Katz & Brosnan since 2009. Her practice focuses on the secondary loan trading markets and on providing advice on the legal issues relating to the purchase and sale of distressed assets and insolvency claims in emerging and established markets in Europe and South America. Elizabeth has been actively involved in the loan trading market since 2003, and has had extensive experience in various types of high-yield transactions throughout the world, including the purchase and sale of distressed and par loans, trade claims and loan restructurings.

Elizabeth Bilbao is a qualified lawyer in England & Wales, Spain and Venezuela.

Jérémie Bismuth
Senior associate, Gide Loyrette Nouel, London
jeremie.bismuth@gide.com

Jérémie Bismuth is a French law qualified senior associate in the banking and structured finance team of Gide Loyrette Nouel's London office. He has substantial experience in banking and structured finance, where he advises financial institutions, private equity funds and corporates on a wide range of asset-backed financing, securitisation and general corporate finance deals.

Ignacio Buil Aldana
Partner, Cuatrecasas, Gonçalves Pereira, London
Ignacio.buil@cuatrecasas.com

A partner at Cuatrecasas, Gonçalves Pereira, Mr Buil is a member of its finance practice. He has been based in the London office since September 2013. He is qualified in Madrid (Spain) and New York.

He has extensive experience in financing and debt-restructuring transactions (in and out of court), and in negotiating financing and refinancing agreements involving a wide range of capital structures, including the refinancing of LBO financings, project finance, real estate finance and corporate finance.

Mr Buil represents borrowers and lenders, and advises financial institutions, hedge funds and private equity funds on financing and refinancing transactions, and distressed investment strategies. He has also participated in several national and multijurisdictional financing transactions and acquisition of NPL portfolios.

He worked as an associate in the New York office of a major American law firm where he represented several debtors and creditors in Chapter 11 reorganisations, including advising on 363 sales and debtor-in-possession financings.

Giorgio Cappelli
Partner, Chiomenti Studio Legale
giorgio.cappelli@chiomenti.net

Giorgio Cappelli is a partner in the banking & finance department of Chiomenti. He graduated in law from the University of Rome, La Sapienza, in 1986; then obtained an LLM at Northwestern University Law School, Chicago (as a Fulbright scholar), in 1989. Giorgio Cappelli was admitted to the Rome Bar in November 1994. He joined the firm in January 1995 and became a partner in 1999. He previously worked for Banca di Roma in the international finance department. Giorgio Cappelli mainly provides assistance to Italian and foreign clients in finance (acquisition and leveraged finance, real estate financing, structured finance, securitisations, covered bonds) and real estate (real estate asset management, real estate funds, real estate securitisations).

Beatriz Causapé
Partner, Cuatrecasas, Gonçalves Pereira
beatriz.causape@cuatrecasas.com

Beatriz Causapé is a partner in Cuatrecasas, Gonçalves Pereira. She has specialised in financial transactions, particularly international transactions.

She has ample experience in leveraged and acquisition finance, syndicated and bilateral loans, real estate finance, corporate finance, securitization deals, project finance, public-private partnerships in infrastructures, structured finance and guarantees and security interests granted in Spain. She has also advised on complex restructuring and refinancing deals at pre-insolvency stages. Now, she is focusing on the secondary loan trading markets.

Gregorio Consoli
Partner, Chiomenti Studio Legale
gregorio.consoli@chiomenti.net

Gregorio Consoli is a partner in the banking and finance department of Chiomenti Studio Legale in Milan. He holds degrees in law and a PhD in business law, and has specialised in structuring and documentation of debt transactions with a focus on structured finance transactions, securitisation of receivables and secured lending transactions.

Since 2009 he has been a leader in the Italian covered bonds market. He has also been heavily involved in a number of securitisation and asset finance transactions and has assisted major banks, investment funds and other investors in the sale and purchase of distressed assets.

Cristóbal Cotta
Partner, Cuatrecasas, Gonçalves Pereira, Madrid
cristobal.cotta@cuatrecasas.com

Cristóbal, a partner in the firm's Madrid office, specialises in refinancing and restructuring industrial, real estate companies and has participated in all stages of complex deals involving reorganisations and restructurings. He also has extensive experience with respect to advising clients on financing projects, all types of infrastructures (PPP and PFI methods), and renewable energies and real estate, using simple, syndicated and structured financing arrangements (eg, sale-and-lease-back and off-balance-sheet transactions).

Recommended by several directories, including *IFLR*, *Best Lawyers* and *Legal 500* in Project Finance, Public Finance and Real Estate.

He lectures in the master in international business law (MIBL) at the Universidad San Pablo CEU, and in a master at the Universidad de Navarra. We highlight his work at the European Investment Bank's legal department.

He is a member of the Madrid Bar Association

Tom Cox
Director, AlixPartners
tocox@alixpartners.com

Tom Cox is a director in AlixPartners' financial advisory services practice with over 12 years' advisory experience working with companies, financial sponsors, and management teams on a wide range of complex financing mandates and more mainstream corporate and leveraged debt raisings.

Tom has extensive experience with lending institutions from both a primary issuance and restructuring perspective, having also been seconded to the restructuring group of a major UK clearing bank, acting on a variety of debt-restructuring and refinancing mandates ranging from £10 million to £1 billion.

More recently Tom advised Monarch Airlines on an asset-based loan transaction following the acquisition by Greybull Capital, and has significant experience in the leveraged buyout market including the private equity buyout financings of Danish waste management operator, MH Gruppen, and the French cold sterilisation business, Ionisos.

Íñigo de Luisa
Partner, Cuatrecasas, Gonçalves Pereira
inigo.deluisa@cuatrecasas.com

Íñigo de Luisa is a partner in Cuatrecasas, Gonçalves Pereira. He has specialised in banking and financing transactions, particularly those with international exposure.

He has advised on complex debt restructuring and refinancing deals at pre-insolvency stages, and has participated in the acquisition of distressed debt and non-performing loan portfolios (both secured and unsecured). More recently, he has regularly participated in bidding processes of loan portfolios and direct lending transactions advising debt funds.

Mr de Luisa lectures at the Faculty of Law of the Universidad Pontificia Comillas (ICADE), and regularly speaks at training courses and conferences specialising in finance, in addition to writing periodically for the journal *International Financial Law Review* (Banking, Spain).

Marie Dubarry de Lassalle
Associate, Gide Loyrette Nouel
Marie.dubarry-de-lassalle@gide.com

Marie Dubarry de Lassalle is an associate in Gide Loyrette Nouel's mergers and acquisitions practice group. She specialises in restructuring and insolvency. Her main areas of expertise are in insolvency proceedings of distressed companies, both in the context of out-of-court and formal insolvency proceedings. She has extensive experience in insolvency-related litigation.

Paul Dunbar
Partner, Vinson & Elkins LLP
pdunbar@velaw.com

Paul Dunbar is a partner in the mergers and acquisitions (M&A) department of Vinson & Elkins in London. He has a broad practice advising clients on M&A, private equity and special situations transactions, including public and private M&A, joint ventures, minority equity and debt investments, and non-performing loan portfolio acquisitions and financings. Paul also advises corporate clients on shareholder activism campaigns and corporate governance matters.

Paul spent six months seconded to TPG Capital and TPG Special Situations Partners as European counsel in 2012.

Paul Durban
Associate, Brown Rudnick LLP
pdurban@brownrudnick.com

Paul Durban is an associate in the financial restructuring and insolvency practice at Brown Rudnick LLP. Paul is involved in restructuring, finance and insolvency matters, including UK and cross-border workouts, new financings and general lending.

He has experience acting for a range of clients in both non-contentious and contentious matters, including financial institutions, bondholders, hedge funds and corporates, and regularly represents major creditors and stakeholders both in the United Kingdom and internationally.

Paul also represents secondary market participants in relation to the acquisition and disposal of debt products using both Loan Market Association standard terms and conditions and bespoke agreements.

Prior to joining Brown Rudnick, Paul worked at Bingham McCutchen as an associate in their restructuring and finance department.

Arturo Gayoso
Director/Head of corporate recovery, Deloitte Financial Advisory
agayoso@deloitte.es

Based in Madrid Deloitte's financial services team, Arturo Gayoso has over 18 years of financial and operational restructuring experience, which includes a significant number of assignments based in Europe, Latin and North America.

Arturo Gayoso has broad experience as an adviser in the energy, consumer business, retail and manufacturing sectors, helping a number of businesses to address both operating and financial issues, focusing on cash management, business planning, performance improvement and financial restructuring (including implementation of turnaround strategies, leading large-scale cost reduction programmes, exit of non-core operations to financial restructurings, etc). He also has experience as chief restructuring officer in companies, helping to overcome financial distress situations.

Arturo holds a degree in business administration and management and a bachelor's in general management from the University of La Coruña, and a degree in international economy from the Open University of Madrid. He also holds a MBA from IE Business School.

Grégoire Hansen
Associate, Brown Rudnick LLP
GHansen@brownrudnick.com

Grégoire Hansen is a French law-qualified associate in Brown Rudnick's bankruptcy and corporate restructuring group based in London. His practice focuses on debt restructuring, corporate financing and cross-border insolvency, as well as English and French law debt workouts. Grégoire acts for bondholders, corporates and investment funds in the UK and in France.

Grégoire is qualified as an *avocat* of the Paris Bar and practises as a Registered European Lawyer recognised by the Solicitors' Regulation Authority.

Grégoire holds a master's degree in business law from the Diplôme de Juriste Conseil d'Entreprise.

Douglas Hawthorn
Senior counsel, Travers Smith LLP
douglas.hawthorn@traverssmith.com

Douglas is senior counsel in the finance and restructuring department at Travers Smith LLP, having previously practised at international law firms DLA Piper and Hogan Lovells. He holds a first class BA in history from the University of Leeds. Douglas specialises in advising on debt and equity restructurings, turnaround and insolvency (including cross-border) situations, acting for private equity sponsors, financial institutions, investors, companies (including listed companies), directors, turnaround professionals and insolvency practitioners. Douglas also has experience in advising on general banking matters.

Jacqueline Ingram
Special counsel, Cadwalader, Wickersham & Taft LLP
Jacqueline.Ingram@cwt.com

Jacqueline Ingram is a special counsel in the financial restructuring group of Cadwalader's London office.

Jacqueline focuses on debt restructuring and special situations financing. She has extensive experience of acting on complex cross-border restructurings, involving a wide range of insolvency and reorganisation processes. Her practice also encompasses direct lending and special situations financing, often involving complex and bespoke debt instruments and intercreditor structures. She has worked with a diverse range of clients including distressed investors, banks, corporates and creditor and noteholder committees.

Jacquie graduated from Nottingham University with a first class BA and studied for the graduate diploma in law and legal practice course at Nottingham Law School. She is admitted to the roll of solicitors of England and Wales.

Graham Lane
Partner, Willkie Farr & Gallagher LLP
glane@willkie.com

Graham Lane is a partner at Willkie Farr & Gallagher LLP based in London. He heads the London business reorganisation and restructuring practice, where he advises stakeholders on a range of restructuring and insolvency matters, with a particular focus on complex cross-border projects.

Graham has gained extensive experience from playing key roles in some of the largest and most noteworthy market-leading restructurings of the last decade, including Eitzen, Travelodge, Klöckner Pentaplast, MF Global, European Directories, Eurotunnel, Sea Containers and Japan Airlines. He is also known for his vast experience in the French market, having been involved in the Vivarte, Latécoère, Solocal, Akerys, Belvedere and Du Fort/Jallatte restructurings, among others. He recently led the UK team in the CORE Entertainment Chapter 11 bankruptcy.

Olivia Locatelli
Associate, Gide Loyrette Nouel, London
olivia.locatelli@gide.com

Olivia Locatelli is a French law-qualified associate in the banking and structured finance team of Gide Loyrette Nouel's London office. She has worked on multijurisdictional international securitisation deals, banking and project financing transactions. She has advised investment banks, corporate borrowers and institutional banks.

Dimitrios Logizidis
Partner, Gide Loyrette Nouel, London
logizidis@gide.com

Dimitrios Logizidis, partner in the London office, specialises in banking and structured finance where he advises financial institutions, private equity funds and corporates on a wide range of asset-backed financing, securitisation, covered bonds and general corporate finance deals. In particular, Dimitrios has acted for arrangers, private equity funds and originators in major whole business and trade receivable securitisation transactions involving amounts of up to €4 billion. He has also been involved in a number of multijurisdictional asset-backed commercial paper conduit deals, including in emerging countries, where securitisation was implemented for the first time.

Dimitrios is qualified both as an English solicitor and a French *avocat*, and advises on English and French law transactions.

Sacha Lürken
Partner, Kirkland & Ellis International LLP
sacha.luerken@kirkland.com

Sacha Lürken is a partner in the restructuring practice group of Kirkland & Ellis in Munich. He holds a law degree from the Ludwig-Maximilians-Universität München and qualified as a lawyer in 2002. Before joining Kirkland & Ellis, he was working in the Corporate Finance as well as in the Litigation & Dispute Resolution practice groups of Clifford Chance in Frankfurt, London and Munich.

Sacha advises financial investors with regards to investments in the entire capital structure of German corporations, mostly in distressed high-yield or bank debt, as well as companies or directors in restructuring and insolvency situations, including in litigation.

Sacha has been a lead or co-lead partner in some of the most prominent German restructuring cases, most recently Scholz Holding, HETA Asset Resolution, IVG Immobilien, PROKON, SolarWorld and Q-Cells.

Iben Madsen
Associate, Willkie Farr & Gallagher LLP
imadsen@willkie.com

Iben Madsen is a senior associate in the business reorganisation and restructuring practice at Willkie Farr & Gallagher LLP based in London. She has experience advising all types of stakeholders (including debtors, creditors and insolvency practitioners) on restructurings, acquisitions and disposals of stressed and distressed businesses.

Iben has played a lead role advising clients on the following significant matters: Eitzen Group, on the international elements of its successful debt-for-equity restructuring; Axcess Financial on the restructuring of Cheque Centre; Evans Easyspace, on behalf of Zolfo Cooper LLP as administrators; the coordinating committee of lenders in relation to Vivarte, on the French clothes and shoe retailer's restructuring; Monier Group in relation to its schemes of arrangement; and GoldenTree, Avenue Capital and Goldman Sachs on the financial restructuring of Travelodge. Most recently, Iben has been a key member of the team advising on the UK elements of the CORE Entertainment Chapter 11 restructuring.

Iben is an associate member of the Insolvency Lawyers' Association.

Damian Malone
Vice-president, AlixPartners
dmalone@alixpartners.com

Damian Malone is a vice-president in AlixPartners' corporate finance practice, with over 11 years' experience in advisory services working with companies, alternative capital providers, private equity firms and management teams on a range of assignments including mergers and acquisitions, debt restructurings and corporate valuations.

Damian is a graduate of University College Dublin, Oxford Brookes University, the University of Oxford and the University of Cambridge.

Additionally, he is a fellow of the Association of Chartered Certified Accountants and holds a diploma in corporate restructuring from the Law Society of Ireland.

Most recently Damian has been involved in the sale of the Co-operative Group's Somerfield business to Hilco Capital and advising on the valuation of a global shipping business. Furthermore, in 2015 he advised on the sale of the Parabis Group and its subsidiaries to multiple acquirers.

Andrea Martino
Senior associate, Chiomenti Studio Legale
andrea.martino@chiomenti.net

Andrea Martino is a senior associate in the banking and finance department of Chiomenti Studio Legale in Rome. He holds a degree in corporate law, and has specialised in corporate and structured finance for a number of years.

In particular, he has been involved in a variety of important domestic and cross-border transactions concerning acquisitions and real estate financings, including asset deals relating to major Italian corporations.

He has also provided legal assistance to arrangers and originators in the structuring of securitisation transactions of performing assets.

Fernando Mínguez
Partner, Cuatrecasas, Gonçalves Pereira
fernando.minguez@cuatrecasas.com

Fernando Mínguez is a partner in Cuatrecasas, Gonçalves Pereira. He is a renowned expert in all areas of banking and finance transactions, particularly in the administrative regulations applicable to credit institutions. He mainly focuses on advising credit and financial institutions on corporate and institutional matters on an ongoing basis.

He is a regular speaker at forums specialising in commercial, banking and financial matters. He also lectures in postgraduate courses and seminars at the IEB and the University of Navarre. He regularly publishes articles in the financial press and articles of opinion on his areas of specialty.

Mr Mínguez is currently on leave from his position as inspector of credit and savings institutions at the Bank of Spain. He is an official auditor (not practising), and he is admitted as a solicitor in England and Wales.

Wolfgang Nardi
Partner, Kirkland & Ellis International LLP
wolfgang.nardi@kirkland.com

Wolfgang Nardi is a partner in the debt finance practice group of Kirkland & Ellis in Munich. He holds a law degree and a master's degree in political science from the University of Regensburg as well as a master's degree in law from the European University Institute in Florence. Wolfgang qualified as a German lawyer (*Rechtsanwalt*) in 2002 and as an English solicitor in 2008. Before joining Kirkland & Ellis, he worked in the banking practices of Linklaters in Frankfurt and Clifford Chance in Munich.

Wolfgang's particular focus lies on advising investors on the financing aspects of private equity transactions and financial restructuring in a private equity environment. He is specialised in finding solutions for the non-consensual refinancing or restructuring of syndicated debt to German debtors.

Wolfgang was the lead or a co-lead partner in some of the most prominent German and Germany-related distressed financing and restructuring cases, most recently Scholz Holding, APCOA Parking, IVG Immobilien and Rodenstock.

Andrea Perelló
Senior associate, Cuatrecasas, Gonçalves Pereira
andrea.perello@cuatrecasas.com

Andrea Perelló is a senior associate in Cuatrecasas, Gonçalves Pereira. She has specialised in litigation and restructuring and insolvency transactions.

She has ample experience on several

bankruptcy proceedings, including some of the most important cases on a national scale, defending the interests of both debtors and creditors.

Throughout her professional career, she has also represented investors' interests in the acquisition of assets and sales of business units within the frame of insolvency proceedings. She also has extensive expertise in debt refinancing transactions (both in and out of court) and corporate restructuring agreements.

Ms Perelló lectures at Universitat Pompeu Fabra in Barcelona.

Nerea Pérez de Guzmán
Senior director, FTI Consulting
Nerea.PerezdeGuzman@fticonsulting.com

Nerea Pérez de Guzmán is a senior director in the corporate finance department of FTI Consulting in Madrid. She holds a degree in business administration and has specialised in advisory services to corporates, financial entities and funds for the last 12 years while based in Madrid and London.

From 2004 she specialised in transaction services in KPMG Madrid and London, where she worked in connection with disposals and acquisitions for domestic, international and private equity houses in a wide range of industries, including manufacturing, media, real estate, retail and leisure.

Since 2008 she has been involved in major debt restructuring cases in Spain, with a high exposure to construction, real estate and retail companies.

Andrew Perkins
Partner, Macfarlanes LLP
andrew.perkins@macfarlanes.com

Andrew Perkins is a partner in the finance team of Macfarlanes LLP in London, and has over 15 years' experience acting for banks, financial institutions, borrowers and sponsors on a wide range of financing transactions, including facilities for investment funds and leveraged buyouts.

Andrew is a market leader in the alternative credit space, and is core counsel to a number of major debt funds. Andrew is also recognised in fund finance and is one of a small group of practitioners able to advise lenders and fund managers of all descriptions on the structuring of complex debt finance into all forms of investment funds.

Andrew has recently acted for (among others) Ares Capital on the acquisition of a portfolio of leveraged loans from Barclays Bank plc and The Royal Bank of Scotland plc on facilities to P2P Global Investments plc.

Giovanna Randazzo
Lawyer
randazzogiovanna84@gmail.com

Giovanna Randazzo is a lawyer specialising in banking and bankruptcy law, she provides legal assistance to companies and individuals and works as bankruptcy receiver. She holds a degree in law and an MA in corporate criminal law.

She worked for a number of years for the legal department of the Italian Banking Association, where she provided legal assistance to the associated Italian banks, mainly in banking and bankruptcy law, and analysed law reforms on the same subjects in order to draft proposals for amendments.

Furthermore, she was an associate in the banking and finance department of Chiomenti Studio Legale in Rome until June 2016. Her main task there was to handle finance transactions. In particular, she has been involved in local and cross-border finance transactions, concerning acquisitions and real estate financings.

About the authors

Rebeca Rodríguez
Partner, Cuatrecasas, Gonçalves Pereira
rebeca.rodriguez@cuatrecasas.com

Rebeca Rodríguez is a partner in Cuatrecasas, Gonçalves Pereira. She specialises in advising credit institutions, investment service firms, financial institutions and insurance companies, particularly on institutional matters and on their financial products. She advises on all kinds of restructuring transactions, financing, issues of securities, acquisition of distressed debt, structures, securitisation and financial agreements. She also advises on developing and implementing investment structures in Spain and abroad.

Ms Rodríguez lectures on the taxation of products and financial transactions in the master in tax consultancy at the Instituto de Empresa and in the master in financial institutions and markets at CUNEF. She also lectures on international tax in the master in business law at the Universidad de Vigo. Additionally, she is a regular speaker at conferences and symposiums at IIR, IFAES and the Fundación de Estudios Financieros.

Íñigo Rubio
Partner, Cuatrecasas, Gonçalves Pereira
inigo.rubio@cuatrecasas.com

Íñigo Rubio Lasarte is a partner in Cuatrecasas, Gonçalves Pereira. He specialises in advising on different financing transactions, particularly, in real estate finance projects, acquisition of non-performing loan and real estate owned portfolios from Spanish financial entities by international investors.

Mr Rubio has ample experience in corporate finance and debt restructuring transactions, having participated in several of the most important and complex refinancing processes in recent years in Spain.

Oded Schein
Partner, Kirkland & Ellis International LLP
oded.schein@kirkland.com

Dr Oded Schein is a tax partner in the Munich office of Kirkland & Ellis International LLP. He holds a degree in law, is a certified tax advisor in Germany, and has extensive experience in German and international tax planning, in particular in the context of cross-border private equity transactions and investments by hedge funds. Oded Schein advises on the formation of investment vehicles for commercial and private investors and has worked on several large-scale international restructuring cases in recent years where he provided tax advice and structural solutions.

Luisa Federica Scialpi
Associate, Chiomenti Studio Legale
federica.scialpi@chiomenti.net

Federica Scialpi is an associate in the banking and finance department of Chiomenti Studio Legale in Milan. She holds degrees in law and is admitted to the Italian Bar. She specialises in structured finance transactions, debt capital market and lending transactions.

She has been involved in a number of securitisation and asset finance transactions and has assisted major investment funds and other investors in the sale and purchase of performing and distressed assets. In addition, she has provided assistance to several banks and arrangers in relation to the structuring of the covered bonds programme.

Mark Sinjakli
Director, AlixPartners
msinjakli@alixpartners.com

Mark Sinjakli is a director in AlixPartners' turnaround and restructuring services practice. He has 14 years' advisory experience, working both for debtors and creditors, on a variety of businesses ranging from UK mid-market concerns to large international groups.

He was recently on secondment to the restructuring department of a major UK clearing bank. He conducted the on-site management of a major UK food factory while it was in administration, including the pursuit of a sizeable insurance claim.

Recently Mark was extensively involved with the Cattles scheme of arrangement, advised a German corporate facing liquidity issues, and oversaw the implementation of a pre-packaged sale of a group of UK bars and restaurants. He has experience of restructuring in industries such as hotels and leisure, real estate, printing, manufacturing and digital media.

Antonio Tavella
Partner, Chiomenti Studio Legale, Milan
antonio.tavella@chiomenti.net

Antonio Tavella joined the firm in 2004 and became a partner in 2013.

He specialises in providing assistance to Italian and foreign clients in finance (structured finance, real estate financing, acquisition finance, project finance, securitisation, covered bonds), insolvency and restructuring (insolvency and pre-insolvency proceedings, financial and corporate restructuring).

He graduated in law from the University of Parma and was admitted to the Italian Bar in 2006.

Antonio Tavella is also a member of the Milan Bar. He speaks Italian and English.

Caroline Texier
Partner, Gide Loyrette Nouel
Caroline.texier@gide.com

Caroline Texier is a partner in Gide Loyrette Nouel's mergers and acquisitions practice group. She specialises in restructuring and insolvency. Her main areas of expertise are insolvency proceedings and debt restructurings. She has long-standing experience in international restructurings of distressed companies, both in the context of out-of-court and formal insolvency proceedings, where she advises all types of stakeholders. Her expertise covers all aspects of restructurings, including insolvency-related litigation.

Fedra Valencia
Partner, Cuatrecasas, Gonçalves Pereira
fedra.valencia@cuatrecasas.com

Fedra Valencia is a partner in Cuatrecasas, Gonçalves Pereira. She is a renowned in the legal management of bankruptcy proceedings, and provides legal advice on corporate and financial-restructuring transactions. She has participated in several bankruptcy proceedings defending the interests of both debtors and creditors, as well as in debt-refinancing transactions (both in and out of court) and corporate-restructuring agreements, which were beneficial for her clients with respect to their creditors. She is also an expert in administrative liability.

She is a professor of bankruptcy law at Universidad Pontificia Comillas-ICADE and lectures at several universities. She speaks regularly at conferences, symposia and seminars.

Luke Vassay
Milbank, Tweed, Hadley & McCloy LLP
LVassay@milbank.com

Luke Vassay is an Associate and Chartered Tax Adviser in the London office of Milbank, Tweed, Hadley & McCloy LLP, specialising in the taxation of a range of corporate and finance transactions.

Jeremy Walsh
Consultant, Travers Smith LLP
Jeremy.walsh@traverssmith.com

Jeremy was until recently a partner and is now a consultant in the finance and restructuring department at Travers Smith LLP. He specialises in advising on finance, restructuring and insolvency, in each case acting for financial institutions, private equity sponsors, investors, borrowers, pensions trustees, directors, insolvency practitioners and turnaround professionals. Jeremy is also a licensed insolvency practitioner.

Sarah Ward
Senior solicitor, Macfarlanes LLP
sarah.ward@macfarlanes.com

Sarah Ward is a senior solicitor in the finance team of Macfarlanes LLP in London. Sarah has over six years' experience advising banks, financial institutions, borrowers and sponsors on a wide range of financing transactions, including advising senior, super-senior and unitranche lenders on all aspects of acquisition financing and facilities for investment funds.

Sarah has recently acted for (among others) Ares Capital on various unitranche and super-senior facilities, including for the refinancing facilities made available to the Claranet Group, and The Royal Bank of Scotland plc on various leveraged buyouts and financings.

Related titles

Restructuring and Workouts
Strategies for Maximising Value, Second Edition
Consulting Editor **Ben Larkin**

European Debt Restructuring Handbook
Leading Case Studies from the Post-Lehman Cycle
Consulting Editors **Ken Asimacopoulos** and **Justin Bickle**

"Several chapters in the book provide practical tools to maximise value in restructuring situations and the market will still undoubtedly provide opportunities for their use.

Bob Wessels
Emeritus Professor of International Insolvency Law, University of Leiden School of Law

"If you want to read an account of some of Europe's most important, and sometimes contentious, restructurings in the recent downturn written by the advisers that actually worked on the deals, then this is the book for you.

Global Turnaround

Go to **www.globelawandbusiness.com** for full details including free sample chapters and reviews.